Shahid Yusuf
Weiping Wu
Simon Evenett

Editors

Local
Dynamics
in an Era of
Globalization

THE WORLD BANK

Local Dynamics in an
Era of Globalization

21st Century Catalysts for Development

Edited by

**Shahid Yusuf, Weiping Wu,
and Simon Evenett**

**Published for the World Bank
Oxford University Press**

Oxford University Press

OXFORD   NEW YORK   ATHENS   AUCKLAND   BANGKOK   BOGOTÁ
BUENOS AIRES   CALCUTTA   CAPE TOWN   CHENNAI   DAR ES SALAAM
DELHI   FLORENCE   HONG KONG   ISTANBUL   KARACHI
KUALA LUMPUR   MADRID   MELBOURNE   MEXICO CITY   MUMBAI
NAIROBI   PARIS   SÃO PAULO   SINGAPORE   TAIPEI   TOKYO
TORONTO   WARSAW

and associated companies in

BERLIN   IBADAN

© 2000 The International Bank for Reconstruction and
Development / The World Bank
1818 H Street, N.W., Washington, D.C. 20433, USA

Published by Oxford University Press, Inc.
198 Madison Avenue, New York, N.Y. 10016

Oxford is a registered trademark of Oxford University Press.

The Chinese characters displayed on the front cover of this book
signify "globalization"—*quan qiou hua*. They were rendered by
Jun Ma in the East Asia and Pacific Region of the World Bank.

Cover design by W. Drew Fasick, ULTRAdesign. Typesetting is by
Barton Matheson Willse & Worthington, Baltimore.

Manufactured in the United States of America
First printing August 2000
1 2 3 4 5 04 03 02 01 00

The findings, interpretations, and conclusions expressed in this
study are entirely those of the authors and should not be attributed
in any manner to the World Bank, to its affiliated organizations, or
to members of its Board of Executive Directors or the countries
they represent. The boundaries, colors, denominations, and other
information shown on any map in this volume do not imply on the
part of the World Bank Group any judgment on the legal status of
any territory or the endorsement or acceptance of such boundaries.

Library of Congress Cataloging-in-Publication Data
Local dynamics in a globalizing world : 21st century catalysts for
development / edited by Shahid Yusuf, Weiping Wu and Simon
Evenett.
    p.   cm.
Includes bibliographical references.
ISBN 0-19-521597-4
   1. Economic development.   2. Globalization.
3. Decentralization in government.   4. Urbanization.
I. Yusuf, Shahid, 1949–   .   II. Wu, Wei-p'ing.
III. Evenett, Simon J.
HD75 .L63 2000
338.9—dc21
                                          00-036342

Preface

In preparing the *World Development Report 1999/2000,* the team responsible for the report commissioned a number of papers to map the several major fields covered by the report, to synthesize significant findings from recent research and to explore issues that were likely to loom large in the early 21st century. These papers, by leading specialists, were reviewed at workshops in Washington, Tokyo, and Singapore, and they served as some of the building blocks for the report. However, from the very outset we saw these papers as having a life of their own—independent of the report—so that all those with an interest in local and global dynamics could draw upon the ideas and information presented in these papers.

This companion volume to the *World Development Report* assembles a selection of papers that relate to the unfolding of local dynamics in an increasingly integrated world environment. A second volume in the World Bank's Discussion Paper Series will provide a further selection on the themes of globalization and urbanization.

All the papers in this volume were extensively revised and edited prior to publication. We greatly appreciate the effort put in by each of the authors in revising their contributions and working closely with us through the lengthy editing process. The research in these papers, the convening of the workshops, and the publication of this volume was supported by a Population and Human Resources Development Grant from the government of Japan. This financial assistance was enormously valuable throughout the preparation of the *World Development Report.* It helped widen the knowledge base of the re-port, the workshops were a rich source of feedback on the themes we were exploring, and the grant has enabled us to make these papers available to a wide readership.

Many people have contributed to the making of this volume. We want to thank our fellow team members Anjum Altaf, William Dillinger, Marianne Fay, Vernon Henderson, and Charles Kenny, who assisted in the commissioning of the papers and in reviewing earlier drafts. We are greatly indebted to Rebecca Sugui for her help in the processing of the papers and, together with Paulina Flewitt and Leila Search, assisting with the logistics of the workshops. Umou Al-Bazzaz provided invaluable assistance in the assembly of the final manuscript. The first workshop, held in Washington during July 1998, helped to launch the *World Development Report.* We owe its success to the effort put in by Jean Ponchamni and Mani Jandu. The two workshops in Tokyo were flawlessly co-organized by the staff of the World Bank's Tokyo office together with the Overseas Economic Cooperation Fund of Japan (now a part of the Japan Bank for International Corporation, or JBIC) and the Foundation for Advanced Studies in International Development (FASID). We would like to thank the director of the Tokyo office, Shuzo Nakamura; Mika Iwasaki; and Tomoko Hagimoto; and staff from JBIC and FASID for the success of these events.

The workshop in Singapore was co-hosted with the Institute of Southeast Asian Studies. Thanks are due to the institute's director, Professor Chia Siow Yue, for providing us with the ideal physical and intellectual environment.

In editing the manuscript, we have been greatly aided by Sandra Hackman.

Contents

Making Decentralization Work in a Global Economy

Building Competitive Cities for the 21st Century

Tables

Figures

Boxes

Maps

The World
of Globalizing
Forces

chapter 1

Local Dynamics in a Globalizing World: 21st Century Catalysts for Development

Shahid Yusuf, Simon Evenett, and Weiping Wu

The
World
Bank

The World Bank and
The Brookings Institution

Virginia
Commonwealth
University

For those who entered the last decade of the 20th century believing that the central elements of the development question had been settled in favor of market capitalism, the ensuing tumult was, to say the least, disquieting. Few anticipated that the melding together of national financial systems would lead to contagion being transmitted across continents. Indeed, when the Berlin Wall fell who would have thought that 10 years later a different type of architecture—the global financial architecture—would be hotly debated in the corridors of power? And yet even these well-discussed global forces pale in comparison to the dynamics unleashed within nations by increased pressures for local autonomy.

Two events in 1999 crystallize the forces that are reshaping the development landscape: the failure to launch a new global trade round at the World Trade Organization's Second Ministerial Conference in Seattle, and the centrifugal—and all too often deadly—forces pulling power away from the central authorities in Jakarta to the regions and islands of the vast Indonesian archipelago. The diverse set of demonstrators at Seattle highlighted just how deep are social concerns aroused by international trade flows. Irrespective of the merits of their case, the ramifications of trade reform for the environment, food safety, working conditions, and democracy received prominent attention in Seattle. In addition, the capacity of the World Trade Organization to accommodate the differing aspirations of a membership that now exceeds 135 members was called into question.

Both the increasingly violent protests in parts of Indonesia[1] as well as the votes in Scotland and Wales for devolution point to a declining faith in the capacity of central governments to deliver high-quality public services, promote sustainable economic growth, and equitably distribute the benefits of such growth. Furthermore, improvements in communications technologies have made it easier for local actors to express and, more important, organize dissent. Though it is a political decision made by individual countries, the devolution of power to subnational entities is widespread.

Managing "localization" is a central challenge for all countries—industrial and developing alike—during the coming decades. For many developing countries this is compounded by the fact that central states have never faced such comprehensive demands to cede powers and resources, even though in many instances local actors may not have the administrative experience to match their aspirations. Furthermore, even though the most embryonic institutional framework may have yet to materialize in order to reconcile the competing demands of disparate elements of society. So strong is the sentiment for local autonomy that discontented regions are seceding in greater numbers: Since 1990 on average 3.1 new nations were born each year, compared to the previous 30 years where on average the number of nations grew by 2.2 per annum.[2]

The objectives of this volume are twofold: first, to analyze how these local dynamics and global forces are transforming the development landscape, are raising new questions for the development agenda, and are altering the scope and effectiveness of policy alternatives. The second goal is to propose ambitious yet feasible measures that will enhance the prospects for developing nations in the 21st century. In rising to these admittedly ambitious goals, the contributors to this volume, all prominent scholars, have drawn upon the experiences of developing and industrial countries from every continent.

A recurring theme in this volume is that traditional frameworks for analysis need to be rethought to take account of greater interdependencies across space, time, and issues. In what follows, perhaps the most prominent example is urbanization, a phenomenon that is spurred on by intensifying local dynamics and where integration of cities into the world economies opens the door to faster growth, by tapping foreign funds and expertise. How these interdependencies evolve over time is of critical importance to humanity as at the turn of the century approximately one-half of the world's population lives in urban areas, and by 2025 this fraction is expected to rise to two-thirds. The new economic geography literature, which analyzes the role of cities and regions in a global economy, is one example of the type of development thinking that could grow in importance.

A second theme, which receives considerable prominence, is that the number of competing decisionmakers on the development landscape will multiply, calling for the reform and often creation of new modes of governance. This involves a shift away from a central, state-led view of development toward a more complex, and potentially untidy, coalition of actors at both supra- and subnational levels who will typically not confine themselves to operating in one arena, such as the local sphere. Given the growing linkages across issues, actors in any one sovereign unit are likely to find themselves dealing with one another on matters that were not previously envisaged when their nation's constitutional arrangements were decided. This enlarges the importance of institutional mechanisms permitting wider participation, the orderly resolution of disagreements, and for inducing compliance with collective decisions.

A third theme is that the combination of local dynamics and global forces can catalyze policy action, enabling regions and cities to accelerate the pace of development. This is especially so for cities which build the appropriate infrastructure and amenities to attract high-valued added service industries and personnel from abroad. Two other implications are also worth noting: Rapid development need not occur and to the extent that it does it may well widen the gap between richer and poorer regions of the world. The difference between success and failure will almost certainly become greater than ever before, and that in and of itself may well focus the minds of policymakers.

Globalization

The term *globalization* is of recent vintage, but the process it describes has been under way for well over a century and even longer if the definition is broadened to embrace political globalization.[3] Growth of international trade and capital flows, which are central to globalization as conventionally understood, accelerated markedly in the latter part of the 19th century. There was a sharp fall in shipping costs between 1870 and 1900 and a substantial narrowing of the spread of staples prices on world markets.[4] Moreover, between 1820 and the first decade of the 20th century, nearly 60 million people migrated to the Americas alone.[5] In fact, several observers maintain that the current phase of globalization has yet to surpass the high point reached around the beginning of the 20th century. But a closer look at evidence indicates significant differences, quantitatively, qualitatively, and technologically.

International commerce now encompasses a much larger share of tradable commodities. This share has risen from 20 percent in the late 19th century to more than 40 percent at the end of the 20th century.[6] Moreover, the trade in services has swelled from insignificance to nearly one-fifth of total trade—it amounts to 40 percent of the value of U.S merchandise exports. It is also growing much faster than the trade in goods. Close to two-thirds of all trade is within production networks created by transnational corporations through alliances and subcontracting relationships. The increase in trade has been supported by the steady reduction in tariff barriers, a result of seven rounds of trade negotiations over the past 50 years. Tariffs on manufactured imports in the industrialized countries have fallen by 90 percent since World War II to an average of 4 percent.[7]

Overseas capital flows into government bonds and corporate debentures rose strongly from the mid-19th century through the first decade of the 20th in spite of periodic panics and crises triggered by the collapse of major private ventures or government defaults. But the current flow of capital is of a different order. The magnitude has increased manyfold and the composition has changed drastically. Financial globalization is reinforcing the impact of the communications revolution on global linkages. In fact, 80 percent of all international data flows are generated by the financial services sector.[8]

Foreign direct investment, mainly by transnational corporations, has emerged as a major item and comprised 48 percent of long-term capital flows to developing countries in 1997.[9] Institutional and individual investors are also a source of the growing volume of private portfolio capital and short-term flows, and these have overshadowed bank lending and investment in government paper. Foreign direct investment is being spurred by the easing of barriers to trade, the advantages of situating production facilities close to major markets, and the greater ease in managing dispersed operations brought about by recent advances in communications. Firms need no longer design, manufacture, assemble, and market a good in the same nation; and developing nations will increasingly find themselves evaluated as a potential location for only stages in production processes, with ramifications for the nature and extent of foreign direct investment that they receive.

The new phase of globalization is also notable for the changes in human mobility. Although the heightened flows of goods and capital, together with advances in communications, might have been expected to dampen human migration, the trend is in the opposite direction. More people are on the move than ever before. Each year between 2 and 3 million people emigrate, with the majority of them going to just four home countries: the United States, Germany, Canada, and Australia, in that order. At the turn of the 21st century, nearly 120 million people are living outside countries of their birth. Better information, the lower cost of transport, increased education, rising incomes, and a readiness to exploit worldwide opportunities are encouraging people to travel and to migrate. The emergence of a global culture and the spread of English as a lingua franca has further reduced inhibitions to movement.[10]

Cross-border migration will be one of the major forces shaping the landscape of the 21st century, for at least three reasons. First, migration is causing dramatic shifts in the demographic profiles of both industrial and developing countries, in particular in industrial and Eastern European nations where fertility rates are low. Second, the movement of highly skilled people from the developing world affects low-income countries and recipient countries alike. Here traditional concerns about the "brain drain" from developing nations are to be weighed against newer research that shows the benefits to developing nations of the remittances from national residents abroad. At present such remittances exceed US$70 billion and are worth 50 percent more to developing nations than official aid. Third, the international diaspora has tremendous business potential, facilitating the dissemination of market opportunities, funds, and best practices across national borders.

Given the accelerated and unpredictable pace of change, the critical question is how to develop rules, institutions, and policies that enable nations to respond to the many opportunities and risks presented by globalization as it unfolds. In this volume, the following four chapters delineate reforms that will raise the likelihood of developing nations benefiting from globalization.

Rules governing international trade. Kym Anderson accounts for the factors that determined the current multilateral trading system, the legacy of the Uruguay Round

of trade negotiations. The Uruguay Round envisaged significant reductions in trade barriers, with sizable potential gains for both industrial and developing countries. But given the complexity of the issues and the political economy underlying the negotiations, a number of items were bypassed or covered only peripherally. Uppermost among these are rules for a phased liberalization of trade in textiles, agricultural commodities, and services. The tensions that surfaced at the Seattle meetings indicated that the members of the World Trade Organization are still struggling to implement the agreements reached through the Uruguay Round. Further lowering of trade barriers in key areas is stoutly resisted by vested interests, and extending multilateral disciplines to encompass producer services is a source of concern, especially for developing countries. In addition, organized groups, particularly the international nongovernmental organizations (NGOs), are agitating to bring environmental and labor-related standards into the ambit of the trading system.

Financial reform and managing capital flows. The increasing frequency of banking and currency crises during the 1980s and 1990s, culminating in the East Asian Crisis of 1997–1998, has highlighted the role of the financial system in economic development. These crises also revealed the effects of capital flows on the growth and stability of financial sectors in industrializing countries and the necessity of making adequate regulatory provisions when removing domestic controls on the banking system—especially where domestic financing is combined with an easing of restrictions on international capital flows. Robert Litan's chapter succinctly reviews the case for actively pursuing financial deepening and containing the risks of increasingly disruptive shocks. To be effective, institution building will have to be conducted simultaneously at three levels: at the level of individual financial entities, which must tighten their information and risk management practices to ensure their viability in a globalizing environment; at the country level through the defining and enforcement of rules that, for instance, set benchmarks for capital adequacy, help sustain franchise value, and orchestrate a process of liberalization; and at the international level through a revamped Basle Accord backed up by monitoring arrangements that will result in commonality of standards and adherence to good regulatory practices.

Coordinating monetary policies. While multilevel regulatory institutions will be essential for stability under conditions of financial globalization, they will need to be complemented by some degree of policy coordination both between major countries and at the regional level where international linkages are greatest. Andrew

Hughes Hallett explores the desirability of and prerequisites for coordination of monetary policies, the recent record, and the most fruitful pathways for the future. During the 1980s and 1990s, exchange rate volatility between key currencies had significant national and regional consequences, but attempts to harmonize macroeconomic policies met with limited success. Hughes Hallett emphasizes that successful international cooperation requires flexible domestic institutions which can accommodate the macroeconomic policies needed to support the cooperative endeavor. Care must also be taken in devising cooperation agreements so that the gains are not asymmetrically distributed across participants.

Harnessing international migration. After providing an overview of the principal trends in international migration, Stephen Castles' chapter discusses the many costs and benefits associated with the movement of people across national borders. Of particular interest are two case studies, on Turkey and the Philippines, where it is argued that migration has contributed more to the latter's development strategy than to the former's. One reason for this difference is that the Philippines has taken extensive measures to facilitate the reintegration of expatriates into their home country. This has encouraged the transfer of funds, essential for establishing small and medium-sized businesses, as well as transferring practices and tapping global contacts. Drawing from these experiences Castles proposes a series of international measures that could enhance the benefits of cross-border migration. Should policymakers wish to redress the striking imbalance between the extensive rules on trade and capital flows and the paucity of such rules on the movement of people, then Castles' chapter provides considerable food for thought.

Localization

Global integration frames and, to a degree, spurs the ongoing localizing tendency. The multiplication of international rules, standards, and conventions; the growing influence of multilateral agencies; transnational corporations and nongovernmental organizations; and the force of global public opinion reinforced by modern communications have all circumscribed the authority of national governments. Greater openness has also enlarged the freedoms enjoyed by subnational entities to exploit trading opportunities, to raise funds on overseas markets, and to cultivate direct relations with international agencies and cities.

The economic effects of openness and easier travel have spurred urban economies, thereby reinforcing urbanization in developing countries. Direct gains have been observed from exports, and indirect benefits from the growth of services and tourism. In some countries, such as China, openness has also prompted rural development by enabling rural producers to attract foreign direct investment, to expand processing industries, and to enter foreign markets.

The globalizing world is a world of cities and their hinterlands. Anthony Venables draws upon the models generated by the new economic geography to explore the spatial structure of development. He shows how an initial clustering of urban activity linked to agglomeration effects could be followed by dispersion as economies open up and expand their trading links, transport costs decline, and congestion offsets the benefits of concentration in one or a few large urban centers. However, he notes that economic development is likely to be an uneven process that is concentrated in a few areas that have been quick to grasp opportunities, create backward and forward linkages, and respond to declining transaction costs. Venables' chapter sets the stage for the four chapters that follow, each of which examines a particular facet of urban development.

Vernon Henderson examines the emergence of a hierarchy of cities and the role of megacities in developing countries. Henderson points out that megacities might initially dominate the landscape but rising costs in such cities along with the building of transport infrastructure can expedite the dispersion of activities to medium-sized cities with a more specialized production structure. Edwin Mills extends the points made by Henderson by showing how the productivity advantages of large urban areas are dependent upon policies that determine the quality of infrastructure and effective management of land use.

Globalization also opens up new markets to hinterland producers previously more tied to domestic markets than producers in the vicinity of coastal regions. Yujiro Hayami discusses how the emergence of trading opportunities was responsible for rural industrialization in Japan and Taiwan (China) in the earlier part of the 20th century and more recently in some of the Southeast Asian economies. He also explores the significance of urban-rural trading linkages that have served as the relays transmitting global demands to the rural areas. Hayami's contribution usefully complements others in this section by showing that the growth impulse deriving from globalization can lead to a more balanced development of rural and urban areas.

Over the past quarter century, another form of urbanization has acquired prominence. Allen Scott analyzes the formation of economic city-regions through a coalescence of growing, outward-oriented metropolitan areas. He also suggests that globalization enhances the possibilities of increased geographic differentiation and locational specialization. A new set of industries, including high-technology manufacturing, business and financial services, neoartisanal industries, and cultural products industries, are becoming especially important in major world metropolises such as New York, London, Paris, and Los Angeles. The economies of scope and scale of city-regions are reinforced by local labor market processes, by innovation and learning effects, and by the conventions, cultures, and interdependencies that constitute intrinsic elements of any active industrial system.

The concentration of economic power in cities and regions has strengthened demands for decentralization—fiscal and administrative—demands that have drawn impetus from political trends in industrial countries, where the momentum toward decentralization has been gathering force for some time. This is now finding an echo in developing countries where central governments are acceding to the pressure to devolve authority to lower levels. However, in several instances, revenue constraints are also encouraging central authorities to shed obligations to subnational entities by way of decentralization.

Political openness and a heightened awareness of ethnic or regional identity also have contributed to the trend toward greater political and administrative responsibilities being placed on the shoulders of local authorities. The importance of local development and governance is further enhanced by the assertiveness of civil society in many countries. Such a focus on local development is conducive to greater participation, as the incentives are stronger and the consequences of action taken are more visible and immediate at the local level. But in order to ensure that newly empowered local governments are in fact responsive and accountable to their constituents, transparency and incentives for democratic participation will be required.

With increased levels of political autonomy and democratic participation, municipalities are now facing greater challenges in delivering services to urban populations. The exclusive responsibility of the public sector to provide a range of services is giving way to private participation, public–private partnerships, and community initiatives. Reaffirming the importance for municipalities of developing appropriate institutions that involve the private sector, community-based organizations, and nongovernmental organizations, promising improvements have emerged in several developing countries in all major sectors of urban services. It is also apparent that for many municipalities the new responsibilities entail considerable financial hardship and stretch, if not exceed, their technical capabilities.

Just as globalization requires the community of nations to devise policies and constitute institutions to deal with the flow of goods, capital, labor, and information among countries, so also localization raises a host of policy and institutional issues relating to decentralization and the creating of competitive and livable cities.

Effective decentralization. This involves a number of steps that distribute responsibilities between the center and subnational entities, assign sources of revenue commensurate with these responsibilities to different levels of government, create administrative capacity to discharge the newly assigned functions, and establish the ground rules for interaction between the center and lower level governments in a decentralized milieu.

Rules for decentralization and recent experience in a number of countries that could guide other economies travelling down this path are the topics of the chapters by Roy Bahl and Paul Smoke. Bahl synthesizes a wide range of experience into 11 rules on the pace and nature of decentralization, taking account of the capacity in most developing countries. He emphasizes a rule-bound process, kept simple and continuously monitored, which gives local authorities significant taxing powers, but then subjects them to hard budget constraints. Similarly, Paul Smoke draws lessons from the decentralization episodes in Brazil, Ethiopia, Indonesia, Kenya, and Uganda; concluding that although there is no single model for fiscal decentralization, seven principles should form the building blocks of any strategy to accommodate increased pressures for local autonomy. But the key rule of decentralization is that it must respond to the specific attributes of the country and local communities.

Successful decentralization also is contingent upon effective local governance. Accountability of local officials to the population determines whether the fruit of decentralization will be realized in the form of more responsive provision of local services and local self-determination. Kengo Akizuki describes Japan's steps toward devolving authority down to prefectures and lower levels of government since the mid-1990s. He discusses the bureaucratic restructuring that this is entailing, the administrative capacity gaps that still exist, but also the alacrity with which prefectures are grasping the possibilities offered by globalization.

Judith Tendler reminds us that decentralization initiatives do not necessarily lead to improved quality of public-service delivery to local constituencies, particularly those less advantaged. She challenges the effectiveness of social funds—programs usually administered by a separate agency within a central government that allocates grants directly to myriad communities—as a safety net for the poor and, more significantly, about the greater desirability of social funds as an alternative to traditional government provision. At best, such funds may represent a deconcentrated version of supply-driven service that constructs small infrastructure projects more quickly at lower costs.

Managing urbanization. As engines of growth, cities are becoming the focal points of global and national economies, despite the likely strain on urban governance and infrastructure.

Ann Markusen's study of secondary cities in Brazil, Japan, the Republic of Korea, and the United States points to some of the prominent contributors to successful urbanization. These include specialization in innovative or income elastic economic sectors, favorable national government policies in such areas as investment and infrastructure, economic development leadership from either local public or private sectors, and flexibility and openness toward new and emerging industrial ensembles. National governments should continue to monitor urban growth patterns, selectively intervening in dynamics that are worsening regional disparities. Adding to this list, Utis Kaothien and Douglas Webster believe that cities must address quality of life, develop human resources, harness global capital flows, and focus on software (policy and programming) instead of hardware (physical systems). But municipalities have difficulty in achieving multiple objectives because of the massive scale of periurbanization—as in the case of Thailand—and the multiplicity of local governments in the extended urban regions.

Successful urban development in the context of decentralization must come to terms with mobilizing financing for municipalities and long-term financing for infrastructure. Municipal revenues are still mainly dependent upon transfers from provincial and central authorities. But there are growing incentives to utilize local tax handles such as property and sales taxes and user charges for municipally supplied services. Success in this regard depends on the building of administrative capacity to levy and collect both taxes and user charges, as exemplified by the experience of the United States in Andrew Reschovsky's chapter. Term financing rests in large part on the ability to tap bond markets. Globalization is enhancing access to such financing, but cities must first fulfill certain criteria and establish a good policy and payment record.

Building livable cities. Urban success requires strategic planning, which can guide key investments and assist in allocating resources. Backed by integrated land use and transport policies that accommodate private initiative to fill the gaps, the process could help cities avoid the worst outcomes of unplanned growth. This has clearly been a key source of Singapore's success, as discussed in the chapter by Sock-Yong Phang. She also credits Singapore's effective implementation of such planning to a network of competent and reliable organizations that implement public policies. However, the transferability of Singapore's experience needs to be juxtaposed with local political and social context because of the island city's unique governmental system and its ability to control the entry of migrants who can impose a strain on urban services.

In comparing two sets of large cities in Southeast Asia, Rimmer and Dick reaffirmed the need for integrated land use and transportation planning. For cities that have applied modern transport technologies piecemeal and uncoordinated by any consistent long-term strategy, the outcome has inevitably been heavy congestion and urban sprawl. The mobility of the urban poor has been impeded and dangers from vehicle traffic worsened. The authors further suggest that although cities of varying sizes often need to focus on different priorities, all would gain from greater access to local resources and more responsiveness to local constituencies. One option for large cities—a technique that Japan has used with success—is to encourage private companies to finance infrastructure by relying on earnings from related development.

Smart cities are efficient at providing services and at putting in place infrastructure sufficient to achieve competitiveness in an open environment. Cross-country experience with municipal development suggests that the quality of local governance, especially the ability of local authorities to establish partnerships with the private sector and community groups and to mobilize organizational skills, strongly influences the degree to which municipalities deliver on their promises. In a revealing chapter on Japan's urban environmental movements, Ryo Fujikura takes up the interlinked issues of governance and environmental quality. In particular, Kitakyushu City's experience shows the importance of public awareness and environmental education, spearheaded by women's groups, in building support for environmental protection. Local leaders also understand their communities better than higher-level governments, and careful advice from local officials to individual firms has solved many problems of industrial pollution.

The issues of service provision by municipalities are further pursued by David Beede and David Bloom, specifically in solid waste management. Economic growth, poverty reduction, and good governance are likely to enhance countries' capacities to address the waste problem. Among the available solutions, recycling and composting may be better alternatives for most developing cities as they also capitalize on the resource value of the waste. But composting will not fulfill its promise until both quality control and demand improve significantly. Many economic schemes—including charging service fees, deposit–refund mechanisms, and private concessions—can help municipalities pay for proper management of solid waste and cut the amount illicitly dumped into the natural environment.

Concluding Observations

The contributions in this volume identify some of the major forces transforming the world economy in the early 21st century. They also provide a framework for thinking about the challenges confronting policymakers. They offer tools for analyzing key problems and suggest policy or institutional initiatives that allow countries to make globalization and localization yield benefits rather than becoming obstacles to development.

The integration of economies through trade, capital flows, and communications, the emphasis on local autonomy, the emergence of regional economic entities, and the growing political and economic salience of urban centers cannot be viewed in isolation. The interrelationships need to be recognized and factored into the making of policy. While each author concentrates on a particular aspect of a large picture, taken together, the 21 chapters offer a wide-ranging perspective on the development opportunities presented by a globalizing world of urban regions.

Notes

1. *Economist* "Brutality and Budgets in Indonesia," January 22, 2000; *Far Eastern Economic Review,* "Bleak Prospects," December 16, 1999, discusses the effects of a breakdown in law and order in Indonesia in its mining industry.

2. Juan Enriquez, "Too Many Flags." *Foreign Policy,* Fall 1999, pp. 30–50.

3. David Held, Anthony McGrew, David Goldblatt, and Jonathan Perraton. 1999. *Global Transformations.* Palo Alto, CA: Stanford University Press.

4. Kevin H. O'Rourke and Jeffrey G. Williamson. 1999. *Globalization and History.* Cambridge, MA: MIT Press.

5. Timothy J. Hatton and Jeffrey G. Williamson. 1998. *The Age of Mass Migration.* New York: Oxford University Press.

6. Michael D. Bordo, Barry Eichengreen, and Douglas A. Irwin. 1999. "Is Globalization Today Really Different than Globalization a Hundred Years Ago?" In Brookings Trade Policy Forum, Washington, D.C.: Brookings Institution.

7. *Business Week,* "Global Growing Pains," December 13, 1999.

8. Graham, Stephen. 1999. "Global Grids of Glass: On Global Cities, Telecommunications and Planetary Urban Networks." *Urban Studies* 36, 5–6 (May): 929–949.

9. World Bank. 2000. *Global Economic Prospects 2000,* Table A2.10, Washington, D.C.

10. David Crystal. 1997. *English as a Global Language.* Cambridge, U.K.: Cambridge University Press.

chapter 2

Globalization, the World Trade Organization, and Development Strategies of Poorer Countries

Kym Anderson

School of Economics and Centre for International Economic Studies,
University of Adelaide, Australia

The pervasive effects of the process of globalization are being felt in poorer economies at least as much as in richer ones. Globalization is also being affected by, and is affecting, international institutions such as the World Trade Organization (WTO). The WTO's evolution in turn is altering the policy options of developing and transition economies. In addition, the ability of those countries to influence the WTO is beginning to increase. This three-way interaction between globalization, the WTO, and the development policy strategies of developing and transition economies is explored in this chapter, with a view toward drawing out implications for further action by governments of the world's developing countries as the next century dawns. Those actions certainly involve getting rid of, or not introducing, certain types of government interventions in markets, especially those whose inappropriateness is increasing with globalization. But attention is also given to the question of what new government actions may be required—at international as well as at national levels—to maintain or improve the smooth functioning of economic and political markets.

The chapter has five sections. The first defines globalization and briefly describes indicators of its growth; the second summarizes technological aspects of globalization of relevance to poorer countries; the third notes the changes in national economic policies that have contributed to globalization; the General Agreement on Tariffs and Trade (GATT) and now the World Trade Organization (WTO) have added significantly to those governmental contributions to globalization, as discussed in the fourth section; and the final section of the chapter explores the implications of these developments for policies and strategies of developing countries, including the poorer economies in transition from socialism. Particular attention is given to rural development strategies because globalization is likely to strengthen urbanization and thereby add to the burden of adjustment that rural areas traditionally bear.

The implications of globalization for poorer countries, and for the poorer rural areas within them, are of significance to people in rich countries as much as to those in poor countries. This statement is true because globalization threatens to increase the gap between the haves and have-nots to such an extent as to cause political tensions within and between countries and even a backlash against a key contributor to globalization, namely, the opening up of national economies. As David Landes (1998, p. xx) put it in his latest book:

> The old division of the world into two power blocs, East and West, has subsided. Now the big challenge and threat is the gap in wealth and health that separates rich and poor. These are often styled North and South, because the division is geographic; but a more accurate signifier would be the West and the Rest, because the division is also historic. Here is the greatest single problem and danger facing the world of the Third Millennium.

Definition and Extent of Globalization

For present purposes, globalization is defined as the decline in transactions costs or barriers to doing business

Table 2.1

Growth in World GDP and Merchandise Exports in Real Terms, 1720–1996

(percent per year)

	1720–1820	1820–70	1870–1913	1913–50	1950–73	1973–90	1990–96
Real GDP	0.8	1.9	2.5	1.8	5.4	2.7	2.9
Export volume	1.4	4.5	3.9	0.5	9.8	4.0	5.9
Export growth/GDP growth	1.7	2.4	1.6	0.3	1.8	1.5	2.1

Source: WTO (1998, p. 34)

or otherwise interacting with people of other nations around the world. Its effect is to enhance the integration of markets for goods, services, technology, ideas, capital, and labor, reducing the differences in prices for those products and factors across space. Both technological and governmental barriers contribute to the costs of interacting internationally. Falling transport costs, the huge decline in communication and information costs, and cuts in tariff and nontariff barriers to trade in goods, services, financial capital, and, to some extent, labor have combined in the late 20th century to accelerate globalization to an unprecedented speed that shows no sign of abating.

The extent of the acceleration in globalization cannot be captured in a single statistic, but several provide partial indications of what is involved. A standard indicator is the comparison between trade and gross domestic product (GDP) growth. As Table 2.1 shows, while merchandise trade has grown faster than output for all periods except between the two world wars, the gap has been larger in the 1990s than in any earlier period since the mid-19th century. More than one-fifth of global output is now exported, double the proportion in the 1950s. Also, annual outflows of foreign direct investment grew more than six-fold between 1983 and 1990 and have continued to grow more than twice as fast as goods trade in the 1990s. Intrafirm trade among multinational corporations is estimated to account for one-third of world trade, and another one-third is multinational corporation (MNC) trade with nonaffiliates. During the 1990s international portfolio investment was growing equally as fast as foreign direct investment (WTO 1996, pp. 44–46). In just the past five years, the annual value of cross-border mergers and acquisitions has trebled, growing from US$100 billion to US$300 billion (UNCTAD 1998, p. 21). Daily foreign exchange transactions now exceed global currency reserves, with international capital flows more than 50 times the value of international trade flows. The 1990s have also seen an explosion in the world's capacity for electronic commerce. Table 2.2 shows a doubling in the

number of telephone lines, a 25-fold increase in the number of cellular phones, a near quadrupling in the number of personal computers, and an expectation that two-thirds of those PCs will have Internet access by 2001.

The Technological Dimension of Globalization

There have been three technological revolutions in transport and communication costs in modern times. The cost of transporting goods was lowered enormously in the 19th century with the advent of the steam engine, which created the railway and steamship. Steel hulls for ships and refrigeration further lowered the cost of ocean transport late in the 19th century, particularly for perishable goods. The telegraph helped as well (O'Rourke and Williamson 1999). The second technological revolution also greatly lowered the cost of moving people. It was dominated in the middle half of the 20th century by the falling cost of transport by car and airplane, caused by mass production of such goods and associated services. Ocean freight rates (helped by containerization) and telephone charges also fell massively over this period.[1] The third revolution in transport and communications technology, at this end of the 20th century, has been digital. Aided by deregulation of telecommunications markets in many countries, the digital revolution

Table 2.2

Growth in Capacity for Electronic Commerce, 1991–2001

(million units)

	1991	1996	2001[a]
Telephone main lines	545	741	1000
Cellular phone subscribers	16	135	400
Personal computers	123	245	450
Internet host computers	1	16	110
PCs with internet access	5	60	300

[a] Projected by the International Telecommunications Union, Geneva
Source: WTO (1998b, p. 8).

has enormously lowered long-distance communication costs, and especially the cost of rapidly accessing and processing knowledge, information, and ideas from anywhere in the world.[2] A side effect of the Internet's expansion has been the growth in the use of the English language. It has been claimed that there are now more people using English as a second language than there are people for whom it is a first language (Cairncross 1997). This too is lowering costs of communicating between countries.

The Governmental Contribution to Globalization

The previously mentioned developments have been reinforced by government decisions to liberalize trade and investment regimes. Following the protectionist interwar period, this liberalization began with the lowering of import tariffs on trade in manufactures between industrial economies. Within Western Europe that trade was especially liberal following the Treaty of Rome and the formation of the European Free Trade Area. In the 1980s trade reform was followed by extensive liberalization of foreign exchange markets and of restrictions on capital flows, leading (with the help of new digital technologies) to the development of new financial instruments. At the same time many non-Organisation for Economic Co-operation and Development (OECD) countries—including China and ultimately the Soviet bloc—began moving away from inward-looking to outward-oriented trade and investment policies. The 1980s also saw the deregulation of domestic markets in a growing number of countries, which reinforced the effects of deregulating transactions at national borders.

These reforms benefit most the countries making them, but they also benefit their trading partners. Hence the more countries open up and reform, the greater is the gain to other countries from doing likewise. In particular, they expand the opportunities for developing and transition economies to access goods and services markets, investment funds, and technologies, thereby raising the payoff to those economies for joining the bandwagon of liberalization. Those that have already done so have grown much faster than the rest and have seen their incomes converge toward OECD income levels (see, for example, Dollar 1992; Edwards 1993; Sachs and Warner 1995; and WTO 1998a, pp. 62–63 for a bibliography). The reasons for faster growth of more open economies have to do with the dynamics of trade liberalization, which are not just predictions derived from new trade and growth theories (Grossman and Helpman 1991) but that are well supported empirically (USITC 1997). However, greater openness can carry some risks, especially if appropriate domestic policies are

not in place. Two examples, to be discussed later, have to do with prudential regulation of the financial sector and environmental concerns. There is also a risk that the market-opening reforms of the postwar period, and especially the past 15 years, could be reversed by governments as domestic political circumstances change. As explained in the next section, during the past 50 years that risk has been contained by the GATT and, since 1995, by the WTO.

Together with the technological revolution, these policy reforms have brought about a more integrated global trading system, a global capital market, and more international transactions that formerly took place between independent entities are being internalized within single firms or corporate alliances. The increasing mobility of the productive assets of firms enables them to minimize their corporate income tax exposure by strategically locating their headquarters and using transfer pricing in their intrafirm international trade. This mobility also encourages governments to compete for the presence of firms with regulatory reforms and investment incentives (including restraints on the adoption of higher environmental and labor standards). On the one hand, this could leave governments with less tax revenue to implement social policies at a time when the demand for such policies is rising with income growth and with disruptions in the market for low-skilled labor. On the other hand, if regulatory reform is growth enhancing and includes the privatization of state-owned enterprises, government revenue could expand.

These technological and governmental revolutions have contributed increasingly to the drift toward urbanization. The first helped launch the industrial revolution in Western Europe, but this was done partly by lowering the cost of exploiting natural resources abroad, which also allowed primary sectors in less densely populated and tropical countries to expand. The second revolution accelerated industrialization in the West and its spread to the Far East, including by means of what Vernon (1966) described as the product cycle. The current revolution is increasing the scope to subdivide the processes of production and distribution into parts that can be relocated anywhere in the world according to ever-increasing changes in comparative advantages over time. That outsourcing can be via various means including subcontracting, licensing, joint ventures, and direct foreign investment by multinational corporations (Markusen et al. 1996).

The resulting productivity growth in the industrial and service sectors is altering the key source of wealth of nations, which is moving ever faster away from natural capital to human capital (that is, from raw materials and physical capital per worker to human skills and knowledge). In particular, wealth creation in the 21st century will depend especially on the ability to access and make productive use of expanding stocks of knowledge and information, and to build on them through creative research and development (World Bank 1998). How well and how quickly people of different countries are able to do that will increasingly determine relative economic growth rates. But for all countries the extent and speed with which economic events abroad are transmitted to domestic markets will increase inexorably, and governments will have less and less capacity to isolate their economies from such trends, as derivatives and electronic commerce have made clear in the cases of international financial flows and a widening range of traded goods and services.

The GATT/WTO's Contribution to Globalization

History shows that the risk of market opening being reversed is much more likely in the absence than in the presence of international constraints on national trade policy actions. For example, the Cobden–Chevalier Treaty of 1860 between England and France contained a most-favored-nation (MFN) clause which required that the agreed cut in the tariff on each item in their bilateral trade was also to be applied to their imports from other countries. This clause also meant that every European country that subsequently signed a trade treaty with either England or France (and most did by 1867) signed onto the MFN treaty. The effect was a network of treaties that greatly lowered the level of tariff protection in Europe (Kindleberger 1975), allowing world output and trade to boom for several decades until the First World War intervened (Table 2.1). Following that war, efforts to restore liberal trade centered on international conferences but did not lead to renewed trade treaties with binding commitments to openness based on MFN. Then when recession hit in the late 1920s, governments responded with beggar-my-neighbor protectionist trade policies that drove the world economy into depression. The volume of world trade shrank by one-quarter between 1929 and 1932, and its value fell by 40 percent. The first attempts to reverse that protection were discriminatory, as with the Ottawa Conference of 1932, which led to preferential tariffs on trade among members of the British Commonwealth.

Out of the interwar experience came the conviction that liberal world trade required a set of rules and binding commitments based on nondiscriminatory principles. While there was not enough agreement to create an international trade organization, at least a General Agreement on Tariffs and Trade was signed by 23 large trading countries in 1947. The GATT provided not only a set of multilateral rules and disciplines but also a forum within which to negotiate tariff reductions and rules changes. It also provided a mechanism to help settle trade disputes. Eight so-called rounds of negotiations took place in the subsequent 46 years, the last one (the Uruguay Round) culminating in the "interim" GATT Secretariat being converted into the World Trade Organization.

The GATT, and now even more so the WTO, contribute to globalization in several crucial ways. The WTO has four key objectives: to set and enforce rules for international trade; to provide a forum within which to negotiate and monitor trade liberalization; to improve policy transparency; and to resolve trade disputes. Apart from the transparency role, these were also the key objectives of its predecessor before the WTO came into being; but the WTO is much more comprehensive than the GATT. For example, GATT's product coverage in practice was confined mainly to manufactures (effectively not including textiles and clothing), whereas the WTO encompasses all goods (including sensitive farm products), services, capital to some extent, and ideas (intellectual property). In addition, following the conclusion of the Uruguay Round negotiations, the interim GATT Secretariat was converted to a permanent WTO Secretariat with greatly strengthened trade policy review and dispute settlement mechanisms. It also has a new role: cooperating with the International Monetary Fund (IMF) and World Bank with a view toward achieving greater coherence in global economic policymaking.

GATT/WTO rules to govern international trade serve at least three purposes. First, they protect the welfare of small and weak nations against discriminatory trade policy actions of large and powerful nations. GATT Articles I (most favored nation) and III (national treatment) promise that all WTO members will be given the same conditions of access to a particular country's market as the most favored member, and all foreign suppliers will be treated the same as domestic suppliers. These fairness rules are fundamental to instilling confidence in the world trading system. In particular, they lower the risks that are associated with a nation's producers and consumers becoming more dependent on foreigners—risks that otherwise could be used by a country as an excuse for not fully opening its borders.

Second, large economies have the potential of exploiting their monopoly power by taxing their trade, but we know from trade theory that the world as a whole is made worse off by such trade taxes. Thus while each large economy might be tempted to impose trade taxes, the effect of many of them doing so simultaneously may well be to leave most if not all of them worse off, not to mention the welfare reductions for smaller countries. Here then is the value of agreeing not to raise trade barriers and instead to "bind" them in a tariff schedule at specified ceiling levels. This rule is embodied in GATT Article II whereby WTO members are expected to limit trade only with tariffs and are obligated to continue to provide market access never less favorable than that agreed to in their tariff schedules. Again, the greater certainty that this tariff-binding rule brings to the international trading system adds to the preparedness of countries to become more interdependent and of business people to invest more.

The third and perhaps most important contribution of multilateral rules disciplining trade policy is that they can help governments ward off domestic interest groups seeking special favors. This comes about partly via Article II, which outlaws the raising of bound tariffs, as well as via numerous other articles aimed at ensuring that nontariff measures are not used as substitutes for tariffs. This benefit of the system is sometimes referred to as the "Ulysses effect": It helps prevent governments from being tempted to "sin," in this case to favor special interest groups at the expense of the rest of their economy.[3]

While no one would argue that GATT rules have been applied without exception, the fact that they are there ensures the worst excesses are avoided. They therefore bring greater certainty and predictability to international markets, enhancing economic welfare in and reducing political tensions between nations. More than that, by promoting interdependence, the GATT/WTO indirectly has raised the price and hence reduced the likelihood of countries going to war.

But why do countries need the WTO to negotiate freer trade? One of the clearest lessons from trade theory is that an economy unable to influence its international terms of trade cannot maximize its national income and economic growth without allowing free trade in all goods and services. Consumers lose directly from the higher domestic prices of importables, while exporters lose indirectly because import barriers cause the nation's currency to appreciate (there is less demand for foreign currency from importers) and raise the price of labor and other mobile resources. More open economies also grow faster. Why, then, do countries restrict their trade, and why do they need to get together to agree to liberalize those protectionist trade regimes multilaterally, when it is in their national economic interests to do so unilaterally?

Numerous reasons have been suggested as to why a country imposes trade barriers in the first place, but al-most all of them are found wanting (Corden 1997). The most compelling explanation relates to a country's political economy. It has to do with the national income redistribution feature of trade policies: the gains are concentrated in the hands of a few who are prepared to support politicians who favor protection, while the losses are sufficiently small per consumer and export firm and are distributed sufficiently widely as to make it not worthwhile for those losers to get together to provide a counterlobby, particularly given their greater free-rider problem in acting collectively (Hillman 1989; Grossman and Helpman 1994; Anderson 1995). Thus the observed pattern of protection in a country at a point in time may well be an equilibrium outcome in a national political market for policy intervention.

That political equilibrium in two or more countries might be able to be altered, however, for the better through an exchange of product market access. If country A allows more imports it may well harm its import-competing producers if there are no compensation mechanisms; but if this liberalization is done in return for country A's trading partners lowering their barriers to A's exports, the producers of those exports will enjoy this additional benefit. The latter extra benefit may be sufficiently greater than the loss to A's import-competing producers that A's liberalizing politicians also become net gainers in terms of electoral support. Likewise, politicians in the countries trading with A may well be able to gain from this trade in market access, for equal and opposite reasons. That is, a new opportunity for trade negotiations can stimulate trade liberalization by altering the incentives to lobby politicians and thereby the political equilibrium in trading nations.[4]

Such gains from trade negotiations involving exchange of market access will tend to be greater nationally and globally, the larger the number of countries involved and the broader the product and issues coverage of the negotiations; hence the wisdom in negotiating multilaterally with more than 100 countries over a wide range of sectors and issues, as in the Uruguay Round, despite the process being cumbersome. Now that there is so much more product coverage under the WTO than under the GATT, and the number and extent of participation by member countries keeps growing, the scope for exchange of market access has increased dramatically. That is especially true for exchanges between more- and less-developed economies now that agriculture, textiles, and clothing are back in the GATT mainstream and services and trade-related intellectual property have been added, making a wider range of intersector tradeoffs possible.

This is not to deny the many challenges confronting the global trading system. Digesting and implementing the agreements that came out of the Uruguay Round negotiations is but one of them. Launching a new round of multilateral trade negotiations next year is another, especially given the lack of agreement on the extent to which new issues should be added to the WTO's agenda. Another obvious and urgent challenge is the Asian financial crisis. This crisis is of interest internationally not just because of humanitarian concern for those directly hurting in East Asia. What it has demonstrated is how volatile short-term private capital can be in an integrated global capital market where herd mentality and panic can take hold and spread quickly thanks to the digital revolution in communications. The consequent risk of contagion to other regions is thus now greater than in even the recent past. Such international spillovers magnify the adverse consequences of the crisis. Among other things, that multiplies the probability that affected countries in Asia and elsewhere will slow or reverse their market-opening policy stance even though the opposite is what is required to resume or sustain growth. The possibility of policy reversals underscores the importance of getting another comprehensive WTO round under way in the year 2000.

Implications for Development Strategies of Poorer Countries

Greater openness of and interdependence between national economies provides wonderful opportunities for poorer economies, but it is not without its challenges. Globalization is raising the rewards to economies choosing good economic governance *but is also raising the cost to economies with poor economic governance.* Just as financial capital can now flow into a well-managed economy more easily and quickly than ever before, so it can equally quickly be withdrawn if confidence in that economy's governance is shaken—as the East Asian crisis has demonstrated all too clearly during 1997–98. In this section just two aspects of good economic governance in the wake of globalization are discussed: commitment to a liberal international trade and payments regime, and growth-enhancing domestic policies that are not biased by sectors. Together these will enable producers to take maximum advantage of new and prospective export opportunities following Uruguay Round implementation.

Commitment to a Liberal Trade and Payments Regime
The previous discussion suggests the first priority for a poor country seeking to achieve sustainable economic development in the 21st century is to practice good economic governance generally, and in particular to com-

mit to a *permanently* open international trade and payments regime and to provide secure property rights (intellectual as well as physical). The stability of the commitment to openness is much more crucial now than even just 15 years ago because otherwise capital inflows and investments will be only short-term in nature and will be susceptible to withdrawal should confidence waver. It is for this reason, and because of the comprehensiveness of the Uruguay Round agreements, that liberal trade policy commitments under the WTO are so important. They are valued by would-be investors because WTO commitments involve (a) legal bindings and (b) most-favored-nation treatment by trading partners. The legal bindings mean a WTO member cannot return to a more protectionist regime by raising tariffs above the bound rates listed in the member's schedules of commitments, nor does that member risk facing higher than MFN bound tariffs in exporting to its trading partners if they are WTO members.

The security of a stable trading environment instills a confidence in investors that is noticeably less in countries that are not WTO members. For such countries a key ingredient in achieving good economic governance is to seek speedy accession to the WTO. Already there are 134 countries that have chosen to join the new organization. The WTO is thus approaching the status of a truly global trade organization except for underrepresentation by two groups: the former centrally planned economies (CPEs) seeking to transform from plan to market orientations, and some of the smallest and poorest economies.

Most of the CPEs not already members are seeking WTO accession, the most notable being China (whose accession would allow Taiwan to join) and Russia. Their accession negotiations have proceeded slowly in part because members want more access to those countries' markets than their governments have been willing to give. This is especially so with respect to bound tariffs, signing the WTO's plurilateral government procurement agreement, and assurances over intellectual property rights. Additional problems include their lack of policy transparency and their high degree of state trading, not to mention the need to overcome political opposition (for human rights reasons) in the U.S. Congress and elsewhere to their joining. In China's case the "concessions" available to developing country WTO members are also being sought. The United States and others are very reluctant to allow China those "concessions," however, because that could effectively make meaningless the negotiated access to Chinese markets (Anderson 1997).

The other group feeling marginalized is the world's least developed countries (LDCs), particularly those that are not yet WTO members. For them the cost of the accession process, and subsequently of maintaining a mission in Geneva that is large enough to cover the expanding number of items of key concern to them, is prohibitive without some financial and technical aid. A program of multilateral assistance does exist and was expanded following a high-level meeting between LDCs, the WTO, and five other international agencies in late October 1997. Many bilateral assistance programs also exist (OECD 1998). But with so many new countries seeking membership and so many more issues to deal with following the Uruguay Round, the budgets for those programs may need to expand further, especially if a new round is launched soon.

In addition to the 30-plus countries currently in the queue for membership, perhaps another 20 will apply soon. Hence within a decade, the WTO will have much the same membership number and composition as the United Nations. The WTO's predecessor, the GATT, began as a club of industrial countries, but by the start of the Uruguay Round those countries' share had fallen to one-quarter and could be as small as one-sixth during the next round.

To understand how well the WTO club is managing its own globalization, consider the following four questions: To what extent are less-advanced economies (1) opening up to trade, (2) able to get their exports into markets of more-advanced economies, (3) engaged in WTO activities such as improving the rules, and (4) able to accede expeditiously?

On the first question regarding openness, the answer is that many developing and transition economies are opening up substantially. During the past decade or so an ever-larger number of developing countries—including those in Africa—have embraced trade liberalization. Some of those reform programs have been adopted with reluctance as conditions for receiving IMF or World Bank loans, while others have been unconditional unilateral decisions. Until they are bound under the WTO, though, there is a risk of backsliding in the future. Furthermore, tariffs need to be bound at levels close to applied rates in order to be taken seriously, unlike during the Uruguay Round when many developing countries just committed to ceiling bindings at several times the level of applied rates.

On the second question of market access for developing country products, the answer is that not enough has been done. The two sectors of most interest to less-advanced economies are agriculture and textiles/clothing, and protection levels in more-advanced economies for those items are as much as ten times the average for other merchandise. Even though commitments have been made in the Uruguay Round to lower agricultural and textile import barriers, only modest reductions resulted by the turn of the century. Pooling of negotiating efforts to open those markets more is one strategy worth pursuing, as the Cairns Group of agricultural exporting countries demonstrated during the Uruguay Round.

On the third question, the answer is that while there are ample opportunities for less-advanced economies to become engaged in WTO activities, such as chairing committees, they are taken up infrequently. Michalopoulos (1998a) suggests that is because poor and especially small countries have few, if any, delegates in Geneva, and those that are there are inadequately serviced by their national capitals and so are always overstretched. The pooling of efforts by members forming a group has been one way of coping, as the Association of Southeast Asian Nations (ASEAN) member countries do, for example. Perhaps further aid funding is warranted for the smallest and least developed countries in order to raise their quality and quantity of representation.

As to the final question concerning the pace of accession of new members, the answer is unclear. Certainly an average time of six years to accede to the WTO sounds long, and certainly politics may have contributed to delays, as with China.[5] But much of the delay appears to be on the part of the acceding country. Sometimes this is because of a lack of internal political support to push ahead with reform commitments. More often it is because of insufficient bureaucratic horsepower to get on top of the issues and to move the necessary papers forward faster (Michalopoulos 1998b). This situation is unfortunate because the reforms required to join the WTO will become even greater during the next round of WTO multilateral trade negotiations. One partial solution is to raise the quantity and quality of trade policy staffing in national capitals, and in particular to boost training. Further education is needed not only about the WTO institution but also in analytical capability and skills in advocating the virtues of liberal markets. The domestic political commitment to do that may not be in place, however, and the question again arises as to whether more development assistance funds need to be directed to that cause.

Growth-Enhancing Domestic Policies That Are Not Biased by Sectors

The extent to which liberalizing one's own trade and payments regime and securing greater market access opportunities for one's exports boosts a developing country's economic growth depends importantly also on domestic policy environment. Sound, predictable, stable macroeconomic policies and taxation policies that are not biased by sectors are essential. Uruguay Round reforms abroad will make agricultural and textile/clothing exports more profitable for developing countries. Trade liberalization at home will tend to reinforce that, because many developing and transition economies have traditionally protected heavy manufacturing industry at the expense of light manufacturing and primary production—a pro-urban industrial bias.

Those past trade and other pro-urban policy biases discouraged investment in infrastructure and human capital in rural areas. Unleashing the productive potential of the rural sector requires major upgrading of essential rural infrastructures, thereby lowering transactions costs of doing business there, and it requires investment in the people involved. The crucial infrastructures include rural roads, electricity, telecommunications, and radio transmission so that costs of transport, communications, and information (about market conditions, new technologies, and the like) become more affordable. Investments in these items probably will be more expensive per capita than in urban areas, but that needs to be weighed against the net long-term benefits from expanding output faster from rural areas. In numerous countries irrigation investments also need to be facilitated, even if they are mostly funded at the local level with the help of loans (which require secure property rights over land use so land can be used as collateral with lenders).

The crucial investments in people include basic schooling (for girls as much as for boys), basic health services, and agricultural research and extension. All the empirical evidence points to the social rates of return from such public investments being very high in developing countries even when price and trade policies discriminate heavily against the rural sector; hence they are likely to be even higher as and when those policies are reformed. If those social rates of return are significantly above private rates, a case might be made for government subsidies (Schultz 1975). Drawing on a great deal of empirical research, Schultz argues that the case is especially strong with human capital investments in rural areas. Such investments not only raise farm incomes and so reduce the need for farmers to leave agriculture, but they also increase the prospects for those who migrate to nonfarm jobs. In both respects, the social tensions that are inevitably associated with rapid economic growth and structural change are lessened.

Efforts to reduce underinvestment in rural infrastructure also would benefit not only agricultural production. With better transport and communications infrastructure and better-educated workers, rural areas would be more attractive to investors in low-skill intensive manufacturing and related service activities. Hence we would see clothing factories and the like becoming more common in rural areas. That would boost off-farm earnings of farm households, allowing a more efficient and fuller use of the rural work force, particularly in nonpeak seasons. In addition to its contribution to output, this rural development strategy would slow the growth of urban pollution and congestion, and reduce the incidence of poverty and hunger (since most of the poor are in or have recently migrated from rural areas).[6]

Conclusion

In conclusion, it is worth reiterating that market responses to trade liberalization at home and abroad may not be sufficient to fully reap the rewards from those reforms. As explained by Krugman (1998), the reason is that history matters: Earlier protection toward heavy industry in developing countries boosted their urban centers, as did the restrictions on those countries' access to rich-country markets for farm products. With the growing importance of scale economies in many nonprimary sectors, and inadequate environmental taxes on negative externalities such as urban pollution and congestion, resources will continue to want to locate in large urban centers. In societies where lobbying politicians has a high payoff, that provides a further reason for capitalists to retain a presence in the capital city. First-best solutions could include imposing environmental taxes and outlawing rent-seeking. But if that is too difficult, second-best measures may well be justified. They could include temporarily subsidizing investments in infrastructure and human capital in rural areas until the centrifugal market forces are sufficient to offset the centripetal forces of geographic concentration, to use Krugman's terminology.

Bibliography

Anderson, K. 1995. "Lobbying Incentives and the Pattern of Protection in Rich and Poor Countries." *Economic Development and Cultural Change* 43(2): 401–23, January.

Anderson, K., ed. 1996. *Strengthening the Global Trading System: From GATT to WTO.* Adelaide: Centre for International Economic Studies.

Anderson, K. 1997. "On the Complexities of China's WTO Accession." *The World Economy* 20(6): 749–72, September.

Anderson, K. 1998a. *Vietnam's Transition Economy and WTO Accession.* Adelaide: Centre for International Economic Studies.

Anderson, K. 1998b. *Lao Economic Reform and WTO Accession.* Adelaide: Centre for International Economic Studies.

Baldwin, R. E., and P. Martin. 1999. "Two Waves of Globalization: Superficial Similarities and Fundamental Differences." NBER Working Paper 6904, Cambridge MA, January (http://www.papers.nber.org/papers/w6904).

Blainey, G. 1966. The Tyranny of Distance. Melbourne: Sun Books.

Bordo, M. D., B. Eichengreen, and D. A. Irwin. 1999. "Is Globalization Today Really Different Than Globalization a Hundred Years Ago?" in S. Collins and R. Lawrence eds. *Brookings Trade Policy Forum* 1999, Washington, D.C.: Brookings Institution.

Cairncross, F. 1997. *The Death of Distance: How the Communications Revolution Will Change Our Lives.* London: Orion Business Books.

Corden, W. M. 1997. *Trade Policy and Economic Welfare,* 2d ed. Oxford: Clarendon Press.

Dollar, D. 1992. "Outward-Oriented Developing Economies Really Do Grow More Rapidly: Evidence From 95 LDCs, 1976–85." *Economic Development and Cultural Change* 40: 523–44, April.

Edwards, S. 1993. "Openness, Trade Liberalization, and Growth in Developing Countries." *Journal of Economic Literature* 31(3): 1358–93, September.

Goldstein, J. 1998. "International Institutions and Domestic Politics: GATT, WTO, and the Liberalization of International Trade." In A. O. Krueger, ed., *The WTO as an International Organization.* Chicago and London: University of Chicago Press.

Grossman, G. M., and E. Helpman. 1991. *Innovation and Growth in the Global Economy.* Cambridge, MA: MIT Press.

Grossman, G., and E. Helpman. 1994. "Protection for Sale." *American Economic Review* 84(4): 833–50, September.

Grossman, G., and E. Helpman. 1995. "Trade Wars and Trade Talks." *Journal of Political Economy* 103(4): 675–708, August.

Hillman, A. L. 1989. *The Political Economy of Protection.* New York: Harwood Academic.

Hoekman, B. M., and M. Kostecki. 1995. *The Political Economy of the World Trading System: From GATT to WTO.* London and New York: Oxford University Press.

Hufbauer, G. C. 1991. "World Economic Integration: The Long View." *International Economic Insights,* May/June.

Kindleberger, C. P. 1975. "The Rise of Free Trade in Western Europe, 1820–1875." *Journal of Economic History* 35(1): 20–55, March.

Krugman, P. 1998. "The Role of Geography in Development." Paper presented to the Annual World Bank Conference on Development Economics. Washington, D.C., April 20–21.

Landes, D. 1998. *The Wealth and Poverty of Nations.* London: Little Brown and Company.

Maddison, A. 1982. *Phases of Capitalist Development.* London: Oxford University Press.

Markusen, J. R., A. J. Venables, D. B. Konan, and K. Zhang. 1996. "A Unified Treatment of Horizontal Direct Investment, Vertical Direct Investment, and the Pattern of Trade in Goods and Services." NBER Working Paper 5696, Cambridge, MA.

Michalopoulos, C. 1998a. "The Participation of Developing Countries in the WTO." Policy Research Working Paper 1906, World Bank, Washington, D.C., March.

Michalopoulos, C. 1998b. "WTO Accession for Countries in Transition." Policy Research Working Paper 1932, World Bank, Washington, D.C.

OECD (Organisation for Economic Co-operation and Development). 1998. *Survey of DAC Members' Co-operation for Capacity Development in Trade.* DCD/DAC(97)24/REV1, Paris: OECD, March.

O'Rourke, K. H., and J. G. Williamson. 1999. *Globalization and History: The Evolution of a Nineteenth Century Atlantic Economy.* Cambridge, MA: MIT Press.

Petersmann, E-U. 1991. *Constitutional Functions and Constitutional Problems of International Economic Law.* Fribourg: Fribourg University Press.

Roessler, F. 1985. "The Scope, Limits and Function of the GATT Legal System." *The World Economy* 8(3): 287–98.

Sachs, J. D., and A. Warner. 1995. "Economic Reform and the Process of Global Integration." *Brookings Papers on Economic Activity* 1: 1–118.

Schultz, T. W. 1975. "On the Ability to Deal With Disequilibria." *Journal of Economic Literature* 13(3): 827–46, September.

UNCTAD (United Nations Conference on Trade and Development). 1998. *World Investment Report 1998: Trends and Determinants.* New York and Geneva: United Nations.

USITC (United States International Trade Commission). 1997. *The Dynamic Effects of Trade Liberalization: An Empirical Analysis.* Publication 3069, U.S. International Trade Commission, Washington, D.C., October.

Vernon, R. 1966. "International Investment and International Trade in the Product Cycle." *Quarterly Journal of Economics* 80: 190–207, May.

World Bank. 1997. *Rural Development: From Vision to Action.* ESSD Studies and Monograph Series 12, Washington, D.C.: The World Bank.

World Bank. 1998. *World Development Report 1998/99: Knowledge for Development.* New York: Oxford University Press.

WTO (World Trade Organization). 1996. *Annual Report 1996.* Geneva: World Trade Organization.

WTO (World Trade Organization). 1998a. *Annual Report 1998.* Geneva: World Trade Organization.

WTO (World Trade Organization). 1998b. *Electronic Commerce and the Role of the WTO.* Geneva: World Trade Organization.

Notes

1. Between 1920 and 1980, the real charge per tonne for ocean freight fell by almost three-quarters and between 1960 and 1980 the real cost of a telephone call from New York to London fell by 90 percent. Meanwhile, between 1930 and 1980 the real cost of air travel fell 85 percent (Hufbauer 1991).

2. Two book titles summarize this 150-year history: Blainey's *Tyranny of Distance* which refers to Australia's early isolation from the Old World prior to steamships, and Cairncross' *Death of Distance* which refers to the latest communications revolution (Blainey 1966; Cairncross 1997). For comparisons of the nineteenth and late twentieth century episodes of globalization, see Baldwin and Martin (1999) and Bordo, Eichengreen and Irwin (1999).

3. Petersmann (1991, p. 83) goes so far as to say that "the primary regulatory function of the GATT.... [is] the welfare-increasing resolution of *domestic* conflicts of interest *within* GATT member countries among individual producers, importers, exporters and consumers." Similarly, Roessler (1985, p. 298) claims that "the principal function of the GATT as a sys-

tem of rules is to resolve conflicts of interest within, not among, countries. The function of the GATT as a negotiating forum is to enable countries to defend the national interest not against the national interests of other countries but against sectional interests within their own and other countries."

4. Elaborations of this economists' perspective can be found in Grossman and Helpman (1995), Hillman and Moser (1995), Hoekman and Kostecki (1995), and Anderson (1996, Ch. 1). Political scientists are beginning to take a similar view. See, for example, Goldstein (1998).

5. In particular, the concern in the United States about human rights in China has often meant the US Congress is unsympathetic to China. One manifestation of that is the high demands on China in terms of policy reform and market opening before the US will conclude its bilateral negotiations on its WTO accession. Vietnam and Laos have similar hurdles to jump in their bids to join WTO, in their cases because of the sensitive issue of US soldiers missing in action during the Vietnam war (Anderson 1998a,b).

6. For more on the benefits of removing the anti-rural bias in many countries' development strategies, see World Bank (1997).

chapter 3

Toward a Global Financial Architecture for the 21st Century

Robert E. Litan

Vice President and Director
Economics Studies Program
The Brookings Institution

Going into the 21st century, the challenge for financial policymakers is to learn from the past while constructing institutions that better enable economies to reap the benefits of modern finance without the pitfalls that have plagued so many countries in this century, vividly illustrated by the Asian financial crisis of the past two years. The task is complicated by the need to anticipate and take account of trends and developments that will continue to shape the financial landscape throughout the world.

This chapter seeks to address this challenge. It begins by surveying the role of finance in both developed and developing economies and its increasing cross-border or global character. It then describes the origins and key features of the recent financial crises, as a predicate for a description of some of the key issues that financial policymakers around the world must now confront. Along the way, it addresses the role for financial supervision, the relative costs and benefits of various exchange rate regimes, and the ways in which international financial institutions may assist in achieving more orderly growth of both the real and financial sectors in the years ahead.

The Economics and Globalization of Finance

Finance is important not just for its own sake but because it is central to the process of economic growth. Financial intermediaries and markets *enhance both saving and investment*, enlarging the capital stock and thus increasing the productivity of workers. In addition, by taking advantage of economies of scale in collecting and evaluating information about investment projects and their sponsors, commercial banks and other financial intermediaries can help efficiently *allocate capital to its most productive uses.*

These are not merely theoretical propositions. Empirical evidence confirms that the level of financial development—measured by, among other things, the size of the banking sector relative to overall economic activity—is highly correlated with economic growth among developing countries, controlling for other factors (Levine 1996). At the same time, if incentives for the efficient use of capital are lacking, then even sophisticated financial systems cannot insulate an economy against adversity, as the Asian crisis demonstrated.

The focus on banking in developing countries is not an accident. Developing economies rely heavily on commercial banks to perform the critical function of intermediating funds between savers and investors. In contrast, nonbanking institutions active in the capital markets play a more important intermediating role in more developed economies. The relative importance of banks and markets as instruments of intermediation is a function, in large part, of the state of economic development. In developing economies, savers tend to lack sophistication in financial matters and are mainly interested in investing their funds in safe vehicles, such as bank deposits. Meanwhile, few borrowers in developing economies are of sufficient size and creditworthiness to justify the expense of floating securities, which in turn reduces the demand for securities markets. However, as economies mature and their firms grow in size and sophistication, so do their capital markets, provided both the private and public sectors erect a suitable technical and legal infrastructure to support them.

Financial intermediation is not confined to national borders. Like water that will flow downhill if given the chance, financial capital will—if allowed—move to projects offering the highest risk-adjusted returns wherever they may be located. In addition, modern portfolio theory demonstrates that there are advantages to investing in a wide variety of projects, even in different countries, provided those endeavors' returns are not perfectly correlated with one another.

These basic theoretical propositions have been put to work in recent decades, as finance has become truly "globalized," through two types of cross-border financial flows. So-called *portfolio capital* consists of investments that are potentially short-term in nature, including loans between banks and investments in traded bonds and equities. Cross-border interbank lending now exceeds US$6 trillion, up from US$1.2 trillion as recently as 1983 (Bank of International Settlements 1992). The globalization of stock markets also has facilitated the movement of portfolio capital between nations. The shares of portfolios invested in foreign stocks and bonds have been rising steadily in the United States, Western Europe, and even Japan (Tesar and Werner 1998).

In contrast, foreign direct investment (FDI) consists of long-term holdings of equity, where the aim is to control or exercise significant influence over local firms. FDI has become increasingly linked to trade as it no longer suffices simply to ship many products across borders to customers waiting in foreign lands. Consumer and business products often require local servicing operations, as well as research and development and marketing enterprises, if they are to be sold effectively in other countries. Moreover, financial and professional services, among others, typically can only be supplied by a presence on the ground in other countries. It is not surprising, therefore, that since the dominant share of trade of developed economies is with other developed economies, a similar pattern has developed with respect to FDI.

The globalization of finance has not been confined to developed economies. One of the more important trends of the 1990s is that investors from developed economies have poured steadily larger sums into developing countries. This process has been facilitated by dramatically lower costs of collecting, analyzing, processing, and communicating information. Figure 3.1 illustrates that as late as 1990, official funds accounted for the majority of the roughly US$100 billion flowing to developing countries. By 1997, about US$300 billion went into the developing world, of which only about 15 percent was supplied officially. FDI accounted for the largest share (40 percent), followed closely by borrowing (34 percent), which

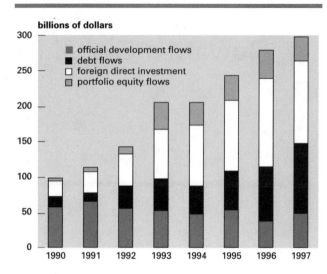

Figure 3.1

Net Long-Term Resource Flows to Developing Countries, 1990–97

billions of dollars

- official development flows
- debt flows
- foreign direct investment
- portfolio equity flows

Source: World Bank Debtor Reporting System.

was up by more than 125 percent from the beginning of the decade. Indeed, during the 1989–96 period, the growth of incoming FDI into developing countries outpaced the growth of trade and gross domestic product (GDP) by a large margin, as well as the growth of incoming FDI into developed countries (Figure 3.2).

An important aspect of the globalization of finance is the increased presence of banks in multiple countries. Table 3.1 highlights the extent to which foreign banks have made inroads into the banking systems of certain developing countries. Notably, none of the countries with a foreign bank share in excess of 20 percent experienced banking and financial problems either directly or indirectly during the Asian financial crisis. Two reasons help explain this fact. Foreign institutions bring cutting edge financial technologies and practices that not only improve the performance and health of financial institutions in the host countries but impart up-to-date knowledge of banking practices to their regulators. Moreover, because they are often active in numerous parts of the world, foreign financial institutions are typically far more diversified in their lending than local institutions, and thus less likely to fail when economic conditions in local markets turn down (for evidence, see Claessens and Glaessner 1998).

Financial integration has not been universal, however. The vast majority of developing countries still receive relatively little private capital (World Bank 1997). Much of the flows have been to Asia, where net foreign portfolio investments rose steadily from US$20 billion in 1990 to nearly US$120 billion in 1993. Since 1993

Figure 3.2
Trends in Global Finance: Growth of GDP, Trade, and FDI, 1989–96

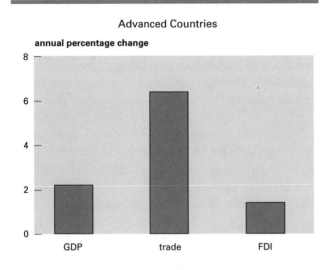

Advanced Countries

annual percentage change

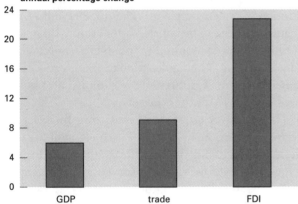

Developing Countries

annual percentage change

Source: World Bank Investment Report, 1997, and World Economic Outlook, May 1998.

Table 3.1
Foreign-Owned Banks

Government	Percentage share of total assets
Hong Kong, China	78.0[a]
India	7.3
Indonesia	3.7
Rep. of Korea	5.1
Malaysia	15.9
Singapore	80.0
Taiwan, China	4.7
Thailand	7.1
Argentina	21.7
Brazil	9.4
Chile	21.4
Colombia	3.6
Mexico	1.2
Venezuela	1.2
Russian Federation	2.2
Israel	0.0
South Africa	3.3
Germany	3.9
Japan	1.8
United States	22.0

Note: Figures refer to latest available year.
[a] Refers to all overseas-incorporated authorized institutions.
Sources: OECD, central banks, ministries of finance, and Goldstein and Turner (1996). Adapted from Goldstein 1997.

portfolio inflows have fluctuated considerably, collapsing to less than US$40 billion in 1998 (International Monetary Fund 1998). Such fluctuations imply that financial integration can be a two-edged sword: If foreign capital comes in too quickly, it can overwhelm the capacity of local financial institutions to put it to productive use, especially where government guarantees distort investment choices. This can sow the seeds of a later financial crisis, especially if local bank failures or other shocks to the economy trigger a loss of confidence in the currency. In that event, portfolio capital tends to run out much more quickly than it came in.

Financial Crises

When it functions well, finance is critical to facilitating economic growth. But when it is managed poorly, espe-

cially in an increasingly global environment, financial crises can lead to significant disruption of real economies. Large-scale banking problems, for example, can contribute to "credit crunches," or severe contractions in the availability of credit at the worst possible time, during a recession. This problem can be especially serious in developing economies, which as already noted, rely much more heavily on banks to perform intermediation than capital markets (Lindgren et al. 1996). Indeed, financial crises have occurred so frequently in some many parts of the world that some economists believe that financial panics (sudden "runs" by investors in capital markets or depositors from their banks) or "near crises" (financial difficulties short of a panic but which nevertheless depress economic activity) are an inevitable feature of market economies (Kindleberger 1978; Minsky 1982).

In the 20th century, the deepest financial crisis occurred during the Depression when thousands of banks failed in the United States and other countries, and stock prices plunged to fractions of their prior levels. For several decades after World War II, the financial arena was relatively free from major difficulty. But since 1980 the industrialized and developing world alike have experienced a rash of banking crises, with notable exam-

Table 3.2
Severe Banking Crises, 1980–96

Country (time of crisis)	Estimate of total losses/costs (percentage of GDP)
Latin America	
Argentina (1980–82)	55
Chile (1981–83)	41
Venezuela (1994–95)	18
Mexico (1995)	12–15
Africa	
Benin (1988–90)	17
Côte d'Ivoire (1988–91)	25
Mauritania (1984–93)	15
Senegal (1988–91)	17
Tanzania (1987–95)	10
Middle East	
Israel (1977–83)	30
Transition Countries	
Bulgaria (1990s)	14
Hungary (1995)	10
Industrial Countries	
United States (1980s)	3–4
Spain (1977–85)	17
Japan (1990s)	10

ples listed in Table 3.2. The crises in the developed world include the well-known savings and loan disaster in the United States, the ongoing difficulties in Japan, and the banking problems that plagued the Scandinavian countries in the late 1980s and early 1990s. The crises in the developing world have been both more numerous and more severe, as measured by the cost of their resolution as a share of local GDP. In all, roughly three-quarters of the IMF's member countries have experienced significant banking problems in the past two decades (Lindgren et al. 1996).

The 1980s and 1990s have been marked not only by banking crises, but by panics in capital markets as well. The October 1987 stock market crash afflicted markets throughout the world, although prices recovered in many markets a year later. That was not true in the case of Japan, whose stock prices collapsed in 1989 and at present stand 40 percent below those prior to the crash. Similarly, stock prices plunged in Mexico during its peso crisis of 1994–95 and throughout Southeast Asian markets during the recent financial crisis there. In all of these cases, the collapse in stock prices was directly or indirectly linked to weaknesses in domestic banking systems.

Some, but certainly not the majority of, financial crises have had international consequences. As just noted, the 1987 stock market crash reverberated around the world. The Mexican and Asian financial crises of the 1990s had international effects because both episodes were characterized by sharp plunges in exchange rates, which inevitably affected trade flows, and because the financial difficulties of these countries stemmed in large part from an inability to service debt linked to or denominated in foreign currencies (sovereign debt in the Mexican case and private borrowings in the Asian case). Similarly, the United States and to a lesser extent other industrialized countries suffered near crises in the 1980s when their large banks suffered losses on sovereign lending to developing (especially Latin American) countries. In most other cases, however, banking crises have had entirely or largely domestic origins and impacts.

Challenges Ahead

Developing sound financial policy is much like managing auto traffic on highways: While there always will be accidents, traffic engineers try to avoid especially costly ones—crashes at key intersections that cause gridlock throughout an entire region. The number and severity of auto crashes can be reduced by educating drivers, designing safer cars, monitoring speed levels, and building safer highways. The market alone cannot carry out all these functions. Countries have found that a helpful hand from government is necessary.

The objectives and tools for controlling financial traffic are similar. The objective of financial policy can be viewed as facilitating the orderly flow of money between actors, wherever they may be located, without experiencing "crashes" resulting in financial gridlock. This, too, requires a combination of market discipline and government oversight. Market participants must have timely access to accurate information; those running financial institutions must be educated in the tools of risk management; mechanisms must be in place to ensure the safety and soundness of individual financial institutions; and the "highways" of finance—the nuts and bolts of the back offices of financial institutions and clearing and settlement systems—must be built to withstand both heavy volumes of traffic and occasional traffic accidents.

While the highway analogy is highly useful, it actually *understates* the difficulties in designing financial systems, especially in an increasingly global financial marketplace. Although automobile accidents may cause highway traffic to back up many miles from the scene, accidents in one part of a county, state, or country do not tie up traffic in other geographic locations. In other words, there is no highway analogy to a "contagious run," which can occur in financial systems when problems in one or more institutions or in the currencies of one or more countries trigger the flight of depositors or investors from other institutions or currencies.

Nonetheless, it is useful to keep the highway analogy in mind in considering the following four trends that are likely to pose challenges to financial policymakers in the years ahead:

- Continued improvements in communications and computer technology will lead to even more rapid transmission of information while increasing both the volume and speed of financial transactions. Here technology may be both a boon and a bane. The gradual implementation of technology-based "real-time gross settlement" systems for clearing and settling funds transfers (including currency trades) between banks will eliminate clearing risk, helping insulate banking and securities markets against chain reactions if one or more large financial institutions fail. The potential downside of technological advances, however, is that precisely because they make it easier to move money from one place and one instrument to the other, they also facilitate more rapid exits from markets when investor moods suddenly shift.

- Financial technologies also will continue to evolve, producing new and even more complex financial instruments and trading strategies. To the extent that the new technologies facilitate risk management by financial institutions and investors, they will enhance the safety of those institutions and of the system as a whole. However, complex new instruments and trading strategies can detract from safety and soundness. It can take time for top management and regulators to fully understand the risks of the newer instruments, especially how they might interact with one another. The risks to individual institutions, and more importantly, to entire financial systems may rise in the meantime. Moreover, while the fact that most customized derivatives contracts are concentrated among the world's largest financial institutions gives some observers comfort, it makes others uneasy, fearing the potential chain reaction-like effects if one or more large counterparties become unable for any reason to honor their commitments.

- Markets will continue to replace banks as vehicles of intermediation, not just in the developed world where this process has been ongoing (especially in the United States), but also in developing and emerging market countries where it is in its relative infancy. Markets disperse lending risks throughout an investment community, potentially worldwide in scope, so that even when prices fall, the impact is diffused widely. In contrast, when lending is concentrated in banks, especially when the banking industry itself is highly concentrated as it is many developing countries, then an economic downturn that renders many borrowers unable to service their debts can significantly weaken the banking system. This in turn can aggravate the recession to the extent that banks are then unable to extend credit.

- Just as commerce continues to "globalize," so will financial institutions. Indeed, many large banks headquartered in developed countries already have followed their corporate customers into the countries in which they have made direct investments. This process will only gather force in the next century as trade expands and firms increasingly cross borders to service existing customers and to develop new markets. The Asian crisis has given a strong impetus to countries that previously had inhibited FDI to relax those restrictions.

Cross-border investment by financial institutions, in developing countries in particular, increases competition and innovation in these markets while helping to stabilize their financial systems. At the same time, however, the globalization of finance throughout both the developed and developing worlds will pose continuing and new challenges to national regulators. As a Group of Thirty report points out, "there is no international framework for dealing with the supervisory, legal and financial problems that would arise in a cross-border insolvency of any kind, and a major cross-border insolvency in the financial sector could therefore pose a substantial risk to the international financial system" (Group of Thirty 1998).

Financial Policy Challenges for Industrial Economies

Industrial economies with relatively sophisticated financial systems that are already open to capital movements of all kinds face challenges that are both similar to and different from those confronting developing countries.

The similar challenge is to maintain and effectively enforce sound capital standards for financial institutions, in particular banks whose deposits are insured explicitly (up to some limit) or implicitly (if the bank is large). This challenge is more complex and difficult than it may appear because capital standards by themselves are merely numbers and useless as a device for disciplining banks against excessive risk-taking, as well as insulating them against economic shocks of various sorts, unless bank assets and liabilities are recorded at levels reasonably close to their market values. Full-dress market value accounting is probably some way off, even in industrial economies, because many bank loans continue to be customized and are not traded (although at some point in the next century, it is likely that some form of market value accounting for banks will be adopted, either at the behest of regulators or the market). Nonetheless, even under historical cost accounting standards, loan loss reserves—which reduce a bank's reported capital—must reflect current conditions if bank capital is to even come close to being an accurate measure of the institution's net worth. This, in turn, requires effective regulatory supervision to ensure the reasonableness of the financial data the banks and their auditors report.

But even accurate information is not sufficient to ensure the effectiveness of a supervisory regime. Both market participants and regulators must *act* on information suggesting bank weakness, and must do so *promptly*. Otherwise, weak and insolvent institutions have strong incentives to continue gambling, especially when they know that because of deposit insurance schemes or their size, the government is likely to guarantee their depositors' holdings. The United States learned the lesson of regulatory "forbearance" the hard way during its savings and loan and banking problems in the 1980s, which ultimately required taxpayer funds amounting to roughly 3 percent of GDP to reimburse depositors (a sum that at the time seemed enormous, but with the passage of time, looks moderate by international standards). Similarly, large U.S. banks that had weakened capital positions as a result of uncollectible loans to less developed countries were not forced by regulators to recognize the full extent of their losses, and instead were allowed to take risky bets—primarily in commercial real estate—that also turned sour and later brought a number of the banks near to insolvency (Litan 1994). As a result of these experiences, the United States adopted a "prompt corrective regime" in its banking law in 1991. A central challenge for the United States in the next century is not to weaken this regime if and when the economy turns down again and political pressure for regulatory forbearance returns.

If there is any doubt about the dangers of regulatory forbearance, the Japanese reaction to its own banking troubles in the 1990s should dispel it. By not taking forceful, timely action at the first sign of trouble to constrain its banks from risk-taking or to require raising additional capital, the Japanese banking authorities have allowed that country's banking problems to grow to vast proportions.

For the most part, banking failures to date have been domestic in nature in that the institutions involved have been engaged primarily, if not exclusively, in their home countries. To be sure, there have been exceptions, such as the failure of the Bankhaus Herstatt in 1974 that led to the creation of the Basle Committee and the more recent collapse of the infamous Bank of Credit and Commerce International (BCCI), which had cross-border ramifications around the world and ultimately led to tightened regulation of foreign banks by the United States and other countries. With the increasing globalization of finance, however, failures of internationally active institutions—with offices and activities located in numerous countries—may become more common. While international failures may pose challenges to financial regulators throughout the world, they should be of special interest to regulators in industrial economies where global financial institutions are likely to be most active.

The rapid changes in financial technologies described earlier also pose special challenges for regulators in industrial economies where those technologies, instruments, and trading techniques are most intensively used. The member countries of the Basle Committee have been attempting to keep up with these fast-paced developments by continuously refining the minimum capital standards to take account of the newer risks these developments may pose (see Box 3.1). But the way they are responding highlights the growing recognition of the limits to detailed regulation in an increasingly complex and fast-moving financial environment.

A key problem confronting the Committee—and indeed all national bank regulators—is the fact that market discipline cannot function effectively in the presence of government guarantees that distort decisionmaking. Although industrial economies have limited the reach of formal deposit insurance protection, the perception remains that their governments nonetheless would protect all depositors, and possibly all creditors, of those large banks whose failure might be perceived to jeopardize financial stability. Even the United States, which formally prohibited government guarantees of uninsured depositors in 1991, left open the possibility for broader guarantees in the event all bank regulators conclude it is necessary to prevent systemic risk. As financial institutions grow in size and scope, often by merger, the so-called *too big to fail* problem is likely to become more pronounced over time. To the extent very large institutions benefit from such implicit government guarantees, they have lower funding costs than their smaller competitors, which constitutes an artificial bias toward concentration within and across markets.

For those countries seeking to address this problem, one possible solution is to require large banks to back a certain portion of their assets with subordinated debt,

Box 3.1
The Basle Capital Accord: A First Step Toward Regulatory Harmonization

The Basle Committee on Banking Supervision was established in 1976 by G-10 countries and Luxembourg in the wake of the failure of the Bankhaus Herstatt, a West German bank whose unfulfilled foreign currency obligations to American banks sent a shudder through the U.S. and other financial systems. For its first decade, the Basle Committee focused on principles for the supervision of internationally active banks and for cooperation among bank regulators to help govern the activities of multinational banks. By the mid-1980s, concern grew among the members both about the inadequate levels of capital at major banks and the seeming unfairness of different capital standards in different countries. Spurred by an initial agreement on capital standards between the United States and the United Kingdom in 1986, the Basle Committee eventually adopted in 1988 the first international capital standards for banks.

The initial standards were "risk-weighted" in that assets of different categories (as well as off-balance sheet liabilities) were given different risk weights (government bonds in the member countries being assigned a zero risk weight, ordinary loans a 100 percent weight) and then capital was computed as a percentage of the risk-weighted total. The minimum standard was set at 8 percent. In subsequent years, the Basle Committee has supplemented the initial standards with separate computations for other types of risk, such as interest rate risk and trading risks.

Most recently, in June 1999 the Basle Committee proposed a sweeping set of revisions to its risk-based standards, adding more risk classifications and tying them to the ratings of borrowers provided by credit rating agencies. The intention behind the proposal was to incorporate more market-based information in setting the risk weights.

However, the June 1999 proposal is open to criticism on several grounds. For one thing, by retaining a complicated set of risk weights, the Basle standards continue to ignore the fact that the best measures of bank risk center on the risks of their entire *portfolios* rather than the sum of the risk-weighted assets. Indeed, the risk weights that the Committee continues to use are arbitrary in nature. These flaws are not corrected by relying in private credit rating agencies, which often lag rather than lead to market developments. Furthermore, many borrowers—especially those outside the United States—are not even rated.

or uninsured instruments "subordinate" to the rights of depositors. Unlike deposits, which can be withdrawn at any time and thus are potential sources of instability, holders of subordinated debt cannot regain their principal until the instruments mature (or only by selling them to other investors on the secondary market). In addition, unlike shareholders who benefit when their banks become more profitable, subordinated debt holders are entitled only to the interest on the bonds, and because their instruments are uninsured, they bear the risk of losing their investments. For all these reasons, subordinated debt holders have powerful incentives to monitor the risks taken by bank managers and shareholders.

A subordinated debt requirement would supplement regulation with market-based discipline and thus implement the "multiple eyes" approach to bank surveillance that one recent World Bank study has recommended for all countries (Caprio 1998). The idea has been recommended in a report of the Treasury Department of the United States (Litan 1997) and has been supported by numerous academic scholars. It is being seriously considered by U.S. regulatory agencies and should be on the agendas of other countries as well (Board of Governors 1999).

Financial Policy Challenges for Developing Countries

Financial policymakers from countries outside the industrialized world, but seeking to join that club as rapidly as possible, confront two sets of challenges in the next century. One will be to upgrade—as quickly as possible—financial laws, practices, and institutions up to minimum standards, such as those embodied in the Core Principles established by the Basle Committee. The second will be to decide at what pace to link their financial systems with the industrialized world, or using the highway analogy spelled out earlier, at what pace to build out and fully pave their financial on-ramps to the global financial turnpike.

Upgrading Financial Supervision
Developing countries have several reasons for upgrading their financial standards and practices. First, the Asian crisis has demonstrated that while it may seem to work for some time, the personalized, nontransparent, and heavily government-influenced credit culture prevalent not only in Asia but in other parts of the world has its limits. When those making credit decisions do not believe they bear any significant risk if they make a mistake, they are likely to lend too much for the wrong purposes, especially when foreign capital rushes in, providing local banks with ample funds with which to make those mistakes. The result is not just that scarce capital ends up being channeled toward unproductive uses, but that in the process, asset prices are bid up artificially, only to collapse when investors suddenly pull out, sending the economy into a recession.

Second, in the wake of the Asian crisis, upgrading financial standards (and enforcing them) will be necessary if developing countries hope to attract direct investment from abroad, which as already noted, holds the best promise for quickly bringing cutting-edge financial expertise to both the private sector and financial supervisors in these economies, as well as for weaning them off official finance. Although many foreign investors jumped into Asian countries in the years preceding the crisis without caring about the lack of transparency or the presence of Western-style bank regulation and supervision, the crisis has since acted as a wake up call: Smart money is not likely to return to Asia nor is it likely to move in great quantities into other developing countries until there is demonstrated progress toward upgrading the financial infrastructure. Moreover, countries saddled with major bank insolvency problems, in Asia and Eastern Europe in particular, have also discovered that they can minimize the taxpayer costs of resolving them if they are able to attract foreign financial institutions to join the bidding for the insolvent institutions and their nonperforming assets.

Goldstein (1997) has laid out a comprehensive agenda for upgrading developing countries' banking supervision systems (see Box 3.2). Significantly, Goldstein's list envisions banks in these countries not just meeting the Basle capital standards, but capital requirements 50 percent more stringent than the Basle rules, to reflect the greater risks currently associated with lending in these economies. In addition, the agenda for reform extends beyond well-enforced capital guidelines to include rules designed to avoid conflict of interest and connected lending of the sort that has contributed to banking problems throughout the world. Indeed, given

the need to upgrade experience within their regulatory agencies, there is a strong case for not mixing banking and commerce in developing countries, and even for separating commercial and investment banking for some transition period in order not to stifle the development of capital markets.

A number of developing countries already have made major strides toward improving their banking systems, notably Argentina and Brazil. Indeed, Argentina is *ahead* of the developed world in being the first country to require its banks to back a certain portion of their assets with subordinated debt, a recommendation advanced earlier in this chapter.

More broadly, it will be in the interest of developing countries to adopt other reforms to strengthen their capital markets so that they can become less reliant on banks for intermediation. Among other things, this will require enforcement of disclosure standards for firms whose securities are listed in exchanges, effective clearing and settlement mechanisms so that trades can be completed promptly without undue risk, and effective bankruptcy systems that can quickly sort out claims of creditors when things go wrong. In addition, it is especially important for governments to develop their bond markets, issuing government debt in maturities extending beyond one year. This should not only make funding of the government more stable but also help develop a longer-term bond market for private securities as well.

It is much easier to spell out what may be required for developing and emerging market countries to do to upgrade their financial supervision and regulation, however, than for these countries actually to implement the necessary steps. For economies that have long operated under different rules and institutions, the transition will be long and difficult. It would be wishful thinking to believe otherwise. Nonetheless, the experience of the United States in overcoming its banking difficulties in recent years provides a beacon of hope to developing countries.

Policy Toward Capital Movements

Precisely because it will take some time for developing countries to improve their systems of financial regulation and supervision, governments in these countries must also determine how open they should be in the meantime to shorter-term *portfolio capital*. Clearly, one telling lesson from the Asian currency crisis is that if a developing country has decided to fix its exchange rate but has a weak financial sector, it runs great risks if it freely allows the influx of short-term funds, especially if they are borrowed and denominated in foreign currency. Moreover, notwithstanding the theoretical case for

---

Box 3.2
Banking Reform Measures for Developing Countries

- Implement and enforce capital standards for banks that are above those for developed countries
- Publish timely, accurate, and audited information on the financial condition of individual banks
- Adopt internationally recognized loan classification and provisioning practices
- Enforce requirements that banks maintain internal procedures and safeguards
- Make government involvement in the banking sector more transparent (through disclosure of government costs involving the banking system, data on nonperforming loans of state-owned banks, and disclosing the nature and extent of government instructions to banks on the allocation of credit)
- Limit bank lending to "connected" parties
- Limit deposit insurance and offset its "moral hazard" through a system of "prompt corrective action" (now embodied in U.S. banking law)

Source: Goldstein (1997).

openness to foreign capital—that it facilitates the efficient allocation of capital around the world—there is little evidence that controls on portfolio capital have penalized economic growth in countries that have used them. At a minimum, therefore, it is prudent for countries with weak banking systems and methods of financial regulation to provide disincentives for banks and private firms to borrow in foreign currency.

What about countries that have been forced off fixed exchange rates, already have heavy foreign currency obligations, weak or essentially insolvent banking systems and meager foreign currency reserves, but so far have allowed portfolio capital to move freely in and out of the country? Should they now reinstate some form of controls on foreign portfolio capital? Or is the proverbial horse already out of the barn?

For countries in the middle of an exchange rate crisis, either having floated or watched the currency plummet, introducing new controls on incoming capital runs a severe risk of aggravating the crisis. After all, in the middle of a currency crisis, governments should want foreign (and domestic) investors to buy or keep their currency rather than sell it.

Furthermore, not all short-term capital is alike in effects. At worst, flows into and out of equity instruments can produce swings in the prices of domestic stocks and may interrupt some public offerings. Nonetheless, foreign investors in the equities of domestic firms know that their investments are risky, and they bear the full consequences of any currency depreciations. Accordingly, there seems little reason for developing countries to restrict portfolio investments in equities.

That is not the case with movements of foreign capital into debt instruments. Foreign capital pouring into banks, in the form of interbank deposits, can fuel lending booms. And if the foreign deposits or bonds are denominated in foreign currencies, as they were in Asia and Russia, they can become an especially heavy burden for domestic borrowers if the currency declines in value, putting the country's financial condition at risk if the domestic borrowers and foreign investors lose confidence in the currency and thus help make their fears a self-fulfilling prophecy.

As will be discussed, countries nonetheless may be able to reduce their risks by not fixing their exchange rates. When exchange rates are flexible, capital controls may be less necessary to insulate the economy against excessive foreign currency borrowing. However, wild swings in investor sentiment about the country's commitment to fighting inflation, among other economic objectives, may produce unwelcome volatility in exchange rates that, in the absence of well-developed forward markets for currencies, disrupt trade. For this reason, even if a country decides not to fix its exchange rate, it may want to provide some buffer to its domestic economy from volatile foreign capital movements.

In that case, allowing foreign portfolio capital to move freely in and out of equities while putting some limits on or disincentives against short-term foreign currency *borrowing* by private sector firms may steer a sensible middle course. Examples of the latter include reserve requirements on short-term foreign currency borrowing that have been applied in Chile and Colombia or direct limits on foreign currency borrowing by banks in particular that have been used in Malaysia (which also has used reserve requirements).

It cannot be emphasized too strongly that any limits on short-term capital movements should not be extended to *foreign direct investment*, which, for reasons already discussed, is an important means by which countries can increase their rate of growth. Indeed, empirical evidence suggests that FDI tends to act as a complement to, rather than substitute for, domestic investment. And not to be forgotten is the fact that the Southeast Asian countries, where the financial crisis first appeared, contributed to their own predicament by restricting foreign direct investment, which provided artificial inducements for banks and private firms to borrow short term in foreign currency instead.

One further caveat is in order. The case for even targeted capital controls on foreign currency borrowing must recognize that the presence of any controls invites rent-seeking and corruption (Summers 1998). The ultimate aim for all countries is to have their economic and financial systems mature to the point where even these limited controls, which can themselves lead to distortions, prove no longer necessary. Indeed, the preferable course for countries seeking to discourage foreign currency borrowing during some transition phase is to avoid quantitative restrictions or prohibitions and to use disincentives instead (such as the Chilean-style reserve requirement or the removal of tax deductibility of interest on such borrowings).

Exchange Rates in the Global Financial Marketplace

No discussion of an appropriate global financial architecture can ignore the question of what exchange rate policy countries should follow. The 20th century has seen various types of exchange rate policies, but essentially they reduce to three: some type of fixed or pegged rate, freely floating rates, and variations in between, sometimes called "managed floating" or adjustable or crawling pegs. It is becoming the conventional wisdom, however, that as capital becomes increasingly mobile, countries will be forced to choose one of the two extremes, in particular monetary union with one or more countries (such as some members of the European Union have decided to do) or purely flexible rates (which comes close to the current policy of the United States and that of Asian countries that have been forced to abandon their pegs).

Choosing between the two extreme exchange rate options, however, is difficult and depends on a host of economic and, perhaps even more important, political considerations (Eichengreen 1994). Generally speaking, it is in the economic interest of small, open economies or larger economies with flexible labor markets to belong to a monetary union—that is, to irrevocably link their currencies to the value of one or more others, or to yield control over their currencies to a multijurisdictional organization. Small countries can benefit by "free-riding" on the reputations of other currencies (in the case of fixed rates) or on the reputations of a multicountry currency block (European Monetary Union). The more open an economy is the more its participants benefit, through lower transactions costs, by having its currency fixed in terms of other currencies. And the more flexible the labor market is, the less countries need flexible rates to adjust real wages between regions experiencing different levels of unemployment (accounting for the benefits of a single currency in the 50 states of the United States where labor mobility is high, but raising a question about the wisdom of European countries adopting a single currency at a time when few citizens of European countries move across national borders to find jobs).

At the other extreme, flexible rates are in the economic interest of countries that have strong institutions in place to contain inflation (and thus do not need the discipline afforded by fixed exchange rates) or are vulnerable to macroeconomic shocks not experienced elsewhere (perhaps requiring changes in monetary policy regardless of their impact on the exchange rate). Even with a flexible rate regime, countries still have a strong interest in ensuring that they and their major trading partners follow sustainable macroeconomic policies that lead to stable inflation and real growth. For it is precisely when macroeconomic policies depart from this objective that financial markets force adjustments in the exchange rates. Along with multimember groupings such as the G-7, the IMF can help countries coordinate their macroeconomic policies so that wild swings in exchange rates are avoided.

In fact, had the Asian countries at the center of the 1997–98 crisis permitted their currencies to float much earlier in the decade, they might never have found themselves in difficulties in the first place. Knowing that the currency could fluctuate, domestic firms and their creditors would have entered into very different borrowing arrangements than actually occurred. Creditors would have demanded higher interest rates to compensate them for the currency risk. Higher rates, in turn, would have discouraged many Asian firms and banks from engaging in "currency arbitrage": borrowing dollars at low interest rates and then investing the proceeds in domestic projects offering potentially much higher returns, but in domestic currency. The net result is that foreign currency borrowing may not have risen so far out of line relative to foreign currency reserves and the crisis could have been avoided (or its severity considerably minimized). In short, the Asian financial crisis has strengthened the case for developing countries to float their exchange rates.

It is important not to oversell the benefits of flexible exchange rates, however. For developing countries in particular—which generally do not have well-developed forward markets enabling parties to hedge their currency risks—the uncertainty associated with movements in flexible rates may impose significant transactions costs on importers and exporters. Moreover, even floating rates can be subject to speculative attack or "bandwagon effects" if, for any number of reasons, domestic or foreign investors engage in panic selling, dumping the currency before they believe it will fall further in value. Alternatively, excessive optimism can lead to speculative bubbles in exchange rates, just as they can with the price of any asset. Fluctuations in exchange rates not justified by underlying fundamental economic conditions can complicate economic policy management as exchange rates affect domestic inflation rates through their effect on import prices. Indeed, a strong argument for fixing the exchange rate—either pegging to another one (or a basket of currencies), adopting a currency board, or joining a monetary union—is that it eliminates this source of domestic inflation.

In the end, political considerations often prove even more important than the foregoing economic factors in determining which exchange rate regime countries choose. A political barrier to monetary union is the demonstrated desire of governments and their citizens to maintain their own currency. That hurdle can be overcome, but only when some other political objective, such as the desire of the European members of the EMU to cement peaceful relations among themselves, assumes overriding importance.

The Role of International Financial Institutions

Finally, what role should the major international financial institutions—the World Bank and the IMF—play in facilitating the construction of resilient global financial architecture? This is a broad topic, but several functions remain especially important and deserve highlighting.

The World Bank

A central objective of the World Bank should be to gradually wean client states off official assistance and encourage them to mature to the point where they are funded entirely by private markets. The funds of the Bank are scarce and so the more borrowers that graduate from the Bank's programs, the more funds become available for the most needy countries. The Bank can best achieve its goals by providing technical assistance, preferably in coordination with the IMF, to help countries upgrade the legal, technical, and managerial infrastructure that is required for financial institutions to participate in global markets.

An equally important job for the World Bank is to provide financial and technical assistance to enable countries to establish better social safety nets, such as unemployment insurance and job training, that are common in the West but not elsewhere. This challenge is much more closely related to the financial agenda than may first appear because financial crises often bring substantial increases in unemployment in their wake. Social safety nets act as a cushion that brakes the impact of such crises on aggregate demand, as well as meeting very real human needs for aid in difficult times (Stiglitz 1998). In the absence of an adequate safety net, political pressures can build within countries to reject movements toward markets.

The Bank and the Fund should work together to promote the adoption and use of the tools for effective bank and financial supervision already outlined. In particular, both institutions can assist regulators in these countries with techniques for valuing loans (especially nonperforming loans) and measuring interest rate and currency risk. They can and should also assist countries with identifying and measuring areas of lending and activity displaying unusually rapid growth, and providing advice about the best means for discouraging excesses in this regard.

IMF

While the IMF remains critical to provide emergency assistance to help stabilize currencies in distress, especially where falling currencies threaten systemic consequences to the global financial system, the Fund also must play a central role in reducing the likelihood of future crises. It can do this by taking steps to minimize the moral hazard entailed in future emergency lending packages, while encouraging the provision of more useful information to private actors on a timely basis so that markets can allocate funds more effectively.

Minimizing Moral Hazard

Although IMF lending packages do not protect investors, in recent years they have tended to insulate foreign creditors from significant losses. The IMF can reduce this well-known source of moral hazard by encouraging improvements in national financial supervision and regulation. But the Fund shouldn't stop there.

Eichengreen and Portes (1995) have outlined a series of possible steps, such as allowing the IMF to lend to countries even when their private banks and other borrowers are behind in their loan payments to foreign creditors (which would reduce the power of those creditors to "hold up" new loans until they are provided government guarantees of their loans) and amending Article 8.2(b) of the IMF Articles of Agreement to authorize the Fund to impose "standstills" on debt payments owed to foreign creditors until the loans are renegotiated.

A more aggressive step would be to condition IMF lending on borrower countries imposing a "haircut" on foreign currency denominated credits to their banks unless the creditors roll over their loans or not withdraw their deposits. Less drastically the IMF could impose higher penalty rates on loans to countries that have not adopted such a system (Shadow Financial Regulatory Committee 1998). The haircut's virtue is that it ensures that foreign currency creditors take some losses, which could be tied to the discount on sovereign debt of the country prior to the IMF lending package or to some preset amount. At the same time, by only imposing the haircut if creditors withdraw their funds, this proposal would supply powerful incentives on creditors not to run once the IMF steps in and thus would exert a stabilizing effect on the currency and the banking system. To prevent domestic governments from using the proceeds of the IMF lending packages to guarantee lenders, IMF loans could also be conditioned on the government not extending guarantees to any more than the net amount of the foreign currency loans (the nominal principal minus the haircut).

An alternative approach to limiting the moral hazard associated with IMF lending is to impose limits on crisis lending. A 1999 Council on Foreign Relations study recommended, for example, that ordinary IMF borrowing be limited to perhaps two or three times a country's credit tranche. Any larger packages—designed to address global systemic risks—would have to be provided by a new facility, subscribed to by large industrialized countries, and approved by a supermajority vote.

One suspects that whether any formal means are adopted to limit IMF lending, the Fund is likely to do so on its own initiative, but on a case-by-case basis. Indeed, the Fund has already shown an unwillingness to provide lending to Russia in 1998 and Ecuador in 1999 because these countries did not change their economic policies in ways that conformed with the Fund's policy recommendations. Given the Fund's limited funds, and the unlikely prospect that industrialized countries will augment them any time soon, the Fund is therefore likely to take a harder line in the future in its emergency lending than it has in the past.

Enhancing Information

A necessary but not sufficient condition for markets to operate properly is for actors to have comprehensive, reliable information on a timely basis to inform their decisions. One response to the Mexican peso crisis was for the IMF to encourage countries to provide more financial information about their economic and financial conditions—indeed, to post it regularly on the Internet. Nonetheless, the Asian crisis demonstrates that information was lacking about two key financial indicators that are highly relevant to investors' perceptions about the status of a country's currency: the country's *net* international reserve position (gross reserves minus forward currency commitments) and the foreign currency debts of the country's domestic firms and their foreign affiliates. These data are not consistently gathered now by many developed economies, let alone those that have been at the center of market turmoil in 1997–98. Nonetheless, the experience over the past two years has amply demonstrated the need for investors to know the reserve and debt positions of countries *in advance*, not after the fact. A major challenge for the Fund, and all its members, will be to put systems in place to gather these data and have them publicly reported on a timely basis.

Conclusion

In sum, there is a continuing role for the International Financial Institutions, as the world enters the 21st century. However, there also is a need for both the World Bank and the International Monetary Fund to concentrate their missions on problems and issues likely to be characteristic of the next century, drawing upon the ample lessons from recent events.

Bibliography

Bank of International Settlements. 1992. "Recent Developments in International Interbank Relations." Basel, Switzerland.

Board of Governors of the Federal Reserve System. 1999. "Using Subordinated Debt as an Instrument of Market Discipline." Staff Study 1972. Washington, D.C.: Board of Governors.

Caprio, Gerard Jr. 1998. "Banking on Crises: Expensive Lessons from Recent Financial Crises." Policy Research Working Paper 1979. Washington, D.C.: World Bank Development Research Group.

Claessens, Stijn and Thomas Glaessner. 1998. *Are Financial Sector Weaknesses Undermining the Asian Miracle?* Washington, D.C.: World Bank.

Council on Foreign Relations. 1999. *Safeguarding Prosperity in a Global Financial System.* Carla Hills and Peter G. Peterson, Co-Chairs, Task Force Report.

Eichengreen, Barry. 1994. International Monetary Arrangements for the 21st Century. Washington, D.C.: The Brookings Institution Press.

Eichengreen, Barry and Richard Portes. 1995. *Crisis, What Crisis? Orderly Workouts for Sovereign Debtors.* London: Centre for Economic Policy Research.

Goldstein, Morris. 1997. *The Case for an International Banking Standard.* Washington, D.C.: Institute for International Economics.

Group of Thirty. 1998. *International Insolvencies in the Financial Sector.* Washington, D.C.

International Monetary Fund. 1998. *Balance of Payments Statistics Yearbook 1998.* Washington, D.C.: International Monetary Fund.

Kindleberger, Charles P. 1978. *Manias, Panics and Crashes.* New York: Basic Books.

Levine, Ross. 1996. "Foreign Banks, Financial Development, and Economic Growth." In Claude E. Barfield, ed., *International Financial Markets: Harmonization Versus Competition.* Washington, D.C.: The AEI Press.

Lindgren, Carol-Johan, Gillian Garcia, and Matthew I. Saal. 1996. *Bank Soundness and Macro-economic Policy.* Washington, D.C.: International Monetary Fund.

Litan, Robert E. 1994. "Financial Regulation." In Martin Feldstein, ed., *American Economic Policy in the 1980s*, pp. 519–557. Chicago, IL: National Bureau of Economic Research and University of Chicago Press.

Litan, Robert E. (with Jonathan Rauch). 1997/1998. *American Finance for the 21st Century.* Washington, D.C.: U.S. Treasury Department, 1997; Washington, D.C.: Brookings Institution Press.

Minsky, Hyman. 1982. *Can "It" Happen Again? Essays on Instability and Finance.* New York: M.E. Sharpe.

Shadow Financial Regulatory Committee. 1998. "International Monetary Fund Assistance and International Crises." Statement No. 145 (see www.aei.org).

Stiglitz, Joseph. 1998. "The Role of International Financial Institutions in the Current Global Economy." Address to the Chicago Council on Foreign Relations, February 27, 1998.

Summers, Lawrence. 1998. "Remarks before the International Monetary Fund." March 9, 1998.

Tesar, Linda L., and Ingrid M. Werner. 1998. "The Internationalization of Securities Markets since the 1987 Crash." In R. E. Litan and A. Santomero, eds., *Brookings–Wharton Papers on Financial Services, 1998*, pp. 281–349.

World Bank. 1997. *Private Capital Flows to Developing Countries: The Road to Financial Integration.* A World Bank Policy Research Report. Washington, D.C.: World Bank.

chapter 4

Prerequisites for Successful International Monetary Policy Coordination

Andrew Hughes Hallett

University of Strathclyde, Glasgow,
and Centre for Economic Policy Research, London

The second half of the 1990s has seen a series of financial crises, first in Central America, but then more seriously in East Asia. These disturbances caused major disruption in terms of falling incomes, currency depreciations, inflation, and losses in investment activity and output. Worse, they spilled over into neighboring countries, until then unaffected, through contagion in the financial markets and disruptions in trade—developments which then exaggerated the crises at home and began to threaten the markets of those who might organize loans or a bailout. This raises the question of whether some form of monetary and fiscal cooperation might not have reduced the severity of the crisis once it had happened, or whether some mild forms of cooperation, involving exchange rate regimes or a redesign of the financial architecture in particular, might not have reduced the probability of a crisis in the first place—or at least have allowed the burden of adjustment to be shared and the risks to be spread. But there are additional features which may also be important: Are the domestic policies well coordinated with each other and with the financial policies of the G8 economies which provide much of the financial and capital flows to these economies? And are there sufficient supporting policies in place to provide the market flexibility needed for making adjustments if a crisis does strike?

This chapter reviews the advantages and likely characteristics of more effective coordination between the economic and financial policies in countries subject to large economic or financial disturbances—particularly those that come through the increased competitive pressures of globalization. Such coordination might be a re-

gional or a worldwide affair, and it might involve agreements on fiscal and monetary discipline or measures of financial support and lender of last resort facilities. But it might also have to deal with issues of policy mix within economies, exchange rate management, market flexibility (competition and trade policies, including policies on market access and corporate control), and structural reforms, as well as with reforms to a country's financial architecture. These are all local issues requiring local decisions, which must be taken in conjunction with the international coordination designed to counter the difficulties created by the effects of increasing globalization.

One objective of this chapter is to evaluate the benefits of monetary coordination for stabilizing and enhancing economic performance among the smaller and developing economies in the face of increasing globalization. We are also interested in what drives those benefits and how they would be distributed. A second objective is to stress that monetary conditions are not the only economic feature that needs to be coordinated. A strengthening and more focused use of local policy instruments is perhaps a prerequisite for successful monetary coordination; that is, we need to ensure sufficient support from competition and free trade policies and from certain structural reforms in the labor and financial markets.

These two objectives create, in effect, a distinction between *absolute* coordination and *relative* coordination. The former has to do with the overall stance of policy in a region or within the G8 countries and is designed to capture the efficiency gains of better-designed policies and a better economic performance. That may well involve greater fiscal and monetary discipline so that, in pursuing their separate interests, countries do not produce excessively tight, loose, or risky conditions for a region as a whole. But against that, we have relative (or internal) coordination, which is concerned with getting the policy mix right and financial stability right within each economy. It tends to focus on exchange rate behavior, market flexibility, market access, trade balances, and supply side reforms.

A Taxonomy of Monetary Coordination

Most people would probably think of economic policy coordination as the business of the G8 world economic summit meetings, the International Monetary Fund (IMF)—World Bank meetings, or regional summits like those conducted by the European Union's council of ministers or by the Asia-Pacific Economic Council (APEC) ministers. However, there is a whole range of simpler and politically more manageable forms of coordination, many of which can be conducted on a routine basis. We describe them next, in ascending order of sophistication. That said, the potential benefits of coordinating policies internationally, or between institutions, will always depend on the level and degree of cooperation between the agencies responsible for overseeing trade, or the capital or financial markets worldwide, and also between the countries that operate in those markets.

Information exchanges. Here countries (institutions) would exchange information freely about their targets, priorities, and information (including expectations) about external events, as well as about how they expect each of those factors to affect economic performance in the countries and markets in their charge. However, given that information and including any announced or proposed policy changes elsewhere, they would continue to make their decisions in a decentralized autonomous way. By coordinating their information, policymakers will improve outcomes by eliminating incomplete or faulty information over the intentions, expectations, or policy responses of others. On the other hand, there is always the danger that by sharing faulty information about external shocks, policymakers could spread those errors around the whole system. Nevertheless, existing research (for example, Hughes Hallett 1986a) has suggested that the major gains come from this aspect of coordination, and that those gains may often be rather robust to shared information errors (Hughes Hallett 1987c).

Crisis management. Here coordination would take place in response to episodes of particular difficulty in the international economy and would involve policy changes particular to that episode. It might involve ad hoc policy adjustments, where misalignments and current national policies or regional policy regimes interact

resulting in a crisis (for example, in the problem of international debt, the Stock Market crash of 1987, German Unification, or the liquidity squeeze following the financial crisis in Asia). The institutional implications of this are that the world's major economies should institute suitable disaster relief plans, hold sufficient financial resources in reserve, or impose suitable surveillance mechanisms and require that certain financial safety measures be observed at all times. But they or their agencies should not interfere in any country's policies or policy stance on a day-to-day basis. Thus a lender of last resort facility (but at a penal rate, and to central banks only in order to minimize moral hazard) or an agreed set of capital adequacy standards for risk management in the financial markets and a jointly operated surveillance system could all be part of this arrangement. But notions of a world central bank, a policy of restructuring banks without a free market in corporate control, or programs of structural adjustment and restrictions on monetary and fiscal policy, or target zones for exchange rates, would not be.

Avoiding conflicts over shared target values. Shared targets arise where countries actually target the same variable (for example, a mutual exchange rate) or where they target variables linked by some identity which is not capable of being relaxed by policy interventions (for example, a set of current accounts). Here coordination could take the form of agreements that prevent countries or institutions targeting mutually inconsistent values for what is actually the same variable, or agreements that prevent them attempting competitive policy changes (for example, devaluations) that cannot all be achieved simultaneously. In either case, policy effort would be saved and better target values achieved for both parties if countries and institutions did not push against each other in vain efforts to improve their own (national) outcomes. Institutional forms of this would include target zone regimes for exchange rates, an absence of capital controls, and an effective scheme for modifying policies so as not to pass current account deficits or liquidity shortages around between trading partners.

Intermediate targeting schemes. Similarly, a limited amount of coordination may be achieved when countries agree to jointly control the variables forming the main links between their economies or that cause the main spillovers (externalities) from one to another. In this case, cooperation is achieved by targeting the link or spillover variables directly. Coordination is therefore achieved by using certain variables that affect the outcomes in several economies, as a surrogate for the targets that policymakers really care about. Such intermediate targets may or may not be shared variables, although the scope for fruitless competition over shared targets make them the most obvious examples. Thus exchange rate targeting would be one example, but monetary targeting and the supply of liquidity or credit would be another, while deregulating markets would be a third, and debt management a fourth.

Partial coordination. Partial coordination takes place when countries cooperate in achieving certain targets, but may choose other targets noncooperatively or according to some preassigned national rules. It is often suggested that countries need to coordinate their monetary policies, leaving fiscal policies to the domestic policymakers. This reflects the thinking in Europe's monetary union. On the other hand, fiscal policy needs to be sustainable if it is not to cause liquidity shortages and high interest rates for others if it becomes excessively expansionary.[1] That implies a minimal degree of fiscal coordination. The latter might be achieved by agreeing on policy assignments: fiscal policy for internal targets (growth and employment) and monetary policy for external and link targets (liquidity, capital, trade). The difficulty here is that a great deal of design work may be needed to devise agreed, but country-specific policy rules that can provide gains for each participant over the best they can attain otherwise. On the other hand, agreed rules make monitoring—and transparency—relatively straightforward.

Full coordination. Full cooperation takes place when countries agree to a certain bargain describing how all their targets and their fiscal, monetary, and exchange rate instruments shall behave. This would aim to maximize the gains over the best outcomes that could be attained from noncooperative policymaking, subject to a reasonable distribution of those gains. As in the previous two cases, the key is that the bargain is between a number of freely contracting parties, be they countries or institutions. That means each party must be able to make gains over what they could achieve with independent policies. However, full cooperation may be very hard because it is politically difficult to reach agreement across all the targets and instruments of policy—especially when there is significant uncertainty about the exact impact of those instruments or whether the external variables will turn out as expected. And, because the policy changes are unlikely to follow any simple rules in this case, monitoring or penalizing those who deviate from the agreement may also be difficult.

Institutional Prerequisites to Secure the Gains from Monetary Coordination

The previous discussion gives an idea of the types of monetary policy coordination, with or without fiscal co-ordination, which might prove important in practice. But it does not say whether coordination can be expected to yield significant benefits overall, or who would gain and why, or whether coordination would be an effective mechanism for absorbing financial shocks and preventing the kind of economic disruptions that we have seen in the Asian economies recently.

Nor, more importantly, does such a classification of policy coordination schemes give any idea how these schemes might actually be implemented in practice. One of the lessons from the G3 and European attempts at coordination is that it is often extremely hard to get agreement on measures that cover all the instruments and targets of policy, or to secure agreement on how to treat those who deviate from their part of the agreement. Similarly, a proper coordination of policy usually makes greater demands on information and modeling of economic responses than do simpler forms of policymaking. It is therefore often thought to be more vulnerable to unexpected shocks or to errors of information or specification. Indeed, it can be very hard to secure agreement on how to respond to such shocks and errors, especially when they are distributed asymmetrically across participants. For all these reasons, it is important to have an idea of how policies may be coordinated, what simplifications are effective in practice, and where the gains are likely to come from.

The Benefits of Full Coordination

Studies that have attempted to evaluate the likely gains from full coordination have generally concluded that those gains exist but are small. However, those studies have been restricted (almost exclusively) to the major industrialized economies. For example, in their pioneering study, Oudiz and Sachs (1984) estimated that of the gains among the Group of Three countries in the mid-1970s, coordination would be worth no more than 0.5 percent of gross national product (GNP) to each country compared with the best noncooperative outcomes. It may, of course, be debated whether 0.5 percent of GNP is only a "small" gain. It would represent a significant amount of extra productive capacity if fully invested in each period. But it is not large compared with annual growth rates. Moreover, if gains of this size are not much bigger than the forecast standard error of the target variables (that is, if the gains are small relative to the imprecision with which policies can be implemented), then it may not be easy to persuade policymakers of their value.

Later studies have confirmed that the gains from coordination among the Organisation for Economic Co-operation and Development (OECD) economies are likely to be small. In studies that allowed for dynamic decisionmaking,[2] Hughes Hallett (1986a, 1986b, 1987a) found the gains to be somewhat larger—between 0.5 percent and 1.5 percent of GNP for the United States, the European Union, and Japan. Subsequent work by Canzoneri and Minford (1986), Minford and Canzoneri (1987), and Currie et al. (1987) have also suggested relatively small gains in the absence of major shocks, based on calculations for the United States and the EU or OECD, respectively. However, all those results have turned out to vary significantly with the size and persistence of external shocks and the perceived reputations of the governments concerned. In fact, persistent shocks and the existence of "reputation" among government and central bank policymakers appear to increase the value of coordination more than anything else (see Currie et al. 1987).

Regrettably, there have been very few exercises that were not concerned with the major industrial economies or with the coordination of the standard instruments of macroeconomic policy. So it is hard to tell how well these "stylized facts" carry over into cases involving developing or newly industrialized countries, or to countries with underdeveloped capital and financial markets, or where there are trade barriers or other market imperfections. However, small gains on average do not always mean small gains for everyone. Coordination tends to be more important for the following:

■ Developing countries, or those on the weaker side of an asymmetric relationship with their trading partners or the suppliers of capital (see Currie and Vines 1988; Hughes Hallett 1988; and Brandsma and Hughes Hallett 1984)

■ Countries subject to persistent shocks or a lack of reputation in policymaking

■ Situations where there are significant market distortions or restrictions, and in particular where free trade is abandoned or where free trade zones discriminate against outsiders (Helkie et al. 1989; Hughes Hallett 1992a; Hughes Hallett 1994a)

■ Situations where coalitions among subsets of players are easily formed

■ Episodes where exchange rate stability is important in its own right, as opposed to it being simply a means to an end (that is, where the exchange rate is an intermediate target designed to achieve a superior performance in the other targets of economic policy; Hughes Hallett 1992b)

■ In cases where *optimal* noncooperative behavior is not the alternative; for example, where large exchange rate fluctuations or large unanticipated shocks disrupt a sequence of rationally chosen policies (for example, in

financial crises, a collapse of export markets, or a liquidity crunch), or where governments need to be restrained from implementing a sequence of entirely inappropriate policies (whether designed for their own private advantage, a general lack of "reputation," or through ignorance of the pressures on their economy).

In any of those cases, coordination may prove more advantageous. We consider each in more detail below.

How the Gains from Coordination Are Distributed

Little work has been done on how the gains from coordination might be distributed (relative coordination), as opposed to how they might be created (absolute coordination). This is a pity since it will be difficult to persuade policymakers to cooperate if the gains are not distributed in a reasonable manner and are not assured to be positive for each participant. In the event, Oudiz and Sachs (1984) found gains distributed roughly 2:1 in favor of Germany, relative to the United States. Hughes Hallett's (1986b) study of the United States and Europe again suggests gains distributed 2:1 in favor of Europe using a wide range of bargaining models. Later work showed this result to be somewhat sensitive to alternative types of exogenous shocks (Hughes Hallett 1987b), although in no case was the position of Europe as main gainer overturned. Hughes Hallett et al. (1989) also found the gains to be asymmetrically distributed among the Group of Five countries in the late 1980s and point out that it can be extremely difficult to find ways of improving the lot of those countries that benefit least from coordination.

These are important results because they suggest that (1) it will be hard to secure and maintain a coordination agreement in the face of significant uncertainties, and (2) if those who make the gains and those who shoulder the burden of adjustment are different sets of people, securing any agreement at all will be politically difficult.

Coordination Substitutes: Information Exchanges

The gains from coordination relative to noncoordination may well be substantially smaller than the gains of efficient noncooperative policies over strategies that ignore predictable foreign policy changes altogether (Hughes Hallett 1986a). Thus, coordination in the sense of *information exchanges*, rather than detailed coordination across all variables, may supply the major part of the improvements available from policy coordination. If this is so, an important function of international forums for policy discussion will be the exchange of information among policymakers concerning their policies and the state of their economies. Interestingly, this conclusion can hold even when the information exchanged is found to contain prediction errors (Hughes Hallett 1987b). It has also been confirmed in a series of experiments carried out by Minford and Canzoneri (1987) on the larger OECD economies. Hence poor information may be less of a problem than a mismatch of policies.

Thus, information exchanges do appear to be a key part of the coordination process, irrespective of the model or time period. One might also suppose that the wider the range of policies reviewed, the greater the benefits of information exchange to the decisions subsequently made (Bryant 1987). Certainly prior consultation would alert policymakers to potential and self-defeating conflicts such as incompatible exchange rate or trade balance targets that would lead to competitive appreciations or depreciations, or inconsistent fiscal and monetary programs. Prior consultation could also help policymakers avoid any losses attributable to conditioning their own decisions on erroneous information about other policymakers' intentions (for example, what priorities they have, what target paths they aim at, what model they use for policy selection). Whatever the difficulty of predicting the true state of the world, errors owing to mistakes should be avoidable, and there is no point in adding them to the unavoidable (genuinely random) errors.

Coordination Substitutes: Exchange Rate Targeting

None of these early studies of policy coordination considered exchange rates to be a target of policy. Yet much of the recent policy debate has been concerned with exchange rate management, with the aim of either stabilizing exchange rates or of making controlled realignments. This may serve as a means of improving relative coordination among countries.

The Hughes Hallett (1992b) study points out that although exchange rates may be included among the targets during policy selection, they can either be included in the associated objective function evaluations (in which case exchange rate stability is a target in its own right) or excluded from those evaluations (in which case exchange rates are just an intermediate target, instrumental in securing improvements elsewhere). If the former holds, the gains from coordination appear larger than before, about 3–6 percent of GNP (equivalent to 10–20 percent improvements in the targets themselves) as estimated across seven multicountry models. If exchange rates are treated merely as intermediate targets, the gains are significantly smaller and much the same as in the earlier literature (1–1.5 percent of GNP).

Perhaps the most interesting result here is that the gains from exchange rate targeting over the policies historically chosen are typically several times larger than the gains of exchange rate targeting over the best non-cooperative alternative without targeting (see Currie and Wren-Lewis 1989; Hughes Hallett 1992b). That suggests that exchange rate targeting yields gains, not because it is a particularly effective substitute for full coordination, but because the historically chosen policies were usually inappropriate for the job in hand. That, in turn, means that the major advantage of exchange rate targeting schemes is that they restrain governments from choosing silly policies—whether in their own private interest or through sheer ignorance. That is a particularly important result in the context of large financial shocks which threaten to pervade the whole system.

However, these results all refer to coordination *including* exchange rate targets. If exchange rate targeting is undertaken with *no* explicit coordination, the gains are much smaller: typically 0.5 percent of GNP, and then not necessarily for all participants (Hughes Hallett et al. 1989). That runs the risk of creating an incentive incompatible, and hence unsustainable, regime. Subsequent studies have been able to confirm *analytically* that exchange rate targeting can be no more than an imperfect substitute for proper economic coordination (Hughes Hallett 1994b), but that there are ranges of circumstances in which it would be a good substitute and others where it would be a poor substitute. For example,[3] exchange rate targeting is helpful in the following circumstances:

- In economies that are structurally dissimilar but subject to symmetric shocks or in economies that are structurally similar but subject to country-specific shocks. This plays off the fact that the potential for gains from coordination is driven (in large measure) by the asymmetries between economic responses (see below, p. 36).
- Also in cases where the exchange rate target can be set to reinforce the positive spillovers between economies (and reduce the negative), so that *either* smaller interventions are needed to support the policy targets (that is, the intervention costs saved allow the instruments to be used more intensively on the targets they are most effective at achieving, and the gains from that are more than enough to pay for the sacrifice required to reach the extra target), *or* that better target values are achieved for the same level of interventions (with the same implication that the target improvements more than pay for the interventions needed to support the extra target).
- Similarly where the shocks are destabilizing (that is, they reinforce the spillover effects between economies; this will happen if, but not only if, the shocks or the responses are asymmetric between countries), but, conversely, exchange rate targeting is unhelpful if the shocks are predominantly stabilizing.

■ Finally, whether exchange rate targeting is helpful or not must also depend on the sensitivity of the exchange rate to policy changes or shocks (because that determines the sacrifice necessary to support the extra target), *and* on the responsiveness of the target variables to the exchange rate (because this determines the potential gains through better coordination), *and* on the target values chosen for the exchange rate path. Some authors have emphasized that exchange rate regimes are very unlikely to be helpful if the target values are chosen far from their equilibrium or "fundamentals" (see Wren-Lewis et al. 1991). That leaves open the question of how best to calculate those equilibrium values.[4] One answer to the latter problem is to make the target values respond to the deviations of other peoples' targets from your own, as well as to your targets and the economic "fundamentals" (Hughes Hallett 1998). It is in the latter case that exchange rate targeting appears to provide a good measure of the gains available from coordination.

Three other observations are important. First, there are obviously circumstances where exchange rate targeting is a poor substitute for coordination—and in particular it only takes one participant to be damaged for the system to break down, whereas all have to benefit if it is to work. So the distribution of gains is crucial. It can be quite difficult to arrange that successfully. Second, symmetry obviously plays a role, but not in a very direct way. There are circumstances where asymmetries make coordination and exchange rate targeting helpful and circumstances where it is damaging. Equally there are cases where symmetry helps and cases where it harms. Nevertheless, it seems that whereas asymmetries typically appear to increase the potential gains from coordination, they tend to exaggerate the characteristics that cause exchange rate targeting to fail. By contrast, symmetries tend to reduce those characteristics. Finally, the degree of commitment by the participating governments is important. Success depends on the commitment of all participants, not just some of them. But the advantage of exchange rate targeting, if it works, is fewer policy conflicts and a reduction in the scale of the interventions needed to resolve domestic or foreign policy problems.

Finally, there is the question of speculative attacks. Any target zone scheme may suffer speculative attacks, although, given a credible commitment to defend the intervention boundaries and a parity in line with the economy's "fundamental equilibrium," there is no particular reason to expect them. An important point, however, is that exchange rate bands that are too tight will invite speculative attacks, since they present speculators with a "one-way bet" in that they need to commit only limited funds to push a currency beyond its intervention boundary. And they may be able to trigger such an attack before the policymakers have had time to mount a convincing counterattack. Widening the bands, by contrast, is unlikely to lead to much deterioration in exchange rate stability because it doesn't present the speculators with such an easy one-way bet. Larger funds will have to be committed to the attack, and there is a much better chance that the authorities will be able to intervene and reverse the attack *before* the currency reaches its boundary. In that case the speculators will lose money, not gain. Knowing this in advance, speculators will be less willing to risk an attack. Moreover, the authorities will have time to mount (and demonstrate their commitment to) corrective policies before the boundary is reached—which is more convincing to the markets than merely saying they would defend those boundaries should the need arise. Speculators are therefore more likely to anticipate a return toward parity rather than speculate on a realignment at the boundary as long as governments have the time to make their policy actions credible and transparent.

Policy Assignments in an Increasingly Globalized Economy

Assigning Your Own Policies to Your Own Targets

One result that appears in almost every study is that coordination seems to generate more stability in the targets and more continuity in the policy interventions (Hughes Hallett 1986a). The explanation, according to Cooper (1969), is that ignoring independence within or between economies leads to oscillations and overshooting because the implied assignments (country by country) ignore the international side effects of decisions made in the domestic interest until after they have appeared. Corrections have then to be applied.

These are the costs of imposing policy assignments on an exclusively national basis (that is, domestic policy instruments to domestic targets). They are analogous to the costs imposed by creating one-to-one policy assignments internally, for example, monetary policy to inflation, and fiscal policy for output stabilization, as happens when the central bank is granted independence. Typically one would expect internal coordination (relative coordination) to be more important than the coordination of policies or regimes between countries, since any changes or shocks go directly through the domestic goods and financial markets in the former case. But in the latter, they have to go through the markets for traded goods or capital movements before they get to the domestic markets. Hence countries that are particularly sensitive to trade flows, exchange rate movements, or capital flows (driven by interest rate differentials, expected devaluations, or the threat of debt, insolvency, or liquidity problems) may find that their stability is also particularly sensitive to international coordination. Conversely, other types of countries would be more sensitive to the advantages of relative (internal) coordination. Thus coordination, both internal and external, is important in the following circumstances:

- When trade contributes a large share of national income
- Where capital inflows or imports are a key component of domestic production, or exports a key element in the development strategy
- Where the exchange rate can be significantly affected by changes in the policy mix in the major trading partners
- And, most of all, where the domestic financial and capital markets are incomplete or too small, with the result that domestic investment and production have to be financed by foreign capital inflows.

Finally, "vertical" coordination, that is, linkages that make elements in the internal coordination problem adjust to support the external one more effectively, can also be important for the final outcomes and their stability. Strengthening an economy's *local* policy instruments to provide that support is therefore a necessary part of any coordination exercise.

It is worth reflecting on the intuition behind these observations. Essentially the message is that assignments, whether internal or international, render domestic policies less effective as policymakers have to correct past "mistakes" and counter the undesired impacts of policies introduced by others for the benefit of others. Moreover, because the strength of these spillovers increases with the degree of interdependence (globalization), the effectiveness of policy in decentralized economies declines along with it. Decreasing policy effectiveness shows up in the size of the policy interventions needed to restore targets to their desired levels and in the speed with which the targets approach their desired levels after a shock. So increasing integration means that in the absence of changes in the way economies are run or policies made, one will suffer either worse outcomes, or longer periods away from equilibrium (exaggerated cycles), or greater intervention costs in the form of what is necessary to restore the targets to their desired values.

The key point is that all this is an unavoidable consequence of increasing globalization, whether in trade, capital flows, technological transfer, or consumption pat-

terns, but it can only be partly fixed by greater coordination at a global level. It also requires increasing coordination and flexibility among policymakers at the *local* level (that is, within countries or within particular markets). Indeed, without the latter, coordination between countries or blocs of countries will become much more difficult. We therefore distinguish between the following:

- No coordination. Domestic instruments are assigned to domestic targets on a one-to-one basis (as in Mundell's assignment of fiscal policy to achieving internal targets, and monetary for achieving external or monetary balance).
- Internal coordination. Domestic instruments are used simultaneously to achieve domestic targets, but they take no account of foreign targets. The assignments are national.
- Full coordination. Domestic and foreign instruments are used together to achieve the set of all domestic and foreign targets.

Thus coordination is an important element in any well-balanced set of policies. The first regime represents decentralization both internally and externally, whereas the other two regimes represent policy arrangements that are noncooperative and cooperative externally. Studies of these different regimes have shown the following:

- Target overshooting and oscillations are removed by internal coordination, which no longer ignores side effects until after they have happened. The same happens if the assignments of national instruments to national targets are eliminated.
- Increasing degrees of coordination (for a fixed degree of interdependence) damp out the transitory effects of shocks more rapidly. On the other hand, increasing degrees of interdependence (with policies fixed) extends the size and duration of the target disturbances. Thus coordination increases the power of policy interventions, while interdependence reduces the effectiveness of policy.
- One example of the increased costs of intervening in an open economy is that interdependence slows the correction of trade imbalances (because other countries take countermeasures such as competitive tight money or competitive depreciations in order to protect their own targets). The result is that one must hold a higher level of reserves to last out the slower adjustments. The required level of reserves or foreign inflows is lower with coordination *both* because the domestic adjustment processes are stronger (policy effectiveness) *and* because smaller interventions mean

that the side effects (externalities) of national policies are reduced.

■ In the wider context of greater integration within and between economies, Mundell's policy assignment proposition only survives in the form of policy specializations between or within interdependent economies. Indeed, the assignment of national policies to national targets is already a generalization of Mundell's original idea, and international coordination is just to exploit the same idea yet further. Moreover, Patrick (1972) has shown that there is no generalization of Mundell's proposition to systems with many targets and instruments or to systems where there is uncertainty over the policy responses. That means we will be compelled to rely on policy specializations rather than exclusive assignments. Thus "comparative policy advantage," defined next, remains the key to successful policies in economies that are interdependent.

Smaller Economies and Financially Dependent Economies

Although set in general terms, much of the discussion here is of particular importance for the smaller and developing economies. Since those economies cannot, by definition, do much to influence world economic conditions or the pace of globalization, it will be especially important for them to preserve and strengthen their policy instruments at the local level. Hence all the arguments here in favor of "localization" or "internal coordination" should be taken to refer to smaller and developing economies in particular, as indeed are the arguments which say that the weaker economies are the ones to gain most from the explicit coordination of economic policies (see the next section). Stronger self-interested responses, carefully coordinated with those of the world's larger economies, will cause little disturbance to the major economies. So the smaller economies should exploit their opportunities for localization as far as possible, without fear of retaliation.

A couple of specific examples make the point. Eichengreen and Rose (1998) find that increases in OECD country interest rates have often enlarged the probability of a financial crisis in the developing economies. In that case localized responses in the developing countries, and a serious attempt at coordination on other issues (since the developing countries won't be able to have much impact on OECD interest rates), would be particularly helpful. In the same way, capital flight is a perennial danger for developing countries. It is likely to be linked to anticipated exchange rate movements, to changes in external (or internal) debt, and to local investment opportunities vs. outside options. Again coordination will be especially important to the smaller and developing countries to prevent sudden changes in those variables.

On the Importance of Internal Coordination

(i) Getting the policy mix right. The previous arguments suggest that internal and vertical coordination—the localization of policy—are likely to be a necessary initial condition for successful coordination at an international level. Hughes Hallett and Ma (1996a) provide examples of why it may be an important necessary condition. They find that the coordination of fiscal and monetary policies within one economy (that is, getting the policy mix right) is important because policy assignments—or at least the absence of mutually supporting or consistent policies—are costly in terms of lost performance and generation of larger oscillations and overshootings in the targets (see also Demertzis et al. 1999a). Not only is that costly for the domestic economy, it can be highly damaging for the neighboring economies. Since the spillover effects between sectors go through the domestic and international markets rather than just the international markets, these effects may be large. And rules designed to deal with policy assignments, short of coordination, will be accident-prone because they depend on particular realizations of shocks. So internal coordination is really the only option.

(ii) Policy conflicts. The problem is not only that uncoordinated policies internally are inefficient and may cause exaggerated swings in output or the exchange rate. There is also a danger that, in a world of competing policy targets and competing policymakers with different preferences over which targets should have priority (growth, employment, and investment vs. currency and price stability or domestic vs. regional stability, and so on), it is likely that uncoordinated policies will compete not only to reach their preferred targets, but also to undo some of the effects of their rival's policies. The danger is that these offsetting interventions will leave the domestic economy to drift without effective policies—at a cost to itself and to the stability of its neighbors.

Thus policy conflicts internally, or where domestic policies are set to undo or overcome the policies in a rival economy, will mean that none of the policymakers will get what they want. That could easily trigger a self-interested political response. And if it does, both the conflicts and economic performance will get worse. In Demertzis et al. (1999b) we find that a more conservative stance by one set of policymakers, for the sake of achieving their own goals, will produce a more nationalistic set of preferences from the voters, and hence governments, in the rival economy or policymaking activity. Hence the electoral mechanism may create further differences in priorities. And the more priorities are made to diverge by the electoral process, the greater the conflicts. Coordination therefore becomes more important when we add in political responses, and the outcomes are likely to get worse, if not more unstable, if there is no coordination.

(iii) An example: Policy mix and the sustainability of debts (see Beetsma and Bovenberg 1997; Beetsma and Uhlig 1999). If monetary policy is increasingly dedicated to controlling inflation in an economy with little internal coordination, it becomes necessary to use fiscal policy more vigorously to achieve output growth, stabilization, and employment. And the larger fluctuations that appear when there is little internal coordination will call for larger fiscal interventions to counteract them. If deficits created in the downturn are not fully repaid by surpluses in the upturn, which is typically the case, then countries will tend to accumulate debt and eventually face an unsustainable fiscal position. The outcome of that could be price jumps (in anticipation of a bailout and monetization) or a default and capital rationing, which could have a devastating effect in the form of contagion because of the liquidity restrictions this can imply both at home and for other countries borrowing in the same financial markets.

Indeed, trying to head off a debt problem before it happens can cause problems unless the policy mix is carefully adjusted, because sharp fiscal contractions to reduce public sector debt will tend to reduce national income at the same time. As a result, the debt *ratio* will not fall by much. It may even rise because revenues will also fall with national income. To fix this problem, countries need to match their fiscal contractions with monetary expansions so that national income and revenues do not fall with the debt. If they don't, they risk a rapid rise in real interest rates as deflation combines with tight money (a liquidity crunch). This will destroy investment as well as output and hence employment and output capacity in the longer term.

Another Example: Policy Deepening, Supporting Coordination with Policies at the National Level

The globalization of markets and investment will tend to reduce prices and increase output through increased competition, scale economies, and a better use of comparative advantage. Where the markets are already competitive and offer free access, there will be relatively little gain to be made. However, where the markets are imperfectly competitive (domestically) or fail to offer free access (internationally), the potential gains will be much larger. As the pressures for globalization build up,

prices will tend to fall further. These pressures will therefore divert trade and investment from inefficient firms and countries while creating it for the efficient ones. So if countries wish to protect themselves and profit from all these changes, they need a strong internal competition policy to keep prices and quantities flexible and to allow their other policies the scope and effectiveness to create the most appropriate internal circumstances given the external pressures. In this sense a strong pro-competition policy is a necessary condition for dealing with globalization and international shocks.

Trade restrictions—be they tariff barriers, quantity restrictions, nontariff barriers, or restrictions on market access (including restrictions in the markets for corporate control)—will have exactly the same effect. It won't help much if an internally pro-competitive policy is matched by external restrictions. Countries and blocs of countries must remain "open" rather than "closed" if they are to remain flexible enough to coordinate their internal affairs properly and reduce their vulnerability to the effects of globalization. A "closed" economy is one in which external barriers are increased or maintained as the internal are reduced; an "open" one is where they too are reduced. Of course trade barriers can be reduced as a unilateral act, but it is obviously more effective if everyone else is doing so as well. That makes low trade barriers, with extensions into services and the financial markets, a multilateral policy requirement from an institutional point of view.

The message here is that we need a "deepening" of the number and type of relationships that can be used for coordination rather than just a "widening" of the existing relationships. In the same way, exchange rate targeting schemes are helpful because they prevent countries from maintaining over- or undervalued exchange rates for strategic purposes and to the cost of their neighbors. Fortunately none of these possibilities is likely to be tremendously important in practice as the long-term benefits of strategic trade policy and exchange rate manipulation appear to be rather limited (Hughes Hallett 1992a). But there may be short-term opportunities to "kick start" changes that way or to manipulate the monetary–fiscal mix to the same end. Hence, given a sustained WTO program, coordination should be used to ensure such policy changes are not introduced at the wrong moment.

The Distributional Consequences of Coordination

One consistent feature in the results cited is that the weaker party to the cooperative bargain gains most, which is a result that is easily explained. In any noncooperative decision game or conflict, the stronger party will always be able to capture the larger part of the benefits for two reasons. First, being stronger means the targets respond more strongly to your instruments, so you can get closer to those targets than others do, and you have to expend less effort deflecting the effects of decisions made abroad. Second, being stronger or larger means that you can influence world monetary or trade conditions and make them more favorable to your own circumstances, perhaps "crowding out" the efforts of others to pull things their way.

Thus a stronger country is bound to make larger gains and exercise a degree of control, as long as things remain noncooperative. But to the extent that there are positive as well as negative spillovers from that better performance, the weaker countries will also benefit—in effect free riding on the ability of the policy leader to choose his policies correctly and improve economic performance for all. This may suggest Stackelberg leadership; but it must be true of Nash noncooperation too, since it depends on the "locomotive" aspects of the world economy being not a lot less than the "beggar-thy-neighbor" aspects. And if the problems of the smaller and less developed economies are a matter of asymmetric dependence through trade and capital flows, then globalization must mean that the locomotive aspects are important even in countries with financial markets that are incomplete or too small.

Thus the weaker countries will benefit from sensibly chosen policies elsewhere, albeit to a smaller extent.[5] If we move now to coordination, it means the weaker countries get a chance to fine-tune their policies against a policy stance in the leading economies, which won't change much through the act of cooperation. At this point the advantage passes to the weaker countries: The stronger countries, having made most of their gains at the noncooperative stage, will have exhausted most of the opportunity to make further gains. However, with most of their chips on the table, they stand to lose more if things go wrong. The weaker countries can therefore exploit their chance to redesign their policies, building on the gains the leaders have already made and extracting some concessions where advantageous—but not up to the point where the leader backs out or retaliates. That explains why we consistently find that the weaker countries gain most from coordination: See, for example, in Hughes Hallett (1986a, 1987a) where the United States "leads" the other OECD countries, and again in Hughes Hallett and Ma (1996b) where the United States is stronger than the rest of the G7 countries, but Germany is the hegemon within Europe. Perhaps the best demonstration is in Brandsma and Hughes Hallett (1984) where the final gains to the weaker party increase steadily as the stronger

party is given a more dominant role—exactly as our explanation would predict. Finally, and of special interest here, it also appears to be true for the less developed or commodity-based countries (the "South") in a game of growth and investment with the industrialized "North," at least until debt repayments from South to North become large enough to drain the South of resources or until the North hits its capacity constraints (Hughes Hallett 1988).

Is there anything more specific to be learned about what drives the size of these gains from coordination? That is a question that has to be answered on a case-by-case basis, but it is quite clear that coordination always induces a degree of policy specialization. In the Hughes Hallett (1986a) exercise, the United States relies on monetary policy, while Europe concentrates on fiscal interventions. Although this is not a policy assignment, it does agree with the relative efficiency of the policy responses in the model: Countries use their policy instruments according to their comparative (policy) advantage. The logic behind this is exactly the same as in international trade theory. By "trading" policies and reallocating intervention effort between the instruments according to their *international* comparative advantage, countries can improve the outcomes in terms of their own utilities that those policies produce. These improvements could take the form of better target values for the same overall level of intervention, or the same target values with smaller interventions, or a mixture of the two. The importance of all these results therefore depends on the asymmetries between economies.

A second result is that cooperative policies produce greater continuity in the instruments and greater smoothness in the target paths compared to noncooperative policies. Cooperation also advances the timing and increases the speed with which targets are achieved. This result confirms Cooper's (1969) arguments: Cooperation damps out shocks more rapidly and reduces the costs of being out of equilibrium.

Third, cooperative policymaking involves smaller interventions as well as better target realizations; that is, for less effort one gets greater success. Cooperation therefore reduces policy "externalities" imposed from abroad. In the exercise quoted, Europe was relieved of the need to block spillovers from U.S. policy, and the United States was freed from the need to stimulate a stagnant European economy. As a result, both countries can better dedicate their instruments to achieving their own targets. Coordination therefore restores policy effectiveness weakened by competitive policymaking.

In summary, cooperation brings improvements because of the following:

■ Coordination restores policy effectiveness, which is weakened by interdependence and by expectations of foreign reactions. This happens because cooperation involves trading reductions in foreign externalities caused by domestic action against reduced externalities from foreign reactions. As a result, smaller interventions can achieve better expected outcomes on average.

■ Coordination speeds up an economy's responses and dampens out the transitory effects or external shocks more rapidly.

■ Coordination enables governments to extend the range of comparative policy advantage, and hence the policy specializations, which they can exploit.

Asymmetries between countries therefore play a crucial role in determining the gains from cooperation. Three kinds of asymmetry are of interest: asymmetric domestic policy responses (which determine policy specialization), asymmetric spillover effects (which determine bargaining strengths), and asymmetric adjustment speeds (which determine the cost of policy responses needed).

What Are the Risks in Coordination?

The previous sections have suggested that we do not need new forms of coordination, but "deeper" coordination and perhaps more robust forms of coordination. If the gains from coordination are not very large in normal circumstances, except for the weaker and more dependent countries, then maybe they can be made to generate more robust outcomes in an uncertain world. The difficulty is that policymakers are not going to want to cooperate if (a) they feel other countries will not wish to stick with their part of the bargain; (b) if they think there are likely to be errors in the exogenous information or assumed shocks that will invalidate their decisions; (c) if they think they may have (or may have been led to) wrongly estimated the preferences of others (a lack of transparency); or (d) if they think that their partners differ in their assessment of how their economies work or that the models they use to evaluate the policy bargains contain errors. We discuss each of these points in turn.

Sustainability

The first issue is whether policymakers will stick to their part of the bargain or cheat by redesigning their future policies once they have got the other participants locked into position. There are two possibilities here. First, one party may find it advantageous to deviate from what was agreed once the other participants have taken up their agreed positions; that is, governments cheat each other. The second is the usual time-inconsistency or credibility problem, discussed in the literature, where govern-

ments cheat the private sector. This does not involve a bargain as such but a breach of what the private sector had been led to expect. One example is that given by Rogoff (1985), who points out that international policy coordination may actually be welfare decreasing if the coordination process eases the constraints on governments engaging in inflationary monetary expansions. Governments may conclude that it pays to join together and cheat the private sector. The point here is that there is really more than one set of actors per economy so that coordination among governments may represent a coalition against the private sectors, wage earners, and so on, but not full coordination. Policy coalitions of this kind must be very common in practice, particularly between governments or governments and institutions. But such situations are not always welfare reducing. Carraro and Giavazzi (1988) produce a different model with three sectors (government, firms, and trade unions) to show that cooperation will be welfare increasing in all circumstances. The only clear message here seems to be that coordination with those with reputation will increase your credibility and hence the effectiveness of your policies.

The question of cheating between governments has received less attention. The argument here is that coordinated policies will be sustainable against cheating if the losses that a country might suffer under retaliation or preemptive cheating by the opponent sufficiently outweigh the gains that the first government might make by cheating. Hughes Hallett (1986b) finds that this condition is easily satisfied in a reflation game between the United States and the European Union; Currie et al. (1987) similarly find that there is little incentive to renege on bargains struck among policymakers.

External Shocks

There is some evidence that forecasting errors or exogenous shocks can cause significant disturbances and affect the incentives to coordinate. But those shocks have to be both large and persistent. Canzoneri and Minford (1986), in a static analysis with an empirical model, show that the mix of shocks can certainly affect the gains from coordination. Currie and others (1987) find the benefits of coordination to be small in the face of temporary disturbances, but those benefits rise steeply as the persistence of the disturbance increases.

These results, and the fact that it is not obvious why noncoordinated policies should be disturbed less than coordinated policies, suggest that coordination may actually *increase* policy robustness. Indeed, coordination may reduce policy errors because decisionmakers try to share the risks rather than offload them onto their rivals. Performance indicators are generally taken to be aggregations of national targets that are affected in different (and often conflicting) ways by externals shocks, while coordinated policies follow by aggregating those national indicators into some global performance index. Coordinated policies will therefore normally be more robust than noncooperative policies, which lack that extra aggregation stage and, hence, the added ability to diversify the risks.

Brandsma and others (1987) look at these robustness arguments explicitly using an example of United States–European Union coordination for the 1974–78 recession, subject to a range of "favorable" and "unfavorable" shocks to each of the target variables. They found that while coordination almost always produced better outcomes, it was not always the more robust strategy unless policymakers learn to revise their policies as they discover more about the disturbances entering their system. But policymakers would almost certainly wish to revise their calculations in the light of past shocks and errors. In that case, coordination quite clearly yielded the more robust policies, and, more importantly, the degree of extra robustness then *increased* with the size of shock.

Liberalization vs. Social Protection

Disagreements about whether the "Washington consensus" for a rapid liberalization of markets, but fiscal austerity and strict monetary discipline in policymaking, would be more appropriate than an approach focusing on social and economic cohesion, financial stability, and arrangements to overcome market imperfections, have done a lot to damage our ability to deal with financial and economic crises. In truth, it is very hard to provide a coordinated response when there is disagreement about the underlying paradigm to be followed.

A number of papers have been written on this theme. Pieper and Taylor (1998) and Stiglitz (1998) are two recent examples. They emphasize that the problem is not so much misguided policies, but that these policies have been recommended on the basis of the wrong framework for understanding how emerging economies work. That means the problem is market and information failures, leading to misguided market reactions and a lack of coordination internally or between different sectors of the economy. But can coordination really work when policymakers disagree on the model?

Frankel and Rockett (1988) examine the consequences of the assumption that governments differ about their view of the world. Using 10 international models in a model comparison exercise, Frankel and Rockett examine all 1,000 possible combinations where the two governments (the United States and the rest of the world) can

subscribe to any of the 10 models, and the true state of the world can in turn be any of the 10 models. Coordination yields benefits in just 60 percent of the combinations; in nearly 40 percent of the combinations, cooperation makes at least one party to the bargain feel worse off. However, this rather pessimistic view of the benefits to be expected from international policy coordination depends on the assumption that policymakers take no account of the different views about which model may be correct when computing the outcomes to be expected under each bargain. If policymakers disagree about the choice of model, they are unlikely to agree to coordinate their policies. However, Holtham and Hughes Hallett (1992) have shown that ruling out "weak" bargains in which either one party or the other expects their rival to be made worse off by the bargain greatly improves the success rate of coordination when it occurs. They argue that risk averse governments would wish to rule out weak bargains because they will be liable to reneging and would jeopardize future coordination attempts. In other words, each government would need to expect gains for all players ex post, as well as ex ante, before entering such a bargain. Ghosh and Masson (1988a, 1988b) similarly show that the presence of model uncertainty may raise the expected benefits of coordination if governments design their policies with explicit regard to the presence of model uncertainty. Governments aware of the adverse consequences of model disagreement would certainly take those consequences into account when choosing their policies, models, and degree of coordination. That would greatly reduce the force of this objection to policy coordination.

Summary

The recent financial and economic crisis in Asia, and the financial difficulties in Russia and Latin America, have shown how globalization without supporting local policies can bring trouble. Can local responses help "insure" the world against the kind of financial and trade shocks we have seen in the 1990s—or at least prevent the propagation of them to the smaller and less financially developed economies?

The answer seems to be "yes," but only up to a point and only if that coordination is constructed right. By that we mean the following:

■ The forces of globalization will make greater regional or international coordination more necessary. But for that coordination to be successful, it *must* be accompanied by explicit "localization" at the same time, that is, by the more effective (or proactive and flexible) use of domestic economy instruments to create the conditions in which international coordination efforts can work effectively.

- Under localization we have highlighted internal coordination (involving policy mix and market flexibility) and "vertical" coordination. Thus wider international coordination needs to be matched by "deepening," meaning a more consistent use of local policies.

- Another way of looking at it is globalization and the harmonization of policies in response to globalization need greater relative coordination too. Financial arrangements and monetary and fiscal discipline belong to the absolute coordination category, as does the fact that recovery in one country is much easier if others are growing than when they are not. But policy mix and exchange rate management belong to the latter category. The international institutions have largely concentrated on the former aspect, without being able to elicit much response on the latter. The consequence has been that the outcomes have been controversial and considerably less successful than they might have been. It would have been better had the institutional arrangements made the associated governments more like partners in the coordination process and less like the recipients of an imposed solution.

- In any case, coordinated policies (or policy rules) must be incentive compatible; the *distribution* of the gains is crucial. Very often the weaker parties stand to gain most over the best alternative, which makes it harder to persuade those who have to carry the burden of adjustment not to impose their own solutions—unless, or until, a crisis breaks out. Then institutional arrangements have to be found which balance the relative coordination gains against the absolute gains or losses.

- In normal G-8 type circumstances, coordination shows small but worthwhile gains. Outside that, coordination, whether formal or informal and limited to exchange rate targeting, has the great advantage of limiting the damage caused by governments following silly policies—whether they are too much in their own private interests, or simply misguided. This suggests that even simple forms of coordination can limit the effect of large financial disturbances and inappropriate responses to them. It's a disciplining device.

- Empirical studies have shown that coordination limits the losses from unexpected shocks: The more so the larger the shocks. Similarly it can help limit the uncertainty and controversies caused by disagreements over the appropriate policy framework. But if coordinated policies are to give the benefits of greater stability, it is important that they are well understood.

Consequently, the information exchanges they require will continue to be the most valuable element.

Bibliography

Beetsma, R., and L. Bovenberg. 1997. "Central Bank Independence and Public Debt Policy." *Journal of Economic Dynamics and Control* 21: 873–94.

Beetsma, R., and H. Uhlig. 1999. "An Analysis of the Stability and Growth Pact." *Economic Journal* 109: 546–71.

Brandsma, A., and A. Hughes Hallett. 1984. "Economic Conflict and the Solution of Dynamic Games." *European Economic Review* 26: 13–32.

Brandsma, Andries S., Andrew Hughes Hallett, and Joop Swank. 1987. "The Robustness of Economic Policy Selections and the Incentive to Cooperate." *Journal of Economic Dynamics and Control* 11: 163–70.

Bryant, Ralph. 1987. "Intergovernmental Coordination of Economic Policies: An Interim Stocktaking." In *International Monetary Cooperation Essays in Honor of Henry C. Wallich, Princeton Essays in International Finance.* No. 169. Princeton, NJ: Princeton University Press.

Canzoneri, Matthew, and Patrick Minford. 1986. "When Policy Coordination Matters: An Empirical Analysis." Centre for Economic Policy Research Discussion Paper No. 119. London: Centre for Economic Policy Research.

Carraro, Carlo, and Francesco Giavazzi. 1988. "Can International Policy Coordination Really be Counterproductive?" Centre for Economic Policy Research Discussion Paper No. 258. London: Centre for Economic Policy Research.

Cooper, Richard N. 1969. "Macroeconomic Policy Adjustment in Interdependent Economies." *Quarterly Journal of Economics* 83: 1–24.

Currie, David A., and David Vines. 1988. *Macroeconomic Interactions between North and South.* Cambridge: Cambridge University Press.

Currie, D. A., and S. Wren-Lewis. 1989. "An Appraisal of Alternative Blueprints for International Policy Coordination." *European Economic Review* 33: 1769–86.

Currie, David A., Paul Levine, and Nic Vidalis. 1987. "Cooperative and Noncooperative Rules for Monetary and Fiscal Policy in an Empirical Two-Bloc Model." In Ralph Bryant and Richard Portes, eds., *Global Macroeconomics: Policy Conflict and Cooperation.* London: Macmillan.

Demertzis, M., A. Hughes Hallett, and N. Viegi. 1999a. "Can the ECB be Truly Independent? Should It?" *Empirica* (Special Issue for the Austrian National Bank, November) 26: 217–40.

Demertzis, M., A. Hughes Hallett, and N. Viegi. 1999b. "An Independent Central Bank Faced with Elected Governments." Centre for Economic Policy Research Discussion Paper No. 2219. London: Centre for Economic Policy Research.

Eichengreen B., and A. K. Rose. 1998. "Staying Afloat When the Wind Shifts: External Factors and Emerging Market Banking Crises." Working Paper 6370. National Bureau of Economic Research, Cambridge, Mass.

Frankel, J., and Katherine E. Rockett. 1988. "International Macroeconomic Policy Coordination When Policy Makers Do Not Agree on the True Model." *American Economic Review* 78: 318–40.

Ghosh, Atish R., and Paul R. Masson. 1988a. "International Policy Coordination in a World with Model Uncertainty." International Monetary Fund, *Staff Papers*, Vol. 35. Washington, D.C.: International Monetary Fund.

Ghosh, A., and P. Masson. 1988b. "Model Uncertainty, Learning and the Gains from Coordination." International Monetary Fund Working Paper. Washington, D.C.: International Monetary Fund.

Helkie, William, A. Hughes Hallett, and J. Marquez. 1989. "Protectionism and the U.S. Trade Deficit: An Empirical Analysis." Centre for Economic Policy Research Discussion Paper No. 286. London: Centre for Economic Policy Research.

Holtham, G.H., and A. Hughes Hallett. 1992. "International Policy Coordination when Policy Markets do not Agree on the True Model." *American Economic Review* 82: 1043–51.

Hughes Hallett, A. 1986a. "Autonomy and the Choice of Policy in Asymmetrically Dependent Economies." *Oxford Economic Papers* 38: 516–44.

Hughes Hallett, A. 1986b. "International Policy Design and the Sustainability of Policy Bargains." *Journal of Economic Dynamics and Control* 10.

Hughes Hallett, A. 1987a. "The Impact of Interdependence on Economic Policy Design: The Case of the U.S., E.E.C. and Japan." *Economic Modelling* 4: 377–96.

Hughes Hallett, A. 1987b. "How Robust Are the Gains to Policy Coordination to Variations in the Model and Objectives?" *Richerche Economiche* (Special Issue on Game Theory and Economics) 41: 341–72.

Hughes Hallett, A. 1988. "Commodities, Debt and North–South Cooperation: A Cautionary Tale from the Structuralist Camp." In David A. Currie and David Vines, *Macroeconomic Interactions between North and South.* Cambridge: Cambridge University Press.

Hughes Hallett, A. 1992a. "Exchange Rates, Protectionism and Commercial Policy: Alternative Strategies for Coordinating the G3 Economies." *Japan and the World Economy* 4: 215–37.

Hughes Hallett, A. 1992b. "Target Zones and International Policy Coordination: The Contrast between the Necessary and Sufficient Conditions for Success." *European Economic Review* 36: 893–914.

Hughes Hallett, A. 1993. "Exchange Rates and Asymmetric Policy Regimes." *Oxford Economic Papers* 45: 191–206.

Hughes Hallett, A. 1994a. "The Impact of EC-92 on Developing Countries Trade." In *The World Bank Research Observer* 9: 121–46.

Hughes Hallett A. 1994b. "The Imperfect Substitutability of Policy Regimes: Exchange Rate Targeting vs. Policy Coordination." In *Economic Letters* 44: 159–164.

Hughes Hallett, A. 1998. "What Makes Exchange Rate Target Zones Work?" *Open Economies Review* 9: 115–39.

Hughes Hallett, A., and C.A. Primo Braga. 1994. "The New Regionalism and the Threat of Protectionism." *Japan and the International Economies* 8: 388–421.

Hughes Hallett, A. and Y. Ma. 1996a. "Changing Partners: The Importance of Coordinating Fiscal and Monetary Policies within a Monetary Union." *The Manchester School* 64: 115–34.

Hughes Hallett, A. and Y. Ma. 1996b. "Transatlantic Policy Coordination with Sticky Labour Markets: The Reality of the Real Side." In M. Canzoneri, W. Ethier, and V. Grilli, eds., *The New Transatlantic Economy.* Cambridge: Cambridge University Press.

Hughes Hallett, A., Gerald Holtham, and Gary Hutson. 1989. "Exchange Rate Targeting as a Surrogate for International Policy Coordination." In Barry Eichengreen, Marcus Miller, and Richard Portes, eds., *Blueprints for Exchange Rate Management.* London and New York: Academic Press.

Minford, Patrick, and Matthew Canzoneri. 1987. "Policy Interdependence: Does Strategic Behaviour Pay?" Centre for Economic Policy Research Discussion Paper No. 201. London: Centre for Economic Policy Research.

Oudiz, Gilles, and Jeffrey Sachs. 1984. "Macroeconomic Policy Coordination Among the Industrial Economies." *Brookings Papers on Economic Activity* 1. Washington, D.C.: The Brookings Institution.

Patrick, J.D. 1972. "Establishing Convergent Decentralised Policy Assignments." *Journal of International Economics* 3: 37–52.

Pieper, U., and L. Taylor. 1998. "The Revival of the Liberal Creed: The IMF, World Bank and Inequality in a Globalised Economy." Centre for Economic Policy Research Working Paper No. 4. New York: New School for Social Research, revised January 1998.

Rogoff, Kenneth. 1985. "Can International Monetary Policy Coordination be Counterproductive?" *Journal of International Economics* 18: 1169–89.

Stiglitz, J. 1998. "More Instruments and Broader Goals: Moving Toward the Post-Washington Consensus." Wider Annual Lectures No. 2. United Nations University, Helsinki.

Woodford, M. 1995. "Price Level Determinancy with Control of a Monetary Aggregate." Carnegie–Rochester Conference Series, 43.

Wren-Lewis, S., P. Westaway, S. Soteri, and R. Barrel. 1991. "Evaluating the UK's Choice of Entry Rate into the ERM." *Manchester School* 59: 1–22.

Notes

1. Woodford's (1995) "fiscal theory of the price level" shows how the experience of, or prospect of, an undisciplined fiscal policy can end up by undermining a carefully designed and well-conducted monetary policy and determining the effective price level (inflation rate). This implies a need for interinstitution (between central banks and governments) as well as intercountry coordination.

2. The distinction here is between making decisions jointly over several time periods, taking into account the predictable dynamic responses of the policy targets, and making the same decisions as a sequence of individual one period decisions, in which case the predictable dynamic consequences of those decisions cannot be incorporated into each calculation.

3. See also Hughes Hallett (1993) for more detail.

4. It is hard to calculate precise equilibrium exchange rate values in practice. They must depend on what you take to be "normal" capital flows, on what you define to be an equilibrium and on what model you take to calculate it, on what "fundamentals" are assumed for productivity trends or outside conditions (for example, U.S. monetary policy, Japanese growth, or the Euro exchange rate), and on what fiscal and monetary policies may be assumed for the domestic economy in the future.

5. The only time this doesn't apply is when the stronger countries cannot choose their policies sensibly, even for themselves, or when they fail to take into account large, unexpected shocks which render those policies ineffective ex post.

chapter 5

The Impacts of Emigration on Countries of Origin

Stephen Castles

Institute of Social Change and Critical Inquiry
University of Wollongong

irtually all the world's 200-plus countries experience some international migration, both arrivals and departures. We speak of a "country of emigration" when departures of citizens substantially exceed arrivals of noncitizens over some years. Emigration can refer to permanent departure to settle in another country or to temporary migration, usually for employment. The notion of a country of emigration also implies that the departure of many citizens has important economic—as well as social, cultural, and political—implications.[1]

For many countries, emigration has become economically vital and a widely accepted economic strategy. This often leads to a "culture of migration" in which going abroad to work becomes a rite of passage for young men and women, conferring not only economic well-being but also enhanced social status. Indeed, the majority of emigrants are young adults at their most productive age. In earlier times, most migrant workers were males. But the last few decades have seen the "feminization of migration": Not only is a growing proportion of primary migrants women, but some major migratory movements today are female-dominated.

Migration has also become a major industry, encompassing an estimated US$7 billion for air fares, interest on loans to migrants, and service fees to recruiters, medical clinics giving health tests, and training centers (Abella 1995b). Emigration involves a transfer of the most valuable economic resource—human capital—usually from a poor country to a rich one. The family, local community, and state of origin bear the costs of raising a migrant to young adulthood. The immigration country reaps the benefits of this investment, and the migrant often returns home to again become the responsibility of the country of origin.

A key question for governments of emigration countries is whether emigration contributes to development or hinders it through "brain drain" and creation of sectoral imbalances. The question is highly complex as emigration exerts far-reaching and long-lasting impacts on every sector of society. But overall, emigration is worthwhile for the home country only if it could not otherwise employ migrants' labor power and skills, it can use the human capital migrants obtain abroad upon their return, and the transfer of income from emigration outweighs the costs of raising the migrant.

International cooperation can play a major role in enhancing the contribution of migration to development. However, efforts and outcomes so far have been disappointing. Emigration and immigration countries often lack policies for maximizing the benefits of migration, exacerbated by the reluctance of immigration countries to increase the cost of migrant labor to employers.

The Extent and Causes of Emigration

Emigration statistics are incomplete and unreliable, even in highly developed countries and especially in developing countries (Boyle et al. 1998; Hoffmann and Lawrence 1996). This arises from the reluctance of governments to monitor departure of their citizens, the high costs of monitoring, a lack of institutional capacity, the difficulty of distinguishing emigrants from people leaving for other purposes, high levels of irregular migration, and a lack of international uniformity in collecting data.

Estimates of annual departures or of the number of nationals abroad may therefore vary widely. The International Labour Office (ILO), the International Organization for Migration (IOM), the United Nations Population Fund (UNFPA), and the Organisation for Economic Co-operation and Development (OECD), as well as regional bodies such as the European Union and the Asia Pacific Economic Cooperation Forum are trying to improve the reliability and comparability of the data, but international figures are only as good as the national sources on which they are based. Despite these gaps, a number of important comparative studies of emigration dynamics have recently been done.[2] However, the level of knowledge is far lower than with regard to immigration countries, and substantial need for documentation and analysis remains.

The most obvious cause of migration is disparities in income, employment, and social well-being among different areas. Demographic differences in fertility, mortality, age structure, and labor-force growth are also important (Hugo 1998).[3] According to neoclassical economic theory, one would expect individuals to maximize their income by moving from low-wage to high-wage economies (Borjas 1989). However, the causes and patterns of international migration are much more complex, owing partly to the family and community nature of decisionmaking, and partly to state barriers to border crossing (Zolberg 1989; Portes and Böröcz 1989). Recent research has shown the enormous influence of social networks in both sending and receiving countries in encouraging and organizing migration.

Thus there is no simple relationship between poverty and emigration. Departures from the very poorest areas may be rare because people lack the economic capital needed to travel, the cultural capital to become aware of opportunities elsewhere, and the social capital (or networks) to find work and cope in a new environment. However, a catastrophe such as a war or environmental disaster may force even the poorest to migrate, usually under very bad conditions.

Emigration is both a result and a cause of development. Development leads to migration because economic and educational improvements enable people to seek better opportunities elsewhere. Research shows that middle-income groups in developing areas are most likely to depart. As incomes rise further, emigration then tends to decline (Rowlands 1998; United Nations 1998). Migration also leads to development when remittances contribute to investment in the area of origin and when migrants return with skills, experience, and attitudes conducive to economic, social, and cultural change.

Emigration is therefore part of the social transformation linked to modernization.

Migratory movements generally arise from prior links between sending and receiving countries stemming from colonization, political influence, trade, investment, or cultural ties (Kritz et al. 1992). Migrations from India, Pakistan, and Bangladesh to Britain were linked to the British colonial presence on the Indian subcontinent. Caribbean migrants have similarly tended to move to their former colonial power—for example, from Jamaica to Britain, Martinique to France, and Surinam to the Netherlands.

Research on Asian migration has shown that families rather than individuals make migration decisions (Hugo 1994). In situations of rapid change, a family may decide to send one or more members to work in another region or country to maximize income and survival. Such decisions are often made by elders (especially men), with younger people and women expected to obey patriarchal authority. Families may decide to send young women to the city or overseas because the labor of the young men is less dispensable on the farm and because young women are often seen as more reliable in sending remittances. Such motivations parallel growing international demand for female labor in precision assembly or as domestic servants.

Migratory chains typically stem from an external factor such as recruitment or military service, or initial movement of young pioneers. Ensuing migrants mainly follow "beaten paths" (Stahl 1993), helped by relatives and friends who provide shelter, work, assistance in coping with bureaucratic procedures, and personal support. Migratory movements thus become self-sustaining: Both migrants and nonmigrants become facilitators, and a "migration industry" emerges consisting of recruitment organizations, lawyers, agents, smugglers, and other middle-people. The emergence of a migration industry with a strong interest in the continuation of migration has often confounded government efforts to control or stop such movements.

The links between migrant community and area of origin may persist over generations. Remittances fall off and visits home may decline, but familial and cultural links remain, and migrants may seek marriage partners in the home country. Migration continues and may increase dramatically in time of crisis, as shown by the mass movement of Yugoslav refugees to Germany during the early 1990s, where they joined compatriots who had migrated 20 years earlier. In the long run, migrations may spawn international networks that affect economic relations, social and political institutions, and the

Box 5.1
The Benefits and Costs of Migration

Benefits

Potential microlevel (individual and familial) benefits:
- Escaping from unemployment or underemployment
- Escaping from repressive situations or threats to life and health
- Improving individual or family income
- Gaining capital to invest in land or in business
- Gaining skills, work experience, and education
- Improving family security through diversification of income
- Improving social status

Potential macrolevel (society-wide) benefits:
- Reducing demographic pressures where population is outstripping resources
- Reducing unemployment where growth in the labor force growth exceeds demand
- Reducing political pressures where economic and social problems are causing discontent
- Using migrant remittances to improve a country's balance of payments and fund imports
- Improving human capital through transfer of skills, work experience, and education
- Contributing to international trade
- Introducing innovative attitudes toward economic development through exposure to more developed societies

Costs

Potential microlevel problems or costs:
- The loss of workers may reduce productivity and income at home
- The high costs of migration (especially in irregular movements) may put an individual or family into debt
- The risk of illness or injury (especially in irregular movements) may involve high costs
- Remittances may be used for nonproductive purposes
- Remittances may exacerbate existing social inequalities or cause local inflation
- Migrants may fail to gain useful skills abroad
- Certain types of migration (especially trafficking of women and children for the sex industry) may lead to individual or family shame

Potential macrolevel problems or costs:
- Emigration is unlikely to reduce demographic pressures but may lead to shortages of young adults in certain regions
- Emigration of skilled workers may cause economic bottlenecks in certain industries
- The import of ideas by returning migrants may increase political pressures for change
- Remittances may occur through irregular channels
- Improvements in human capital may be minimal and outweighed by loss of highly skilled personnel
- Loss of control of migratory movements may encourage corruption and organized crime
- The need for people to go abroad to seek a decent livelihood may be seen as a "national shame"

culture and national identity of all countries concerned (Basch et al. 1994).

The Migration Transition

Much as the "industrial transition" refers to the shift from agriculture to manufacturing to services and the "demographic transition" entails falls in both mortality and fertility, a "mobility or migration transition" links the preceding transitions with population movements (Zelinsky 1971). Emigration frequently rises at the beginning of the industrialization process owing to population growth, a decline in rural employment, and low wages. This was the case in early-19th-century Britain, late-19th-century Japan, and Korea in the 1970s. As industrialization proceeds, the labor supply declines and wage levels rise. Emigration then falls, and immigration occurs and then predominates (Martin et al. 1996; Skeldon 1997; Amjad 1996).

Countries often experience simultaneous emigration and immigration during the transition, usually of workers with different types of skills. For instance, some Malaysian workers migrate to Taiwan and other countries while some highly skilled personnel (especially of

Chinese ethnic background) seek work elsewhere. But Malaysia also attracts large numbers of low-skilled workers from Indonesia, the Philippines, and Bangladesh as well as expatriate experts from developed countries.

The notion of a migration transition is helpful in evaluating the long-term results of emigration. If the benefits help support the economic and demographic transitions and reduce the need for future emigration, then the process can be seen as conducive to development. However, if emigration perpetuates economic and demographic imbalances and reduces pressure for change on governments, it can hinder development.

Weighing the Benefits and Costs of Emigration

The potential benefits and problems arising from emigration include microlevel effects on individual migrants, families, and communities, and macrolevel effects on economies and societies (see Box 5.1). Most individuals that emigrate and governments that encourage emigration obviously conclude that the benefits outweigh the costs. However, microlevel and macrolevel cost-benefit calculations may conflict. Governments often encourage emigration to reduce unemployment, gain remittances, and transfer skills, but these expectations are not always realized. In some cases, the calculation is based on short-term factors while the costs to the economy and society are long-term.[4]

Many governments facilitate the movement of workers abroad to provide employment, obtain remittances, and mollify social discontent. Other governments are skeptical of such benefits and do their best to restrict emigration, with varying degrees of success. Some governments doubt the merits of emigration but find that they cannot prevent it and therefore try to regulate movements and protect their citizens abroad. Indeed, strict limits on emigration may be counterproductive if a state lacks the capacity to enforce them: They can simply lead to irregular movements, which hurt both migrants and the sending country.

Abella (1995b) found that most Asian countries guarantee the right of their citizens to move freely out of their country and back in again, but that they may use high fees, complex procedures, or other barriers to deter such movements or select who pursues them. For example, Pakistan, Bangladesh, India, Indonesia, and the Philippines set a minimum age for women seeking employment abroad. Cultural factors can also come into play: Women from Pakistan and Bangladesh rarely migrate for employment, while Sri Lanka, Indonesia, and the Philippines encourage female labor migration.

Most Asian governments have set up special departments or agencies to manage labor emigration, such as Bangladesh's Bureau of Manpower, Employment and Training (BMET) and India's Office of the Protector of Emigrants within the Ministry of Labour. The governments of China and Vietnam organize labor migration through state-owned firms that contract with foreign states or companies, and Bangladesh, Indonesia, and Thailand have also negotiated directly with foreign governments. India, meanwhile, licenses private recruitment firms to hire and deploy workers while seeking to regulate their fees and ensure that they treat workers fairly (Abella 1995b). In South Asia, emigration bureaus review the contracts of emigrants to ensure that their terms are satisfactory (Shah 1994).

However, governments find it difficult to control recruitment firms, and cases of abuse and exploitation are widespread. For example, agents in Pakistan charge four times the permitted fee or even more (Shah 1994). In fact, the number of irregular migrants within Asia may exceed the number of regular ones (Lim and Oishi 1996), and the same is certainly true in Africa, Latin America, and even in Eastern and Southern Europe. Irregular migration gives rise to exploitative employment and may take extreme forms such as the trafficking of women and children for prostitution.

Remittances from emigrants working abroad can constitute a major contribution to the balance of payments of countries with severe trade deficits. For instance, Pakistani workers remitted over US$2 billion in 1988 (not including unofficial transfers or consumer goods), which covered 30 percent of the cost of imports (Abella 1995a). Indian workers remitted US$2.6 billion in 1988—the equivalent of 15 percent of imports (ILO 1991). Most emigration countries encourage workers to send remittances through official channels by setting up banking facilities in countries of employment, providing special exchange rates, or by other inducements. Failure to provide accessible financial services and realistic exchange rates often leads emigrants to repatriate funds through irregular channels, which may reduce their benefits to the home economy.

Most emigration countries maintain policies to prevent the abuse or exploitation of their citizens abroad and provide assistance in case of illness, accident, death, legal trouble, disputes with employers, or other emergencies. Emigration countries typically station labor attachés and welfare workers at consulates and may also fund welfare centers or support nongovernmental organizations (NGOs) that run them. Some also provide advice and counseling services before departure—sometimes in cooperation with immigration countries. Migrant workers must often cover the costs of such services, usually as part of the fee to obtain travel documentation.

Measures and services for protecting emigrants are frequently ineffective. They are not available to the large numbers of irregular migrants, and even legal migrants are so dependent on finding and keeping employment abroad that they hesitate to complain about abuses. Staffing and regional coverage abroad is often inadequate to meet the need, and sending authorities hesitate to antagonize authorities and employers in immigration countries. In a situation of global oversupply of low-skilled migrants, market power lies with recruiting countries.

Large numbers of migrants return to their countries of origin after varying stays abroad. Some benefit from reintegration assistance from either the receiving country or the country of origin. However, most are left to their own devices, and they frequently face difficulty in finding employment commensurate with skills they have acquired abroad. Their potential input to their country is thus diminished, if not lost. Even though return migration occurs in many countries on a large scale, authorities possess limited knowledge and concern regarding these conditions.

The 1998 United Nations Technical Symposium on International Migration and Development found that monitoring of return migration and research on its consequences is insufficient to understand its contribution to development. In some cases returnees appear to have contributed little to sustainable development, while in others they appear to have had positive effects. However, adequate counseling and information as well as help in obtaining investment credits do seem to help returnees reacclimate successfully and maximizes their positive effects on development. Returnees are more likely to be successful if advised and supported by governmental agencies and NGOs, and social networks in the home country are also crucial. Cooperation between sending and receiving countries and with international organizations and NGOs can play an important role, especially when significant numbers of emigrants return over a short time (United Nations 1998).

Case Study: Turkey

Turkey was a major source of labor for Western Europe's postwar boom until the 1970s. Rather than undergoing a "migration transition," the country has since developed new types of emigration.

Unlike the Southern European countries that sent workers to Western Europe after 1945, Turkey had no tradition of international labor migration. Agreements between the German Federal Government and the Turkish government in 1961 and 1964 initiated organized movement. The latter hoped to relieve domestic unemployment and obtain foreign exchange, while the migrants themselves sought to escape poverty, unemployment, and dependence on semifeudal landowners. The country also expected that money and skills gained abroad would encourage economic development and hoped to gain access to the European Community.[5]

Migration to Germany was highly organized. The German Federal Labour Office (Bundesanstalt für Arbeit—BfA) set up recruitment offices in Turkey in collaboration with authorities. Employers requiring both unskilled and skilled manual employees paid a fee to the BfA, which selected workers, tested their skills, provided medical exams, and screened police records. The workers were brought in groups to Germany, where employers had to provide initial accommodation. Although bi-lateral agreements regulated working conditions and social security, as many as 20 percent of employees migrated irregularly (Martin 1991).

The Netherlands recruited Turks in much the same way as Germany had, and migrants moved spontaneously to France, Belgium, Austria, and other countries. The peak movement occurred from 1968 to 1973, with 525,000 workers traveling through official channels, and many more unofficially (Martin 1991). This was guestworker migration: The workers were not meant to bring in dependents or stay for long periods. In the event of an economic downturn, the system was designed to allow quick repatriation. Despite the restrictions, about one-quarter of Turkish emigrants were women, often traveling before their men to get jobs in factories looking for light assembly workers. Once in Germany or the Netherlands, they would try to persuade employers to recruit their husbands by name. This facilitated family reunion, despite official policies (Castles and Kosack 1973 and 1985; Castles et al. 1984). By 1972, half of Turkish workers had their families with them in Germany (Martin 1991).

The German government stopped recruiting in 1973 in response to the oil crisis, hoping that surplus workers would leave. In fact, many Turks stayed, and family reunion continued. By 1974 the country housed over 1 million Turkish residents among a total foreign population of 4.1 million. Their number grew to 1.6 million by 1982 and to over 2 million by 1995. Political unrest leading to the 1980 Turkish military coup generated waves of asylum seekers, who found shelter in Turkish communities in Germany. Clearly, the chain migration process was more powerful than German policies. Mass deportation, though debated, was never a real option for a democratic state. By pursuing family reunion and permanent settlement, the Turks lost their attractiveness as a flexible labor force: They became largely permanent settlers who needed housing, schools, and social amenities.

Turkish expectations of the benefits of labor migration were also unfulfilled. Many of the migrants selected by the German recruitment offices were not unemployed "surplus population" but skilled workers. Since they were generally given unskilled jobs in Germany, they gained few qualifications relevant to Turkish industrialization. Worker remittances, which ran at US$1.5–2 billion per year in the 1980s, certainly helped the Turkish balance of payments, but they were mainly used for consumption or to establish small tertiary businesses such as taxis, cafés, and shops rather than for productive investment (Martin 1991). When Turkey applied for full EC membership in 1987, there were strong reactions in Germany because of fears of an uncontrolled flood of workers. EC membership was refused in 1989, although negotiations reopened in the mid-1990s.

Thus Turkish migration to Western Europe did little to promote economic development. Since rapid demographic growth continued and the labor market was unable to absorb all Turkish young people, pressure for emigration continued. At the beginning of the 1990s some 20–40 percent of young adults professed interest in migrating to EC countries (Martin 1991). Because this possibility had largely closed, new emigration flows developed to the Gulf oil states, especially Saudi Arabia, as well as to Russia and other Soviet successor states. Many of these new migrants were skilled workers. By 1996, 3.45 million Turks were living abroad—the equivalent of 5.4 percent of Turkey's population. Yet Turkey's labor market was still incapable of providing enough jobs: 1 million more people had applied for emigration. Turkey's proportion of surplus labor is expected to reach 15 percent by 2000 (OECD 1998).

Why did Turkey's large-scale emigration program fail to spark economic development? Beginning in the 1970s, the German government and Turkish authorities developed measures to help workers reintegrate, including promoting new companies and establishing credit funds. But a longitudinal study by the German Institute for Employment Research (IAB) showed that only half of male respondents were still economically active in Turkey in 1988, with 90 percent self-employed. There was almost no relationship between occupations in Turkey and in Germany: Most returnees were farmers or retailers or worked in transport occupations. The majority worked in small enterprises. Few had acquired qualifications in Germany, and those that had had rarely been able to use them on return. Hardly any returnees had received counseling about return or investment, and return seemed to have made little contribution to development, although there might have been exceptions at the regional level. Migrants did appear to have invested considerably in educating their children, which might have promoted development indirectly. The IAB's analysis concludes that better measures to prepare returnees for economic reintegration and encouraging investments in specific regions and economic sectors are essential (Hönekopp and Tayanç 1998).

Apparently emigration itself does not spur economic development. However, this result must be seen in the context of a strained economy and a society deeply divided along political, ethnic, and religious lines. Emigration is an expression of such problems and will not provide a solution unless it is part of an integrated development strategy.

Case Study: The Philippines

Just as the Mediterranean periphery fueled Western European industrial expansion until the 1970s, China, South Asian countries, and the Philippines and Indonesia have more recently become major labor providers. The Philippines is the contemporary labor exporter *par excellence* (rather like Italy a generation ago), with over 4 million of its people scattered across the world (Battistella and Paganoni 1992). About half are permanent settlers, residing mainly in the United States, while the rest are overseas contract workers (OCWs)—both legal and illegal—residing in the Gulf states and Asia, including Japan, Malaysia, Singapore, and Hong Kong. In 1994 a total of 565,000 Filipinos were recruited to work in other countries, and a further 154,000 took jobs as sailors on foreign-owned ships.

Labor export is crucial to the economy of the Philippines: Unemployment levels might be 40 percent higher without it. Official remittances from migrants in 1994 totaled US$2.94 billion, which financed 50 percent of the country's external trade deficit (Amjad 1996). Workers remitted a total of US$23.4 billion between 1975 and 1995, with the largest source being the United States (Go 1998). (These figures include only remittances through the formal banking system; transfers are also made as cash or consumer goods.) By the early 1990s, 16 percent of Filipino households were receiving remittances from abroad (Saith 1997).[6]

Women have played a growing part in emigration from the Philippines—at least half of temporary migrant workers are now female. Most migrant women take jobs as domestic workers, entertainers (often a euphemism for prostitution), restaurant and hotel staff, and assembly-line workers in clothing and electronics. These jobs are low in pay and status, offer poor working conditions, and are associated with patriarchal stereotypes such as docility and willingness to give personal service. Domestic service leads to isolation and vulnerability for young women, who often have little protection against the demands of their employers (Lim and Oishi 1996). Female migrants from the Philippines, Thailand, and Sri Lanka also often travel as "mail-order" brides to Europe, Australia, and Japan (Cahill 1990). According to Saith, both supply-side and demand-side factors underlie Philippine migration. The former include rapid growth of the population and the labor force amid a long period of economic stagnation, which has led to low-quality employment and unsustainable forms of agriculture. Such emigration pressures found an outlet because of the high levels of education and occupational training, familiarity with the English language, and female participation among the Filipino labor force. Saith's study found no sign of economic development in the foreseeable future that could reduce emigration pressures. The study also found that migration gains accrue disproportionately to richer regions and higher income groups, exacerbating existing imbalances (Saith 1997).

Overseas employment became an official program of the Philippine government in 1974. At first it attempted to follow the South Korean model by setting up an autonomous Overseas Employment and Development Board with a near-monopoly on recruitment. However, this approach was unsuccessful, and the government established the Philippine Overseas Employment Administration (POEA) to maintain "positive controls" over the private recruitment industry. The POEA has become a major agency, with numerous offices and a budget for 1988–95 of 576 million pesos—some 7.6 percent of the budget of the Department of Labour and Employment (Tomas 1998). People who wish to seek work abroad must register with the POEA, and premigration training and certification requirements for entertainers, domestic workers, and some other categories have been tightened to prevent abuse.

The country also established the Overseas Workers' Welfare Administration (OWWA) to assist workers in emergencies and protect them from exploitation. Officials at Filipino consulates in labor-importing countries also help migrants, yet in 1993 only 31 labor attachés, 20 welfare officers, and 20 coordinators were available to respond to the needs of millions of migrant workers in 120 countries (Lim and Oishi 1996). Philippine officials often find themselves powerless against unscrupulous agents and abusive employers who may have the backing of the police and other authorities in receiving countries, especially the Persian Gulf.

An important receiving country, especially for women, is Singapore. Owing to attractive job opportunities for Singaporean women, employment of foreign domestic servants is high: In 1993 the city-state housed some 81,000 foreign domestic servants, of whom 50,000 were from the Philippines, 17,000 from Sri Lanka, and 10,000 from Indonesia. Fees for recruitment (mainly through specialized agencies) ranged from US$1,000 to US$2,000, usually deducted from the employee's wages. Frequent cases of abuse reported to Philippine authorities led to a ban on recruitment in 1987, but this was circumvented by the Singaporean authorities, who admitted Filipinas as tourists and then gave them work permits

(Wong 1996). Public concern in the Philippines came to a head in 1995 when a Filipina maid, Flor Contemplacion, was hanged in Singapore after being found guilty of murder. The case strained relations between the two countries and led to a heated debate concerning the 700,000 Filipinos who go to work overseas each year. The Philippine government again banned migration of domestic workers to Singapore, but this ban, too, was largely circumvented.

However, in June 1995 the Philippines passed the Migrant Workers and Overseas Filipinos Act to improve the welfare of OCWs. Protecting the dignity and human rights of Filipinos was to come before economic objectives. And rather than exporting Filipino labor, the government adopted a policy of managing labor outflows while developing a comprehensive employment strategy at home (Lim and Oishi 1996). Specific measures included a policy of selective deployment and measures to improve information for prospective migrants as well as cooperation between POEA, OWWA, the Technical Skills and Development Authority, and the Department of Foreign Affairs (Go 1998).

It is difficult to assess the success of the new policy. Certainly dramatic cuts in emigration and substantial improvement in conditions of Filipino OCWs did not seem to have occurred by 1997. Since then the effects of the Asian crisis on labor migration make comparisons difficult. However, it's important to note that return migration and cuts in flows to receiving countries are likely to cause considerable hardship. Böhning (1998) points out that women migrants originate disproportionately from poorer regions of the country, and loss of their earnings can be disastrous for the families who depend on them.

Substantial emigration also affects Philippine national identity. For emigration countries, admitting to permanent loss of substantial groups of emigrants can be seen as a "national shame" because the nation is incapable of providing an acceptable life for its people. This has become a major theme in the Philippines, especially regarding settlement in the United States. Permanent emigrants may be seen as members of a diaspora who retain links with the homeland (even after becoming U.S. citizens), but also as people who betray the nation by exporting their energy and skills (Aguilar Jr. 1996).

One way of dealing with this dilemma is to create a special status for expatriates. The Philippines established the category of *Balikbayans*—"people coming back home to the Philippines"—as early as the 1970s. *Balikbayans* may be overseas contract workers, permanent

U.S. residents, or even U.S. citizens of Filipino origin. Programs that facilitate their return include special travel documents, tax privileges, and import concessions. Such official recognition of diasporas treats people who live abroad as a part of the national community, yielding both economic and political benefits (Blanc 1996). Indeed, a key focus of contemporary migration studies is the emergence of international networks linking emigrants to their countries of origin.

Has large-scale emigration contributed to economic development in the Philippines? At the microlevel, remittances have provided resources to improve agricultural enterprises or establish other types of enterprise. At the macrolevel, remittances have provided a substantial amount of foreign exchange. And returning Filipinos have often brought new skills as well as experience in a wide range of economic activities. However, without effective policies to maximize these benefits, resources have often gone into unproductive or unsuccessful ventures. The most common investment has been in small-scale enterprises in transport, catering, and other services, with skills gained abroad often wasted for lack of relevant opportunities. What's more, by providing individual escape from economic stagnation, emigration may well have reduced pressures for economic and social change.

In view of such problems, Go suggests major initiatives to achieve the benefits of migration, including efforts to sustain Filipino economic growth, more and better-trained personnel and financial resources to protect the rights and welfare of Filipinos abroad, and more education and training to enable Filipinos to keep pace with changes in the local and global economy (Go 1998). These far-reaching suggestions clearly imply that efforts to manage emigration must be closely linked to economic and social development. Implementing such policies requires political will as well as institutional capacity for effective action.

Improving the Conditions for Return Migration

Despite the knowledge gaps, some policies clearly help maximize the gains from emigration and return migration. An effective strategy begins during the decision-making period before departure: Governments, communities, and individuals need to plan to use the economic and cultural capital they hope to gain through work abroad. There is considerable evidence that many migrants and their families do make such long-term calculations. Governments, in contrast, often concentrate mainly on short-term economic and political aspects and neglect long-term strategies.

Policies to maximize long-term gains from return migration might include the following elements:

Preparing for migration. Authorities should use their consuls and labor attachés in destination countries to collect information on working and living conditions for migrant workers and their families. Governments can then employ counseling and other forms of information to help potential migrants make well-informed choices. Authorities should also provide counseling on repatriating earnings and savings and investing them to improve economic well-being, health, education, and social welfare.

Controlling actual movement. Authorities should take all possible steps to ensure orderly migration, including organizing recruitment and deployment or regulating private agents. Bilateral or multilateral agreements, or at least discussions, with receiving countries are important. Experience has shown that rigid regulations that fight market forces, such as prohibitions of cross-border movement, are often counterproductive. Governments are more likely to achieve orderly movements by providing regulatory frameworks and services.

Offering consular and social services abroad. It is vital for countries of origin to take responsibility for migrants. This requires provision of consular and social services in the event of legal problems, disputes with employers, or accident and illness. Emigration countries need to adequately fund special agencies; the Filipino experience provides a useful model.

Transferring remittances. Orderly transfer of remittances is essential for countries to realize development benefits; otherwise migrants will transfer their earnings in the form of cash or consumer goods. Orderly transfer ensures direct benefits to national accounts as well as safety for migrants. Realistic exchange rates, low bank charges, and reliable financial services in countries of both employment and origin are vital. Special investment schemes to encourage migrants to combine their savings to establish companies or fund infrastructure projects in home communities are worthwhile. Companies set up by Turkish migrants in the 1970s were not particularly successful, but this experience should be evaluated to learn its lessons.

Providing education and training. Countries of origin should ensure that migrants receive education, vocational training, and work experience relevant to occupational needs at home. This requires cooperation with governments and employers in the receiving country as well as appropriate counseling for migrants. However, migrants will be motivated to accumulate human capital only if they see a real chance of using it on return. Such measures therefore must be closely linked to domestic economic and labor-market policies.

Maintaining links. Research has shown that the most successful returnees maintain economic and community links at home. Returnees who have lost local contacts and knowledge or members of the second generation often have great difficulty relating to local customs and participating in social networks. Governments can foster such networks by facilitating regular visits home and efficient and affordable telecommunications, and by supporting social and cultural associations in receiving countries. Counseling and services should emphasize the need for maintaining local business contacts while abroad if migrants wish to establish businesses on return.

Offering prereturn advice. Authorities from emigration countries should provide comprehensive services to prepare migrants for return. Consular officials or social workers employed by the government can provide such services, but social and cultural associations of migrants may prove more effective. Such services should include advice on social reintegration and family matters as well as employment opportunities and investments at home.

Repatriating and investing savings and assets. Governments should encourage returning migrants to repatriate their savings and assets by adopting policies such as realistic exchange rates and waiving of fees and customs duties. Migration agencies should also ensure that returning migrants maximize the benefits of their economic and human capital to foster sustainable development. One technique is to provide targeted credit mechanisms such as low-interest rates to returnees who invest their savings in economically useful ways.

Emphasizing nondiscrimination. Finally, a word of warning: Services for migrants and returnees should be designed and delivered so that they do not seem unfair to nonmigrants. Credit mechanisms and similar measures should be built into wider strategies for economic and social development for the whole population.

Fostering International Cooperation on Emigration

Although international cooperation between sending and receiving countries could help maximize the benefits of emigration, immigration countries tend to view labor migration as a source of short-term economic benefit rather than as an aspect of cooperation on development. Labor-importing countries also often see migrants as "cheap labor," using them to meet skill shortages that would otherwise lead to bottlenecks or wage inflation. Measures such as training to improve migration's contribution to the country of origin would make it more expensive, and therefore reduce employers' motivation. In any case, a large proportion of migrating labor moves through irregular channels.

As an example of such problems, the Philippines has concluded labor agreements with Jordan, Iraq, and Qatar but not with the most important recruiting countries

(Go 1998). Japan set up the Japan International Training Organization (JITCO) to work with government agencies, employers, unions, and international organizations on recruitment and training (Abella 1995b). But such training schemes sometimes merely undermine restrictions on the import of low-skilled workers, and the training is often limited.

International cooperation often occurs when the immigration country wishes to encourage repatriation. Just as Germany tried to assist reintegration of Turkish workers after 1973, France and migrant-sending countries in North and West Africa made similar arrangements. The European Union has also helped facilitate return migration and maximize its benefits. For example, in 1975 France and Senegal began encouraging the voluntary return of migrants, offering training to returnees and funding reintegration projects. However, Senegal has apparently been more successful in ensuring transfers of migrants' savings than in utilizing their skills. One study suggests facilitating access to microfunding and financing for small-scale enterprises—a "bank of the poor" based on models in Bolivia, Bangladesh, and Tunisia (Diatta and Mbow 1998).

International organizations—notably the ILO and the IOM—have played an important role in improving cooperation between sending and receiving states, and regional organizations such as the European Union (EU) and the Asia-Pacific Economic Council (APEC) also seek to harmonize regulations regarding migrant workers. The International Covenant on Civil and Political Rights and the International Covenant on Economic, Social and Cultural Rights apply to migrants as much as to anyone else, but more specific measures are needed. ILO conventions No. 97 of 1949 and No. 143 of 1975 do specify minimum standards of treatment for migrant workers and their dependents, but as of 1993 only 40 and 17 countries, respectively, had ratified the conventions (Stalker 1994). In 1990 the United Nations adopted a Convention on the Rights of Migrant Workers and Members of Their Families, but only a handful of emigration countries and no significant immigration countries have ratified it.

International organizations also offer technical assistance. For example, from 1989 to 1991 the ILO, in collaboration with the POEA and the Commission of the European Communities, pursued a program called Entrepreneurship on Migrant Earnings in the Philippines. The project identified training, advisory, and financial services to help former migrants establish businesses. However, the success of would-be entrepreneurs depended on the local economic, political, and social climate (ILO 1991). Another important scheme is the

IOM's Return of Talents Program, which encourages highly skilled emigrants to take temporary positions in their countries of origin to aid development.

Despite such efforts, relatively little bilateral and multilateral work is focusing on protecting migrants and helping migration stimulate economic development in sending countries. The following steps may help:

Ratifying and improving multilateral regulations. Major elements of an international regulatory framework already exist in ILO conventions and the 1990 United Nations Convention on the Rights of Migrant Workers and Members of Their Families. Labor standards laid down by the World Trade Organization also relate to the conditions of migrant workers. These standards need to be linked into a comprehensive framework to regulate the rights and conditions of migrant workers. However, the main task is to persuade more countries to ratify these instruments and to take steps to implement them. A world intergovernmental conference on migration could raise awareness of the need for such action.

Establishing an effective international agency for migration. An international agency, possibly within the United Nations framework, could play a major role in boosting the effectiveness of international regulation of migration and in developing multilateral approaches to using migration to aid economic development. Such an agency could be built on the existing International Organization for Migration (IOM—an intergovernmental organization which has existed since the 1940s), but would need to greatly enhance its responsibilities, funding, and standing.

Improving monitoring and research. Most countries lack effective systems for monitoring international migration, and definitions, and statistical categories vary considerably. Effective monitoring and comprehensive, comparable statistics are essential for effective multilateral action. An international agency for migration could assume such a task. Countries and analysts also know far too little about the long-term economic and social consequences of emigration. Greatly increased research at the local, national, and international levels is essential.

Implementing regional agreements. Regional economic integration and political cooperation often includes a focus on labor migration. Some regional bodies have highly developed policies on movements among member countries—particularly the European Union, which has introduced almost totally free movement for citizens of member states. However, no regional body has introduced comprehensive policies regarding migrants from third countries, although EU countries have begun to harmonize national rules. Common policies on migration from both member states and third countries should be essential to regional economic integration as well as to international cooperation on development.

Cementing bilateral agreements. Emigration countries frequently seek to make bilateral agreements with immigration countries; such agreements did much to improve the social security and rights of migrant workers and their families in Western Europe in the 1960s and 1970s. However, immigration countries have recently proved reluctant to conclude such agreements. International efforts should encourage such agreements by underscoring their benefits for all parties. Migrants gain through greater social security—for instance, through transferability of pension entitlements gained while abroad. Emigration countries gain because such agreements facilitate transfer of remittances and make it harder for agents and recruiters to cream off profits. Immigration countries gain through improved control of migration and the creation of a more stable and better-trained workforce.

Cooperating on training and education. Such cooperation should be an important part of multilateral, regional, and bilateral agreements on migration, and a major aspect of efforts to support international development. Such programs would increase the cost of migrant labor somewhat, but short-term gains in productivity for host countries and long-term gains for countries of origin would offset this cost.

Linking foreign direct investment to migration strategies. One way to maximize gains from international migration is to link it to foreign direct investment. Foreign investment in a less-developed country can create opportunities for workers to migrate temporarily to the headquarters country to gain industrial experience and training. This process not only provides a source of temporary labor for the company but also produces well-trained workers for less-developed countries, while the workers gain through both training and enhanced earnings. Many companies already follow such practices, but they need to expand and develop them systematically.

Expanding "return-of-talents" schemes. The IOM has encouraged highly skilled emigrants to make their skills available for development projects in their countries of origin. International institutions should develop this approach—a way to reverse the effects of "brain drain"—on a much larger scale.

Bibliography

Abadan-Unat, N. 1988. "The Socio-economic Aspects of Return Migration to Turkey." *Revue Européenne des Migrations Internationales* (3): 29–59.

Abella, M. 1993. "Labor Mobility, Trade and Structural Change: The Philippine Experience." *Asian and Pacific Migration Journal* 2(3): 249–68.

Abella, M. I. 1995a. "Asian Migrant and Contract Workers in the Middle East." In R. Cohen, ed., *The Cambridge Survey of World Migration*. Cambridge: Cambridge University Press.

Abella, M. I. 1995b. "Policies and Institutions for the Orderly Movement of Labour Abroad." In M. I. Abella and K. J. Lönnroth, eds., *Orderly International Migration of Workers and Incentives to Stay: Options for Emigration Countries*. Geneva: International Labour Office.

Aguilar, F. V. Jr. 1996. "The Dialectics of Transnational Shame and National Identity." *Philippine Sociological Review* 44(1–4): 101–36.

Amjad, R. ed. 1989. *To the Gulf and Back, Studies on the Economic Impact of Asian Labour Migration*. New Delhi: ILO/ARTEP.

Amjad, R. 1996. "Philippines and Indonesia: On the Way to a Migration Transition." *Asian and Pacific Migration Journal* 5(2–3).

Appleyard, R. ed. 1995. *International Migration: Special Issue on Emigration Dynamics in Developing Countries*. Geneva: International Organization for Migration.

Appleyard, R. 1998. "Emigration Dynamics in Developing Countries: Case Study on South Asia (IOM/UNFPA Project)." In P. Brownlee and C. Mitchell, eds., *Migration Research in the Asia Pacific: Theoretical and Empirical Issues*. Wollongong, Australia: Asia Pacific Migration Research Network Secretariat.

Basch, L., N. Glick-Schiller, and C. S. Blanc. 1994. *Nations Unbound: Transnational Projects, Post-Colonial Predicaments and Deterritorialized Nation-States*. New York: Gordon and Breach.

Battistella, G. and A. Paganoni. 1992. *Philippine Labor Migration: Impact and Policy*. Quezon City: Scalabrini Migration Center.

Blanc, C. S. 1996. "Balikbayan: A Filipino Extension of the National Imaginary and of State Boundaries." *Philippine Sociological Review* 44(1–4): 178–93.

Böhning, W. R. 1998. "The Impact of the Asian Crisis on Filipino Employment Prospects Abroad." Geneva: International Labour Office.

Borjas, G. J. 1989. "Economic Theory and International Migration." *International Migration Review* Special Silver Anniversary Issue, 23(3): 457–85.

Boyle, P., K. Halfacree, and V. Robinson. 1998. *Exploring Contemporary Migration*. Harlow, Essex: Longman.

Cahill, D. 1990. *Intermarriages in International Contexts*. Quezon City: Scalabrini Migration Center.

Castles, S., H. Booth, and T. Wallace. 1984. *Here for Good: Western Europe's New Ethnic Minorities*. London: Pluto Press.

Castles, S. and G. Kosack. 1973 and 1985. *Immigrant Workers and Class Structure in Western Europe*. London: Oxford University Press.

Castles, S. and M. J. Miller. 1998. *The Age of Migration: International Population Movements in the Modern World*. 2d ed. London: Macmillan.

Diatta, M. A. and N. Mbow. 1998. "Releasing the Development Potential of Return Migration: The Case of Senegal." Paper presented at United Nations Technical Symposium on International Migration and Development, 29 June–3 July 1998. The Hague, Netherlands: unpublished.

Go, S. 1998. "The Philippines: A Look into the Migration Scenario in the Nineties." In *Migration and Regional Economic Integration in Asia*. Paris: Organisation for Economic Cooperation and Development (OECD).

Gunatilleke, G. 1991. *Migration to the Arab World: Experience of Returning Migrants*. Tokyo: United Nations University.

Hoffmann, E. and S. Lawrence. 1996. "Statistics on International Labour Migration: A Review of Sources and Methodological Issues." Geneva: International Labour Office.

Hönekopp, E. and T. Tayanç. 1998. "Releasing the Development Potential of Return Migration: The Case of Turkey." Paper presented at United Nations Technical Symposium on International Migration and Development, 29 June–3 July 1998. The Hague, Netherlands: unpublished.

Hugo, G. 1994. *Migration and the Family*. Vienna: United Nations Occasional Papers Series for the International Year of the Family, no. 12.

Hugo, G. 1998. "The Demographic Underpinnings of Current and Future International Migration in Asia." *Asian and Pacific Migration Journal* 7(1): 1–25.

ILO 1991. "Entrepreneurship on Migrant Earnings in the Philippines: Results and Experiences from an ILO Project." Geneva: ILO.

Kritz, M. M., L. L. Lin, and H. Zlotnik, eds. 1992. *International Migration Systems: A Global Approach*. Oxford: Clarendon Press.

Lim, L. L. 1996. "The Migration Transition in Malaysia." *Asian and Pacific Migration Journal* 5(2–3).

Lim, L. L. and N. Oishi. 1996. "International Labor Migration of Asian Women: Distinctive Characteristics and Policy Concerns." *Asian and Pacific Migration Journal* 5(1): 85–116.

Martin, P., A. Mason, and T. Nagayama. 1996. "Introduction to Special Issue on the Dynamics of Labor Migration in Asia." *Asian and Pacific Migration Journal* 5(2–3).

Martin, P. L. 1991. *The Unfinished Story: Turkish Labour Migration to Western Europe*. Geneva: International Labour Office.

Massey, D. S., J. Arango, G. Hugo, A. Kouaouci, J. E. Taylor, and A. Pellegrino. 1993. "Theories of International Migration: A Review and Appraisal." *Population and Development Review* 19(3): 431–66.

Massey, D. S., J. Arango, G. Hugo, and J. E. Taylor. 1994. "An Evaluation of International Migration Theory: The North American Case." *Population and Development Review* 20: 699–751.

OECD 1997. *Trends in International Migration: Annual Report 1996*. Paris: OECD.

OECD 1998. *Trends in International Migration: Annual Report 1998*. Paris: OECD.

Paine, S. 1974. *Exporting Workers: The Turkish Case*. Cambridge: Cambridge University Press.

Portes, A. and J. Böröcz. 1989. "Contemporary Immigration: Theoretical Perspectives on Its Determinants and Modes of Incorporation." *International Migration Review* 28(4): 606–30.

Rowlands, D. 1998. "Poverty and Environmental Degradation as Root Causes of International Migration: A Critical Assessment." Paper presented at United Nations Technical Symposium on International Migration and Development, 29 June–3 July 1998. The Hague, Netherlands: unpublished.

Saith, A. 1997. *Emigration Pressures and Structural Change: Case Study of the Philippines.* Geneva: International Labour Office.

Shah, N. M. 1994. "An Overview of Present and Future Emigration Dynamics in South Asia." *International Migration* 32(2): 217–68.

Skeldon, R. 1997. *Migration and Development: A Global Perspective.* Harlow, Essex: Addison Wesley Longman.

Stahl, C. 1993. "Explaining International Migration." In C. Stahl, R. Ball, C. Inglis, and P. Gutman, eds., *Global Population Movements and their Implications for Australia.* Canberra: Australian Government Publishing Service.

Stalker, P. 1994. *The Work of Strangers: A Survey of International Labour Migration.* Geneva: ILO.

Tomas, P. S. 1998. "Enhancing the Capabilities of Emigration Countries to Protect Men and Women Destined for Low-Skilled Employment: The Case of the Philippines." Paper presented at United Nations Technical Symposium on International Migration and Development, 29 June–3 July 1998. The Hague, Netherlands: unpublished.

United Nations. 1998. "Report of the United Nations Technical Symposium on International Migration and Development, The Hague, Netherlands 29 June–3 July 1998." New York: United Nations.

Wong, D. 1996. "Foreign Domestic Workers in Singapore." *Asian and Pacific Migration Journal* 5(1): 117–38.

Yukawa, J. 1996. *Migration from the Philippines 1975–1995: An Annotated Bibliography.* Quezon City: Scalabrini Migration Center.

Zelinsky, W. 1971. "The Hypothesis of the Mobility Transition." *Geographical Review* 61(2): 219–49.

Zolberg, A. R. 1989. "The Next Waves: Migration Theory for a Changing World." *International Migration Review* 23(3): 403–30.

Zolberg, A. R., A. Suhrke, and S. Aguayo. 1989. *Escape from Violence.* New York: Oxford University Press.

1. Countries of emigration may also be referred to as migrant-sending countries or countries of origin. These terms are used synonymously.

2. A comparative project of the United Nations University on Asian migration to the Gulf oil states produced important findings (see Amjad 1989, Gunatilleke 1991). A major joint project of the International Organization for Migration and the United Nations Population Fund, which started in 1993, has already produced major reports, most of which have been reported in special issues of the IOM's journal *International Migration* (Appleyard 1995 and 1998). The OECD's annual *Trends in International Migration* contains regular reports, mainly from European emigration countries (OECD 1997).

3. For overviews of migration research and theory see: (Massey, et al. 1993); (Massey, et al. 1994); (Skeldon 1997); (Boyle, et al. 1998), Chapter 3; (Castles and Miller 1998), Chapter 2.

4. A good discussion of the costs and benefits of emigration can be found in Skeldon 1997, chapter 6. Each cost and benefit is highly complex, and migration studies generally attempt to analyze them for each migration system.

5. There is a considerable literature on Turkish emigration and its effects on the economy and society. An early economic study is Paine 1974. Turkish scholars have published many works, notably Professor Nermin Abadan-Unat (for instance, Abadan-Unat 1988). Martin 1991 provides a valuable overview, which is used extensively here.

6. Here too, considerable literature is available. For a bibliography on the Philippines, see Yukawa 1996. Much material can be found in the *Asian and Pacific Migration Journal,* published in Manila since 1992. See, for instance, Abella 1993.

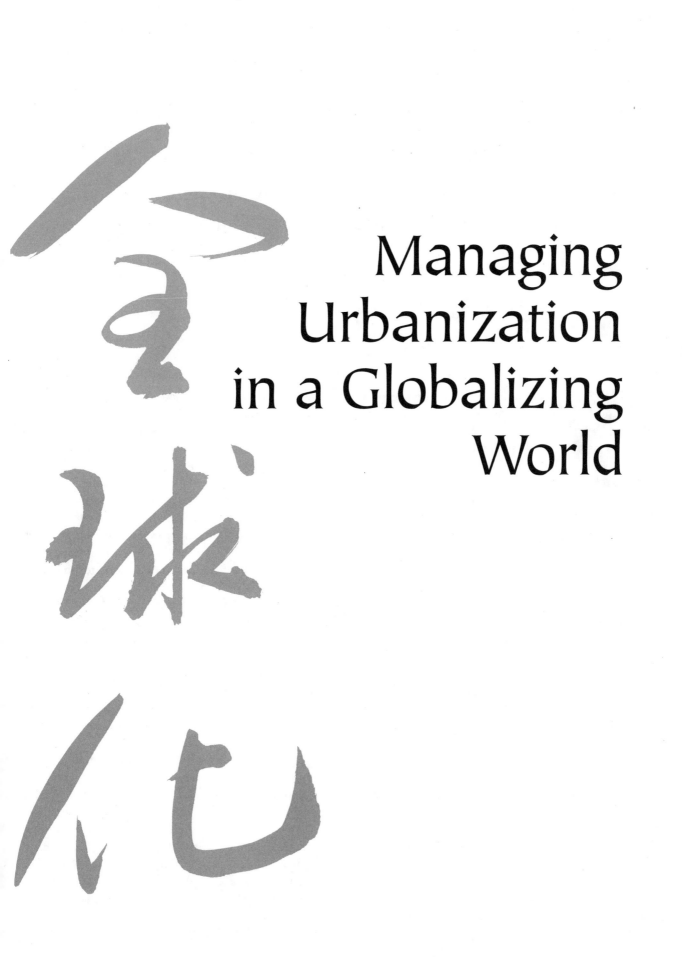

Managing Urbanization in a Globalizing World

chapter 6

Cities and Trade: External Trade and Internal Geography in Developing Economies

Anthony J. Venables

London School of Economics and Centre for Economic Policy Research

The evolution of the economic geography of developing countries, in particular the process of urbanization, is well documented (for example, Rosen and Resnick 1980; United Nations 1991), but perhaps less well understood. The proportion of the population in urban centers increases with development (World Bank 1999), but how is this urban population distributed between cities of different types and in different locations? What factors determine the size structure of cities in developing countries, and why does the largest city tend to be so dominant? Is this concentration of activity good for growth, or would countries be better served by a more dispersed structure of economic activity? To answer these questions we also need to understand the functional structure of cities and the extent to which they specialize in different activities.

Empirical research indicates that prime cities in developing countries are much more dominant than similar cities in high-income countries are—or were. It also indicates that the dominance of the prime city tends to peak during the development process (Williamson 1965; more recently confirmed by Wheaton and Shishido 1981 and Henderson 1998). Determinants of the factors that lead to dominance are researched by Ades and Glaeser (1997), who show that trade barriers, poor internal transport, and the concentration of political power all contribute to the dominance of the largest city. The deconcentration of activity that can occur in later stages of development is nicely illustrated by the Korean example. Henderson et al. (1998) show how increasing urban congestion and infrastructure improvements led to the deconcentration of manufacturing from Seoul to outlying cities. This research also addresses the question of what functions are performed by cities; Seoul maintained a diversified manufacturing base, but as activity moved out of Seoul to other cities, so these tended to specialize in particular sectors (see Henderson, Chapter 7).

This shifting balance between concentration and dispersion—both of activity as a whole and of particular sectors—arises from the interplay of a number of different forces. Marshall, writing in 1890, listed three forces that encourage concentration of activity: technological externalities ["the mysteries of the trade become no mystery but are, as it were, in the air . . ." (Marshall 1890)]; benefits arising from thick labor markets, such as labor market pooling effects and externalities in training; and forward and backward linkages that occur between firms that are linked through the production and supply of intermediate goods and services.[1] Recent research has outlined the benefits that come from concentration of research activities (for example, Audretsch and Feldman 1996), from being in close-knit production networks (for example, Porter 1990), and from locating in cities. In a recent *Journal of Economic Perspectives* paper reviewing evidence on the subject, Quigley (1998) concludes, "it remains clear that the increased size of cities and their diversity are strongly associated with increased output, productivity and growth. . . ." (See Mills, Chapter 8.)

These forces foster spatial concentration, but the world is not a single megacity. Forces for concentration are opposed by "centrifugal" forces that encourage dispersion of economic activity. Chief among these are supplies of immobile factors (such as land and possibly labor) which lead to spatial variations in rents and wages, the presence of external diseconomies such as congestion costs and pollution, and the need for firms to meet demand from spatially dispersed consumers.

Although economists have researched these separate forces, little has been done to see how they all interact to determine the actual location of economic activity.[2] The omission is now being rectified by recent research on "new economic geography." Taking into account the components just outlined, the research shows how concentrations of economic activity can arise and evolve. It shows how, even if locations are broadly similar in their underlying characteristics, they may nevertheless develop very different economic structures as concentrations of activity form. This process may go on at different levels. At the urban level it can account for the formation of cities, while at the international level it goes some way to explain the concentration of economic activity in the "North" and consequent North–South income inequalities.

At each of these levels there are a number of common features.[3] First, very small initial differences between locations may become magnified through time, as processes of "cumulative causation" drive growth. Second, spatial inequalities can be very large; furthermore, they are likely to be largest at "intermediate" stages of development. Third, once established, spatial structures may become "locked in" and persist for long periods of time, although when they do start to break down, change may be quite abrupt (a phenomenon akin to the "punctuated equilibria" of evolutionary theory). And finally, economic growth and development will not take the form of the smooth convergence of income levels of different regions. Instead, it is more likely to involve rapid growth of a few regions, while others are left behind. Essentially, the rich club expands to include more members, but gaps between the rich and the poor remain.[4]

The objective of this chapter is to show how ideas from this new economic geography literature can be brought to bear on the questions we have posed concerning the city structure of developing economies. The chapter is a speculative exploration of issues rather than a definitive piece of research, but nevertheless provides a number of insights. The analysis suggests that in the early stages of economic development countries are likely to have a monocentric structure, with manufacturing concentrated in a single dominant economic center, but that this will evolve into a multicentric structure as development proceeds. Furthermore, policies that inhibit the development of this structure are likely be economically damaging. Openness to international trade brings benefits both from facilitating deconcentration of population and from allowing the agglomeration of

particular industries in which linkages are relatively strong.

Analytical Framework

My approach is based on a new economic geography model which is described informally here, referring the reader to Fujita et al. (1999) for full development. In order to focus on the tension between forces for agglomeration and dispersion the model abstracts from many issues that are usually regarded as important in economic development. We consider just two countries and assume that they have the same relative endowments of two factors of production, labor and land. One country is large, and we call it the Outside country—it can be thought of as the rest of the world. We focus on the other country, which we call Home, and assume to be divided into two regions. Each Home region has the same amount of land, and Home labor is mobile between the two regions. Within each region there is a single city (or potential city site).

There are two production activities, agriculture and manufacturing. Agriculture takes place in all locations, using land and labor to produce a perfectly tradable output.[5] Manufacturing can operate in any of the locations; our analysis will establish the locations in which production actually takes place. Manufacturing has the usual characteristics of increasing returns to scale (at the firm level), product differentiation, and monopolistic competition. Firms use labor and intermediate goods as inputs, and their output is used both as a consumer good and as an intermediate. This input–output structure gives rise to forward and backward linkages between firms, as each firm uses output supplied by other firms (a forward linkage) and sells some of its output to other firms (a backward linkage). Shipping manufacturing output incurs transport costs. On internal trade between the two Home regions the transport cost per unit shipped is denoted T, and on external trade between either of the Home regions and Outside the cost per unit imported or exported is T_O. Notice that the two Home regions are constructed to be identical—neither has the benefit of proximity to the outside world.[6]

This structure tends to generate concentrations of both manufacturing activity and population. They arise because firms want to be close to other firms supplying intermediate goods (in order to save transport costs on these intermediates). They also want to be close to a large market, which again means being close to other firms in order to meet demands for intermediate goods. As firms cluster in one location, so too does labor—the firms' employees—further increasing market size. Working against these agglomeration forces, we assume that there are some congestion diseconomies that increase with the size of the region's population. These have to be offset by firms in the congested region paying higher wages, and this in turn counts against the attractiveness of this region as a base for manufacturing. The actual location of manufacturing—and of manufacturing workers—is determined by the balance of these forces. We will see some cases in which all manufacturing is concentrated in a single location and others in which it spreads out, giving a less concentrated spatial structure. Our task is to identify the key determinants of this spatial structure.

We take as a starting point in our experiments an initial situation in which all manufacturing is concentrated in the Outside country. Outside consequently appears to be a developed economy, and the demand for labor in manufacturing means that Outside's wage rate is higher than Home's. However, despite this wage gap, it is not profitable for any single firm to relocate from Outside to Home because if it were to do so, it would forego the benefits of forward and backward linkages to other Outside firms.

Economic Development and Internal Geography

In this framework economic underdevelopment is simply a corollary of the spatial agglomeration of manufacturing, and development occurs if the agglomeration breaks down or spreads to new locations. Let us now see how changing trade costs can cause the Home country to attract manufacturing, and see also how Home's internal economic geography evolves during this process.

Internal Trade Costs

Our first experiment captures the effects of Home infrastructure improvement, represented by a reduction in internal transport costs between the two Home regions. Results are illustrated in Figure 6.1, which has internal transport costs on the horizontal axis, and the share of each region's labor force employed in manufacturing on the vertical. (This and subsequent figures come from numerical simulation with particular functional forms and parameter values; they are illustrations of possibilities, not general results.)

At high levels of internal transport costs the economy is in the initial situation—neither Home region has any manufacturing employment. Reducing the internal transport barrier has the effect of making Home a more attractive location, since a firm can now supply the entire Home market more cheaply, and the figure shows that there is a level of transport costs below which Home starts to attract manufacturing industry. Reducing internal transport costs therefore triggers industrial devel-

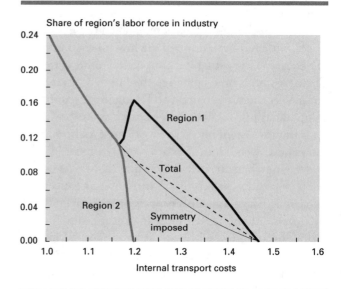

Figure 6.1
Internal Transport Costs and Regional Industrialization

opment. What else do we learn from the figure? The key point is that, over a range of trade costs, only one of the Home country's regions industrializes, despite the fact that the regions are constructed to be symmetric.[7] Why should development lead to this monocentric structure? The answer is that a situation in which development occurs in both regions simultaneously is unstable; if one of the regions got slightly ahead, then the forward and backward linkages from its firms would create an advantage that would cumulate over time. With the symmetric structure of this model there is nothing to determine which region industrializes, but because of the benefits of agglomeration, it cannot be both. The region that attracts manufacturing also attracts population, as labor demand from industry brings in-migration until real wages, net of congestion diseconomies, are the same in both regions.

As Figure 6.1 shows, the monocentric internal geography occurs only for a range of internal transport costs. As these costs are reduced further, there comes a point at which industry spreads to the second location. This happens for two reasons. First, forward and backward linkages become less geographically concentrated as transport costs fall, making it less costly for a firm to move to the other location.[8] And second, congestion diseconomies increase the wages that must be paid by firms in the industrialized location to retain workers, and thereby create an incentive for firms to leave. The pattern we see then, is that at early stages of industrialization, there is a monocentric structure, but at later stages (in this example, at lower internal transport costs), a duocentric structure develops.

This example shows how the primacy of one region may occur as industrialization takes off. Does this outcome lead to earlier development or higher income levels than one in which activity is more uniformly distributed? The dashed line in Figure 6.1 gives the share of the entire Home labor force in industry, and the light line is the share if we *force* the two locations to be identical. The point at which industrialization starts is the same in both cases. But during the monocentric phase, forcing duocentricity would reduce the overall share of the labor force in manufacturing and consequently reduce real income. The reason is that forward and backward linkages are lost, and these linkages are good for industrialization and real income.

How does this story change if there are more than two Home regions? The answer is that we see industry start first in one region, then spread into a second, then a third, and so on, as industrialization occurs in regions sequentially, not simultaneously. Forcing simultaneous development of all regions is even more costly, since no region has enough industry to reap the benefits of agglomeration.

Internal Geography and External Trade

We now consider a second experiment in which the driving force for industrialization is the Home economy's openness to international trade. Figure 6.2 illustrates possibilities, mapping out the share of manufacturing employment in each region as a function of external trade costs, T_O.

Several striking points emerge from this example. When Home is relatively closed (high T_O), it will have a substantial amount of industrial employment, but this will be concentrated in a single location. The reason Home has industry is simply the need to supply local consumers who, at very high trade costs, do not have access to imports. The reason for the monocentric structure is the one given by Krugman and Livas (1996). With high external trade costs firms and consumers are inward looking, purchasing largely from local firms, and this makes the internal linkage effects very strong.

At intermediate trade costs Home has less industry because the economy is now more open to imports, and this benefits the existing agglomeration of industry in Outside. However, as external trade costs fall further, so Home starts to attract industry. To understand why, note that a firm moving into the country from the existing Outside agglomeration pays lower wages but foregoes forward and backward linkages with firms in the agglomeration. At low trade costs the cost of foregoing these linkages is small—intermediate inputs can be imported and Outside demand met by exports.[9]

Figure 6.2
External Trade Barriers and Regional Industrialization

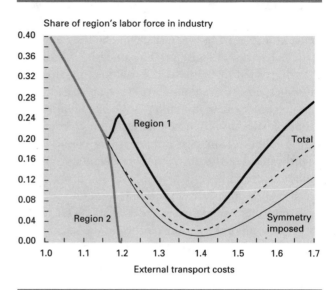

As this more outward-looking industrialization occurs it initially gives rise to a monocentric internal geography because (like the previous case studied) having industry in both locations is unstable. However, as external trade costs are reduced and levels of industrial employment increase, so industry spreads to region 2 and the economy develops a duocentric structure. The reasons for the spread are that the diseconomies of urban concentration have become stronger, while more outward orientation reduces linkage strength within the economy.

As in the previous case then, we see that industrialization, which is driven by closer integration in the world economy, first involves a monocentric structure and then evolves into a more uniform duocentric structure. We can study the costs and benefits of the monocentric structure by comparing it with a situation in which a symmetric duocentric structure is imposed. As before, the light solid line illustrates the share of employment in manufacturing if the two Home regions are forced to be identical, and comparison with the dashed line indicates lower manufacturing employment and lower welfare.

Regional Integration

An alternative to multilateral external trade liberalization (falling T_O) might be regional integration—preferential tariff reductions within a regional trading bloc. By reinterpreting the regions in our model we can offer some predictions about the likely effect of such a policy on the location of industries in the member states. Suppose that the two regions in our model are two countries in a trading bloc and that T, the internal transport cost, is now reinterpreted as the internal tariff between the countries. What happens if there is a preferential liberalization, reducing this tariff while holding external trade barriers, T_O, constant? The analysis is similar to that illustrated in Figure 6.1. Intrabloc liberalization promotes industrialization—firms in the bloc gain from better access to a larger market—but, as in Figure 6.1, industrialization will occur in just one country (or region). The reason is as before; if one country gets slightly ahead of the other, then its advantage will cumulate as firms benefit from forward and backward linkages with other firms in the same location.

Two further remarks are in order. First, the likelihood that formation of the trading bloc will cause unequal development is larger the higher is the external tariff (T_O). A high external tariff forces firms to be more dependent on other local firms, so increasing the strength of forward and backward linkages. Second, our model assumes that labor is mobile between regions—an assumption that is unlikely to be correct for countries within a trading bloc. If labor is immobile, then the likelihood of agglomeration is reduced, but not removed.

The prediction that regional integration might promote inequalities between members of the bloc fits well with at least some historical experience. The East African Community collapsed because of the perception that the Nairobi region was capturing all of the benefits; Abidjan and Dakar are attracting a very high proportion of the new economic activity developing in the Economic Community of West Africa; and Paraguay is now claiming that it is losing industry to its larger South American Common Market (MERCOSUR) partners, Argentina and Brazil.[10]

City Specialization and Hierarchy

In the discussion so far we have assumed that linkages occur at the level of manufacturing as a whole. This means that growth of one industry benefits all others by demanding output or providing a supply of intermediates, either directly or indirectly. However, some linkages operate at a much narrower level than this, for example, linkages between firms within a specialized industrial sector. If we move to a multi-industry setting in which the input–output linkages occur primarily within particular industries rather than between them, then what sort of economic geography develops?[11] Can we shed light on the evolving pattern of city specialization accompanying development?

To address these questions let us suppose that there are two manufacturing industries and that Home's total

employment in each of them is fixed.[12] Although total employment in each industry is fixed, its location is not, and we want to see how this is determined. Will each industry operate in a different location or will they be divided in some way between locations? There are three main forces. First, firms will want to locate close to other firms in the same industry in order to exploit forward and backward linkages; this is a force for the clustering of each industry separately. Second, firms will want to locate in the region with the larger demand from consumers; this is a force for agglomeration of manufacturing as a whole, since the location with the more firms will have more workers and a larger consumer demand. Third, if there are congestion diseconomies, then we have a force pushing in the opposite direction, encouraging dispersion of activity.

Figure 6.3 illustrates how the balance between these forces may depend on external trade barriers. The horizontal axis is this external trade cost, T_O, and the vertical is the share of manufacturing employment by region and industry, with subscripts referring to Home regions (1 and 2) and superscripts referring to industries (A and B). Thus L_1 is the share of the manufacturing workers located in region 1 ($L_1 + L_2 = 1$), and L_1^A is the share of manufacturing workers located in region 1 and working in industry A.

The figure shows that the two regions have a hierarchical structure that evolves as trade barriers change. At high external trade costs most of the manufacturing labor force is in region 1 (L_1 is much larger than L_2) because of the tendency of inward-looking firms to

Figure 6.3
External Trade and Internal Economic Geography

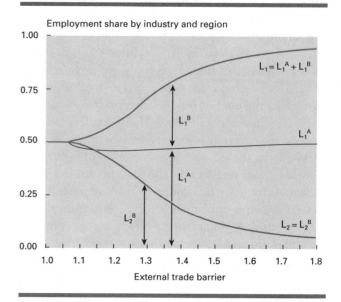

Employment share by industry and region

$L_1 = L_1^A + L_1^B$

L_1^B

L_1^A

L_1^A

L_1^A

L_2^B

$L_2 = L_2^B$

External trade barrier

agglomerate, although full agglomeration is prevented by congestion costs. Given that most industry is in region 1, what do we know about the industrial structures of the regions? Because firms want to locate close to other firms in the same industry, one industry will be completely concentrated and correspondingly one region completely specialized. In this example region 2 is specialized in industry B, while region 1 has all of industry A (since $L_2^A = 0$) and also some of industry B.

Reducing trade costs has two interesting effects. It leads to spatial *deconcentration* of population and *concentration* of particular industries. The deconcentration of population arises for the reasons we have already noted (following Krugman and Livas); greater outward orientation makes linkages less strong compared to congestion costs; it shows up as the decline in L_1 and increase in L_2. Deconcentration of population equalizes the size of the regions, and this facilitates the clustering of each industry—region 2 gains a large enough population to accommodate the whole of industry B, so we see L_2^B increasing and L_1^B falling. As trade costs are reduced the process continues until at low enough trade costs the hierarchical regional structure breaks down completely and the regions have the same population size and complete industrial specialization.

This story is consistent with the experience of Korea that we have previously noted (Henderson et al. 1998). The theoretical modeling enables us to infer the real income effects of the changes, and it turns out that there are two important sources of gain. On top of the usual benefits of trade liberalization (the direct effects of reducing trade costs and any comparative advantage or pro-competitive gains from trade), there are also gains from the reorganization of the economy's internal economic geography. Deconcentrating population reduces congestion costs, and clustering of particular industries gives the benefits from intraindustry linkages.

Conclusions

Standard techniques of economic analysis are good at dealing with situations in which diminishing returns to activities yield "smooth" outcomes. However, the outstanding feature of economic geography is that outcomes are extremely "lumpy." This shows up in the formation of cities, in the contrasting performance of different regions, and in spatial income inequalities in the world economy. It also shows up in countries' growth performance where the long-run picture is of divergence, not convergence, of economic performance (Easterly and Levine 1999).

The "new economic geography" literature addresses these issues and takes seriously the implications of increasing returns to scale and linkages between the location decisions of firms and workers. This program of research is in its infancy, and in this chapter we have suggested how it may be applied to analyze the effects of trade—internal, external, and regional—on the economic geography of developing countries. Our analysis suggests the following answers to the questions posed in the introduction. First, economic development should not be regarded as a smooth process of convergence, but rather as the uneven spread of clusters of activity. It then follows that development may typically involve the concentration of activity in dominant cities or regions. This concentration is beneficial insofar as it raises the level of industrialization and real income (net of congestion costs). Second, the internal economic geography that develops is sensitive to levels of transport costs and other barriers to trade; reducing transport costs promotes industrialization and also facilitates the spread of industry to new Home locations. Thus, the models support the idea that concentration will increase in the early stages of development and then decline, as suggested by the empirical work of Williamson and others. Finally, there are important gains from external openness. In addition to the usual gains from trade, we see that openness may lead to a rearrangement of internal economic geography. It may promote deconcentration of population, while at the same time facilitating clustering of particular industries in which linkages are strong, both these changes being sources of real income gain.

Bibliography

Ades, A. F., and E. L Glaeser. 1997. "Trade and Circuses: Explaining Urban Giants." *Quarterly Journal of Economics* CX(1): 195–227.

Audretsch D., and M. Feldman. 1996. "R&D Spillovers and the Geography of Innovation and Production." *American Economic Review* 86(4): 253–73.

Easterly, W., and R. Levine. 1999. "It's Not Factor Accumulation: Stylized Facts and Growth Models." Washington, D.C.: World Bank.

Fujita, Masahisa, P. R. Krugman, and A. J. Venables. 1999. *The Spatial Economy: Cities, Regions and International Trade.* Cambridge, MA: MIT Press.

Glaeser, E. 1998. "Are Cities Dying?" *Journal of Economic Perspectives* 12: 139–60.

Henderson, J. V. 1999. "The Effects of Urban Concentration on Economic Growth." Processed, Brown University.

Henderson, J. V., T. Lee, and Y.-J. Lee. 1998. "Externalities, Location and Industrial Deconcentration in a Tiger Economy." Processed, Brown University.

Krugman, P. R. 1991. "Increasing Returns and Economic Geography." *Journal of Development Economics* 49(1): 137–50.

Krugman, P. R., and G. Hanson. 1993. "Mexico–U.S. Free Trade and the Location of Production." In P. Garber, ed., *The Mexico U.S. Free-Trade Agreement.* Cambridge, MA: MIT Press.

Krugman, P. R., and R. E. Livas. 1996. "Trade Policy and the Third World Metropolis." *Journal of Development Economics* 49(1): 137–50.

Krugman, P. R., and A. J. Venables. 1995. "Globalization and the Inequality of Nations." *Quarterly Journal of Economics* CX: 857–80.

Marshall, A. 1890. *Principles of Economics*. London: Macmillan.

Porter, M. E. 1990. *The Competitive Advantage of Nations*. New York: Macmillan.

Puga, D. 1998. "Urbanisation Patterns: European vs. Less Developed Countries." *Journal of Regional Science* 38: 231–52.

Puga, D., and A. J. Venables. 1996. "The Spread of Industry: Agglomeration in Economic Development." *Journal of the Japanese and International Economies* 10: 440–64.

Puga, D., and A. J. Venables. 1998. "Trading Arrangements and Industrial Development." *World Bank Economic Review* 12: 221–49.

Quigley, J. M. 1998. "Urban Diversity and Economic Growth." *Journal of Economic Perspectives* 12: 127–38.

Rosen, K. T., and M. Resnick. 1980. "The Size Distribution of Cities: An Examination of the Pareto Law and Primacy." *Journal of Urban Economics* 8: 165–86.

United Nations. 1991. *World Urbanization Prospects 1990*. New York: United Nations.

Venables, A. J. 1999. "Regional Integration Agreements: A Force for Convergence or Divergence." World Bank Policy Research Paper No. 2260. Washington, D.C.: World Bank.

Wheaton, W., and H. Shishido. 1981. "Urban Concentration, Agglomeration Economies and the Level of Economic Development." *Economic Development and Cultural Change* 30: 17–30.

Williamson, J. 1965. "Regional Inequality and the Process of National Development." *Economic Development and Cultural Change* 3–45.

World Bank. 1999. "Entering the 21st Century: World Development Report 1999/2000." Washington, D.C.: World Bank; New York: Oxford University Press.

This chapter was originally a background paper written for the 1999 World Development Report, "Entering the 21st Century." Thanks to Simon Evenett for valuable comments.

Notes

1. For a recent and more comprehensive discussion of these forces see Glaeser (1998).

2. Part of the reason for this is the technical difficulty of analyzing situations with clustering. Often the attraction of a city arises not from its exact location, but simply from the fact that it is a city. Thus, there is a degree of indeterminacy in the analysis—many sites are perfectly suitable places to build a city, but once established it becomes "locked in" to the selected site.

3. See Fujita, Krugman, and Venables (1999) for a synthesis of models in each of these contexts. Puga (1998) has analyzed an urban model in a developing country context. Krugman (1991) sets out a regional model, and Krugman and Venables (1995) and Puga and Venables (1996) develop international models.

4. See Easterly and Levine (1999) for empirical support for this position.

5. The "agricultural" sector should be interpreted as a composite of the perfectly competitive "rest of the economy."

6. We use the usual "iceberg" transport costs; thus T denotes the number of units that have to be shipped for one unit to arrive at its destination. $T = 1$ is perfectly costless trade.

7. When T lies between 1.2 and 1.45, region 1 has manufacturing employment and region 2 does not.

8. Other sources of agglomeration—for example, knowledge spillovers—may be less sensitive to transport costs than are the input–output links assumed here.

9. Quite generally in models of this type agglomeration forces are strongest (relative to other locational forces) at intermediate levels of trade barriers. At very high trade barriers the need to supply immobile consumers prevents agglomeration, and as trade barriers go to zero the spatial dimension of linkages go to zero, so the presence of any centrifugal forces prevents agglomeration.

10. For further development of these ideas see Puga and Venables (1998), and Venables (1999).

11. This material is drawn from Chapter 18 of Fujita, Krugman, and Venables (1999).

12. In other words, we abstract from the question of whether the economy has industry or not. We assume that it has, and study only where it locates.

chapter 7

On the Move: Industrial Deconcentration in Today's Developing Countries

Vernon Henderson

Eastman Professor of Political Economy
Brown University

Countries that have been developing during the past half-century have followed an urban growth pattern that differs from that of earlier industrializing countries, which urbanized much more slowly. The recent model consists of three stages: initial rapid population growth and industrialization of a main city, such as Jakarta until the mid-1970s or Seoul in the 1960s and early 1970s; decentralization or suburbanization of population and manufacturing into the core city's outer rings and satellite cities, as in Jakarta today and in Seoul from the mid-1970s to the mid-1980s; and decentralization of manufacturing—and to a lesser extent population—from the major metropolitan area into the rest of the country, as in Seoul since the early 1980s or São Paulo post-1970.

Does concentration in the core main city and its metropolitan area go too far before deconcentration sets in? Are megacities in developing countries too large or growing too fast? Might earlier industrialization of medium-sized and smaller cities be desirable? Why have markets not produced better outcomes, if deconcentration is delayed too long?

Several concerns motivate these questions. First, econometric analysis suggests that an optimal degree of urban concentration exists in countries, which first increases as national per capita incomes grow from low levels, peaks, and then declines with further income growth, as the three stages just outlined suggest (Henderson 1999). This analysis estimates that deviations from the best degree of urban concentration at any income level are reflected in significantly lowered growth

rates. It also finds that many countries tend to have excessive concentration; many have reasonable concentration; and few are underconcentrated. Why does excessive concentration lead to growth losses?

One reason involves a country's ability to participate in world markets, as well as a high overall level of industrial efficiency. Megacities become inordinately expensive locations within which to produce many products. Another reason is the quality of life in a country's megacity, especially its environmental quality: In large congested areas, poor water quality and related diseases, long commuting times, and the inequality of these effects on the urban poor are major problems. A third concern—related to the quality of life—is the lack of technical expertise and managerial resources to effectively plan, govern, and operate megacities. Fourth, and also related to environmental quality, enormous investment burdens need to be undertaken in providing adequate infrastructure in megacities.

The first concern—the interaction between industrial competitiveness and efficiency and the urbanization process—is particularly important in determining the economic vitality of developing countries.

Production Efficiency in Megacities vs. Medium-Sized Cities

Studies suggest that in higher-income countries, research and development, corporate headquarters, financial, business, and professional services that are exchanged across cities, and experimental stages of manufacturing operate most efficiently in very large metropolitan areas, with their skilled labor forces and diverse economic activity. Once production of a brand line becomes standardized, the need for a diverse, skilled force in a large metropolitan center diminishes. Producers then want to take advantage of the low-cost labor and land found in smaller, more specialized cities. Kolko's work (1999) on the United States shows how the percentage of local employment in manufacturing rises as city size declines, being greatest in United States "rural" areas, and how the percentage of business and financial services rises with city size, being largest in megacities. The variation in percentages is over twofold for services and almost twofold for manufacturing, between rural areas or small urban areas and the largest cities.

One explanation for the variation in manufacturing activity is that scale economies in standardized manufacturing appear to result from localization, not urbanization—that is, from the level of activity within an industry, not from city size or diversity. Only new high-tech industries appear to rely on large, diverse urban economies (Henderson, Kuncoro, and Turner 1995). For recently developed products, John Hekman has documented the relocation of standardized production to smaller cities in the United States (1982). Other studies have found similar results on scale economies and the location of activities for countries such as Japan (Nakamura 1985), Brazil (Henderson 1988), and Korea (Henderson, Lee, and Lee 1999). Fujita and Ishii (1994) have described this location pattern for Japanese electronics companies (Table 7.1), which suggest these forces are at work.

In less-developed countries, much of the incubation stage of modern manufacturing production may entail importing and adapting foreign technologies. Such development may best focus on one or two metropolitan nodes where foreign contacts and indigenous, highly skilled labor concentrate. However, as in wealthier countries, once domestic production of a commodity is well established, and perhaps standardized, a strong incentive

arises for industry to move out of the dominant metropolitan area. For example, Hansen (1983) specifically shows this pattern for São Paulo State in the early 1980s.

Why do plants move out? Living costs, such as housing, can be two to three times higher in megacities than in smaller cities. Wages must therefore be at least twice as high if workers with comparable skills are to earn similar real wages. What's more, for production to be as viable in megacities as in small cities, the former must have much higher capital–labor ratios and output per worker—typically twice as high (Henderson 1988). For most standardized production, the difference in productivity between megacities and small cities is not great enough to support the higher wages and land rental costs.

How Fast and How Far?

If deconcentration of manufacturing and industrial development of medium-sized cities is a natural process of a country's growth, what key factors determine the rate at which deconcentration occurs? What might inhibit the process, and when might it occur later than desirable?

Investment in intercity infrastructure. For manufacturing in developing countries to migrate outside megacities, producers must have access to major ports—which are typically in megacities—and other transport nodes, so they can transfer inputs and outputs and manage inventories efficiently. A world of just-in-time production and e-business based networks requires excellent transport and communications. Thus only if regions invest in widespread transport facilities and telecommunications can industry substantially deconcentrate.

Studies show a significant negative econometric relationship between industrial concentration and crude measures of transportation systems such as the density of the national rail system, road system, and waterway system (Henderson, 1999; Rosen and Resnick, 1978). Country examples also demonstrate the relationship.

Table 7.1
Distribution of Plants in the Japanese Electronics Industry

Japan		Abroad	
Percentage of plants inside Japan in Japan's metropolitan areas, for each category (total plants in each category)		Percentage of plants outside Japan that are in North America, the European Community, and newly industrialized nations, of all overseas plants (total overseas plants in each category)	
Headquarters and basic R&D	100 (70)	Regional headquarters	100 (13)
Development R&D	70 (54)	R&D	91 (32)
Trial production	91 (21)	Production	59 (335)
Mass production	43 (333)		

Source: Fujita and Ishii 1994.

Table 7.2
Shares of Population and Manufacturing for Selected Regions of the Republic of Korea, 1983 and 1993
(percentage)

	Seoul, Pusan, and Taegu (Seoul)		Satellite cities in the provinces containing Seoul, Pusan, and Taegu	
	1983	1993	1983	1993
Population	37 (23)	39 (25)	14	20
Urban population	59 (37)	53 (34)	n.a.	n.a.
Manufacturing employment	44 (21)	28 (14)	30	30

n.a., Not applicable.
Source: Henderson, Lee, and Lee 1999.

Deconcentration of manufacturing in São Paulo since the 1980s followed widespread infrastructure investments in the late 1960s and early 1970s. In Indonesia, rapid deconcentration of industry from Jakarta into the Botabek suburbs corresponded with construction of highways east and west from Jakarta during the late 1980s and early 1990s. And in the Republic of Korea, industrial deconcentration followed infrastructure investments in roads and in communications during the late-1970s and early-1980s (Table 7.2). For example, communications infrastructure capital stocks had a 235 percent differential between Seoul and the rest of the country in 1972. By 1991 the differential had shrunk to 25 percent. Korea blanketed the country with infrastructure in the late 1970s and early 1980s. As a result, between 1983 and 1993, in rural areas and smaller metropolitan areas, the share of manufacturing employment outside the main three metropolitan areas and their satellite cities climbed from 26 percent to 42 percent, even though population in those areas declined by 9 percent.

State-owned industry, red tape, and economic liberalization. Many central governments in developing countries favor development of megacities, often the capital cities. Planners observing the higher productivity— higher value added per worker—may assume that production is always more efficient in larger cities, without recognizing the disadvantages of steep labor and land costs. In Brazil, this belief may have been partly responsible for the high historical concentration of state-owned industry in São Paulo, Rio de Janeiro, and the axis between them, while corresponding private production

concentrated in cities in the interior. In China, strong beliefs regarding urban hierarchies of production have led state-owned industries—which are not very competitive—to locate in the largest metropolitan areas, while more private industry thrives in smaller cities.

Red tape surrounding financing and production, import and export licenses also appears to foster industrial concentration. The slow speed of deconcentration of production from Seoul into Kyonggi province—its immediate hinterland—in the 1970s appeared to be linked to red tape. The acceleration of deconcentration within Kyonggi in the early 1980s has been linked to dismantling of these constraints.

However, economic liberalization does not always remove the red tape joining production to megacities. In the early 1980s, Indonesia opened up banking and export markets, enabling smaller producers to obtain production loans and export licenses. But firms had to apply for the major loans and licenses in Jakarta or a few other major metropolitan areas. Thus the small firms could realistically obtain the loans and licenses only if they maintained a strong presence in Jakarta or other large urban areas. Liberalization with strings attached appears to have provoked the sharp reconcentration of small firms in the major metropolitan regions of Indonesia during the early and mid-1980s (Henderson and Kuncoro, 1996).

Fiscal decentralization. For manufacturers to move production in developing countries to smaller-sized metropolitan areas, they must be able to find skilled workers and managers there. The key to attracting skilled workers to hinterland cities at reasonable wages is the public services and amenities such workers and their families demand and can get in big cities, including high-quality schooling and medical care. Such consumer services are part of a larger package that includes services for the firms themselves, such as reliable local power and local transport facilities, including containerization, rail facilities, and roads for trucking.

What is the best way to deliver such services and facilities to firms and consumers in hinterland areas? One model is fiscal decentralization. The Charles Tiebout notion is that if localities can raise revenues and choose the level of public services they provide, they will invest in attributes that make their regions attractive to specific industries and types of workers. National governments can foster fiscal decentralization by permitting political decentralization. As countries urbanize, the central government finds it increasingly difficult to manage emerging large cities; those cities develop their own political bases and demands for greater autonomy.

A key constraint on emerging local governments is financing, particularly financing of long-term infrastructure investments. The national government can help by offering revolving-door loans for long-term investments to local governments. Revolving-door loan programs require localities to pay back loans to replenish the fund, so loans can then be made to others (the revolving door). While experience with revolving-door loans in some countries (Indonesia and India) has not been good because the loans are never repaid, there have been positive results in recent years in Brazil. At the same time, more sophisticated cities with strong finances may be able to issue long-term bonds as a financing method. For such bond markets to work well, the national government needs to be strict about not backing these debts in general, a policy which seems to encourage localities to effectively default. That destabilizes the national budgetary process, as experience in parts of Latin America has shown. National governments can also help by developing local technical and managerial expertise in urban planning, local taxation, and service delivery.

Two major issues related to fiscal decentralization remain. First, it is unclear to what extent such decentralization affects economic growth and income inequality. Henderson (1999) finds no relationship between increased political decentralization and economic growth. Second, international agencies attempting to implement decentralization have often been insensitive to local political realities, producing questionable results. It is unclear that half-hearted and poorly designed decentralization is a good solution.

Globalization. Because megacities have the facilities and skilled labor that enables firms to conduct international business and adopt foreign technologies, globalization may initially heighten regional inequality. To operate successfully in medium-sized cities, international enterprises and joint ventures need excellent transport access to coastal cities, reliable global telecommunications, access to domestic capital markets, and ready access to the domestic bureaucracy for required licenses.

However, globalization also opens up new markets to hinterland producers previously more tied to domestic markets than coastal producers. The array of new markets for hinterlands may thus promote industrial deconcentration, especially in countries with reasonably sound interregional transport and telecommunications.

Conclusions

The form that urbanization takes in a country affects its development and economic growth. While some degree of urban concentration is essential for exploiting the gains from scale economies, as well as, under certain circumstances, initial gains from globalization and technology transfer, it appears that there can be a tendency towards excessive concentration in many countries. Interregional infrastructure investments, political decentralization, and a spatially neutral regulation of the economy seem critical to ensuring a desirable level of urban concentration and urban development.

Bibliography

Fujita, M., and T. Ishii. 1994. "Global Location Behavior and Organizational Dynamics of Japanese Electronic Firms and Their Impact on Regional Economics." Paper prepared for Prince Bertil Symposium on the Dynamic Firm, Stockholm, June 1994.

Hansen, E. R. 1983. "Why Do Firms Locate Where They Do?" International Bank for Reconstruction and Development, No. UDD25.

Hekman, J. 1982. "Branch Plant Location and the Product Cycle in Computer Manufacturing." University of North Carolina Working Paper.

Henderson, J. V. 1988. *Urban Development: Theory, Fact, and Illusion.* New York: Oxford University Press.

Henderson, J. V. 1999. "The Effects of Urban Concentration on Economic Growth." World Bank Working Paper. Processed. Washington, D.C.

Henderson, J. V., and A. Kuncoro. 1996. "Industrial Centralization in Indonesia." *World Bank Economic Review* 10: 513–40.

Henderson, J. V., A. Kuncoro, and M. Turner. 1995. "Industrial Development in Cities." *Journal of Political Economy* 103: 1067–90.

Henderson, J. V., T. Lee, and J.-Y. Lee. 1999. "Externalities and Industrial Deconcentration Under Rapid Growth." Mimeo, Brown University.

Kolko, J. 1999. "Can I Get Some Service Here: Transport Costs, Cities, and the Geography of Service Industries." Mimeo (March), Harvard University.

Nakamura, R. 1985. "Agglomeration Economies in Manufacturing." *Journal of Urban Economics* 17: 108–24.

Rosen, K., and M. Resnick. 1978. "The Size Distribution of Cities, the Pareto Law, and the Primate City." Mimeo, Princeton University.

chapter 8

The Importance of Large Urban Areas— and Governments' Roles in Fostering Them

Edwin S. Mills

Kellogg Graduate School of Management
Northwestern University

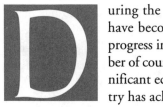 uring the past 50 years, urban areas have become centers of growth and progress in all of the increasing number of countries that are achieving significant economic growth. No country has achieved sustained economic growth without accompanying massive urban growth. Some 75 or 85 percent of the population in the highest income countries is urban, compared with 10–15 percent in the poorest countries.[1] This strong correlation between economic growth and urbanization is as close to a natural law as almost any social process in human history. And this correlation will continue in the future.

Yet in many countries, there is strong ideological opposition to large urban areas—in government, among the media, and in academic institutions. One of life's ironies is to be lectured on the evils of large urban areas by an academic, government official, or media writer who has lived his or her entire life in New York, Tokyo, or Bombay and who could hardly imagine living anywhere else. Perhaps a part of the same ideology is the widespread belief that poor residents should be sent back to rural areas where it is thought that they would be better off.

In fact, overwhelming evidence shows that the poor gain from rural–urban migration. In rapidly urbanizing middle-income countries, urban wages may be two to four times rural wages (Mills and Becker 1986; Mazumdar 1987). Even after adjusting for cost-of-living differences, this gap remains large and is a primary motive for migration. Urban workers have higher wages because they concentrate in growing industrial and service sectors as opposed to stagnating agricultural sectors. Urban workers are also typically better educated than rural workers; indeed, educational opportunities are often an initial reason for rural–urban migration.

Why Large Urban Areas Are More Efficient

Land prices in large urban areas may be 50 to 100 times as high as in rural areas less than 100 kilometers away. Why do nonagricultural producers concentrate in big cities instead of scattering throughout the available space?

The proximity of large numbers of workers, consumers, and producers clearly enables people, goods, and information to move economically. Producers compensate for high land prices by building upward, as offices or residential complexes outbid other users for the most expensive land. Vertical expansion allows large markets for many goods and services in major urban areas, enabling firms to realize economies of scale and scope in many sectors. In large urban areas, many input purchases and output sales also can be made locally, and there is a better match between workers and jobs. As a result, both sectoral outputs and plant sizes are greater in large urban areas than in small ones.

The high density and proximity in urban areas promote efficiency in nonbusiness sectors as well. Urban areas are centers of higher education, technology, and innovation. Proximity permits economies of scale and scope in these sectors and interaction within and between the sectors. For the same reasons, urban areas are centers for the arts. Finally, urban areas are centers for political reform. It is no accident that black Americans' demands for civil rights became effective only as large numbers of blacks migrated from southern farms to urban areas. Demands for political reform in the Republic of Korea were centered in Seoul and demands for reform in China were centered in Beijing.

Similar effects apply to the movement of information. Modern economic activity is highly specialized, requiring a high volume of communication among business units. And face-to-face meetings are important for some kinds of communication. Indeed, because modern technology permits almost cost-free communication over long distances, only the need for face-to-face communication justifies the extremely high office densities and land values in central business districts and suburban subcenters.

Large urban areas economize not only on internal movements of goods, people, and information but also on movements to other large urban areas. Scale economies in producing and operating road, rail, water, and air transport make exchanges more efficient. Even small urban areas do not provide the same advantages, as high transport costs eat up savings from large-scale production.

Some popular writers have forecast that the spread of information technology will mean the demise of large urban areas. But the correlation between the expansion of electronic communication and massive urbanization undermines that theory. Indeed, the telephone, available for a century, appears to have promoted urban growth. Today the availability of faxes, word processors, photocopiers, and e-mail in business hotels worldwide suggests that electronic communication complements rather than substitutes for face-to-face communication (Gaspar and Glaeser 1998).

Globalization reinforces the advantages of large urban areas. Globalization implies international specialization and trade resulting from electronic communication and reduced government trade barriers. These processes will spread the benefits of large urban areas to developing countries.

Technological change originates and spreads more easily in large urban areas, as Alfred Marshall and Jane Jacobs hypothesized and several scholars have confirmed (Glaeser 1997). The geographical concentrations of high-tech firms in Silicon Valley, along Route 128 outside Boston, and in Research Triangle Park in North Carolina provide informal but strong evidence of this effect. More formal evidence comes from the fact that patent issues and various other proxies for technological change and innovation tend to concentrate geographically.

Major U.S. technology centers abut large urban centers partly because they contain research-oriented universities with which they interact closely. Universities, in turn, pursue research linked to technological change and provide industrial laboratories with teachers and students who produce new technology. In low-income countries, universities train scientists and engineers to evaluate and adapt imported technology to local markets and conditions. When governments locate research laboratories or universities far from large urban centers, the distance imposes a barrier to research, and especially to translating results into industrial technology.

Schools themselves benefit from locating in large urban areas, just as other activities do. Student commuting distances are shorter, the schools can realize scale and scope economies, and users can better exchange information concerning school quality and student achievement. Urban areas may also see greater competition among public schools and between public and private schools.

Thus urban areas are centers of higher education, technology, arts, and innovation because proximity permits interaction and economies of scale and scope. We can best measure the difference in efficiency between urban and rural areas by comparing inputs and outputs—or what is called total factor productivity. When applied to urban areas, such analyses are usually referred to as studies of agglomeration economies. Virtually all careful estimates of agglomeration economies have found that large urban areas have higher total factor productivity than small urban areas (Eberts and McMillen 1999; Shukla 1996). Doubling the size of a sector or urban area typically produces a 5- to 10-percent increase in total factor productivity. (However, see Chapter 7 by Vernon Henderson.)

Is there a limit to the size of urban areas that can show greater productivity than smaller urban areas? Most authors assume that congestion and environmental deterioration will inevitably limit productivity gains. But in fact, congestion and pollution are not inevitable; they are the result of failed government policies. Even in large urban areas, appropriate investment in transportation, as well as appropriate prices, can prevent congestion. Unfortunately, government involvement in infrastructure all too often fails to produce sound pricing and investment.

Governments and Infrastructure

Categorizing a service as infrastructure sometimes implies that government should supply it. However, the private sector provides virtually all kinds of infrastructure somewhere in the world. Private companies efficiently supply almost every aspect of urban transportation, for example. Cars, trucks, and two-wheeled vehicles tend to be privately owned. Governments often own and operate buses, but in some countries the private sector performs these functions. Similarly, governments commonly own and operate fixed-rail commuter systems, but private entities build and operate a few, and private companies sometimes operate government-owned systems.

Inadequate investment in urban transportation systems and poor operation and pricing of these systems can bring urban transportation almost to a standstill—and has, to some degree, in cities such as Jakarta, Bangkok, Taipei, and Seoul. But no magic is entailed in creating and maintaining a high-quality urban transportation system. Many countries, international lending institutions, and consulting firms maintain high-quality planning staffs, and international institutions offer loans for planning, building, and operating transportation systems. What's more, the returns on upgrading poor-quality systems are enormous.

But government corruption and favoritism toward locally powerful groups often yield inappropriate investments. Indonesia is an example of such poor policymaking. The government spent billions of dollars planning domestic production of motor vehicles and aircraft at a time when Jakarta was choking on traffic and had little traffic control, almost no public transit, and dramatically underpriced road use.

Governments interfere with investment in communications in a similar way because they invariably try to control the flow of information. Governments have often maintained the telephone system as a public monopoly, for example. Charges are typically low but installations are limited to politically favored institutions. Private families without political influence often wait years to obtain telephone service, and the service that does exist is sometimes so poor that people send messengers instead.

Several private phone companies worldwide have long been willing and able to install and operate phone systems anywhere. As with other infrastructure, the social returns to a high-quality phone system in large urban areas are enormous. Of course, the full social returns to phone and other electronic communications systems can be realized only when large numbers of people and businesses are connected. But the extremely rapid spread of private electronic systems wherever governments permit them shows that this is a minor limitation. Fortunately, governments have become more tolerant of private phone companies as private cellular phones, fax machines, e-mail, and the Internet have made it more difficult for them to control information.

Arthur Lewis (1978) believed that economic growth should concentrate in small urban areas because low land values make infrastructure much less expensive. But that idea is without merit. First, infrastructure is not necessarily more expensive in large urban areas. Highways cost more to build per lane per kilometer in large urban areas, but not per person per kilometer traveled, as the roads see heavy use.

Second, pricing infrastructure services correctly can cut their effect on land values. Governments tend to underprice gas, electricity, clean water, and telephone services. Some developing countries as well as the United States also price highway use by motor vehicles far below cost. Fuel taxes are quite efficient for financing and controlling road use: Many Organisation for Economic Co-operation and Development (OECD) countries levy fuel taxes to approximate highway user costs; $3–4 per U.S. gallon, including taxes, is probably the right range in most of the world's large urban areas.[2]

When governments resist charging for infrastructure services, they deprive themselves of market discipline on investment. Although careful benefit–cost analysis of major projects could overcome this blind spot, such analyses are even scarcer than adequate pricing. The problem is that in most countries high levels of government finance and plan local projects. The United States is typical: Federal or state governments plan and finance most highway, water supply, and sewage treatment projects. If local governments were required to finance locally beneficial projects with locally raised taxes, residents would vote and lobby for projects that had substantial local benefits.

Residents and businesses in each urban area invariably want more infrastructure if it is financed by national taxes. People who favor limits on large urban areas also often want to locate the most heavily subsidized fixed-rail commuter system and the best and most heavily subsidized universities in the largest urban areas. High-quality benefit–cost analysis of alternative government investments could improve infrastructure allocation within and among urban areas. Better pricing of infrastructure services—with financing based on user fees—as well as private operation of infrastructure services would help limit demands for excessive infrastructure. Most urban infrastructure has local benefits. In such cases, infrastructure should be planned and financed at the local level.

Problems with Land Use Controls

Government land use controls exist in all countries where private property is permitted. An important distinction is the level of government at which land use controls are formulated and administered. In most countries, provincial and local governments have little autonomy, so land use controls are formulated at the national level even though local governments administer them and may have some discretion as to their detailed content. In a few countries, including India and the United States, provincial or state governments have some constitutional autonomy and land use controls are at least partly delegated to local governments.

As with infrastructure, governments all too often use land use controls to interfere with the urbanization process. For example, many governments, especially in Asia, place severe controls on converting land from rural to urban uses. In Korea, greenbelts—privately owned areas where governments prohibit development—surround large urban areas. In high-income countries where further urbanization is occurring slowly, the effects of land use controls may be relatively minor. But in developing countries where the urban population is growing at two to four times the national rate, such restrictions result in extremely high urban land and housing prices. These excessive values hamper the expansion of the large urban areas on which national growth depends.

A comparison between Canada and the United States is telling. The two countries have similar incomes, house types, and housing construction and finance sectors. Both have slowly growing urban areas and large supplies of land. Yet the ratio of house values to residents' incomes is 50 percent higher in Canada than in the United States. Canada has much more stringent land use conversion controls than does the United States (Malpezzi and Mayo 1997).

Why do governments restrict the conversion of land from rural to urban uses? One purported rationale is that they protect people from adverse effects that private agreements cannot mediate. Polluting discharges are the classic example. However, the appropriate policy is to abate or treat these discharges, not to move them around by controlling land use. The rationale also sometimes includes the need to limit pollution, congestion, the costs of infrastructure, and the need to preserve farmland. But the growth of large urban areas actually economizes on rural land, since population density is greater the larger the urban area.

Governments also justify land use controls and related building codes as necessary to protect people from shoddy or dangerous construction. That rationale is unassailable—provided that the codes are fair and fairly administered. The worst abuse of building codes is undoubtedly the practice in some developing countries of making illegal the only housing that the poorest 10–30 percent of people can afford. This practice criminalizes poverty and prevents poor people from living in urban areas.

One can argue persuasively that minimal land use controls—say, those segregating residential neighborhoods from factories that may generate noise and dangerous road traffic—are good second-best policies. However, many U.S. urban areas take that claim too far: Restrictions keep virtually all commercial and industrial land use apart from high-income suburbs, resulting in excessive commuting and other automobile use. In small

suburban jurisdictions some land use controls prohibit construction of the high-rise apartments or other multi-family dwellings that lower-income citizens can afford.

Evidence from Boston, Vancouver, and some Northern European cities suggests that land use controls also slow the response of housing development to demand, destabilizing housing prices. For example, when excessive regulations mean that developers require months or years to obtain permission to build, construction slows and housing prices rise rapidly during periods of high demand. When dwellings finally come on the market, growth has often ceased, and housing prices drop sharply.

The economic solution to excessive government controls on conversion of land from rural to urban use, and on types and locations of urban housing, is easy: stop. The political problems of mobilizing citizens to urge governments to adopt appropriate policies are much more difficult and beyond the scope of this chapter.

Conclusion

Large urban areas are among the greatest social inventions of all time. They are important and productive parts of every modern economy. Governments should stop trying to limit and control them and concentrate instead on making them more productive. Toward that end, they should reduce controls on the growth of large urban areas and on the production, location, financing, and types of housing. And they should increase private-sector participation in creating and operating infrastructure.

Bibliography

Barro, Robert. 1996. "Determinants of Economic Growth: A Cross-Country Empirical Study." NBER Working Paper 5698. National Bureau of Economic Research, Cambridge, MA.

Becker, Charles, and Andrew Morrison. Forthcoming. "Urbanization in Transforming Economies." In Paul Cheshire and Edwin Mills, eds., *Handbook of Regional and Urban Economics* Vol. 3: *Applied Urban Economics.* New York: North-Holland.

Becker, Charles, Jeffrey Williamson, and Edwin Mills. 1992. *Indian Urbanization and Economic Growth Since 1960.* Baltimore, MD: The Johns Hopkins University Press.

Eberts, Randall, and Daniel McMillen. 1999. "Agglomeration Economies and Public Infrastructure." In Paul Cheshire and Edwin Mills, eds., *Handbook of Regional and Urban Economics* Vol. 3: *Applied Urban Economics.* New York: North-Holland.

Fischel, William. 1985. *The Economics of Zoning Laws.* Baltimore, MD: Johns Hopkins University Press.

Gaspar, Jess, and Edward Glaeser. 1998. "Information Technology and the Future of Cities." *Journal of Urban Economics* 43(1): 136–56.

Glaeser, Edward. 1997. "Learning in Cities." NBER Working Paper 6271. National Bureau of Economic Research, Cambridge, MA.

Gyourko, Joseph, Matthew Kahn, and Joseph Tracy. 1999. "Quality of Life and Environmental Comparisons." In Paul Cheshire and Edwin Mills, eds., *Handbook of Regional and Urban Economics* Vol. 3: *Applied Urban Economics.* New York: North-Holland.

Lewis, W. Arthur. 1978. *The Evolution of the International Economic Order.* Princeton, NJ: Princeton University Press.

Malpezzi, Stephen, and Stephen Mayo. 1997. "Housing and Urban Development Indicators: A Good Idea Whose Time Has Returned." *Real Estate Economics* 25(1): 1–11.

Mazumdar, Dipak. 1987. "Rural(Urban Migration in Developing Countries." In Edwin Mills, ed., *Handbook of Regional and Urban Economics.* Vol. 2: *Urban Economics.* New York: North-Holland.

Mills, Edwin. 1998. "The Economic Consequences of a Land Tax in Land Value Taxation," edited by Dick Netzer. Cambridge, MA: Lincoln Institute of Land Policy.

Mills, Edwin. 1998. "Excess Commuting in U.S. Metropolitan Areas." In Larx Lindquist, Lars-Goran Mattson, and Tschargo Kim, eds., *Network Infrastructure and the Urban Environment.* Berlin: Springer-Verlag.

Mills, Edwin, and Charles Becker. 1986. *Studies in Indian Urban Development.* New York: Oxford University Press.

Shukla, Vibhotti. 1996. *Urbanization and Economic Growth.* Delhi: Oxford University Press.

Small, Kenneth. 1992. *Urban Transportation Economics.* Chue, Switzerland: Harwood Academic Publishers.

Notes

1. These figures exclude a few countries that are essentially city-states.

2. Adjustments can be made in fuel taxes for fuel burned predominantly outside large urban areas. See Mills 1998a.

chapter 9

Toward a New Model of Rural–Urban Linkages under Globalization

Yujiro Hayami

Foundation for Advanced Studies on International Development

rbanization in developing economies has concentrated largely in megacities, often one per country. The result has been mushrooming slums, formidable congestion and pollution, and social, political, and economic disruption.

However, contrary to widespread belief, urbanization is not an inevitable result of globalization. The urbanization process in developing economies today is largely the product of specific development strategies rather than the inevitable consequence of modern technology and market forces. The integration of domestic with international markets does stimulate the growth of industrial and service activities. Yet those activities do not have to locate in a metropolis.

In fact, Krugman and Livas Elizondo (1996) have shown that trade liberalization can promote industrial decentralization because it gives entrepreneurs in the hinterland access to international markets for products and inputs. A cross-country study by Ades and Glaeser (1995) found a negative link between openness to international trade and concentration of population in a metropolis.

However, trade liberalization alone is unlikely to prevent urban concentration, as these economists imply. Rural-based industrialization in Meiji Japan (1868–1912) as well as the striking success of balanced rural-urban growth in Taiwan, China, after the Second World War show that globalization through liberalization can be a powerful means of inducing industry to locate outside the urban center—if it is accompanied by other important national policies. These historical experiences suggest a new model of rural–urban linkage under globalization.

From Colonialism to Import Substitution

The high concentration of population and economic activities in developing economies today stems from development policies of the 19th century. Indeed, this result was the product of globalization. As colonial powers integrated tropical economies into a network of international trade, they began to specialize in cash crops and minerals, not only because of local comparative advantage in natural resources but also because the colonial powers used imported capital and labor to exploit them—the "vent-for-surplus" development of Hla Myint (1971).

Often colonial powers not only allocated available virgin lands exclusively to colonial planters of export crops, but they also transferred arable lands already under cultivation by native peasants to white planters. Publicly funded research on agricultural technology concentrated on cash crops grown in plantations, to the neglect of subsistence food crops. Investments in infrastructure such as ports, railways, and roads mainly facilitated the transport of cash crops and minerals for export. Peasants shouldered a significant share of the cost of such infrastructure through various taxes and levies such as the poll tax. This taxation forced cashless peasants to seek wage employment, expanding the labor supply for colonial enclaves. All these policies increased the comparative advantage of cash crops and minerals over both subsistence crops and domestically manufactured commodities (Myint 1965; Lewis 1970).

This process produced large port cities, typically one in each colony, linking domestic economies with international markets, not only for trade but also for financial and other services as well as migrating labor. Such cities were usually the site of colonial administration. Strong agglomeration economies worked among all these services, which included close connections between private firms and government offices. Consisting of colonial government officials, traders, shippers, and financiers, plus a large number of native employees including a swarm of coolies, these cities grew to a size incomparably larger than precolonial towns.

Rural deindustrialization accompanied the development of megacities. Competition from commodities produced in modern factories in the West typically destroyed production of indigenous manufactures of farm households and cottage industries for local consumption—"Z-goods," according to Hymer and Resnick (1969). The disappearance of Z-good production was especially pronounced in countries with vent-for-surplus growth, such as Malaysia, Thailand, and the Philippines (Resnick 1970). Because governments kept the incomes of native peasants and wage laborers low, demand for relatively inexpensive and easy-to-make goods requiring no sophisticated skill to manufacture did not justify domestic production. Meanwhile, demand from high-income planters, traders, and other service providers in the capital city for "elite commodities" leaked out of the domestic economy to home countries.

In the later stage of colonial development, modern manufacturing began to respond to rising domestic demand stemming from growing population as well as the incomes of peasants who participated in cash crop production despite many regulations against them. However, with commercial, financial, and other services well established in the capital city and rural non-farm entrepreneurship largely destroyed, new manufacturing establishments tended to locate in the metropolis. Rural deindustrialization did not reverse, and the rural sector continued to specialize in the supply of food and export cash crops as well as labor to the ever-growing urban center.

After World War II, newly independent nations almost unanimously made industrialization a top priority. The most popular strategy was import substitution, geared to protect domestic industries from competition. This doctrine was based on strong pessimism regarding the export of primary commodities because of sharp declines in their prices during the World Depression. The policy also received wide popular support because it was designed to break the inequitable colonial system.

Under import substitution, countries commonly used tariffs and quotas on imports to protect large-scale modern industries, such as assembly of consumer durables and capital equipment and manufacture of synthetic fibers and chemical fertilizers. The tariffs and quotas served to raise domestic prices of these products. Meanwhile, countries also allocated imported capital and intermediate goods to those industries, whose costs were low owing to the overvaluation of domestic currency. The victims of this policy were consumers as well as unprotected industries, as both were forced to purchase commodities at elevated prices.

Agriculture and small- and medium-scale industries especially suffered (Little et al. 1970). For example, when countries protected synthetic fiber industries, high yarn prices undermined garment industries usually run by small and medium enterprises using labor-intensive technology. Note that weaving and garment making are among the most suitable manufacturing activities for rural households and cottage industries. Protection of the manufacture of chemical fertilizers had the same negative effect on farmers. Subsidies for credit and imports such as tractors partly compensated large estate farmers, but small farmers and manufacturers suffered from state trading monopolies and prohibitions on the production and processing of plantation crops by smallholders (Sahn and Sarris 1994). Rural-based industrialization narrowed further and industrial activities concentrated among large urban-based producers. Ironically, a policy intended to break the colonial economic system instead further strengthened the inequitable and urban-biased system.

Strengthening Farm–Nonfarm Linkages

As the comparison between the globalization-oriented colonial system and the autarky-oriented import-substitution system has shown, globalization per se does not promote or prevent urban concentration, but rather different policies produce different outcomes. The question is what policies can curb pathological urban growth and promote an equitable and efficient balance between rural and urban sectors. The colonial and import-substitution systems, when compared with the historical experiences of Japan and Taiwan, suggest policies to correct their failures.

The opening of Japan to international trade in the late 19th century under threat from Admiral Perry's fleet produced an outcome very different from that of the colonial system. In fact, nearly four decades of economic growth after the Meiji Restoration produced vigorous expansion of rural-based industries. This rural industrial growth occurred under virtual free trade and heavy reliance on export of primary and semi-primary commodities such as silk and tea.[1] The sharp contrast between Japan and colonized tropical economies both under the liberal trade regime clearly shows that free trade alone does not promote industrial decentralization outside the urban center, contrary to the predictions of Krugman and Livas Elizondo (1996).

In Japan, the government of the newly established nation-state actively attempted to boost the productivity of food crops, especially rice, by investing in development and extension of new varieties and cultural practices as well as improvements in irrigation and drainage facilities. Major increases in rice yields per hectare outpaced those elsewhere. The new technology was designed to save both land and capital, and it was also largely neutral with respect to operational scale—if anything, it favored family farms (Hayami and Yamada 1991). Small farm producers spent a significant share of their rising incomes on locally produced goods and farm machinery and implements crafted by village blacksmiths and local town workshops.

Peasant agriculture not only provided strong backward linkages to local manufacturers but also provided forward linkages by increasing the supply of cash crops for industrial processing, such as silk and tea. Unlike in tropical economies, smallholders instead of large plantations produced those cash crops in Japan. Hand reeling of silk continued to be a major cottage industry even after World War I, coexisting with factories using modern machinery that were also located mainly in rural towns. Developments in commerce, transport, storage, and other services—also mostly rural-based and small-scale, using labor-intensive organization and technology—supported these intense links between agriculture and manufacturing (Kawagoe 1998; Itoh and Tanimoto 1998). The simultaneous development of industrial and service activities based on rising productivity in smallholder agriculture greatly increased the rural sector's ability to hold population.

Postwar industrialization in Taiwan, China, followed a similar pattern with respect to parallel growth of rural and urban enterprises. Indeed, during the extraordinarily rapid industrial growth from 1956 to 1980, rural- and urban-based manufacturing employment grew at almost exactly the same rate. This experience represented a sharp contrast with the Philippines, where the growth of manufacturing employment in rural areas was much less than half that in urban areas (Table 9.1). Strikingly, Taiwan, China, achieved not only a good interregional balance but also much faster overall growth, suggesting that rural–urban balance and a high rate of economic growth can be complementary.

Table 9.1

Annual Growth of Employment in Manufacturing in Taiwan (China) and the Philippines

(Percent)

	Rural	Urban
Taiwan		
1956–66	4.99	4.94
1966–80	10.28	9.40
Philippines		
1967–75	0.57	1.42
1975–88	2.03	4.81

Source: Ranis and Stewart (1993, p. 94).

As in the case of Meiji Japan, the key to Taiwan's success with rural-based industrialization was public support in the form of agricultural research, extension, and irrigation services for smallholders who provided strong linkages to local industries, trade, and other services (Ho 1977, 1979). Public support for improved rice farming began under the Japanese colonial regime and strengthened after World War II under the Kuomintang (Nationalist Party). This support produced sustained increases in rice yields beginning in the mid-1920s (except for wartime disruption). In the Philippines, where colonial development efforts concentrated on plantation crops, rice yields did not grow significantly until the 1970s.[2]

Structuring Linkages between Rural Producers and Urban Trade Centers

The problem with import-substitution industrialization, as practiced widely for almost three decades after World War II, is that both farmers and small-scale manufacturers were taxed in a highly distortive manner without compensating public support for their activities. Large implicit taxes on small producers were dissipated for bureaucratic consumption as well as to support high-cost protected industries, including the wages of unionized labor. The policy thus choked off the possibility of national development through labor-intensive activities by small producers, which have comparative advantage in labor-abundant and capital-scarce developing economies.

The inefficient and inequitable nature of import-substitution industrialization became increasingly visible throughout the 1960s and 1970s. Then the economic crisis in developing economies resulting from the 1981 collapse of the second oil boom, together with pressure from the International Monetary Fund (IMF) and World Bank, forced them to adopt structural adjustments designed to liberalize their markets. The success of the new policy in promoting economic growth through labor-intensive production was especially remarkable in economies such as Indonesia and Thailand, which were important components of the East Asian economic miracle (World Bank 1993). In Indonesia, for example, currency devaluations and deregulation of trade and foreign direct investment during the 1980s sparked rapid increases in the production and export of labor-intensive manufactures—as well as sharp decreases in poverty. These effects ended only with the recent financial crisis.

But although market liberalization and deregulation opened the door to the effective utilization of abundant labor in response to rising demand for labor-intensive commodities from high-income economies, such production located disproportionately within major cities or their outskirts—with severe accompanying congestion and pollution. This situation is different from the experiences of Meiji Japan and postwar Taiwan, China, which developed rural towns and villages as the location of industrial production for export.

Critical to enabling rural-based industries to participate in global economic activities is the trade network linking small producers to international demand, usually transmitted through urban centers. In Meiji Japan, if an urban trader received an order of cotton or silk cloth for export, for example, he usually made contracts with local collectors in rural areas to assemble the needed amounts from a large number of small weavers living in their places. In order to meet the export demand, a large amount of products to meet a certain quality standard specified by a foreign buyer must be collected by a specified delivery date. If his collectors violated the contracts by mistake or opportunism, the trader was bound to lose reputation among his customers, hence, lose future business opportunity in export trade. Thus, he normally endeavored to establish a mutual trust relationship with collectors through repeated transactions over time as well as interlinking commodity trades with credit and other transactions so as to avoid the prisoners' dilemma game solution.

The same applied for local collectors in relation with weavers operating in rural villages and towns. Typically a local collector developed putting-out contracts with weavers by advancing yarn and collecting cloth at a prescribed piece rate. Long-term, repeated contracts were usually applied to suppress opportunistic behaviors such as embezzlement of yarn by means of weaving cloth at lower density than agreed upon. For the same reason, personal connections such as relatives, friends, and neighbors were preferred in the selection of contracting partners. Opportunism was suppressed significantly by the expectation that possible contract violation would

be punished socially through malicious gossips and ostracism in the small rural community. Once community sanction reduced opportunism, small-scale, family-based rural enterprises became more efficient than large firms because of the farmer's advantage in monitoring labor at a lower cost in light industries with weak scale economies (Hemi 1997).

Japanese automakers' subcontracts with parts suppliers are a prime example of the application of relational contracting to capital-intensive industries. Kiichiro Toyota, founder of the Toyota Motor Company, intended in the 1930s to build "a pastoral factory" in Korma (today's Toyota City)—then a rural town with few manufacturing activities (Wada 1998). Kiichiro's idea was not only to locate the factory in a pastoral environment but also to surround it with trusted parts suppliers connected by community spirit. Toyota initially tried to contract with manufacturers receptive to Toyota's guidance, even if they had no previous experience in the precise, sophisticated work of automobile manufacturing. Kiichiro's idea apparently stemmed from his experience as a supplier of automatic looms for rural-based weaving entrepreneurs. His idea bears fruit today as Toyota's highly efficient modern subcontracting system known as *Kanab* (just-in-time).

The network of relational contracts between urban traders, local collectors, and rural manufacturers was an innovation designed to organize local labor to produce commodities to meet large-scale national and international demand. Indeed, this network of long-term, multistandard contracts tied by mutual trust across urban principals and rural agents substituted for intensive information flows in urban agglomeration economies. If such a system had not proved effective, traders might have opted to build and manage factories for mass-producing standardized commodities in an urban location, even if manufacturing costs were lower in the hinterland. The effective use of a rural–urban trade network to fully exploit the opportunities for rural-based development created by globalization rested upon the active participation of rural entrepreneurs. Thus the links between industrial producers in the hinterland and international markets under liberalized trade assumed in the Krugman–Livas Elizondo model depend critically on a domestic trade network.[3]

Such an active role of rural entrepreneurs contrasts with the traditional image of indigenous people, especially peasants subsisting in rural villages, as inherently passive, with neither the desire nor the ability to participate in commercial or industrial activities. This view found typical expression in Clifford Geertz's anthropological study in Indonesia. He concluded that entrepreneurship in the nonfarm business activities that induce social modernization cannot emerge from "the immediate purview of village social structure" but is limited to populations with "extra-village status," such as ethnic Arab traders in East Java and traditional rulers in Bali (Geertz 1963).

However, my observations of agricultural marketing in Indonesia reveal local marketing systems consisting of petty traders and processors in rural villages who use scarce capital efficiently and local resources intensively, especially labor, while developing adequate linkages with urban traders and manufacturers (Hayami and Kawagoe 1993). The entrepreneurs who organize this system use community relationships to ingeniously design trade practices and contracts for sharing risk and minimizing transaction costs. Rural areas of the Philippines and Thailand reveal similar entrepreneurship in the garment and weaving industries (Kikuchi 1998; Ohno and Jirapatpimol 1998), as do rural communities in India (Bhatt 1998). Somewhat similar organizations are emerging in China, with "township–village enterprises" developing linkages with state or foreign enterprises through trade contracts, including financial support and technical guidance (Liu and Otsuka 1998; Otsuka et al. 1998).

The major question is thus not whether the potential for rural entrepreneurship exists, but rather how developing countries can fully exploit it to achieve balanced rural–urban growth under globalization.

Policies for Rural-Based Development

How can countries intensify farm–nonfarm linkages at the local level and rural–urban linkages at the national level along the historical paths of Japan and Taiwan? Liberalization of both international and internal markets has clearly been indispensable for promoting the activities of small farmers, manufacturers, and traders, as illustrated by an episode during the early Meiji period when Japan was deprived of tariff autonomy as a part of unequal treaties with Western powers (Hayami 1997).

In the 1870s and 1880s the Japanese government tried to develop rural cotton-spinning industries to rescue cotton producers about to succumb to imports of cotton yarn and cloth. The government imported relatively small-scale plants with 2,000 spindles for lease or sale at subsidized prices to entrepreneurs in inland cotton-farming areas. However, factories equipped with these small machines failed to produce yarn at competitive prices from high-priced domestic cotton. But cotton spinning soon after developed into a major export industry as private entrepreneurs established large modern factories equipped with machines composed of 15,000 spindles or more using cotton imported from India and the United States. If Japan had been able to set its own tariffs, the government would likely have protected inefficient cotton-spinning mills as well as farmers by imposing high tariffs on imported cotton and yarn and would have lost the opportunity for cotton spinning to become a major Japanese export industry. Indeed, the dramatic development of the Japanese cotton textile industry—which soon outcompeted Britain and India—occurred with virtually no government protection and subsidy. This experience is clearly inconsistent with the assertion that government subsidies are indispensable for late-industrializing economies hoping to foster export manufactures, including textiles (Amsden 1989).

Foreign direct investment can also be an important support for small and medium-scale rural industries. Taiwan, China, illustrates this relationship most clearly. Unlike the Republic of Korea, Taiwan, China, liberalized foreign direct investment relatively early, and small and medium-sized enterprises contracted with foreign firms, which offered trade credits and technical guidance. The former developed into the dominant export sector, with firms with less than 300 employees accounting for as much as 65 percent of manufactured exports during the mid-1980s (Wade 1990). Compared with Korea, Taiwan's industrialization produced different sizes of manufacturing activities as well as better urban–rural balance (Ho 1979, 1982).

Of course, free trade and direct foreign investment alone do not assure the success of rural-based industrialization. Otherwise, tropical economies under the colonial system would have achieved industrial development similar to that of Meiji Japan. Part of the difference stemmed from Japanese government support for smallholder agriculture, but equally significant was public support for small manufacturers and traders. Japan actively pursued applied industrial research, development, and extension and provided information services such as industrial fairs, exhibitions of foreign products and machines, and newsletters from consulates on overseas markets. The government also encouraged small producers to form industrial associations to distribute technical and market information and organize product grading and quality inspection (Kiyokawa 1995; Minami et al. 1995). Under the colonial system assistance to domestic manufacturers was not only absent but often suppressed.

Public infrastructure such as roads, communication systems, and rural electrification is also key to widely diffusing industrial and commercial activities in rural areas with strong urban links. Even more basic is providing education to rural residents, including primary and midlevel vocational education. Taiwan faired exceptionally well in providing such supports to rural people (Ranis and Stewart 1993).

In terms of remarkable growth in township–village enterprises, the development of postreform China may appear analogous to the historical experience of Japan and Taiwan. However, this development is rather special as it has been supported by strong regulation on labor migration from rural to urban areas, in addition to liberalization in commodity trade and foreign direct investment (Byrd and Lin 1990; Lin et al. 1996). It appears that China will need a major expansion in rural infrastructure, especially for transportation, to further rural industrialization at the speed to prevent the rural–urban disparity from widening.

On the Applicability of the Japan-Taiwan model

Rural-based industrialization in Meiji Japan depended on relatively well-developed roads and irrigation systems inherited from the feudal Tokugawa period,[4] and postwar development in Taiwan depended on public infrastructure built under the Japanese colonial regime (Ranis and Stewart 1993). One might question whether low-income economies today, especially those in sub-Saharan Africa, can replicate this experience without such a favorable initial condition. Indeed, it will be extremely difficult to mobilize enough public resources to support numerous small farmers, manufacturers, and traders in the vast hinterland in economies with much lower population density than in Asia.

However, one great advantage to developing economies today is the availability of advanced electronic communications. The use of personal computers backed by satellite systems can enable small rural producers to integrate their activities with national and international markets, given relatively modest investment. And e-mail and cellular phones can facilitate formation of relational contracts linking rural manufacturers with urban traders. For rural producers, the new communications technology can thus substitute for urban agglomeration economies based on intensive information flows.

Technological advance can also help supply other infrastructure. Local power generation based on solar, wind, and biomass energies can greatly facilitate rural electrification, for example. Such locally generated electricity could eliminate the need for large-scale, high-cost systems for transmitting power. The combined effect of advances in communication and power generation technologies may be similar to the situation in Meiji Japan, which benefited from the development of small electric motors and hydrobased electrification. Small rural workshops relied on those technologies to offset the scale

economies achieved by producers using steam engines, thereby strengthening their competitive position vis-à-vis large-scale urban factories (Minami 1976).

Another legitimate question is whether the simultaneous development of smallholder agriculture, rural manufacturing, and services in Japan and Taiwan stemmed from relatively egalitarian distribution of farmland. After all, rice-growing villages consisted of stable and relatively homogeneous family farms, providing a nursery for contracting based on mutual trust and cooperation and intensive local interaction. If so, developing economies with highly skewed land distribution, such as the Philippines and Latin American countries, may not be able to follow a similar development path without drastic land reform.

However, less severe measures can help redistribute land. In Japan, unequal distribution of land in the early 16th-century Tokugawa period improved with the development of labor-intensive technology and previously prohibited land-rental contracts (Smith 1959). This process continued in the Meiji period. Large, wealthy farmers monopolized cocoon production until the early Meiji period, for example. But with technological innovations such as hybrid silkworms and summer–fall rearing practices, together with institutional innovations such as cooperative rearing of young worms, small farmers could profitably pursue sericulture (Nghiep and Hayami 1991).

Developing economies today could similarly rely on technological and institutional innovations to correct great inequality in land distribution. In fact, significant scope exists for reorganizing large plantations into small family farms. The plantation system was originally established under the colonial regime to exploit tropical lands through export crops. Opening new lands for export production required huge capital outlays for infrastructure such as roads and docking facilities, and farms had to be large for investors to gain from such investments. However, as population density and infrastructure grew, the scale diseconomies of centrally managed estate farms began to emerge, much as with collective farms in socialist economies.

Because agricultural production is performed over wide space and subject to the vagaries of nature, monitoring wage laborers is inherently difficult. This makes family farming most efficient at the field level (Binswanger and Rosenzweig 1986; Hayami and Otsuka 1993). Today the merit of the plantation lies mainly in its ability to coordinate the supply of agricultural raw materials (such as sugar cane) with large-scale processing (using a centrifugal sugar mill). However, efficiency can rise if an agribusiness manages processing and marketing and provides technical guidance, credit, and other services to smallholders in return for their pledged supply of farm products. The principle of this contract farming system is similar to that of traders (or a larger factory) who rely on relational contracts to organize a network of small manufacturers.

Production of sugar and canned pineapple in Thailand based on such a system has recently been outcompeting Filipino production based on the plantation system. Thailand has supported such production by investing in rural infrastructure, especially roads. In fact, inducing plantations to reorganize into contract farming by providing public infrastructure and services, as well as by reducing favorable tax treatments and access to public lands for plantations, will likely prove more efficient than coercive land redistribution (Hayami et al. 1990; Hayami 1994).

Unlike in developing Asia, where comparative advantage stems from labor-intensive manufacturing such as textile and footwear, relatively land-abundant economies in Africa and Latin Africa are likely to find comparative advantage in high-valued agroindustry products. High-income economies have accelerated their demand for such items, including exotic tropical fruits, cut flowers, wines, and leather goods. Contract farming has proved effective in organizing small rural producers to grow such high-valued commodities (Braun et al. 1989; Hayami and Kawagoe 1993).

Transferring the Japan–Taiwan model to economies in sub-Saharan Africa may seem impossible given economic, social, and cultural barriers (Platteau and Hayami 1998). However, it was not too long ago that a distinguished anthropologist, Clifford Geertz, expressed dire pessimism about the entrepreneurship of Indonesian peasants in commerce and industry. Such a perspective was widespread among scholars on tropical Asia before the East Asian miracle. The pessimism regarding Asian peasantry, including Indonesia, did not stand up to historical test.

Yet Geertz's representation of Indonesian peasants may actually have been valid in the early 1950s. At that time the Indonesian economy had not yet recovered from the devastation of Japanese occupation followed by a war of independence against the Dutch. The rural sector was cut off from a wide market and peasants' activities were of necessity subsistence-oriented. In the four decades since then until the outbreak of the recent financial crisis, the country had established law and order, improved transportation and communication systems, and widely diffused primary education as well as the official Indonesian language, breaking down barriers among different regions and ethnic groups. Peasant en-

trepreneurs demonstrated their latent entrepreneurship by pursuing market transactions. Rural villages and towns were progressively integrated with national and international markets, especially after the country liberalized trade and devalued its currency in the 1980s. If peasants in Indonesia as well as other Asian countries considered totally incapable of market activity only a few decades ago could follow the same path as Meiji Japan, is there any reason their African counterparts could not follow a similar path, given stronger national and international support?

Toward Balanced Rural-Urban Growth

Today globalization supported by communications technology makes possible rural-based developments in commerce and industry as well as agriculture in developing economies. Market liberalization has emancipated small farmers, manufacturers, and traders from the yoke of discriminatory regulation against their activities, so pervasive under the import-substitution strategy. The ability of rural producers to organize production in response to international demand has recently become apparent in Latin American countries such as Chile, which successfully produced high-value agroindustry goods for export. If the present momentum strengthens with adequate supports, it could reverse the growing imbalance between rural and urban sectors. The needed supports include general and vocational education, applied research and extension for both agriculture and local manufacturing, roads and communication infrastructure, and rural electrification, among others.

And the budget necessary for providing enough local public goods to achieve rural–urban balanced growth will be large, even given significant cost savings from technological innovation. The need may well exceed the finances of low-income developing economies where the pathology of urban growth is especially severe given high population growth and where local infrastructure has been grossly underdeveloped, such as in sub-Saharan Africa.

The challenge is to make efficient use of scarce public resources. Relying on the central government to allocate such resources to remote hinterlands will prove highly inefficient. Decentralizing decisionmaking to the prefecture level and further to the township and village levels will be necessary. Municipal governments and local industry associations can run experiment stations and extension services much more efficiently than a central government. In fact, Japan has traditionally pursued such a decentralized strategy (Itoh and Urata 1994). Appropriate coordination between central and local governments is the major challenge facing developing economies hoping to achieve balanced rural–urban growth.

In this connection, serious thought must be given to allowing rural people, especially farmers, to share the cost of developing local infrastructure and public services. While postwar Taiwan, China, and Meiji Japan provided public support to farmers, those in Japan shouldered high land taxes, and farmers in Taiwan, China, had to exchange rice for fertilizers under state monopoly at a barter ratio much more unfavorable than the prevailing international price. Taxation of farmers is not inherently antiagricultural or antirural provided that it does not unduly distort market incentives and that at least some of the taxes return to farmers in the form of infrastructure and services expected to produce high economic returns. The important considerations are designing the least distortive tax scheme and concentrating scarce public funds to best support rural producers.

In the past, so many distortive measures have been used to tax rural producers, and scarce public resources were often used not to support but rather to suppress their activities. Such policies have partly been the result of the political elite's rent-seeking activities, but they were also adopted as the result of policymakers' ignorance and distrust of the ability of small informal producers in the countryside. In designing appropriate policies to promote rural–urban balanced growth in the 21st century, we must keep in mind the following remark:

> Most governments under-invest in this infrastructure and over-invest in their own enterprises and efforts to carry out agricultural marketing directly. If policymakers trusted their peasants more and feared middlemen less, this government bias could be reversed. Most policymakers have never met a peasant, much less one with entrepreneurial skills engaged in risky trading activities (Timmer 1993).

Surely this statement applies not only to peasants but to all informal rural entrepreneurs engaging in commerce and industry in developing economies.

Bibliography

Ades, Alberto F., and Edward L. Glaeser. 1995. "Trade and Circuses: Explaining Urban Giants." *Quarterly Journal of Economics* 110(1): 195–227.

Amsden, Alice. 1989. *Asia's Next Giant: South Korea and Late Industrialization*. New York: Oxford University Press.

Bhatt, V. V. 1998. "On the Relevance of East Asian Experience: A South Asian Perspective." In Yujiro Hayami, ed., *Toward the Rural-Based Development of Commerce and Industry: Selected Experiences from East Asia*, pp. 267–91. Washington, D.C.: World Bank.

Binswanger, Hans P., and Mark R. Rosenzweig. 1986. "Behavioral and Material Determinants of Production Relations in Agriculture." *Journal of Development Studies* 22(3): 503–39.

Braun, Joachim von, David Hotchikiss, and Maarten Immink. 1989. "Nontraditional Export Crops in Guatemala: Effects on Production, Income, and Nutrition." IFPRI Research Report No. 73. Washington D.C.: International Food Policy Research Institute.

Byrd, William A., and Qingsong Lin, eds. 1990. *China's Rural Industry: Structure, Development, and Reform*. Oxford: Oxford University Press.

Geertz, Clifford. 1963. *Peddlers and Princes*. Chicago: The University of Chicago Press.

Hayami, Yujiro. 1994. "Peasant and Plantation in Asia." In G.M. Meier, ed., *From Classical Economics to Development Economics*, pp. 121–34. New York: St. Martin's Press.

Hayami, Yujiro. 1996. "The Peasant in Economic Modernization." *American Journal of Agricultural Economics* 78(5): 1157–67.

Hayami, Yujiro. 1997. *Development Economics: From the Poverty to the Wealth of Nations*. Oxford: Oxford University Press.

Hayami, Yujiro, ed. 1998. *Toward the Rural-Based Development of Commerce and Industry: Selected Experiences from East Asia*. Washington, D.C.: World Bank.

Hayami, Yujiro, and Toshihiko Kawagoe. 1993. *The Agrarian Origins of Commerce and Industry: A Study of Peasants Marketing in Indonesia*. New York: St. Martin's Press.

Hayami, Yujiro, and Keijiro Otsuka. 1993. *The Economics of Contract Choice: An Agrarian Perspective*. Oxford: Clarendon Press.

Hayami, Yujiro, and Vernon W. Ruttan. 1985. *Agricultural Development: An International Perspective*, rev. ed. Baltimore: Johns Hopkins University.

Hayami, Yujiro, Agnes R. Quisumbing, and Lourdes A. Adriano. 1990. *Toward an Alternative Land Reform Paradigm: A Philippine Perspective*. Quezon City, Philippines: Ateneo de Manila University Press.

Hayami, Yujiro, and Saburo Yamada, with associates. 1991. *The Agricultural Development of Japan*. Tokyo: University of Tokyo Press.

Ho, Samuel P. S. 1977. *Economic Development of Taiwan, 1860–1970*. New Haven, CT: Yale University Press.

Ho, Samuel P. S. 1979. "Decentralized Industrialization and Rural Development: Evidence from Taiwan." *Economic Development and Cultural Change* 28(1): 77–96.

Ho, Samuel P. S. 1982. "Economic Development and Rural Industry in South Korea and Taiwan." *World Development* 10(11): 973–90.

Hymer, Stephen, and Stephen Resnick. 1969. "A Model of an Agrarian Economy with Nonagricultural Activities." *American Economic Review* 59(4): 493–506.

Ishikawa, Shigeru. 1967. *Economic Development in Asian Perspective*. Tokyo: Kinokuniya.

Itoh, Motoshige, and Masayuki Tanimoto. 1998. "Rural Entrepreneurs in the Cotton-Weaving Industry of Japan." In Yujiro Hayami, ed., *Toward the Rural-Based Development of Commerce and Industry: Selected Experiences from East Asia*, pp. 47–68. Washington, D.C.: World Bank.

Itoh, Motoshige, and Shujiro Urata. 1994. "Small and Medium-size Enterprise Support Policies in Japan." Policy Research Working Paper 1404. Washington D.C.: World Bank.

Kawagoe, Toshihiko. 1998. "Technical and Institutional Innovations in Rice Marketing in Japan." In Yujiro Hayami, ed., *Toward the Rural-Based Development of Commerce and Industry: Selected Experiences from East Asia,* pp. 23–46. Washington, D.C.: World Bank.

Kikuchi, Masao. 1998. "Export-Oriented Garment Industries in the Rural Philippines." In Yujiro Hayami, ed., *Toward the Rural-Based Development of Commerce and Industry: Selected Experiences from East Asia,* pp. 89–129. Washington, D.C.: World Bank.

Kiyokawa, Yukihiko. 1995. *Nihon no Keizai Hatten to Gijutsu Fukyu* (Economic Development and Technological Diffusion). Tokyo: Toyokeizai Shimposha.

Krugman, Paul, and Raul Livas Elizondo. 1996. "Trade Policy and the Third World Metropolis." *Journal of Development Economics* 49(1): 137–50.

Lewis, W. Arthur, ed. 1970. *Tropical Development, 1880–1913: Studies in Economic Progress.* London: Allen & Unwin.

Lin, Jutin Yifu, Cai Fang, and Li Zhou. 1996. *The China Miracle: Development Strategy and Economic Reform.* Hong Kong: The Chinese University Press.

Little, Ian M. D., Tibor Scitovsky, and Maurice Scott. 1970. *Industry and Trade in Some Developing Countries.* Oxford: Oxford University Press.

Liu, Dequiang, and Keijiro Otsuka. 1998. "Township–Village Enterprises in the Garment Sector of China." In Yujiro Hayami, ed., *Toward the Rural-Based Development of Commerce and Industry: Selected Experiences from East Asia,* pp. 161–86. Washington, D.C.: World Bank.

Minami, Ryoshin. 1976. *Doryoku Kakumai to Gijutsushimpo* (Power Revolution and Technological Progress). Tokyo: Toyokeizai Shimposha.

Minami, Ryoshin, Kwan S. Kim, Fumio Makino, and Joung-hae Seo. 1995. *Acquiring, Adapting and Developing Technologies: Lessons from the Japanese Experience.* London: Macmillan.

Myint, Hla. 1965. *The Economics of the Developing Countries.* New York: Praeger.

Myint, Hla. 1971. *Economic Theory and the Underdeveloped Countries.* New York: Oxford University Press.

Nghiep, Le Thang, and Yujiro Hayami. 1991. "The Tradeoff between Food and Industrial Crops: Summer–Fall Rearing of Cocoons." In Yujiro Hayami and S. Yamada, with associates. *The Agricultural Development of Japan,* pp. 175–98. Tokyo: University of Tokyo Press.

Ohno, Akihiko, and Benja Jirapatpimol. 1998. "The Rural Garment and Weaving Industries in Northern Thailand." In Yujiro Hayami, ed., *Toward the Rural-Based Development of Commerce and Industry: Selected Experiences from East Asia,* pp. 131–59. Washington, D.C.: World Bank.

Otsuka, Keijiro, Degiang Lia, and Naoki Murakami. 1998. *Industrial Reform in China: Past Performance and Future Prospects.* Oxford: Oxford University Press.

Pingali, Prabhu, Mahabub Hossain, and Roberta V. Gerpacio. 1997. *Asian Rice Bowls: The Returning Crisis?* Wallingford, U.K.: CBS International.

Platteau, Jean-Philippe, and Yujiro Hayami. 1998. "Resource Endowments and Agricultural Development: Africa versus Asia." In Yujiro Hayami and Masahiko Aoki, eds., *The Institutional Foundation of East Asian Economic Development,* pp. 357–410. New York: St Martin's Press.

Prebisch, Raul. 1959. "Commercial Policy in the Underdeveloped Countries." *American Economic Review* 49(Supplement): 251–73.

Ranis, Gustav and Frances Stewart. 1993. "Rural Nonagricultural Activities in Development: Theory and Application." *Journal of Development Economics* 40(1): 75–101.

Resnick, Stephen. 1970. "The Decline in Rural Industry under Export Expansion: A Comparison among Burma, Philippines and Thailand, 1870–1938." *Journal of Economic History* 30(1): 51–73.

Sahn, David E., and Alexander Sarris. 1994. "The Evolution of States, Markets, and Civil Institutions in Rural Africa." *Journal of Modern African Studies* 32(2): 279–303.

Smith, Thomas C. 1956. "Landlords and Rural Capitalists in the Modernization of Japan." *Journal of Economic History* 16(2): 165–68.

Smith, Thomas C. 1959. *The Agrarian Origins of Modern Japan.* Stanford, CA: Stanford University Press.

Smith, Thomas C. 1988. *Native Sources of Japanese Industrialization, 1750–1920.* Berkeley and Los Angeles: University of California Press.

Timmer, C. Peter. 1993. In Yujiro Hayami and T. Kawagoe, *Agrarian Origins of Commerce and Industry,* foreword. New York: St. Martin's Press.

Wada, Kazuo. 1998. "The Formation of Toyota's Relationship with Suppliers: A Modern Application of the Community Mechanism." In Yujiro Hayami, ed., *Toward the Rural-Based Development of Commerce and Industry: Selected Experiences from East Asia,* pp. 69–86. Washington, D.C.: World Bank.

Wade, Robert. 1990. *Governing the Market: Economic Theory and the Role of Government in East Asian Industrialization.* Princeton: Princeton University Press.

World Bank. 1993. *The East Asian Miracle.* Oxford: Oxford University Press.

Notes

1. Under the unequal treaties closed between the Tokugawa Shogunate and Western powers (first with the United States in 1858), all Japanese tariff rates were fixed at 5 percent *ad valorem*. Japan was "semicolonized" in a fashion similar to China in the sense that it lost tariff autonomy and was forced to concede Western control on legal affairs over certain areas of port cities. From 1899 Japan was allowed to change tariff rates under the condition that it obtain Western nations' consent. Not until 1911 was tariff autonomy fully restored. Thereafter, the Japanese government began to promote heavy and chemical industries by means of border protection, resulting in a reversal of rural-based industrialization centering on light industries.

2. The collaborative efforts of the International Rice Research Institute and national research/extension systems resulted in the successful development and diffusion of modern high-yielding varieties of rice, first in the Philippines, followed by other economies in Southeast Asia as well as in South Asia (Hayami and Ruttan 1985). There is little doubt that this so-called "Green Revolution" in the 1970s to 1980s was an important support to the "economic miracle" in Southeast Asia. It is disquieting to observe that the recent economic crisis in Southeast Asian economies was shortly preceded by significant deceleration in the growth in rice yield, presumably because of exhaustion of yield potential opened up by the Green Revolution (Pingali et al.

1997). One important condition for revitalizing those economies appears to be further intensification of agricultural research involving not only the increased allocation of public funds to agricultural research but also institutional innovations in the coordination between national and international research institutions as well as between public and private research.

3. In the Krugman–Livas Elizondo model, international firms are assumed to serve domestic producers in the urban center and the hinterland equally well, so that free trade establishes equality in product and input prices between the two locations. Such an assumption might be a valid representation for the relationship between Mexico City and the export-processing zones on the country's northern border with the United States. However, that model is irrelevant and unrealistic for most developing economies where domestic producers link with foreign markets only through a megaport city such as Bangkok in Thailand and Manila in the Philippines. In such a case the prices of imported commodities are higher and those of domestic commodities for export are lower in the hinterland than in the center. Also, it is totally unrealistic to assume that international firms can directly serve a large number of small informal producers in the hinterland.

4. During the three centuries of peace under the hegemony of Tokugawa Shogunate, which saw growing population pressures, villages in Japan continued to organize communal work projects and stipulated regulations for conserving and improving local commons, such as forests, grazing lands, irrigation systems, and roads (Hayami 1997). The irrigation infrastructure, already well established by the end of the Tokugawa era, was an important basis for the development and diffusion of high-yielding rice varieties in the Meiji period (Ishikawa 1967; Hayami and Ruttan 1985).

10

Global City-Regions
and the New World System

Allen J. Scott

Department of Policy Studies and Department of Geography
University of California, Los Angeles

Contrary to many recent predictions, geography is not about to disappear (cf. O'Brien 1992). Even in a globalizing world, geography does not become less important. It becomes more important—because globalization tends to heighten geographic differentiation and locational specialization. In fact, a worldwide archipelago, or mosaic, of diverse city-regions has been emerging forcefully since the end of the 1970s. These city-regions are beginning to function as the basic pillars of the new world system that has been taking shape in recent decades (Scott 1998; Veltz 1996). The internal and external relationships of these peculiar agglomerations and their complex dynamics present extraordinarily perplexing challenges to researchers and policymakers alike as we enter the 21st century.

There is an extensive literature on "world cities" and "global cities" by authors such as Castells (1996), Friedmann and Wolff (1982), Hall (1966), Knox (1995), and Sassen (1991), to name only a few. This literature focuses above all on the large cosmopolitan city as a center of advanced services and information flows and as a command post for multinational corporations. I propose to use the term *global city-regions* to capture similar phenomena while extending the term's meaning to include a wider range of contextual characteristics and social implications.

In simple geographic terms, a global city-region can be said to comprise any major metropolitan area, or contiguous set of metropolitan areas, together with a surrounding hinterland—itself a locus of scattered urban settlements—whose internal economic and political affairs are intricately bound up with far-flung and intensifying extranational relationships. I shall refer to these extranational relationships as a symptom of "globalization," though my rather casual use of this term admittedly does injustice to many conceptual niceties and debates (cf. Hirst and Thompson 1996; Krugman 1996). In parallel with these developments, global city-regions are consolidating into political-geographic units as contiguous local governments form coalitions to deal with both the threats and the opportunities of globalization. Far from being dissolved away as definite geographic entities by globalization, city-regions are by and large thriving, and if anything becoming more central to the conduct and coordination of modern life (Taylor 2000).

We can provisionally identify existing global city-regions by referring to a world map of large metropolitan areas (Figure 10.1). The figure plainly shows that large-scale urbanization is of major importance in today's world, and that it is characteristic of both economically advanced and economically developing countries. In fact, contrary to numerous prognostications, large cities all over the globe continue to grow in size. In 1950 there were 83 cities in the world with populations of more than 1 million (two-thirds of them in the economically advanced countries). In 1990 there were 272 such cities (two-thirds of them in economically developing countries). The United Nations' assessment of population trends in the world's 30 largest metropolitan areas indicates that this growth will continue over at least the next few decades (Table 10.1).

However, not all large metropolitan areas are equally caught up in processes of globalization, and not all global city-regions can be equated with existing large

Figure 10.1

World Distribution of Metropolitan Areas with Populations Greater than One Million

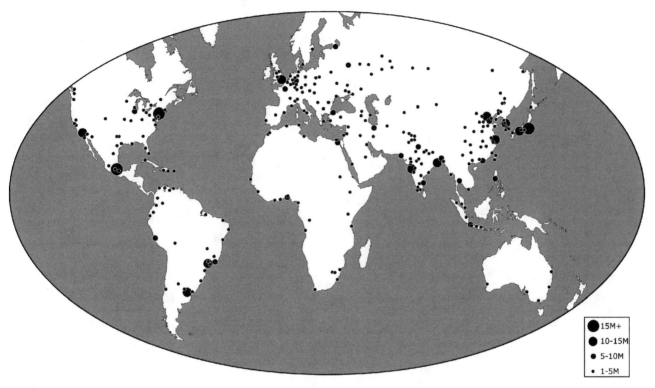

● 15M+
● 10-15M
● 5-10M
· 1-5M

Source: United Nations 1995.

metropolitan areas. A more effective understanding of global city-regions calls for an inquiry into what we might call *a new regionalism* in contemporary capitalism.

Globalization and the New Regionalism

In the immediate post-World War II decades, almost all the major capitalist countries were marked by strong central governments and relatively tightly bordered national economies. These countries constituted a political bloc within a *Pax Americana* underpinned by a rudimentary network of international institutions and arrangements, including the World Bank, the International Monetary Fund (IMF), and the General Agreement on Tariffs and Trade (GATT), through which they sought to regulate their relatively limited—but rapidly expanding—economic interrelations. Over much of the postwar period the most prosperous of these countries constituted a core zone of the world economy, surrounded by a peripheral zone of Third World nations, with a complex set of interdependencies running between the two (as described by world system theorists such as Wallerstein 1979).

Today, after much economic restructuring and technological change, significant transformations of this older order have occurred, creating the outlines of a new world system and a new social grammar of space (Badie 1995). One of the outstanding features of this emerging condition is the apparent though still inchoate formation of a hierarchy of economic and political institutions, from global to local.

Four main aspects of this state of affairs call for immediate attention:

1. Huge and growing amounts of economic activity occur in the form of cross-border relationships, including input–output chains, migration streams, foreign direct investment by multinationals, and monetary flows. Such activity is in large degree what I mean by globalization, though it remains far from any ultimate point of fulfillment. As globalization moves forward, it creates conflicts and predicaments that prompt a variety of political responses and institution-building efforts. Practical expressions of such efforts include a complete reorganization of international financial arrangements, along with a restructuring and reinforcement of international forums of collective decision-making and action such as the G7/G8 group, the Organisation for Economic Co-operation and Development (OECD), the World Bank, the IMF, and a newly streamlined GATT, now known as the World Trade Orga-

Table 10.1

The World's 30 Largest Urban Areas Ranked by Estimated Population in the Year 2000

Population (millions)

	Urban Area	1950	1970	1990	2000 (estimate)	2015 (estimate)
1	Tokyo, Japan	6.9	16.5	25.0	27.9	28.7
2	Mumbai, India	2.9	5.8	12.2	18.1	27.4
3	São Paulo, Brazil	2.4	8.1	14.8	17.8	20.8
4	Shanghai, China	5.3	11.2	13.5	17.2	23.4
5	New York, USA	12.3	16.2	16.1	16.6	17.6
6	Mexico City, Mexico	3.1	9.1	15.1	16.4	18.8
7	Beijing, China	3.9	8.1	10.9	14.2	19.4
8	Jakarta, Indonesia	n.a.	3.9	9.3	14.1	21.2
9	Lagos, Nigeria	n.a.	n.a.	7.7	13.5	24.4
10	Los Angeles, USA	4.0	8.4	11.5	13.1	14.3
11	Calcutta, India	4.4	6.9	10.7	12.7	17.6
12	Tianjin, China	2.4	5.2	9.3	12.4	17.0
13	Seoul, Rep. of Korea	n.a.	5.3	10.6	12.3	13.1
14	Karachi, Pakistan	n.a.	n.a.	8.0	12.1	20.6
15	Delhi, India	n.a.	3.5	8.2	11.7	17.6
16	Buenos Aires, Argentina	5.0	8.4	10.6	11.4	12.4
17	Metro Manila, Philippines	n.a.	3.5	8.0	10.8	14.7
18	Cairo, Arab Republic of Egypt	2.4	5.3	8.6	10.7	14.5
19	Osaka, Japan	4.1	9.4	10.5	10.6	10.6
20	Rio de Janeiro, Brazil	2.9	7.0	9.5	10.2	11.6
21	Dhaka, Bangladesh	n.a.	n.a.	5.9	10.2	19.0
22	Paris, France	5.4	8.5	9.3	9.6	9.6
23	Istanbul, Turkey	n.a.	n.a.	6.5	9.3	12.3
24	Moscow, Russia	5.4	7.1	9.0	9.3	n.a.
25	Lima, Peru	n.a.	n.a.	6.5	8.4	10.5
26	Teheran, Iran	n.a.	n.a.	6.4	7.3	10.2
27	London, U.K.	8.7	8.6	7.3	7.3	n.a.
28	Bangkok, Thailand	n.a.	n.a.	5.9	7.3	10.6
29	Chicago, USA	4.9	6.7	6.8	7.0	n.a.
30	Hyderabad, India	n.a.	n.a.	n.a.	6.7	10.7

Source: United Nations (1995)
n.a. = data not available.

nization (WTO). While these political responses to the pressures of globalization remain limited in scope and severely lacking in real authority, they are liable to grow and consolidate as world capitalism continues its expansion.

2. As a corollary of these pressures, multination blocs such as the European Union (EU), North American Free Trade Agreement (NAFTA), South American Common Market (MERCOSUR), Association of South-East Asian Nations (ASEAN), Asian-Pacific Economic Cooperation (APEC), Caribbean Community and Common Market (CARICOM), and many others have proliferated. These blocs, too, can be seen as institutional efforts to capture the benefits and control the negative effects of the steady spilling over of national capitalisms beyond their traditional political boundaries. The blocs remain in various stages of formation, with the EU in the vanguard. Because such blocs involve only small numbers of participants, they are more manageable as political units (transactions-costs problems are relatively restrained) compared with actual or putative global organizations.

3. Sovereign states and national economies remain prominent, indeed dominant elements of the global landscape, but they are clearly undergoing many sea changes. Individual states no longer enjoy the same degree of political autonomy they once possessed, and under intensifying globalization find themselves less able or willing to safeguard all the regional and sectional interests within their jurisdictions than they once were. Also, national economies have been subject to massive debordering, so it is increasingly difficult, if not impossible, to say precisely where, for example, the American economy ends and the German or Japanese economies begin. As a result, some of the regulatory functions formerly carried out by the central state have been drifting to higher levels of spatial resolution, while other functions have been drifting downward (Swyngedouw 1997).

4. Accordingly, and most importantly in the present context, there has been a resurgence of region-based forms of economic and political organization, with the most overt expression being the formation of large city-

regions. These constitute a global mosaic that is beginning to override the core–periphery relationships that have hitherto characterized much of the macrogeography of capitalist development.

The propensity of many types of economic activity—manufacturing and service sectors alike—to gather into dense regional clusters or agglomerations appears to be intensifying. This renewed quest for collective propinquity on the part of all manner of economic agents can be interpreted as a strategic response to heightened (global) economic competition, in the context of a turn to post-Fordism in modern capitalism. Propinquity is especially important because it is a source of enhanced competitive advantage for many types of firms (Porter 2000; Scott 1988; Storper 1997). As a corollary, large regional production complexes are starting to function as platforms for contesting global markets.

At the same time, the diminishing capacity of central governments to deal with the nuanced policy needs of each region within their borders means that many regions are now faced with the choice of either passive subjection to cross-border pressures or active institution-building, policymaking, and outreach to try to turn globalization to their advantage. Regions that take the latter course are likely to face many new tasks of political coordination and representation. These tasks are of special urgency at a time when large city-regions function more and more as poles of attraction for low-wage migrants from all over the world, so that their populations are heavily interspersed with polyglot and often disinherited social groups. Hence, many city-regions today are confronting pressing issues related to political participation and the reconstruction of local political identity and citizenship.

The Economic Order of Global City-Regions

One of the seeming paradoxes of contemporary geography is that whereas dramatic improvements in transportation and communication are bringing all parts of the world into ever-closer contact, dense urban agglomerations continue to grow in size and importance. These apparently incompatible trends turn out on closer scrutiny to be two mutually reinforcing faces of the network structures (that is, transactional interdependencies) that constitute the basic scaffolding of economic and social life. These economic and social networks are characterized by an intrinsic duality: they possess a definite spatial structure, signifying that any bilateral or multilateral transaction will exact some locationally dependent cost; they also represent social organizations marked by bonding and interaction effects that often produce synergistic outcomes. The latter are exemplified by the increasing-returns effects that typically appear when firms work in collaborative association or the knowledge spillovers that occur in day-to-day business dealings.

Consider two opposing hypothetical situations. First, in an economy marked by uniformly high spatial transactions costs and simple organizational bonds, where all exchanges are purely additive and lacking in synergy, we would expect to observe limited forms of urban and regional development. The kinds of transport-cost minimizing outcomes described by classical Weberian or Löschian location theory would be the main kind of outcome here. In another and purely fictional economy where the time and money costs of spatial transacting are zero, we would expect to observe a state of geographic entropy or randomness no matter what forms of organizational interaction may be present.

In contrast to these two cases, the world that we actually inhabit is one in which the spatial costs of transacting are sometimes extremely high (for example, many kinds of face-to-face exchanges), and sometimes extremely low (for example, international monetary flows). Ours is a world, too, in which the organizational bonds between different economic agents are frequently imbued with multiple synergies. Moreover, as post-Fordist forms of productive organization take deeper hold in economic and social affairs, new synergistic relations seem to be multiplying (Cooke and Morgan 1998; Scott 1998). I shall now attempt to show that this state of affairs leads to the formation of new urban superclusters or city-regions.

The leading edges of the post-Fordist economy are represented by sectors like high-technology production, neoartisanal manufacturing, cultural-products industries, the media, and business and financial services—that is, by sectors that persistently take the form of intricate networks or complexes of producers. These sectors are important sources of increasing-returns effects, and hence of competitive advantage, in that they exhibit high levels of specialization and complementarity so that firms tend to interlock organizationally with one another and to develop relational asset specificities. Specialization and complementarity also provide insurance against critical supply failures due to sudden or unpredictable input needs—an important feature in flexible economies, where long-run planning of production schedules is extremely difficult. The many traded and untraded interdependencies among producers in these networks continually generate new information and practical know-how, leading in turn to learning effects and to high levels of innovation. These effects are complemented by the network-specific skills and habits that workers acquire, which become part of a common pool of human resources upon which employers can draw. Relationships like these are the lifeblood of dynamic economic systems, enabling them to achieve capacities as a whole that are much greater than the sum of their component parts. In this situation, there is a strong likelihood at the outset that the geography of production will be resolved as a series of sizable agglomerations.

Because traded and untraded interdependencies are always geographically extensive, the transactions costs that they incur have a spatial dimension, and in the contemporary world, these costs tend to vary enormously, depending on what is being transacted. For many interrelated groups of producers (especially in post-Fordist sectors), some transactions depend on locational proximity of all participants if they are to be successfully carried out (notably where transacting involves frequent, unpredictable, and constantly shifting face-to-face encounters). Other transactions incur such low unit costs that they can effectively span an unlimited geographic range. Additionally, the rich synergies and increasing-returns effects typical of producer networks tend to magnify any basic proclivity to physical agglomeration due to high transactions costs. This state of affairs is exemplified by the motion picture industry of Hollywood, where actual production occurs mostly within a geographically circumscribed network of transactions that is also the site of many interfirm synergies, whereas final products circulate with ease around the globe (Storper and Christopherson 1987). The net result will be a tendency for urban superclusters to spring forth.

In brief, the clustering of economic activities will usually be especially pronounced where three sets of relationships come into mutual interaction. First, where there are selectively high transactions costs on the production side, interlinked firms will tend to converge toward their own center of gravity. Second, if spatially dependent transaction costs on certain outputs are low and markets are expanding (due to globalization, for example), the agglomeration will tend to grow and differentiate internally via the division of labor. Third, increasing-returns effects embedded in traded and untraded interdependencies among producers will reinforce agglomeration and ensure that growth leads to more growth (cf. Romer 1986).

The superclusters that result from these processes are the core functional units of global city-regions. To be sure, large-scale urban or regional growth also brings a variety of negative externalities that (in the absence of remedial action) set in motion centrifugal tendencies. What we normally observe in response to this situation, however, is regulatory action on the part of local authorities to bring such externalities under at least approximate control.

As large-scale agglomeration occurs, diverse other outcomes result, underpinning the dynamics of convergence and growth. Among the more important are the formation of dense physical infrastructures typically supplied out of public funds as cities expand, the development of dense local labor markets and the concomitant emergence of extended webs of residential services, and the gradual consolidation of conventions and cultures that enhance the capacities of individuals to perform in the local economic environment (Storper 1997). Above all, agglomeration has many positive effects on the ability of cities to function as centers of learning, creativity, and innovation. Precisely because cities are transactions-intensive foci of many interdependent activities, they are also places in which new social encounters and experiences endlessly occur, and in which enormous quantities of information are daily created and circulated. These processes unfold informally in many small, unrecorded events and encounters, but they cumulatively function as important foundations of local innovative energy and successful entrepreneurial effort. They are all the more pervasive in large cities because of the countless kinds of interpersonal encounters that can occur, and out of which may flow serendipitous forms of creative action (Scott 1999). Large cities, as a result, are invariably important centers of resourcefulness and invention for all sectors of production (especially, perhaps, for the neoartisanal, fashion, and cultural-products industries that are to be found within them in increasingly significant concentrations).

Because of these processes, large cities or city-regions have become a more insistent element of the geographic landscape than at any previous time in history. Over the past few decades and across the globe, numerous urban centers have been transformed into superclusters whose extent and growth are due above all to the condition that many of the leading sectors of capitalism today are organized as intensely localized networks of producers with powerful endogenous growth mechanisms and an increasingly extended market reach.

The Political Order of Global City-Regions

The world system is thus in a state of rapid economic flux, leading to many adjustments in political geography. On the one side, profound economic changes are prompting diverse responses and experiments in regulatory coordination, from the global to the local. On the other side, the new regulatory institutions that are now beginning to assume clearer outline on the world map help channel economic development into spatial structures running parallel to the fourfold political hierarchy described earlier. While the political shifts occurring at each level in this hierarchy pose perplexing problems, the new global mosaic of city-regions is certainly one of the least well understood. Moreover, precisely because individual regional units are the basic motors of a rapidly globalizing production system, much is at stake as they sharpen their political identities and institutional foundations.

We may well ask how these regions are to be defined as political-*cum*-territorial units with greater or lesser powers of coordinated action. In many instances, of course, the boundaries of city-regions will tend to coincide with a preexisting metropolitan area. But how will these boundaries be drawn when several metropolitan areas lie in close proximity—as, for example, on the northeast seaboard of the United States? And how far into its hinterland will the political mandate of any city-region range? In fact, the final geographic shape of any given global city-region is apt to be indeterminate in a priori terms because so much depends on how adjacent territorial units interact politically, and on their ability or willingness to enter into durable political coalitions. That said, we can already see some of the outlines of things to come in the new regional government systems that are being put into place in a number of European countries and in the maneuvering (some of which may bear fruit, some of which will lead nowhere) that is currently gathering steam around prospective municipal alliances such as San Diego–Tijuana in the United States and Mexico, Cascadia in the northwestern United States and western Canada, the Trans–Manche region in northeast France, western Belgium and southeast England, Padania in northern Italy, Singapore–Johore–Batam, and Hong Kong–Shenzen. Some of these alliances involve cross-border agreements.

Much of the political change occurring in the world's large city-regions represents a search for structures of governance capable of securing and enhancing competitive advantage in a globalizing economic order. Agglomerated production systems are the arenas of region wide synergies, but because these synergies so frequently assume the guise of externalities, they will always exist in some suboptimal configuration as long as individual decisionmaking and action alone prevail in the economic sphere. These synergies have enormous relevance to the destinies of all the firms and workers in the immediate locality, and they assume dramatic importance in a world where the continued spatial extension of markets gives each city-region vastly expanded economic opportunities but where the same extension also greatly heightens outside economic threats. The economies of large city-regions are thus intrinsically overlain by a domain of collective order defined by these synergies, and this constitutes a crucial domain of social management. Such management may assume various institutional forms

such as agencies of local government, private–public partnerships, and civil associations. But it derives its force and legitimacy from the positive role that coordinating agencies can play by promoting and shaping critical increasing-returns effects that would otherwise fail to materialize or that would be susceptible to severe misallocation. The kinds of tasks that agencies such as these might perform include the fostering of agglomeration-specific technological research, providing high-risk capital to small start-up firms, protecting infant industries, upgrading workers' competencies, cultivating collaborative interfirm relationships, and promoting export markets for local products. There is also, of course, a continued urgent need for more traditional types of urban planning to ensure that periodic land use and transportation breakdowns do not cut too deeply into local economic performance and social life.

The prospect of a mosaic of global city-regions, each characterized by an activist collectivity seeking to reinforce local competitive advantage, brings up additional questions and problems. Rising levels of regional activism can destabilize and politicize interregional relations, both within and across national boundaries. Such predicaments are already manifest in the formation of regional alliances (such as the Four Motors of Europe Program and the recent linking of the London and Frankfurt stock exchanges), leading to complaints from outsiders about unfair competition.

Another predicament resides in attempts by representatives of some regions to lure assets of others into their own geographic orbit, often at heavy social cost. Similar problems ensue when different regions push to secure a decisive lead as the dominant center of some budding industry. These interregional collisions also afford multinational corporations expanding opportunities to play one region off against another in competitive bidding wars for new direct investments, a phenomenon particularly pronounced in contemporary Brazil (Rodríguez-Pose and Tomaney 1999).

As the new regionalism takes deeper hold, stresses and strains of these types are likely to be magnified, and a need for action at the national, plurinational, and eventually global levels of political coordination is foreseeable to establish ground rules for interregional relations (including aid to failing regions) and to provide forums for interregional problem solving. The European Committee of the Regions, established under the terms of the Maastricht Treaty, may represent an early expression of this dawning imperative.

A further question arises as to what macropolitical or ideological formations will provide a framework for the institution-building and policymaking projects that can now be ever more strongly envisioned at different spatial levels. Giddens (1998) has forcefully argued that two main political principles appear to be fighting for position, certainly in the more economically advanced parts of the globe. One is the dominant neoliberal view prescribing minimum government interference in, and maximum market organization of, economic activity—a view that is sometimes erroneously considered to be an inescapable counterpart of globalization. In light of the pressing need for collective action in global city-regions (not to mention other domains of economic activity), neoliberalism, certainly in the version that crudely advocates laissez-faire as a universal panacea, seems to offer a seriously deficient political vision. The other approach is a renascent social democracy, which, especially in Western Europe, has enjoyed notable electoral success of late. On the economic front, social democracy is prepared to acknowledge and work with the efficiency-seeking properties of markets where these are consistent with standards of social fairness and long-term economic well-being, but to intervene selectively where they are not. A social democratic politics would seem to be well armed to build the social infrastructures and enabling conditions at every geographic level, which are becoming more critical to high levels of economic performance. At the city-region level, in particular, these tasks can be identified with the compelling need to promote local levels of efficiency, productivity, and competitiveness that markets alone can never fully secure.

There is a further argument in favor of a social democratic approach to the governance of global city-regions, one that is associated with the need for remedial collective action in local economic affairs, but that also goes well beyond this particular objective. Issues of representation and distributional impact are always in play in any political community, especially where social management of the local economy is under way (Mouffe 1992). The question of local democratic practice and how to establish effective forums for popular participation is inescapably linked to the more technocratic issues raised by the challenges of economic governance in global city-regions.

This question takes on special urgency in view of the role of large global city-regions as magnets for low-wage immigrants, many undocumented, with significant segments of their populations often composed of marginalized and politically dispossessed individuals. Beyond considerations of equity and social justice, enlarging the sphere of democratic practice is an important practical means of registering and dealing with the social tensions that invariably occur in dense social communities. The mobilization of voice in such communities is an important first step in constructively treating their internal dysfunctionalities. Large city-regions, with their rising levels of social distress resulting from globalization, confront urgent political challenges in this regard, not only because their internal conviviality is in jeopardy, but also because any failure to act is likely to undermine the effectiveness of purely economic strategies.

From all of this, it follows that some reconsideration of the everyday notion of citizenship is long overdue. An alternative definition of citizenship, one more fully in harmony with the unfolding new world system, would presumably assign basic political entitlements and obligations to individuals not so much as an absolute birthright, but as a function of their changing allegiances in different geographic contexts. In fact, traditional conceptions of the citizen and citizenship are vigorously in question at each geographic level of the world system, for we all simultaneously participate in local, national, plurinational, and global communities. Perhaps nowhere is the urge to participate more immediate or pressing than in the case of large global city-regions (cf. Holston 2000; Keating 2000). Even though only a few tentative and pioneering instances of pertinent reforms are as yet in evidence in such regions (the case of Amsterdam being perhaps the most advanced), increasing numbers of experiments in local political enfranchisement will no doubt proceed as city-regions start to deal seriously with the new economic and political realities that they face. In a world where mobility is continually increasing, individuals may one day freely acquire citizenship in large city-regions many times over, in conjunction with their movements from place to place over the course of their lifetimes.

Coda

Globalization has potentially both a dark, regressive side and a more hopeful, progressive side. If the analysis presented here turns out to be broadly correct, then the views expressed in some quarters that deepening globalization is a retrograde step for the masses of humanity can be taken as a warning about a possible future world—but by no means as a representation of *all* possible future worlds. Insistent globalization under the aegis of a triumphant neoliberalism would no doubt constitute something close to a worst-case scenario, leading to rising social inequalities and tensions within city-regions and greater discrepancies in growth rates and development potentials among them. Alternative and realistic possibilities can be advanced, however, and I have tried to sketch out some of them here. Globalization, indeed, is the potential bearer of significant social benefits. At this stage in history its future course is open-ended, and it will certainly be subject in the future to many different kinds of political contestation, some of which will mold it in decisive ways. In particular, globalization raises important new questions about economic governance and regulation at all spatial levels, and some form of social market politics seems to offer a viable, fair, and persuasive way of facing these questions.

I have said little or nothing in this account about the less-developed countries, but I see no reason—with due acknowledgment of the enormous difficulties posed by the vicious circles in which they are often caught—why at least some of them cannot benefit from the processes of urbanization and economic growth brought into focus here. These processes suggest that some of the more urbanized regions in these countries will eventually join the expanding mosaic of global city-regions, just as Seoul, Taipei, Hong Kong, Singapore, Mexico City, São Paulo, and others have done, and are doing, before them.

Bibliography

Badie, B. 1995. *La Fin des Territoires: Essai sur le Désordre International et sur l'Utilité Sociale du Respect.* Paris: Fayard.

Castells, M. 1996. *The Rise of the Network Society.* Oxford: Blackwell.

Cooke, P. N., and K. Morgan. 1998. *The Associational Economy: Firms, Regions, and Innovation.* Oxford: Oxford University Press.

Friedmann, J., and G. Wolff. 1982. "World City Formation: An Agenda for Research and Action." *International Journal of Urban and Regional Research* 6: 309–44.

Giddens, A. 1998. *The Third Way: The Renewal of Social Democracy.* Cambridge: Polity Press.

Hall, P. G. 1966. *The World Cities.* London: Weidenfeld and Nicolson.

Hirst, P., and G. Thompson. 1996. *Globalization in Question.* Cambridge: Polity Press.

Holston, J. 2000. "Urban Citizenship and Globalization." In A. J. Scott, ed., *Global City-Regions.* Oxford: Oxford University Press.

Keating, M. 2000. "Governing Cities and Regions: Territorial Reconstruction in a Global Age." In A. J. Scott, ed., *Global City-Regions.* Oxford: Oxford University Press.

Knox, P. L. 1995. "World Cities and the Organization of Global Space." In R. J. Johnston, P. J. Taylor, and M. J. Watts, eds., *Geographies of Global Change: Remapping the World in the Late Twentieth Century,* pp. 232–47. Oxford: Blackwell.

Krugman, P. 1996. *Pop Internationalism.* Cambridge, MA: MIT Press.

Mouffe, C. 1992. "Democratic Citizenship and Political Community." In C. Mouffe, ed., *Dimensions of Radical Democracy,* pp. 225–39. London: Verso.

O'Brien, R. 1992. *Global Financial Integration: The End of Geography.* London: Pinter.

Porter, M. 2000. "Regions and the New Economics of Competition." In A. J. Scott, ed., *Global City-Regions.* Oxford: Oxford University Press.

Rodríguez-Pose, A., and J. Tomaney. 1999. "Industrial Crisis in the Centre of the Periphery: Stabilisation, Economic Restructuring and Policy Responses in the São Paulo Metropolitan Region." *Urban Studies* 36: 479–98.

Romer, P. M. 1986. "Increasing Returns and Long-run Growth." *Journal of Political Economy* 94: 1002–37.

Sassen, S. 1991. *The Global City: New York, London, Tokyo.* Princeton: Princeton University Press.

Scott, A. J. 1988. *New Industrial Spaces: Flexible Production Organization and Regional Development in North America and Western Europe.* London: Pion.

Scott, A. J. 1998. *Regions and the World Economy: The Coming Shape of Global Production, Competition, and Political Order.* Oxford: Oxford University Press.

Scott, A. J. 1999. "The Cultural Economy: Geography and the Creative Field." *Media, Culture and Society* 21: 807–17.

Storper, M. 1997. *The Regional World: Territorial Development in a Global Economy.* New York: Guilford Press.

Storper, M., and S. Christopherson. 1987. "Flexible Specialization and Regional Industrial Agglomerations: The Case of the U.S. Motion-Picture Industry." *Annals of the Association of American Geographers* 77: 260–82.

Swyngedouw, E. 1997. "Neither Global nor Local: Globalization and the Politics of Scale." In K. R. Cox, ed., *Spaces of Globalization: Reasserting the Power of the Local,* pp. 137–66. New York: The Guilford Press.

Taylor, P. J. 2000. "World Cities and Territorial States under Conditions of Contemporary Globalization." *Political Geography* 19: 5–32.

United Nations. 1995. *World Urbanization Prospects: The 1994 Revision.* New York: United Nations.

Veltz, P. 1996. *Mondialisation, Villes et Territoires: L'Economie d'Archipel.* Paris: Presses Universitaires de France.

Wallerstein, I. 1979. *The Capitalist World Economy.* Cambridge: Cambridge University Press.

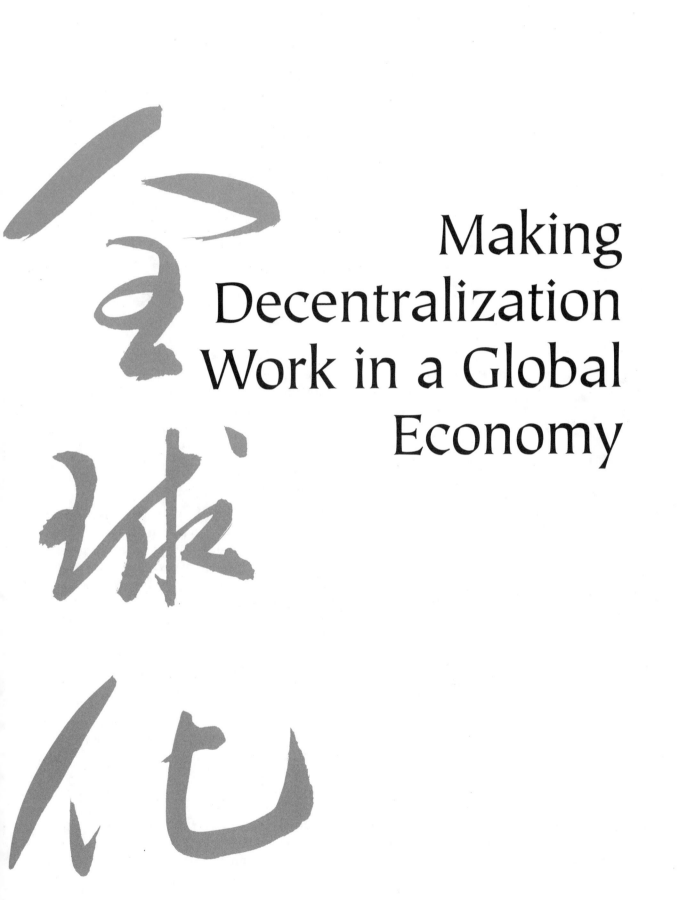

Making Decentralization Work in a Global Economy

chapter 11

How to Design a Fiscal Decentralization Program

Roy Bahl

Dean of the Andrew Young School of Policy Studies
Georgia State University

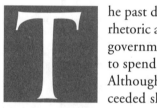he past decade has been replete with rhetoric about endowing subnational governments with more autonomy to spend as well as collect revenues. Although decentralization has proceeded slowly, more and more governments around the world are coming to power on a platform of citizen participation, and decentralization is becoming difficult to resist. One important lesson of the past two decades, learned especially well in East Asia, is that strong central governments cannot sustain themselves without granting appropriate decisionmaking autonomy to their subnational governments. Economic development has also dramatically improved the capabilities of local governments, and recognition is growing that granting local governments some autonomy is preferable to breaking up nation–states into smaller entities. Yet even as signs appear that some countries are ready to move forward, poorly conceived decentralization policies could prevent progress.

The major problems with most decentralization programs are, first, that the government is often committed more in rhetoric than in fact, and second, that the design is usually too narrow and does not focus on all of the components. These are of course related issues because to do fiscal decentralization "right," a major shift in the balance of fiscal power is involved. The tendency in too many countries is to take a much narrower view in order to escape most of the hard decisions about reassigning tax, expenditure, borrowing, and budgetary powers.

But suppose a country did want to implement a program that would pass significant fiscal powers to subnational governments, in the context of the new global economy. How would it design such a program to have maximum chances for success? This chapter offers a set of normative guidelines about the design for a comprehensive fiscal decentralization program.[1]

Guideline 1. Consider all three levels of government.

A key issue is whether a central government's decentralization program will include local as well as state governments.[2] There are good arguments that it should. In some countries provincial governments are too large to allow citizen participation and ensure that voters will hold government officials accountable, so fiscal decentralization must include a lower level of government. For example, eight Chinese provinces have populations of more than 50 million, which would rank them among the 20 largest countries in the world.

While it is essential that the lower tiers of government be explicitly recognized as a component of the fiscal decentralization program, there are choices about how this should be done. The most common arrangement is for each province to define the intergovernmental fiscal relations with its local governments (as in Russia and the United States). A second approach, preferred by centralists, would require all provincial governments to mandate a nationally uniform set of relations with their local governments. A third approach, growing out of some suspicion that provincial or state governments will not "do the right thing," involves the central government prescribing safeguards to protect the rights of local governments (for example, in India, Nigeria, and the United States in the 1970s).

Guideline 2. Match the fiscal system to the administrative capacity of local governments.

Many countries believe that effective decentralization requires giving uniform powers and responsibilities to all subnational governments. However, local and even provincial governments vary widely in their capacity to deliver and finance services, and thus may not fit well into a uniform system of taxing, spending, and borrowing powers. In fact, the decentralization process may work best if larger local governments are assigned significant fiscal powers at the outset while smaller ones grow into it. Kenya, for example, classifies municipal governments and gives them differential fiscal powers, and many U.S. states distinguish among local governments in terms of the taxing powers they assign to them.

Guideline 3. Ensure that central governments keep the fiscal decentralization rules they set.

Provincial and local officials in many countries believe that the central government will not hand over funds when times are hard, nor will it honor its pledge to permit local autonomy. In fact, central governments oftentimes do violate or compromise the principles they establish. There are few developing or transition countries that cannot recite instances of "broken promises" by central governments. Examples of such behavior include:

- Imposing unfunded mandates on subnational governments
- Underfunding promised revenue transfers to subnational governments
- Reassigning expenditures without reassigning revenues
- Abolishing or restricting subnational government taxes.

If decentralization is to have a chance, the central government must adhere to the rules it sets. The President and the Parliament must guarantee that fiscal promises are kept. This means that central governments must take care to design programs that include only those fiscal promises that can be kept. Otherwise, subnational governments will build this uncertainty into their fiscal decisionmaking process, and the result may be inefficient budgetary planning and actions based on the perception of a soft budget constraint.

Guideline 4. Maintain a strong central ability to monitor and evaluate decentralization.

Despite the need for flexibility in adapting plans to local conditions, central governments will have to impose a uniform system of financial accounts and audit rules, and at least set disclosure requirements for governments that borrow. Central governments must also provide technical assistance to local governments in accounting, treasury, tax administration, data processing, and project evaluation. A corollary to the guideline just outlined is that the central government will make the rules of decentralization, and they must also monitor the subnational governments to make sure the rules are obeyed.

Because developing and transition countries are by definition changing rapidly, the intergovernmental system will also change. A central fiscal monitoring system must be in place to guide restructuring of the grant system, detect early warning signs of cities in financial trouble, monitor borrowing limits, decide when a local government is ready to graduate to the next level of autonomy, and so on. There is also a need to set up special provisions to assist subnational governments facing fiscal distress (for example, financial control boards as are being set up in South Africa) or mechanisms of intergovernmental assistance to cover debt service costs, as are being used in some Latin American countries.

Guideline 5. Impose a hard budget constraint on local governments.

Provincial and local governments must balance their budgets without any end-of-year assistance from the central government. This guideline is particularly important because fiscal discipline will occur only if subnational governments believe they are on their own. Enemies of this rule include year-end grants to cover revenue shortfalls or project overruns, and bailouts of subnational governments that are delinquent on debt payments. A good case in point is the Russian regional governments, where some intergovernmental transfers from the center are not known until the end of the fiscal year, and even then are determined partly on an ad hoc basis. This lack of transparency leads to a dependence of the lower level governments on the center to provide the regular "bailout" (Bahl et al. 1999).

The absence of a hard budget constraint on local governments has important consequences. First, the consolidated government deficit will be higher because subnational governments will have an incentive to overspend. Second, increased tax effort by subnational governments will be discouraged. Finally, subnational government officials will be held less accountable by their constituents for imprudent fiscal behavior because the national government will also be seen as culpable.

Guideline 6. Assign local governments significant taxing powers.

Voters will hold their elected officials more accountable if local governments finance services largely through local taxes rather than transfers of funds from the central government. It is important that these local taxes be (a) visible to local voters, (b) large enough to impose a noticeable burden, and (c) not easily exported to residents of other jurisdictions. Nuisance taxes and minor levies, the preference of many centralists for assignment to subnational governments, will not lead to adequate accountability of government officials. Those who say that the feasible set of provincial and local government taxes is very limited are mistaken, as is suggested by the following list and discussion of possible subnational government revenue sources (Bahl and Linn 1992; Bird 1999).

Individual income taxes are a good choice for subnational governments, either as a piggyback on the national income tax or as a standalone tax on local payrolls. Local income taxes fulfill the criteria for an appropriate tax: Local residents shoulder the burden and administration is feasible.

Taxes on foreign trade and taxes on corporate income do not meet the exportability and "easy administration" tests, and thus are probably a poor choice for subnational governments. Few developing countries allow subnational governments much discretion in setting the rate and base of the company income tax.

General sales taxes have always been thought a difficult choice for subnational governments, either because of administrative difficulties or because the tax burden would be exported. However, there is now a flurry of interest in subnational value-added taxes, for example, at the state level in India (Bird and Gendron, 1998). McLure (1999) reviews the administrative arrangements under which a broad-based VAT could work at the subnational level (a nationally uniform tax base and a well-functioning VAT operating at the central government level). Many developing and transition countries also find *retail sales taxes* impractical because of the difficulty of collecting taxes from small vendors. However, in Russia, for example, some regional governments impose retail sales taxes on big-ticket luxury items. Other countries, including the Philippines and South Africa, target the retail sector by taxing businesses' gross sales.

Excise taxes can be an appropriate state and local revenue source—but not on goods for which a natural monopoly exists, for example, petroleum production, possibly beer and cigarette producers, and some natural resources. That's because taxing monopoly goods would impose a burden on people who do not gain the benefits derived from the public services supported by the tax. Revenues from monopolies that happen to locate in their districts thus encourage those provincial or local governments to overspend.

Taxes related to the use of *motor vehicles*—such as license fees, tolls, parking taxes, and taxes on motor fuels—are an excellent revenue source for subnational governments because they fall on people who reap the benefits, and they are relatively easy to administer (Bahl and Linn, 1992). A local tax on motor fuel, for example, especially in urban areas, can charge motorists for the marginal costs of the congestion and pollution they generate and the road services they use. The *property tax*, on which local governments in most countries rely, is also a quasibenefit tax in that it is used to provide services to property owners and occupants. What's more, the tax is highly visible in the local area, its burden is not easily exported to outside residents, and it allows local assessors to identify and tax local wealth.

Finally, *user charges* for local services are especially appropriate because governments can determine the costs of many such services and fully recover them—or privatize the services.

To further enhance the ability of state and local governments to raise revenues, central governments should provide incentives for them to *borrow* funds to finance major infrastructure projects and other long-lived capital assets. The duration of bonds used to finance these projects should match the expected life of the assets. However, if provincial and local governments are to be given borrowing powers and some degree of autonomy, then central governments need to lay down strict rules about the conditions under which such borrowing can take place, including disclosure requirements, senior claims, and actions that may be taken in the event of nonpayment.[3]

Guideline 7. Match the system for transferring funds between central and local governments to the goals of decentralization.

Despite the theoretical appeal of provincial and local taxation, revenue transfers from national to state and local governments are often the most important decentralization tools. Each system for transferring funds has different impacts on local governments, yet countries often design their grants without fully exploring those impacts.[4]

The impacts of such transfers depend on two factors: how the central government determines the total resource pool, and how it distributes this pool among local governments. International practice suggests three basic approaches to the former (see the column headings in Table 11.1). Once the size of the pool is determined, developing countries and transition economies typically use four methods to allocate the funds (see the row headings in Table 11.1). This taxonomy yields 12 potential grant types (Bahl and Linn 1992).

Consider the shared tax column in Table 11.1. Under a *type A* grant, the subnational government is allowed to

Table 11.1
Forms of Intergovernmental Grant Programs

Method of allocating the pool	Method of determining the total divisible pool[a]		
	Specified share of national or state tax	Ad hoc decision	Reimbursement of approved expenditures
Regional or local origin of collections	A	E	n.a.
Formula	B	F	n.a.
Total or partial reimbursement of costs	C	G	K
Ad hoc	D	H	n.a.

n.a. Not applicable.
[a]Grant types are described in the text.
Source: Bahl and Linn (1992).

keep a share of national taxes collected within its boundaries. Most transition economies and many developing countries use this approach.[5] Under a *type B* grant, a formula governs the distribution of a defined amount of national taxes among local governments. For example, the Philippines distributes 40 percent of nationally collected revenue among local governments on the basis of population, land area, and an equal share for each recipient. Under *type C* grants, a fixed percentage of a national tax reimburses local governments for the costs of public projects or needs such as teachers' salaries.

The second column in Table 11.1 lists types of grants awarded after an ad hoc political decision—such as a yearly budget process—establishes the total pool of funds. Under a *type H* grant, the central government makes all decisions concerning which entities receive the funds and how much. Under *type E, F,* and *G,* the central government distributes grants according to objective criteria. The *type G* grant is conditional, while the others are not.

Under a *type K* grant in the third column, a central ministry decides the amount of funding local governments will need to pursue specific projects and whether they meet prescribed eligibility requirements. Examples include grants for infrastructure projects, teachers' salaries, and transfers to individuals to cover income maintenance costs.

These very different types of grants exert very different effects. *Type A* and *B* grants are arguably the most decentralizing because they guarantee local governments a specified share of national revenue and usually carry no conditions. However, even these two transfers have very different impacts. The *type A* grant favors subnational governments with strong tax bases, whereas the *type B* grant can redistribute funds to subnational governments according to the local characteristics that the central government most wants to reward. The ad hoc transfers are the most centralizing because they allow the

national government maximum flexibility in deciding how much to distribute to the local public sector each year. The *type C, G, and K* grants are also centralizing in that they give central government ministries significant control over how money will be spent and allow them to establish standards for construction projects, salary rates, and delivery of services.

Countries often mix these grant types, with the result that some grants in the system are decentralizing and some are centralizing, some are equalizing and some are counterequalizing, some encourage increased tax effort while others discourage it, and so forth. The potential for such offsetting effects is a very important problem in grant design and one that few countries have been able to avoid.

Guideline 8. Keep it simple.

Provincial and local administrators often cannot handle complicated arrangements for intergovernmental transfers that impose significant compliance requirements on them, nor can they meet the requirements of complicated expenditure mandates or collect taxes with complicated definitions of the tax base. It is well to remember that central governments may add to their own problems by designing an intergovernmental fiscal system that they cannot monitor or support. Well-meaning policy analysts often introduce complexities such as:

- Complicated formulas and conditions for allocating grants that require provincial and local governments to supply demographic and economic information that they do not have or that impose heavy costs on the central agency that must allocate the funds and monitor the compliance.
- Local taxes structured to accomplish goals other than revenue raising, for example, property taxes that include special provisions to encourage homeownership

or suburban locations, or to subsidize the construction of certain types of buildings.

■ Expenditure mandates that are difficult to monitor and with which are difficult to comply. For example, requirements that x rubles per patient be spent on hospital meals or that classrooms be built to certain specifications and be used in only certain ways.

This is not to say that simplicity alone should drive intergovernmental reform. Some complicated rules are essential, such as establishing disclosure requirements for governments that borrow funds, and establishing uniform accounting systems and auditing procedures. But the objective should be to limit the goals that each policy instrument is designed to accomplish and to consider the administrative capacity of both the central and the subnational governments. Simpler arrangements will reduce the resources that provincial and local governments must allocate to administration as well as lower monitoring and evaluation costs for the central government.

Guideline 9. Recognize and plan for the fact that intergovernmental systems are always in transition.

Regional disparities, infrastructure quality, investment priorities, and local capacity all change over time. Fiscal decentralization programs must be designed to accommodate these changes. A major factor that will affect decentralization is the global economy. Provincial and local governments, especially those in large urban areas, will increasingly be able to tax a base of industry that is easier to assess and collect, but is more footloose. It also will face more demands for workforce development and for developing an IT infrastructure. Giving subnational governments the ability to respond to these new needs is a major challenge in designing a fiscal decentralization policy. Central governments must therefore keep their decentralization plans flexible while also transparent— that is, the process by which the system changes should be open and obvious. Possible approaches include:

■ Establishing a commission that reviews the allocation of intergovernmental transfers every few years and recommends changes. This approach is flexible yet enables local governments to plan their finances over a multiyear period. Australia and India follow such an approach.

■ Allowing changes in the local tax structure to reflect economic changes. As some areas develop and urbanize, for example, they may piggyback new local taxes onto central revenue collections, tax sectors such as the self-employed and small shops, or impose dedicated revenue raisers such as tolls or special land as-

sessments. Central governments should encourage such improvements in tax structure.

■ Providing a specified timetable for review to determine whether a subnational government can graduate to the next level of fiscal autonomy.

■ Minimizing the degree to which the detail of the fiscal decentralization program is laid down in the constitution.

Guideline 10. Approach fiscal decentralization as a comprehensive system.

Piecemeal reform encompassing only one element of a decentralized system, such as revenue sharing between central and subnational governments, is not likely to succeed. As is noted in Table 11.2, there are many dimensions to a fiscal decentralization plan, beginning with the need for a popularly elected local government and a locally appointed administration. Without this feature, accountability will be "up" to the higher-level government rather than "down" to the voters, and the potential gains from fiscal decentralization are not likely to be realized. It is essential that those making the plan for fiscal decentralization have all of the necessary components involved in the discussion.

Guideline 11. Build an internal champion.

Fiscal decentralization often has involved more rhetoric than action in developing and transition countries because some interest groups must give up power. However, successful decentralization requires a strong domestic champion who understands the costs and benefits for those who must approve and implement the system. A "scorecard" that might help in identifying the potential champions is presented in Table 11.3.

Table 11.2
The Components of a System of Fiscal Decentralization

Necessary conditions	Desirable conditions
• Elected local council	• Freedom from excessive central expenditure mandates
• Locally appointed chief officers	• Unconditional transfers from higher-level governments
• Significant local government discretion to raise revenue	• Local borrowing powers
• Significant local government expenditure responsibilities	
• Budget autonomy	
• A hard budget constraint	
• Transparency	

Table 11.3
The Champions of Fiscal Decentralization

Potentially Strong Supporters	Comments
The people	Often demand more participation in governance at the local level.
The president	Because decentralization is popular the president often supports it, but must be very mindful of national stability as that affects his or her political standing.
The Parliament or Congress	Members would like to claim credit for specific local projects, so they will favor a less transparent, more ad hoc system.
Urban local governments	Urban local governments want to expand their autonomy and gain access to their tax base.
External donors	They provide encouragement and some technical assistance but are no substitute for an in-country champion.
Potentially Weak Supporters	
Ministry of finance	To stabilize a country's economy, these officials want to continue the ministry's hold on fiscal tools and strictly limit decentralization.
Ministry of economy	These officials want to control how and where a country invests its revenues. They are typically interested in programs with national payoff rather than local benefits.
Line ministries	These officials would like to control standards for delivery of public services, and often like to approve transfers of funds to local governments.
Ambivalent Supporters	
Local government	These officials favor a guaranteed share of revenues for local governments and want to control their distribution.
Weaker local governments	These officials would like a guaranteed transfer of resources from urban and wealthier local governments. More interested in a transfer system than in local taxation.

Conclusion

Fiscal decentralization has not yet become the centerpiece of economic development programs that many expected. The advantages of centralization and the political power of the centralists have been too strong. But as the world changes, the case for decentralization becomes more and more irresistible. It may be slowed by an unstable world economy, as the East Asian crisis demonstrated, but its time may have come. Governments around the world are increasingly elected, and increasingly on a platform of citizen participation in governance, economic development has eroded some of the arguments in favor of fiscal centralization, and the service delivery capabilities of local governments have improved dramatically. Moreover, much of the world has come to see that granting some form of local autonomy is better than separatism as a policy direction. The greater enemy of progress now is poorly conceived decentralization policies. Design must match objectives, and implementation must face up to the many dimensions of decentralization. This chapter has been an attempt to stimulate that discussion.

Bibliography

Bahl, Roy W. 1999. *Taxation and Intergovernmental Fiscal Relations in China.* Ann Arbor, MI: The 1990 Institute and the University of Michigan Press.

Bahl, Roy W. 1999a. *Implementation Rules for Fiscal Decentralization, Working Paper No. 10.* International Studies Program, Andrew Young School of Policy Studies, Georgia State University.

Bahl, Roy W. 1999b. "Fiscal Decentralization as Development Policy." In *Public Budgeting and Finance,* pp. 59–75, Summer.

Bahl, Roy W., Galina Kouriandskaia, John Mikesell, Sally Wallace, Natalia Golovanova, Dmitry Shiskin, Andre Timofeev, Alexander Derugin, Yelena Nikolayenko, Inna Verbina, and Natasha Minkova. 1999. "Intergovernmental Fiscal Relations in Leningrad Region." International Studies Program, Andrew Young School of Policy Studies, Georgia State University.

Bahl, Roy W., and Johannes Linn. 1983. "The Assignment of Local Government Revenues in Developing Countries." In Charles E. McLure, Jr., ed., *Tax Assignment in Federal Countries.* Canberra: Centre for Research on Federal Financial Relations, Australian National University.

Bahl, Roy W., and Johannes Linn. 1992. *Urban Public Finance in Developing Countries.* New York: Oxford University Press.

Bird, Richard M. 1999. "Rethinking Subnational Taxes: A New Look at Tax Assignment." Working Paper, International Monetary Fund (IMF) Fiscal Affairs Department.

Bird, Richard, and Pierre-Pascal Gendron. 1998. "Dual VATS and Cross-Border Trade: Two Problems, One Solution?" *International Tax and Public Finance* 5: 429–42.

Bird, Richard M., Robert D. Ebel, and Christine I. Wallich, eds. 1995. *Decentralization of the Socialist State.* A Regional and Sectoral Study, Washington, D.C.: World Bank.

Bird, Richard M., and Francois Vaillancourt, eds. 1998. *Fiscal Decentralization in Developing Countries.* Cambridge: Cambridge University Press.

Dillinger, William. 1994. *Decentralization and Its Implications for Urban Service Delivery.* Urban Management Program Series 16, Washington, D.C.: World Bank.

Dillinger, William. 1991. *Urban Property Tax Reform: Guidelines and Recommendations.* Urban Management Program Discussion Paper Series 1. Washington, D.C.: World Bank.

IADB (Inter-American Development Bank). 1997. *Latin America After A Decade of Reforms: Economic and Social Progress.* Baltimore, MD: Johns Hopkins University Press.

Litvack, Jennie, Junaid Ahmad, and Richard Bird. 1998. *Rethinking Decentralization in Developing Countries*. A Sector Studies Series. Washington, D.C.: World Bank.

Martinez-Vazquez, Jorge, and Robert McNab. Forthcoming. "The Tax Reform Experiment in Transitional Economies." *National Tax Journal*.

McLure, Charles. 1999. "Implementing Subnational Value Added Taxes on Internal Trade: The Compensating VAT." Unpublished paper, The Hoover Institution.

McLure, Charles E., Jr., Jorge Martinez-Vazquez, and Sally Wallace. 1999. *Fiscal Transition in Kazakhstan*. Manila: Asian Development Bank.

Peterson, George. 1999. "Building Local Credit Systems." Urban Management and Municipal Finance Program Paper 25. Washington D.C.: World Bank.

Prud'homme, Remy. 1995. "The Dangers of Decentralization." *The World Bank Research Observer* 10(2): 201–20.

Spahn, P. Bernd. 1997. "Decentralized Government and Macroeconomic Control." Paper prepared for the International Institute of Public Finance 53rd Congress (August, 1998), Kyoto, Japan.

Tanzi, Vito. 1996. "Fiscal Federalism and Decentralization: A Review of Some Efficiency and Macroeconomic Aspects." In Michael Bruno and Boris Pleskovic, eds., *Annual World Bank Conference on Development Economics 1995*. Washington, D.C.: World Bank.

Wong, Christine. 1995. "Overview of Issues in Local Public Finance in the PRC." In Christine Wong, ed., *Financing Local Government in the People's Republic of China*, Manila: Asian Development Bank.

Notes

1. A much longer discussion of these rules appears in two recent papers, Bahl, 1999a, 1999b.

2. Some countries transfer funds among more than three levels. In the Philippines, the central government explicitly includes submunicipal Baranguays in the grant distribution system.

3. For a thorough discussion of borrowing by local governments, see Peterson (1999).

4. The definition of an intergovernmental transfer is often debated. While grants to lower-level governments are clearly intergovernmental transfers, confusion arises in the case of taxes and tax expenditures. If the local government can control either the rate or base of a levy, it is a tax. If the rate and base are determined by the higher-level government and revenue collections are assigned to the local government, it is a transfer. If the central government allows deductibility of property taxes from central income tax liability, this is also a form of transfer.

5. For a discussion of shared taxes in transition countries, see Bahl (1999), Martinez-Vazquez and McNab (forthcoming), and Bird, Ebel, and Wallich (1995). The sharing of revenues derived from the taxation of natural resources is a special case of shared taxes.

chapter 12

Strategic Fiscal Decentralization in Developing Countries: Learning from Recent Innovations

Paul Smoke

International Development and Regional Planning Program
Department of Urban Studies and Planning
Massachusetts Institute of Technology

iscal decentralization emerged as one of the most pervasive global development trends of the 1990s. Rapid economic, political, and technological changes—along with disappointing and uneven progress in meeting key public sector objectives—have forced many countries to think beyond traditional top-down approaches to development and to rely more heavily on lower levels of government.[1]

Conventional theory and some limited empirical evidence suggest various potential benefits of fiscal decentralization.[2] Some analysts, however, caution that decentralization may result in negative macroeconomic effects, diminished opportunities for interregional redistribution, and other possible problems.[3] In fact, fiscal decentralization is neither inherently desirable nor undesirable—the appropriate degree and form depends on the context of a particular country. A common failure to recognize this reality has resulted in many unsuccessful or disappointing reform efforts. With few exceptions, the academic literature and development agency publications are dominated by reports of weak local governments and costly fiscal decentralization programs that have made only modest progress toward meeting their goals.[4] Even cases cited as successful typically focus on the importance of "good leadership" or "effective stakeholder participation" without providing much insight about how these mechanisms work or how other countries can replicate them.

Barriers to Reform

Several key factors underlie the modest performance of fiscal decentralization programs in developing countries.

Reform Origins: Many recent fiscal decentralization programs have been undertaken in response to economic and political difficulties, commonly under pressure from international development agencies. The perceived urgency results in programs that are hastily defined and initiated without developing a minimum enabling framework or carefully thinking through implementation requirements. Such programs tend to be superficial, focusing on textbook solutions derived from the fiscal federalism literature.[5] This literature provides a useful analytical entry point, but its development in the context of industrialized countries suggests a need for careful reflection in applying it to developing countries.[6]

Reformers preoccupied with normative models and rapid results fail to recognize that attitudes concerning the way the public sector works change slowly. Central officials are commonly used to making major fiscal decisions unilaterally and controlling local authorities extensively. Local governments are often comfortable with central subsidization, and they may not feel particularly accountable to the electorate. Finally, local government constituents are often not accustomed to paying for services or to expecting much from local governments. Such mindsets and resulting patterns of behavior require years and careful planning to change.

Institutional Realities: The institutional environment in which decentralization and local government reform programs must be implemented suffers from a number of weaknesses that hinder success.[7] First, systems, procedures, incentives, and capacity tend to be inadequate at all levels of government. Good performance is often not well defined or rewarded, poor performance is rarely punished, and job satisfaction is often low.[8]

Second, the institutional framework in which decentralization must be designed and implemented is complex and poorly coordinated. Most developing countries appoint a central agency to oversee local governments, but powerful coordinating ministries, such as Planning and Finance, often have greater control over decentralization. Key sectoral ministries—public works, transport, health, education, energy, and so on—also typically have some jurisdiction over local services under their general expertise. The situation is particularly problematic when responsibilities are dispersed across several powerful agencies with different views of what decentralization means.

Third, whatever the economic and political impetus to decentralize, there are rarely strong bureaucratic incentives to do so.[9] Central ministries generally do not want to decentralize major responsibilities, thereby undermining their own control over substantial resources. They also tend to protect their own institutional interests as reforms proceed, complicating coordination.

Fourth, well-developed local government accountability to a constituency is rare in developing countries, although generally better in Latin America.[10] Even where local councils are elected, they may not be genuinely autonomous or adequately empowered, and they may be dominated by local elites. In any case, local accountability means little if the center can override the results of local democratic processes, which often occurs in developing countries.

Structure of Decentralization Initiatives: Decentralization initiatives can generally be classified as two types. The first is unworkably comprehensive, overwhelming technical capacity at all levels and threatening bureaucratic and political tolerance at the center.[11] The second is unduly limited, focusing on narrow technical activities that are not conceived as part of a broader fiscal reform agenda.[12] Neither comprehensive nor limited reforms take into adequate account the wider scope of bottlenecks previously discussed that make institutional change so difficult. To complicate matters, many initiatives are led by a single central agency perceived as a rival by other agencies whose cooperation is required for successful decentralization.

Another serious design concern is that decentralization programs tend to treat all local governments (or classes—large urban, small urban, rural, and so on) as similar in capacity and staffing. Treating those with weak capacity as if they can handle new responsibilities invites failure. Providing technical assistance to those that do not need it wastes resources. Standardized decentralization programs that have similar expectations of all local governments also tend to define performance in terms of rigid technocratic steps. The circumstances under which local staff function, however, can differ widely, so that standardization may prevent them from achieving key objectives rather than helping them to do so.

A final structural weakness of many recent decentralization programs is their excessive focus on greater consultation with the consumers of public services. Few development analysts would deny the need to increase citizen participation and to improve accountability, but a demand-side emphasis without adequate consideration of supply-side deficiencies in public service provision is unlikely to improve performance.

International Agency Objectives: The interests of international donors are not necessarily well served by decentralization. For reasons already outlined, such efforts are time-consuming and difficult, and, therefore, likely to cause substantial delays in donor efforts to start new projects and to move funds. Given spending pressures, substantial donor funds continue to flow for decentralization, even if recipient governments do not have the capacity to ensure that the funds will yield sustainable benefits.

A second concern is that donors often try to avoid the complexities of cross-donor and sectoral coordination by limiting their decentralization support to particular sectors or local units. Since donors tend to adopt their own individualized systems and procedures, the process of building a consistent intergovernmental system may be hindered by such fragmentation. Moreover, because donors often develop individual client relationships with rival ministries or local governments, they may exacerbate competition. Donor agencies recognize the need to focus more on institution building than on moving money, and they also support coordination. To date, however, there has been only limited concrete action on these fronts.

Recent Cases of Improved Performance and Innovation

Although the barriers outlined here may seem overwhelming, a number of countries have been managed to make progress in recent years.[13] Their experiences provide ideas for other countries about how to approach decentralization.

Ethiopia and Uganda: Building a Solid Foundation for Reform

In contrast to many developing countries, Ethiopia and Uganda have established strong enabling environments for decentralization.[14] They have been able to do so because changing political conditions created a strong internal incentive for reform.[15] Donor agencies were invited to assist only after the respective governments determined the general direction of reform.

The Ethiopian and Ugandan experiences suggest a number of critical components of a sustainable enabling environment for fiscal decentralization. First, both countries have developed robust constitutional and legal provisions for decentralization and the reform of lower levels of government. The 1995 Ethiopian Constitution and various laws provide for a federal system, with clear service provision and revenue responsibilities for federal and regional governments. In Uganda, the Local Governments Statute of 1993, the 1995 Constitution, and the Local Governments Act of 1997 provide considerable detail about local service and revenue powers.

Second, both Ethiopia and Uganda have reduced the coordination problems previously discussed by developing special-purpose, somewhat more "neutral," and high-level mechanisms to oversee and coordinate decentralization. In Ethiopia, the Regional Affairs Department in the Office of the Prime Minister has substantial responsibility in this regard, and a Decentralization Secretariat was set up for similar purposes in Uganda. Although the Secretariat reports to the Permanent Secretary for Local Government, staff members are not civil servants, and they are in principle detached from the normal government bureaucracy. In addition, the Local Government Finance Commission, a constitutionally mandated independent body that reports directly to the President, has considerable influence over local revenue and intergovernmental transfer design.

Third, rather than thinking of decentralization as a way to reduce pressures on the central budget, both Ethiopia and Uganda recognize that effective local governments must have adequate resources to meet their responsibilities under decentralization. Accordingly, both countries have developed significant transfer programs that account for substantial proportions of total central revenues (around 30 percent in the Uganda case and more than 40 percent in the Ethiopia case).

While these positive features of the decentralization frameworks in Ethiopia and Uganda legitimately distinguish them from many other countries, implementation has been less impressive. First, although there is a strong legal and constitutional basis for decentralized government rights and responsibilities in both countries, neither has a clear process or pragmatic timetable for the gradual transferring of functions.[16] This is partly due to an initial lack of appreciation for the complexity of decentralization. Equally important is the weakness of the coordination bodies, which apparently have inadequate authority to mandate cooperation from ministries reluc-

tant to decentralize or to work cooperatively with other ministries.[17]

Second, neither country's decentralization program adequately recognizes the severe capacity constraints that must be overcome. In both Ethiopia and Uganda, at least some functions and resources are being decentralized to regional and local governments with little capacity to manage them. Moreover, the need for technical assistance to local governments as they assume new duties far exceeds the capacity of the relevant central agencies to deliver it in both cases.

Third, more emphasis has been given in both Ethiopia and Uganda to the development of intergovernmental transfer programs than to improving local revenue sources, and in neither country are there adequate incentives in the transfer formulas to encourage local revenue generation. Local revenue yields have generally increased under the decentralization programs in both countries, but much less than expected, and grants still account for the bulk of local revenues and increasingly substantial portions of the central government budgets.

Fourth, although both countries are moving toward greater local participation and/or democratically elected councils, there is a lack of explicit linkage between the development of local administration and the development of local democracy. In both Ethiopia and Uganda, civil society has been historically weak, and there is little recognition that people must learn over time how to be good citizens and how to interact with their local governments.[18]

In summary, both Ethiopia and Uganda have established a constitutional, legal, and fiscal basis for decentralization programs that could serve as models for other countries. Their perceived political imperative to decentralize, however, has led to attempts to move forward more rapidly and less strategically than a complex process like decentralization merits.

Indonesia: Building a Decentralization Process in a Highly Centralized System

Indonesia, a Southeast Asian nation of more than 14,000 dispersed islands with the world's fourth largest population, has long suffered from many of the decentralization obstacles we have outlined. Numerous central agencies with conflicting visions about local government roles are involved. They have generally been reluctant to decentralize, allegedly because of weak local capacity, but no doubt equally because they control a substantial volume of "decentralization" program resources, which have been largely provided through heavily fragmented donor initiatives. The real challenge in this case was how to begin the contentious process of loosening up top-heavy control in a system with several powerful central actors.[19]

In response to disappointing progress of their decentralization efforts, the Indonesian authorities initiated an experimental government-led effort in 1993 to decentralize strategically, based on local government capacity. The process of evaluating local capacity brought together key central ministries under a coordinating committee chaired by a nonthreatening "neutral" agency with no direct stake in decentralization. The committee intended to repeat the evaluation process regularly. Although the process was not institutionalized because of interministerial disagreements and the onset of political and economic crisis, the fall of Suharto has opened new opportunities for reform based on the principles of this experiment.

The Indonesia approach, which was piloted in three provinces before being abandoned, has several positive features. First, it exposed an underlying agreement among bureaucrats in competing agencies on the ability of some local governments to manage their fiscal affairs more independently. Second, it stimulated extensive dialogue on the meaning, scope, and pace of decentralization. Third, the process was structured to reduce control of more capable local governments, freeing up resources to target technical assistance to weaker ones. Fourth, the implementation approach was pragmatic, such that tasks were to be decentralized gradually to more capable local governments. Fifth, the evaluation process provides incentives for good performance if repeated periodically. Finally, the experiment allowed the government to take fuller control of decentralization agenda from donors, who were excluded from the process.

Given the severity of the current economic and political crisis, it is hard to know what the future will hold for Indonesia. Several developments, including the loss of East Timor as a province and the increasing uncertainty of the situation in Aceh (North Sumatra) and other areas, have placed increasing pressure on the new Wahid government to move forward with economic and political reforms. Decentralization has clearly emerged as a genuine high-priority element of the reform program, and in 1999 the government laid the basic legislative groundwork for a new attempt at decentralization. There can be little doubt that a long-term, gradual, and strategic process that builds on the experiment discussed here is the likely way forward.

Kenya: Negotiating Decentralization Reforms and Technical Assistance Programs

Kenya is a country with a long history of local government, but the system was weakened and heavily controlled by the center after independence, primarily in the name of national unity. There were many efforts in the 1980s and 1990s to reinvigorate local governments, but most were donor-driven and not a priority for the national authorities. As a result, local revenue yields and services deteriorated substantially. In recent years, however, fueled by political and economic pressures, some genuine attempts to strengthen local governments are under way.[20]

Given the number of local authorities and the magnitude of their problems, the government recognized that not all of the necessary reforms could be undertaken at the same time or in all places. Accordingly, the Small Towns Development Program (STDP), the first of a new generation of reform efforts based in the Ministry of Local Government (MLG), involved experimentation with about 15 local authorities. This project, which was jointly funded by the Kenyan and German (GTZ) governments, defined several broad common reform goals for the participating local authorities, but the exact steps each took and the pace at which they took them were negotiated. During implementation, a mobile technical assistance team worked periodically on site with local officials to implement gradually, and, as necessary, to modify, the negotiated program of reforms. Local citizen participation mechanisms were required as part of the reform process for certain types of activities, and some training opportunities were provided for local officials. Local governments that met their agreed goals were rewarded in various ways, such as greater access to funding and reduced MLG interference in their decisions. Most participating local governments improved their fiscal performance considerably.

The STDP has several advantageous features. First, because it built on earlier efforts and slowly evolved over several years in close consultation with MLG officials, STDP developed strong credibility with the local counterparts, who increasingly accepted an approach based on limited, gradual, individually tailored reforms. Second, the negotiation, rather than imposition, of reforms placed some responsibility on local governments to meet the goals they agreed to. Third, virtually all technical assistance personnel were local rather than foreign consultants, raising acceptance and credibility of the initiative among Kenyans. Fourth, STDP efforts generated information that assisted the MLG to create procedural manuals and training materials for different types of local governments. These helped convince central and local officials to accept the use of standards in making basic fiscal decisions. Finally, the ongoing efforts of the STDP over more than a decade raised the visibility of local governments and demonstrated that, with adequate assistance and incentives, they could improve their long-unacceptable performance.

The Kenyan government, with substantial World Bank funding and technical assistance, has recently embarked on a broader program of reform—the Kenya Local Government Reform Program (KLGRP)—largely based on STDP experiences. The premise of KLGRP is that successful fiscal decentralization requires phased and integrated fiscal, legal, institutional, technical, and procedural reforms at central and local levels. An Inter-ministerial Task Force on Local Government Reform manages KLGRP, building it gradually and systematically in a series of manageable, mutually reinforcing steps. Most KLGRP functions are the responsibility of civil servants, who also continue to perform many of their regular duties. This establishes KLGRP as an integral and mutually reinforcing part of government functions rather than a separate activity.

The configuration of KLGRP involves three major phases. The first phase, which is essentially completed, solidified agreement on key reforms, including local managerial and procedural reforms, local tax reforms, intergovernmental tax harmonization, the evaluation of options for intergovernmental transfers, and the resolution of a serious intergovernmental debt problem. The second phase, which started in 1999, involves implementing basic initial reforms defined in the first phase, including basic organizational and managerial reforms, harmonization of key central and local revenues, and establishment of a simple intergovernmental grants program. The third phase will involve implementation of a physical infrastructure program. Funding for basic infrastructure will begin after minimal reform requirements defined in the previous phases are met. As a precondition to more substantial funding, an increasingly comprehensive set of reforms at both the central and local level must be satisfactorily undertaken.

Although the Kenyan government's relationship with the international community has deteriorated in 1999–2000, this program continues to move forward slowly with donor support. Kenya's experience illustrates that a gradual approach and negotiated packages of reform, supported by carefully targeted technical assistance, can have substantial benefits. This approach also recognizes that decentralization involves slowly changing attitudes about what central and local governments should do, and building their capacity to do it.

Brazil: Altering Intergovernmental Relations and the Work Environment

The State of Ceará, located in Brazil's poor northeast region, had a long history of clientelism and poor revenue collection and service delivery. Since the mid-1980s, Ceará has completely turned its negative reputation around.[21] It has been heralded as a success in the international press and development literature because of its recent efforts to reform certain decentralized services, including health care, agricultural extension, business extension, and employment-creating public works.

Many of the major factors underlying this impressive reversal are related to the altering of state–local relations and improving the environment in which public servants function. First, the state played a significant role, rather than the typically prescribed reduced role, in providing the "decentralized" services. This included substantial control over hiring and management of local government employees in key sectors, the creation of strong performance incentives, and the strengthening of local civil society in a way that led to a substantial increase in public pressure for improved local government performance.

Second, in contrast to the conventional emphasis of decentralization reformers on simple, standardized procedures, local employees were given considerable discretion in how to perform their responsibilities, and this often resulted in undertaking service delivery activities in more expansive, complex, and individualized ways. This was possible because workers were judged on the end results of their efforts—that is, services actually being delivered to and well received by local residents—rather than on the specific means they used to provide services.

Third, the increased pressures from the state government and from civil society—partially fueled by agents of the state government—instilled a greater sense of job commitment and engendered greater personal job satisfaction for local government employees. Local staff who performed well were publicly recognized and rewarded, enhancing their prestige.[22] The efforts made by the state to create greater visibility and legitimacy for the services being decentralized and the civil servants responsible for them also resulted in more informed and careful monitoring by local government constituents.

This brief exposition greatly simplifies the story of Ceará's success, but it does highlight a situation in which some of the common prescriptions of "mainstream" decentralization reform were absent, but good results were achieved. A higher level of government (the state) played a strong role in controlling local behavior and educating citizens. Local governments were given discretion about how to undertake responsibilities because the state judged performance on results rather than on adoption of specific procedures. Finally, the state ensured that local civil servants were given recognition for good performance. Together these factors created an environment that was conducive to better performance and enhanced local capacity over time.

Cambodia and Vietnam: Balancing Public Service Demand and Supply Mechanisms

As noted here, many recent decentralization efforts have focused on the development of demand-driven mechanisms, forcing participation to extremes and all but ignoring the role of the supply side in providing information, standards, and technical assistance for local governments. In contrast, Cambodia and Vietnam have been experimenting with a decentralization mechanism that tries to balance the demand and supply sides while incorporating elements of the gradual, strategic approach embodied in the Indonesian and Kenyan cases.

The Cambodia and Vietnam experiences are based on the "Local Development Fund" (LDF) approach developed by the United Nations Capital Development Fund (UNCDF).[23] The LDF shares some characteristics with a number of other types of programs used to support locally generated and managed investments, including small town/rural development programs, the older family of Community Development Funds, and the more recent Social Investment Funds and Micro-projects programs. These programs typically have a poverty alleviation focus, share a "demand-driven" approach, and target local investments (health and education facilities, roads, water supply, income-generating community projects, and so on) of a similar type and scale.

Under most of these programs, various types of local groups [local governments, nongovernmental organizations (NGOs), community groups, and so on] can access resources for projects (typically though a program-specific planning process) by applying to a fund, usually based in a national or a regional capital, that is often largely independent from the government structure. In contrast, LDFs provide resources only to local governments, "entitling" them with an objectively defined block allocation of resources (rather than a project-specific grant) from a fund managed by a higher level of government, with technical assistance. The LDF also introduces a simple participatory local planning process, but local governments use it to plan beyond the use of LDF resources, making requests for larger-scale projects to higher levels of government and applying for other available sources of funding. This process is demand driven, but technical, institutional, and political standards must be met before funds are released. Local governments have access to resources to obtain technical assistance to meet these standards. They decide whether to obtain assistance through conventional channels (agencies of higher level governments), private firms, or

NGOs. Thus, the LDF approach focuses on the development of local governments, which are given some choices, but they are subject to a degree of quality control from higher levels on technical, financial, and governance matters, as in the Kenyan and Brazilian cases.

This basic approach is followed in both cases, but the specific design accounts for cross-country differences. For example, the LDF in centrally planned Vietnam is under the Ministry of Planning and Investment, and commune-level governments, which have a long history of administrative responsibility, serve as the focal institution locally. The LDF in Cambodia, which has a recent history of ineffective central government that has at times been hostile to the people, was initially set up under an interdepartmental management structure at the provincial level, essentially bypassing the center.[24] In addition, the lowest tier of government, villages, which are closest to the people and were allowed to elect representative committees before communes, initially played the dominant local role in Cambodia's LDF.[25] Thus, basic LDF principles can guide decentralization in countries where resources are limited and local governments are poorly developed, but the design must be tailored to local context.

Tentative Lessons and Conclusions

There is obviously no single approach to effective fiscal decentralization that applies to all countries. Reforms must be determined in a particular case, given available resources and capacity, as well as the institutional, social, and political realities that govern an appropriate and realistic scope and pace for decentralization. Most countries, however, face some similar problems and constraints in moving forward. A number of countries around the world have managed to develop in recent years a variety of mechanisms that help to overcome, even if modestly, some of the formidable obstacles outlined earlier. A number of broad tentative lessons about approaching decentralization, many of which are interrelated, can be drawn from these experiences.

Policy Framework: A solid policy framework that defines and guarantees the rights and responsibilities of local governments can be an important starting point for an effective decentralization program. The Ethiopian and Ugandan cases demonstrated, however, that such a framework and the commitment to implement it are not enough to ensure that decentralization will progress smoothly in practice.

Process and Consensus Building: Developing a process to build consensus about the appropriate extent, form, and pace of fiscal decentralization is at least as important as—and initially often more important than—

defining an "end-product" system that conforms to the normative decentralization models. This is particularly critical in highly centralized countries where there is no unified vision of decentralization, and responsibilities for local development are fragmented across central agencies, as in the Indonesian case. Such a process, if properly structured, representative of the key stakeholders, led by a trusted or neutral agency, broadly perceived as fair, and adequately empowered, can help to define a realistic starting point for fiscal decentralization. A domestically led process can also reduce the risk that the decentralization agenda will be dominated by outside experts bearing substantial funds.

Coordinating Reforms: Given the complexity of decentralization, there are many opportunities for its opponents to undermine progress or its proponents to move too quickly. Coordination is essential to ensure that decentralization proceeds in a rational and controlled manner. Responsibility for coordination can be under the same type of interinstitutional mechanism that was recommended above to negotiate the initial decentralization reforms. Such a mechanism would need to develop checks and balances among the various interested organizations to reduce power imbalances that can undermine decentralization. Once agreed upon, the responsibilities of all relevant actors should be formalized, and an effective system of monitoring and enforcing compliance is required.

Strategic Implementation: An effective decentralization program requires a strategic implementation approach, as in all of the cases discussed here. Even though a clear vision of longer-term reform is needed, initial steps should be modest and logically phased. Reforms that have the greatest possibility of relatively rapid success should be undertaken first, primarily simple tasks that don't immediately threaten in a significant way the central power base or overwhelm local capacity. In addition, it can be useful to differentiate among local governments, a highlight of the Indonesian and Kenyan approaches. Some are more capable and can be given greater responsibility, while others will require substantial technical assistance and oversight. Starting carefully and modestly should raise the prospects for initial success, creating a stronger base on which to build.

Integrating Reforms: Effective fiscal decentralization normally requires a focus broader than conventional fiscal concerns. Increasing local spending responsibilities and access to revenues will be unlikely to result in improved performance unless supporting institutional and political reforms are also undertaken. Many countries fragment different types of decentralization reform, but an integrated approach that involves a mutually reinforcing set of reforms, as illustrated in various ways by the Kenyan, Brazilian, Cambodian, and Vietnamese cases, is more likely to yield better results.

Balancing Roles among Levels of Government: Fiscal decentralization means more than just shifting power from central to local governments. In fact, decentralization typically involves an increased initial role for central or regional agencies. This reflects the need for a greater balance between reforms on the supply and demand side of service provision, as in the Brazilian, Cambodian and Vietnamese cases. Consulting the consumer on public expenditures can be critical, but reforming procedures for delivering particular types of services in an appropriate and cost-effective way is equally important for success.

Building Capacity and Governance: A decentralization program must build the commitment and capacity of local governments to assume new responsibility on behalf of their constituents. Disillusioned local residents have to be gradually convinced that their local governments can and will respond to them, and this requires some concrete results in the form of improved services, as in the Brazilian and Cambodian cases. As already noted, such improvements are more likely to be attainable if decentralization reforms are phased in with capacity building and incentives, making it clear to local governments what they must accomplish before receiving additional responsibility or resources, as in the Kenya case. Without increased local accountability and capacity through political and procedural reform, decentralization is ultimately a meaningless exercise.

Ensuring Adequate Flexibility: A pragmatic fiscal decentralization program should judge service providers and employees on the basis of results, not on slavish adherence to rigid bureaucratic procedures. This requires a process that provides incentives for good performance, but that also allows flexibility, so that local governments can operate in a customized way if this is appropriate. The potential success of such a strategy was particularly highlighted by the Brazilian case.

As economic and political pressures for decentralization and local government reform continue to escalate and forces driving democratization continue to develop, many countries will feel an increasing urgency to formulate decentralization policies that produce good results. There is much to learn from the cases and principles discussed here, but there are still many gaps in our understanding of how to design and implement effective decentralization policies. The numerous decentralization activities currently under way around the world provide a significant opportunity for further experimentation and research to improve our knowledge of how to approach this challenging and potentially productive type of public-sector reform.

Bibliography

Bahl, R. 1997. "Fiscal Federalism in Uganda." World Bank, Washington, D.C. Processed.

Bahl, R., and J. Linn. 1992. *Urban Public Finance in Developing Countries.* Baltimore, MD: Johns Hopkins University Press.

Barnes, N. 1998. "How Local Can We Go? Lessons from Fiscal Decentralization in Uganda." Cambridge, MA: Department of Urban Studies and Planning, MIT.

Bird, R. 1993. "Threading the Fiscal Labyrinth: Some Issues in Fiscal Decentralization." *National Tax Journal* 46(2), pp. 207–227.

Bird, R., and F. Vaillancourt 1998. "Fiscal Decentralization in Developing Countries: An Overview." *Discussion Papers*, No. 11. Toronto, ON: International Center for Tax Studies, University of Toronto.

Cohen, J. 1995. "Ethnic Federalism in Ethiopia." *Development Discussion Paper.* Cambridge, MA: Harvard Institute for International Development.

Cohen, J., and S. Peterson 1999. *Beyond Administrative Decentralization: Strategies for Developing Countries.* West Hartford, CT: Kumarian Press.

Dillinger, W. 1995. *Better Urban Services: Finding the Right Incentives.* Washington, D.C.: World Bank.

Fisher, R. C. 1996. *State and Local Public Finance.* Chicago, IL: Irwin.

Khellaf, A. 1992. "Decentralization and Centralization of Local Public Services in Tunisia." Cambridge, MA: Department of Urban Studies and Planning, MIT.

Leonard, D.K. 1987. "The Political Realities of African Management." *World Development* 15(7):899–910.

Litvack, J., J. Ahmad, and R. Bird. 1998. *Rethinking Decentralization in Developing Countries.* Washington, D.C.: World Bank.

Manor, J. 1998. *The Political Economy of Decentralization.* Washington, D.C.: World Bank.

Ndegwa, P., et al. 1987. *Management for Development: Priority Themes for Africa Today.* Nairobi: Oxford University Press.

Oates, W. 1972. *Fiscal Federalism.* New York: Harcourt, Brace, and Jovanovich.

Prud'homme, R. 1995. "The Dangers of Decentralization." *The World Bank Research Observer* 10(2), pp. 201–220.

Rasheed, S., and D. F. Luke, eds. 1995. Development Management in Africa: Toward Dynamism, Empowerment and Entrepreneurship. Boulder, CO: Westview Press.

Smoke, P. 1989. "Is Local Public Finance Theory Relevant for Developing Countries?" *Development Discussion Papers*, No. 316. Cambridge, MA: Harvard Institute for International Development.

Smoke, P. 1994. *Local Government Finance in Developing Countries: The Case of Kenya.* New York: Oxford University Press.

Smoke, P. 1999. "Fiscal Decentralization in Developing Countries: A Review of Current Concepts and Practice." Geneva: United Nations Research Institute for Social Development.

Smoke, P. Forthcoming. "Rebuilding Local Government in Kenya." In J. Wunsch and D. Olowu, eds., *Building Democracy in Africa: Polycentric Strategies and Experiences.* Boulder, CO: Westview Press.

Smoke, P., and B. Lewis. 1996. "Fiscal Decentralization in Indonesia: A New Approach to an Old Idea." *World Development* 24(8), pp. 1281–1299.

Tanzi, V. 1995. "Fiscal Federalism and Decentralization: A Review of Some Efficiency and Macroeconomics Aspects." *Proceedings of the Annual World Bank Conference on Development Economics*, pp. 295–316.

Tendler, J. 1997. *Good Government in the Tropics.* Baltimore, MD: Johns Hopkins University Press.

Tiebout, C. M. 1956. "A Pure Theory of Local Expenditure, *Journal of Political Economy* 64(5), pp. 416–424.

Raimondo, H. J. 1992. *Economics of State and Local Government.* New York: Praeger.

UNCDF (United Nations Capital Development Fund). (1996) *Local Development Funds.* New York: United Nations Development Programme.

UNCDF 1999. *Taking Risks.* New York: United Nations Development Programme.

Wilson, R. H., and R. Cramer. 1995. *International Workshop on Good Local Government.* Austin, TX: Johnson School of Public Affairs, University of Texas.

Notes

1. The cases discussed here are based on programs financed by the World Bank, the United Nations Capital Development Fund (UNCDF), the United Nations Development Program (UNDP), the Deutsche Gesellschaft für Technische Zusammenarbeit (GTZ), the U.S. Agency for International Development (USAID), and various governments. Some findings are based on work conducted for the Management Development and Governance Division of UNDP. The perspectives expressed here are those of the author and should not be attributed to any of these organizations.

2. A substantial literature on the benefits of decentralization dates back to the 1960s. Much of it is reviewed in Smoke (1994). More recent literature is discussed in Smoke (1999).

3. See, for example, Bird (1993), Prud'homme (1995), And Tanzi (1995).

4. Much of this literature is reviewed in Smoke (1994). Other relevant literature includes Dillinger (1995); Tendler (1997); Litvack, J., J. Ahmad, and R. Bird (1998); and Cohen and Peterson (1999).

5. These models originated with a few seminal works, including Tiebout (1956) and Oates (1972). Reviews of how these basic models have been applied, expanded, and empirically tested are found in Bahl and Linn (1992), Raimondo (1992), and Fisher (1996).

6. See Smoke (1989 and 1994), Linn (1992), Bird (1993), Prud'homme (1995), Tanzi (1995), and Bird and Vaillancourt (1998).

7. Many of these weaknesses are elaborated in Smoke (1994); Litvack, Ahmad, and Bird (1998); Manor (1998); and Cohen and Peterson (1999).

8. See Leonard (1987), Ndegwa (1987), and Rasheed and Duke (1995).

9. There are some cases in which significant political motives for decentralization have developed, including Ethiopia, Indonesia, South Africa, and Uganda.

10. See Manor (1998).

11. See Khellaf (1992); Smoke (1994); and Litvack, Ahmad, and Bird (1998).

12. An example would be the reform of local government accounting practices.

13. Some of the cases discussed here are more detailed than others are, either because more information was available or because certain aspects of their performance were considered particularly relevant.

14. There are several good references on Ethiopian and Ugandan decentralization policy, including Cohen (1995); Bahl (1997); World Bank public expenditure reviews for Ethiopia and Uganda, 1994–98; and a 1999 World Bank study on regionalization in Ethiopia.

15. Both countries independently adopted decentralization to hold their ethnically fragmented nations together during a period of crisis. This central government attitude toward local governments is particularly interesting because the historical (post-independence) trend in many postcolonial developing countries, particularly in Africa, has been to increase state control in order to build national unity.

16. In the Ethiopian case, there is also inadequate specificity in the constitution and relevant legislation about the functions to be decentralized to tiers below the regions (the zones and *woredas*). There is no reference to the municipalities, which are important in the urban areas.

17. In some sectors, constitutionally mandated decentralization occurs slowly because a ministry delays moving forward, such as the case of public works in Ethiopia. In other sectors, responsibility has been devolved too rapidly by ministries attempting to comply with the letter of the law, overwhelming the capacity of local governments, such as the case of education in Uganda.

18. A recent study of "successful" local governments in Uganda, for example, demonstrated that local government revenue yields and local service expenditures increased after decentralization. See Barnes (1998). Further analysis, however, revealed that people paid local taxes primarily because they were being forced to do so by aggressive enforcement officers rather than because they were satisfied with the types and levels of services being provided. Thus, in this anecdotal example,

decentralization was technically occurring, but without developing the links between local governments and their constituents that underlie the public choice models used to justify decentralization. The situation is almost certainly worse in Ethiopia.

19. The Indonesia experience is examined in Smoke and Lewis (1996).

20. See Smoke (1994) and Smoke. (forthcoming).

21. The Brazilian experience is examined in Tendler (1997). Tendler links her major findings closely to the literature on industrial performance and workplace transformation.

22. A key element in recognizing good local performance was a system of competitive prizes. Similar mechanisms are used in a number of countries. See, for example, Wilson and Cramer (1995).

23. The LDF approach is discussed in considerable detail in UNCDF's 1996 publication *Local Development Funds.* UNCDF's 1999 publication, *Taking Risks,* reviews experiences with the LDFs to date. As of mid-1999, LDF programs have been or are being designed in more than a dozen countries (Vietnam, Cambodia, Bangladesh, and Nepal in Asia; Palestine in the Middle East; Ethiopia, Uganda, Tanzania, Malawi, Zambia, Equatorial Guinea, Mozambique, and Senegal in Africa). Because UNCDF can focus only on the least developed countries, the LDF is designed primarily to promote decentralization of rural and small-town infrastructure—primarily through grant mechanisms, but the basic model for building capacity and accountability has broader relevance.

24. The Cambodian LDF is now being "mainstreamed" under an interministerial mechanism at the central level that is to be funded by multiple international agencies and the Cambodian government.

25. This will change when commune governments are elected under a decentralization law that is expected to take effect in the year 2000. As of May 2000, the Law on Commune Administrative Management had passed the Council of Ministers and was being referred to the Parliament. The Law on Commune Elections was still being finalized by the Ministry of Interior.

chapter 13

Decentralization Comes to Japan

Kengo Akizuki
Kyoto University

lobalization tends to weaken the credibility of national governments and their willingness to intervene in local government. Japan, which has maintained one of the world's most centralized governmental systems, at least on paper, is no exception.

The Japanese intergovernmental system has undergone fundamental reform since the mid-1990s, with the basic trend to loosen central control. The country's prolonged economic difficulties have undermined the central bureaucracy's credibility, and the public has become more aware of bureaucratic corruption. Most important, globalization has limited the ability of the national government to control movement of the country's population, information, capital, services, and goods. According to a common slogan, it is high time for Japan to shift "from the days of uniformity under centralization to variety under decentralization."

In May 1998, the cabinet formally authorized a Decentralization Promotion Plan, proposed by the Committee for Promotion of Decentralization (CPD), which affects virtually all ministries and agencies. This scheme entails amending at least 500 laws, decentralizing authority, and deregulating functions from the public to the private sector. The most symbolic yet best known reform entails abolishing "agency-delegated functions" (*kikan i'fnin jimu*), a legal concept that enables the national government to require local governments to do its bidding outside the purview of local assemblies. Instead, the national government will give technical advice, ask for reports, and if necessary, even provide direction, but the relationship between the two levels will

no longer be that of master and servant. Local governments will now perform "legally entrusted functions" (*hotei jutaku jimu*), such as administering national elections, collecting statistical data, and implementing national welfare programs. In cases of conflict the CPD proposes a system of mediation, and parties not content with the results may initiate lawsuits. The commission has been strongly criticized for not addressing the issue of financial dependence of local government on the central government—the most difficult challenge of all—but some members say the commission will do so by the end of its tenure in 2000.

In response to such changes, many localities are pursuing new approaches to governance that tap the worldwide exchange of information but that promise to produce winners and losers, threatening Japan's postwar commitment to economic equality. Japan's experience reflects its own strengths and idiosyncrasies as well as the challenges that all governments, central and local alike, confront under globalization.

National Party Conflict Drives Decentralization

The reform process resulted from political turmoil in the central government, beginning when the Liberal Democratic Party slipped from the ruling position in 1993 for the first time since its birth in 1955. This turmoil brought several political aspirants to the top before they had become completely "nationalized." Until then, a candidate for a cabinet post had to serve at least six terms in the Lower House of the Diet; a candidate for prime minister had to hold office for 25 years and assume important posts such as minister of finance or international trade and industry. The new prime minister, Morihiro Hosokawa, was young and lacked legislative experience—he had served as governor of Kumamoto Prefecture—and made clear that decentralization would be his top priority. When the LDP regained control in 1995 by forming an unlikely coalition with the Socialist Party, Tomiichi Murayama, a veteran Socialist politician originally from a local government union, became prime minister.

Murayama established the CPD and appointed its members, who largely represent business, academia, and the press and favor decentralization. Six nationwide groups of local leaders have voiced support for the commission and maintain pressure for reform. The commission has concentrated on refuting the "who-would-fill-the-vacuum" argument advanced by skeptics of local autonomy. Decentralization sounds fine, these skeptics say, but localities need guidance and protection from the national government to get the job done.

Because of such doubts, former would-be reformers often felt they had to revamp the three-tiered Japanese system of government—which includes national, prefectural, and local levels—into two or four tiers and hope that somebody or something would fill the vacuum. Those ideas never won acceptance. But the CPD maintains that there is no need to change the number of tiers, rewrite the Constitution to reflect a federal system, or combine prefectures into regional governments. The current actors, says the CPD, can fill the vacuum. For example, the CPD calls for more active local assemblies in formulating policy and overseeing the local bureaucracy and chief executives. And instead of relying on the national government to supervise the activities of local governments, citizens will do so through information disclosure and referendum and recall.

Prefectural Government—Is It Local?

The CPD focuses on prefectural governments as key to coordinating the activities of cities and towns and delegating authority from the national to the local level, and from the public to the private domain. This represents the first time that postwar governmental reform does not propose abolishing or merging prefectures. Two preemptive moves have convinced the CPD and the national government to make prefectures a partner of the center. Two prominent ex-governors, one an urban liberal with leftist leanings, and another a former rural police bureaucrat, sit on the commission. And prefectures have initiated studies and issued proposals on how to cope with the coming decentralization since the mid-1980s.

Japan has 47 prefectures. Their number and borders have remained largely unchanged since Aritomo Yamagata formulated the prefecture system in the Meiji era.

(The legal status of the Tokyo metropolitan government has fluctuated, and the U.S. military once controlled Okinawa; both are now prefectures.) However, postwar reforms driven by U.S. occupying forces did bring significant changes such as the direct election of prefecture governors.

The performance of the prefectures has often drawn criticism. Some doubt that dividing Japan into 47 pieces can yield administrative efficiency; the business sector has been the most eloquent critic in preferring regional government. Some experts in forestry conservation, river improvement, and other environmental issues also maintain that convincing prefectures to address such concerns is difficult. Critics further maintain that prefectures play a double-edged role, representing and supporting cities and towns but also controlling them—a plausible criticism given the exchanges of personnel between national and prefectural governments.

Despite these criticisms, prefectures have played an important role in Japanese democracy. One dramatic change occurred when leftists took over virtually all important prefectural governorships in the 1960s and 1970s. These so-called progressives could not be considered mere national agents, and kept the intergovernmental games going through careful negotiation—and sometimes confrontation. They also responded to citizens' demands for consumer and environmental protection, partly by retaining access to the national government through the bureaucrats dispatched to them.

The profile of prefecture governors is rising these days, and they are now acting even more boldly. For example, the governor of Saitama, formerly the speaker of the Upper House of the Diet, sent back the personnel dispatched from the national government. Some governors are pursuing an alternative strategy of recruiting national bureaucrats to serve the prefecture directly.

Thus, prefectures have benefited from evolution as well as consistency. To increase their administrative capacity, villages amalgamate to become towns, and towns become cities, constantly changing names, size, and legal status. Citizens usually identify themselves with prefectures. "Character of prefecture" (*Kenminsei*) is a common notion: Men from Kochi prefecture drink a lot, people of Shiga are stingy, and the wives of Gunma rule their families. Doctors' organizations, bar associations, and farmers' unions also organize along prefectural boundaries. The CPD's decision to put prefectures in charge of decentralization formally confirms this status.

The Changing Style of Japanese Governance

Although Japan clearly maintains more central control and overlapping jurisdictions than many countries,

Table 13.1
Percentage of Public Revenue after Fiscal Transfer

	National	local	state/ province	county/ city/town
	Federal			
USA	39	61	33	28
Canada	38	62	43	19
FRG	39	61	32	29
	Unitary			
UK	71	29		
France	72	28		

			Prefecture	city/town/ village
Japan	38	62	30	32

Source: Mikiko Iwasaki, *Politics of Subsidies in Japan* (1990).
Notes: Fiscal year 1985 for Japan, 1986 for other countries.

transfers of funds from central to local governments are also higher than in most countries, and the system clearly allows for local initiative. In fact, Japan's fiscal responsibilities clearly follow the pattern of countries with a federal system (Table 13.1). However, that record leads to another difficult challenge: Each level of government must cut the significant public-sector deficit.

All levels of government are, therefore, now attempting to restructure the bureaucracy, privatize some functions, and rely on partnerships between citizens and nonprofit groups for providing services and collecting information. Prefectures may well serve as coordinators and shock absorbers during this process, as some American states did during the federal budget cuts of the Reagan era.

However, new styles of governance are rapidly emerging among Japanese localities which go well beyond the need for budget cuts. Because the national government will no longer protect localities, these are trying to satisfy their other bosses—their inhabitants. Because localities do not possess enough financial resources to simply expand services, they are experimenting with new tools, many invented in Anglo-Saxon countries.

Two approaches to administrative evaluation (*gyosei hyoka*) are becoming popular among local officials. Today large construction projects are encountering public resistance. The Kobe municipal offshore airport, for instance, a longtime pet project of city government, is under serious attack from citizens as well as outsiders. More than 30 percent of the city's voting population has signed a petition favoring a public referendum on the project. Questions posed by local governments, community leaders, and citizens and landowners have also halted construction of several dams planned by the central Ministry of Construction. Critics maintain that fiscal difficulties and environmental issues preclude such

megaprojects, and they oppose not just the specific schemes but also the fact that once initiated, these schemes are almost impossible to stop. Even if some projects are rational responses to credible needs, critics say, these needs may evaporate during the decade or more needed to complete these projects.

In response, Hokkaido prefecture has initiated a new approach called "assessment by time," as well-known writer Soh Kuramoto nicely named it. A committee headed by the governor evaluates projects according to four standards: necessity, validity, priority, and effect. The committee releases the results and posts them on the Internet. The Hokkaido government has so far selected only seven big projects for review but pledges eventually to apply this scheme to all projects.

In another approach, Mie and Shizuoka prefectures have formulated an evaluation system that attempts to weigh the purpose and progress of virtually all government tasks. Every agency must make an inventory three times a year of the goal of every task, the time period and person-hours required to complete it, and the funds entailed. Since Mie Governor Masayasu Kitagawa began this system in 1996, the prefecture has eliminated 740 tasks. Shin-ichi Ueyama, a consultant with the international firm McKinsey & Company and the leading proponent of such schemes, criticizes these two efforts because they exclude private citizens and public interest groups from directly participating. However, he applauds the prefectures' willingness to disclose the information.

Local Japanese government is considered severely limited in its ability to revamp itself, as laws require localities to have at least one vice-mayor, for example. However, in 1997, Shiga prefecture upset the conventional wisdom that localities cannot reorganize without help or a nod from the central government by creating a new division called the Lake Biwa Environment Bureau. Encompassing 674 square kilometers, Lake Biwa is the largest lake in Japan and supports the daily life of more than 13 million people in seven prefectures. Shiga had been seeking more comprehensive policymaking authority over the lake because it occupies one-third of the prefecture, yet four different bureaus, all associated with national agencies, controlled it. The new bureau combines sections from those four agencies and asserts Shiga's priority in protecting the lake and its surroundings. Although Shiga expected strong opposition to this initiative from central bureaucracies, they remained silent.

Mechanisms for Change

A prefecture's ability to retrain its staff is essential to such administrative reforms. All prefectures and some cities maintain independent training programs and facilities—particularly important for rural areas. The programs have also strengthened connections between local governments and universities and colleges. These universities provide teachers and policy consultants and help develop new ideas or governance. A typical case is Shizuoka prefecture, which tapped a university professor to organize its evaluation scheme.

Leadership by governors is another key to reform, as in Shizuoka, where the governor urged bureaucrats to publicize their assessments. Mie Governor Kitagawa, formerly a successful Diet member, presented a clear agenda of administrative reform and is now considered a champion of such efforts. In fact, driven by top leadership, some local governments seem to be giving birth to a new management class composed of specialists from consulting firms and universities. Whether this coalition will supplant older coalitions of labor, bureaucrats, and service providers depends on circumstances unique to each locality—the front lines of this significant political battle.

Many Japanese localities study local experiments in foreign countries, from benchmarking in Oregon, which projects the future of the state by designating 92 indicators and setting numerical targets for each indicator, to administrative reform in New Zealand. Books, conferences, the Internet, and informal networks of public officials allow the exchange of ideas as well as results. Some skeptics say it is absurd to follow in the wake of countries with different cultures, histories, and institutions. They are usually right. However, total quality management (TQM), which local Japanese governments are now discussing, is proving worthwhile investigating. As is widely known, TQM was conceived of in the United States but further developed in Japan. In today's hyper-globalized world of ideas, even overly cautious public officials in Japan are looking into this new venture.

Some localities are also aggressively taking up the globalization challenge. Kanazawa and several other cities have established closer ties with Russia (Siberia), for example, while Osaka, Fukuoka, and other western cities have invited investment from China. This kind of strategy is not confined to industrial areas: Shiga sponsored the World Lake Conference while the city of Kyoto organized the Historical Cities Roundtable—both designed to enable localities rather than central governments to confer on common problems.

Winners and Losers

Japan's postwar intergovernmental system has committed itself to the idea that no regions or communities should be losers, but decentralization emphasizes competition and tends to produce winners and losers. Is Japan ready for intercity competition and regional economic disparity?

The nation is already talking about pioneers and late-comers in improving governance. Pioneers tend to be suburban/semirural prefectures. Where is Tokyo metropolitan government—the largest in population and finances? Where is Osaka City, known for its ambitious prewar development policy and postwar high-speed growth? These big urban localities grew by initiating new programs, expanding their functions, and employing more officials. They have strong unions, formidable and contentious assemblies, a critical local press, many local actors, and proud governmental staff. This accumulated tradition could work against them.

In the past, local competition did occur, such as when localities fought to win the designation of "new industrial city" in the 1960s, but this race occurred in an era of increasing expansion. Today market forces will choose which localities can deliver effective policies, and decentralization will determine outcomes in arenas ranging from environmental policy and consumer protection to taxes and finance. Localities can expect more autonomy, but they will receive much more scrutiny.

Local governments, especially prefectures, occupy a strategic position in Japan, yet converting that position into effective policymaking presents a formidable challenge. No one can ensure competent political leadership. Democracy, after all, does not provide answers but rather demands ongoing efforts from the governing elite, midlevel officials, as well as the voting public.

Bibliography

Akizuki, Kengo. 1995. "Institutionalizing the Local System: The Ministry of Home Affairs and Intergovernmental Relations in Japan." In Hyung-ki Kim, T. J. Pempel, Kozo Yamamura, and Michio Muramatsu, eds., *The Japanese Civil Service and Economic Development*. Oxford: Clarendon Press.

Akizuki, Kengo. Forthcoming. "Partnership in Controlled Decentralization: Local Governments, The Ministry of Home Affairs, and Intergovernmental Linkages in Postwar Japan." Washington, D.C.: World Bank.

Omori, Wataru. 1998. *Bunken Kaikai to Chiho Gikai (Decentralization Reform and Local Assembly)*. Tokyo: Gyosei (Japanese).

Osborne D., and T. Gaebler. 1992. *Reinventing Government*. Reading, MA: Addison-Wesley.

Peters, B. Guy, and D. J. Savoie, eds. 1997. *Governance in a Changing Environment*. Montreal: Canadian Centre for Management Development.

Reed, Steven R. 1986. *Japanese Prefectures and Policymaking*. Pittsburgh, PA: University of Pittsburgh Press.

Rhodes, R. A. W. 1997. *Understanding Governance: Policy Networks, Governance, Flexibility and Accountability*. London: Open University Press.

Samuels, Richard J. 1983. *The Politics of Regional Policy in Japan*. Princeton, NJ: Princeton University Press.

Stoker, Gerry. 1998. "Governance as Theory: Five Propositions." UNESCO paper, Oxford.

Ueyama, Shin-ich. 1997. *Gyosei Hyoka no Jidai (The Age of Public Evaluation)*. Tokyo: NTT Press (Japanese).

chapter 14

Why Are Social Funds So Popular?

Judith Tendler[1]

Department of Urban Studies and Planning
Massachusetts Institute of Technology

hy are Social Funds (SFs) so popular among international donors, who have committed more than US$3 billion to their creation and perpetuation in 40 countries since the late 1980s?[2] Ostensibly, SFs seem to do several things that are dear to our hearts. They are said to reduce poverty and unemployment and to bring services and small works projects to myriad poor communities in a way that is decentralized, demand-driven, participatory, low in cost, and fast-disbursing. By the donors' own accounts, however, SFs do not live up to the faith placed in them. This chapter explores this conundrum. More important than any particular judgment on SFs,[3] it seeks to assess the SF experience in a way that contributes to the larger debates about improving the quality of public-service delivery in developing countries.

Social Funds started in Latin America in the mid-1980s as a temporary antidote, according to the lore, to the adverse impact of structural adjustment programs and other reforms on the poor.[4] Originally, the programs were meant to provide quick employment through public-works projects and emergency social services, particularly in rural areas and towns, and partly in lieu of the increasingly faltering presence of fiscally strapped line ministries. Some were designed explicitly to compensate for layoffs caused by downsizing of the public sector and its state enterprises. By the early 1990s, donors judged the SFs to be so effective at temporary relief, and so appealing as a different and low-cost model of public-sector service delivery, that they provided follow-on funding to several SFs and started new ones, expanding first to Africa, and then to Eastern Europe and Southeast Asia.

Since 1987, the World Bank (WB) has committed US$1.4 billion worldwide to SFs, the Inter-American Development Bank (IDB) has committed almost the same in Latin America (US$1.3 billion), and in Latin America alone, the European donors have committed US$570 million. The pace of commitment shows no sign of slackening, with a new round of SFs cropping up in reform packages for crisis-afflicted Asian economies. Roughly one-third of SFs go to economic infrastructure; another third to education, health, nutrition, and population activities; and another third to miscellaneous activities such as microfinance, training, and environmental interventions. Social Funds are administered by a separate agency or unit within a department of the central government. They allocate grant funds directly to myriad communities for projects often chosen by them; the funding passes through local governments in only a minority of cases. Some of the acclaimed strengths of SFs are based on a general set of arguments about the superiority of more decentralized and "demand-driven" approaches in contrast to traditional public-service supply, with its "supply-driven" set of problems—overcentralization, rigid and top-down bureaucracy, and insensitivity to service users.

At the start, donors and the borrowing governments viewed SFs as a safety net for ameliorating the harsh effects of structural adjustment on the poor. More recently, SFs have also come to be seen as a refreshing new model of service delivery for poor communities, with their more independent project agencies or units and their involvement of beneficiary communities in choosing, monitoring, and financing projects. In typical descriptions, donor narratives commend the SFs as "an imaginative effort to make government actions and resources more beneficial to the poor"; as having "considerable potential . . . for *sustainable* service delivery . . ." (italics mine); and as succeeding, often, "in targeting the poor and in providing basic services more cheaply[5] and speedily than public sector agencies that have traditionally been charged with these functions."[6]

This chapter draws mainly on evidence about SFs from the donors themselves,[7] in addition to findings from outside researchers[8] and from my own research experience with four SFs in northeast Brazil.[9] The evidence raises questions about the effectiveness of SFs as a safety net for the poor and, more significantly, about the presumed greater desirability of SFs as an alternative to traditional government supply, or reformed versions of it. I therefore question the large amounts of funding and enthusiasm dedicated to SFs, as well as the distraction of attention and the diversion of resources from other paths toward these ends.

Many SF goals and shortcomings are not peculiar to them. Some of their main problems also plagued earlier, more supply-driven and centralized public programs, as well as recent attempts to decentralize power and responsibility to local governments, to rely more on market mechanisms and nongovernmental providers at the local level, and to involve citizens in user choice and monitoring. I hope, then, that this chapter will interest the development community in expanding its thinking beyond SF-type models to other ways of improving government performance. These ways may not be as new and exciting as SFs but, at the least, they would seem to have no more frailties than SFs do.

The Claims

Although SFs vary widely across countries, they tend to have several common components. First, they make grant funds available to enable communities or municipal councils to choose among a menu of possible projects (such as a well, a health center, a school, a grain mill, or road repair). Second, project design and construction are partly outsourced to local actors ("partially privatized")—private firms, nongovernment organizations (NGOs), community associations, and sometimes local governments; community groups themselves find and contract a design or construction firm or equipment supplier, monitor project execution, and/or take some responsibility for operating and maintaining the project. Third, a local contribution is often required, roughly 10–15 percent of project costs. Together, these features add up to the "demand-driven" moniker by which these programs are often described.[10]

Donor evaluations characterize the SF success as a fast, flexible, and low-overhead model of service delivery—just the opposite of the stereotypical government agency.[11] Several organizational traits are considered key to this success. As noted previously, SFs are often run by semiautonomous units or agencies operating outside line agencies, sometimes newly created, and often close and accessible to the office of the country's president. They also work outside civil service regulations, particularly in hiring, firing, and setting salaries. They have therefore often been able to recruit excellent managers with experience in the private sector or to lure to their staffs the best of the public or NGO sector. They have also succeeded in operating outside government procurement regulations, simplifying and speeding up the construction of small works projects.

Social Funds vary considerably from one country to the next, sometimes even on the aforementioned key traits.[12] Although the variety among SFs sometimes makes it difficult to describe this group of programs in uniform terms, I follow the convention of the donors in treating and praising these projects as a single category called Social Funds. To the extent that this chapter dwells on issues relating to sustainability, participation, and demand-driven decisionmaking, it relates more to the ongoing or more permanent funds than to the earlier temporary and emergency funds. (Many of the latter evolved into the former.) In the same vein, I pay relatively more attention to the claims about SFs as a service delivery model—sustainable, decentralized, demand-driven—than to their effectiveness as a safety net for the poor.

For all the talk of SFs as decentralized, they are in some ways the opposite of real decentralization, even when they are demand-driven. They are run by entities of the central government (state government in my Brazilian cases), which are often newly empowered and transformed by their association with international donors and by the corresponding direct support they receive from the president of the borrower country. The majority of SFs do not formally devolve power and responsibilities to local governments. As agencies of the central government, they try to reduce their overhead and personnel costs by deploying some of their staff outside the capital and devolving some responsibility to community groups and local providers. But this is described more accurately as "deconcentrating" rather than as "decentralizing" responsibilities and finances. Deconcentration, of course, shares some of the traits and purported advantages of decentralization. But "deconcentration" does not have the cachet that decentralization has: It does not fit the image, now so popular, of "taking power away" from central government, of moving from a "top-down" to a "bottom-up" style.

In the small number of cases where SFs do work through local governments, they often do so ad hoc, not as part of a larger decentralizing effort nor following the fixed criteria of geographical allocation typical of systems of revenue sharing with local government. In the former cases, SFs channel resources only through some local governments, while avoiding others. This happens according to one or two informally held sets of criteria; one involves the perceived capability and "seriousness" of the particular government, and the other with whether it is run by the same party of the government or the opposition. Where a local government is run by the opposition party, the political calculus of the central government may dictate that the SF circumvent it and work directly with communities—or not operate there at all—while working through local governments in the districts headed by the party faithful.[13] It is for this reason, among others, that some view SFs as working at cross-purposes to decentralization reforms, or at least not advancing the cause of decentralization more generally.

The Evidence: Reducing Poverty and Unemployment

By the donors' own accounts, SFs do not live up to the faith placed in them. They have contributed only insignificantly to the reduction of unemployment and poverty in the countries where they operate, even when compared to other programs with the same goal. The Latin American SFs are reported to have "created relatively few jobs" and reached only a small fraction of the labor force (in the Latin American case, less than 1 percent at best).[14] They also devoted only 30 percent of their expenditures to labor costs, a low share for programs dedicated to employment creation.[15] Jobs offered by the SFs were temporary, of low quality, and provided little or no training. Most of the better jobs went to skilled laborers brought in from elsewhere by outside contractors; skilled labor, for example, accounted for 42 percent of labor expenditures in the Nicaraguan SF.[16] Several employment-creation programs in Latin America, Africa, and Asia, which antedated the SFs, created significantly more jobs, employed a larger share of the labor force,[17] and elicited much greater budgetary resources from their respective governments. In comparison to the SFs, most of these programs were supply-driven, run by traditional public agencies, and funded by their governments rather than donors (at least initially).

Wages paid by SFs, although often set at the legal minimum, have nevertheless been typically lower than subsistence, and sometimes significantly so.[18] The wage in the Nicaraguan SF, for example, represented only 57 percent of a basic family food basket. Granted, most employment-creating programs deliberately set wages so low as to not draw labor away from private-sector employers and to keep the nonpoor from applying for these jobs. At the same time, however, the lower-than-subsistence level plus the short-term nature of the job add up to a weak instrument for reducing poverty and unemployment in a more sustained fashion. In the same vein, the voluntary labor often required of communities for SF projects, although meant to serve the goal of reducing costs and eliciting community "ownership" of the project, represents a regressive tax on the poor.[19]

The donor evaluations do not really bear out the claim that SFs are particularly good at reaching poor communities, or the poor within them.[20] Higher per capita SF expenditures often go to communities or provinces that are better off than to the poorer or the poorest.[21] In its 1997 study of four countries with SFs (Bolivia, Egypt, Sri Lanka, and Zambia), the World Bank found that "the higher poverty headcount index of the province, the lower was the actual per capita SF expenditure it received; or the actual expenditures lagged behind allocations in the areas with the highest poverty index while they far exceeded allocations in areas with low poverty indices."[22] Even in the "star" Bolivian SF, the richest of five income areas received two-and-a-half times as much SFs funds per capita as the poorest five (US$25 vs. US$10).[23] There are some exceptions,[24] though most of the data cannot distinguish between poor and rich within municipalities or other administrative units.

Some researchers comparing SFs to other programs have found that certain more traditional targeted programs have actually had more identifiable impacts in reducing poverty. They refer to employment-guarantee schemes, food stamp programs, food commodity programs, and school feeding programs in particular countries.[25] Others have pointed to broader entitlement or transfer programs, such as the extension of social security to poorer persons and rural areas, as having had significantly greater impacts in reducing poverty. Indeed, the magnitude of these latter impacts simply dwarfs the achievements of SFs in this area.[26] Although SFs are not direct-transfer programs like those just mentioned, these researchers nevertheless warn that the resources and confidence lavished by donors on SFs as a safety net have diverted attention, funding, and research to measures with only a fraction of the payoff of other measures affecting poverty and unemployment.

Despite the continued characterization of SFs as safety nets in donor documents, their evaluations report that the available data and its quality do not permit judgments as to whether SFs contributed to reducing poverty.[27] In most cases, it is not possible to determine whether poverty has been reduced or income increased in the regions served by SFs, or, even when such changes are detected, it is not possible to determine whether they are attributable to the program.[28] "[W]e have no way," a WB study concludes, "of comparing how well [SFs] target poverty compared with other programs."[29]

With respect to SFs' reputation for combating unemployment and poverty, then, they have "created relatively few jobs and generated little additional income for the poor,"[30] even though many of them included income and employment generation among their stated objectives. They were not "effective safety nets in any significant scale," and many countries therefore did not have "an effective mechanism to protect the poor from output, employment, and price risks."[31] "The message is clear," the IDB evaluators conclude, "that if these funds had an impact on poverty, it cannot have been from employment creation and income generation for the poor."[32] Despite these findings, all Latin American countries with SFs gave them a "high profile and a central role in the campaign to reduce poverty."[33]

The Evidence: Service Delivery

The SF track record as a model of service delivery is, at best, mixed. A World Bank tracking of the performance of SF projects in relation to more traditional supply-driven programs found no clear superiority for SFs, though it nevertheless concluded on a positive note about the SF as a model.[34] The IDB evaluators report that evidence was not sufficient to form a judgment as to whether SFs have actually made a difference in the availability of basic economic and social services in the various communities where they operate.[35] In addition, they found that the most successful and innovative of the SFs were those conceived *without* donor input and financing (Chile, Costa Rica, and Guatemala), and were different from the typical SF in other important ways.[36] (More on the Chilean case appears later in this chapter.)

Both major donors themselves gave distinctly low marks to the SFs for "sustainability" and for "ownership" of the projects by the communities in which they were placed.[37] The WB evaluators could find no data on the extent to which SF projects were being operated and maintained.[38] At the same time, frequent reports appeared about health clinics without refrigerators for vaccines, school buildings without textbooks, and wells that were not maintained. What's more, the evaluators noted that ownership of these projects by communities often required distinctly different technical designs, at least for economic infrastructure. But a large number of the SFs were found to have been designed without issues of sustainability in mind.[39] It was "not clear" if communi-

ties even knew what the operating and maintenance costs and responsibilities would be, according to the evaluators, before they chose their project. And only a small percentage of the SFs turned out to have actually required community contributions, even though the SF projects presented for approval to the WB Board of Directors (the "appraisal reports") always included an estimate for upfront contributions from communities. Little ex-post information on such contributions was available.[40]

Social Funds financed many activities—such as schools, clinics, and wells—that needed sustained support from line ministries or other agencies of government, once completed. But either no formal arrangements were made or those that were made were not respected.[41] In many cases, no operating funds came through for staff and maintenance, particularly for schools and health.[42] According to the logic of decentralization, however, this should not have been a serious problem, at least for some types of projects: The demand-driven features of the SF should have led inexorably to ownership of the new projects by communities, who would have willingly taken responsibility for operations and maintenance themselves or have successfully pressured local governments to do so. But this kind of ownership was not forthcoming.[43] If, as the evaluators report, neither the donors nor the recipients designed many of these programs with sustainability in mind—especially the earlier ones—then it is not fair to judge them by these criteria. But the donors themselves have made strong claims for these programs as successful, *ex-post*, on the grounds of community involvement. Indeed, they have hailed the SFs as models of "sustainable" service delivery, as attested to by the aforementioned quotations.

With respect to sustainability and ownership at the national level, finally, both donors lament the fact that most SF programs, 10 years after they were started, continue to be dependent for most of their financing on outside donors.[44] After noting that most Latin American governments with SFs have financed less than 20 percent of their SF operations, the IDB evaluators warn that "[d]onors cannot claim that the funds are successful and sustainable" until countries make a greater contribution. "[D]onors cannot be expected to provide 80–90 percent of the cost of fund operations indefinitely."[45]

The disappointing record of SFs in targeting poor communities may result from the demand-driven dynamics unleashed by the SF model itself. Poor communities are handicapped in responding to SF-like initiatives in that they require prior organizing, preparation of project proposals, and choosing and monitoring of outside contractors.[46] These communities are often less organized, less linked to official networks, and are spoken for more by single clientelistic figures than by inclusive community groups. The communities are often difficult to access, and they tend therefore to be less visited by private providers and NGOs. Whether for reasons of necessity or of maximizing profits and efficiency, these providers concern themselves with keeping down the costs of transport, salaries, per diems for travel, and time spent preparing proposals. In some cases, and with the best of intentions, the SF agency painstakingly mapped poverty and deficiencies of social services in the region served by the SF. But this still did not counteract the comparative advantage of communities that were better off—*within* the "poor-designated" municipalities or subregions—in competing for funds.[47] All this explains why it is often not the communities that choose project choices and designs, but firms, politicians, or SF staffs.

Some of the SFs' very strengths seem to be the sources of their weaknesses, which does not augur well for correcting the latter. For example, the flexibility and speed of SF disbursement frequently causes communities to have less choice, not more—undermining their ability to gather information about options for alternative projects, and to deliberate and choose among them. What's more, the prized autonomy and special privileges of SFs also reduce the opportunities and likelihood of their working complementarily with existing institutions of government, whose lack of involvement partly explains the frequent failure of maintenance and operation. Also problematic, the same donor accounts that laud the more flexible and speedy disbursement of SFs point disapprovingly to these traits as causing SF-served communities to have *less* choice—with less information about options, and less time to deliberate.[48] Finally, SF autonomy does not necessarily translate, as claimed, into more "apolitical," technocratic, or "private-sector-like" management styles. The less noted flip side of this autonomy is the SFs' vulnerability to political manipulation.

Turning Assumptions into Questions

The evidence on SFs and other decentralizing experiences is somewhat muddied by the fact that many accounts treat as assumptions matters that should be treated as questions. For example, decentralization and outsourcing to local providers are assumed to create a special dynamic leading to better service—a dynamic that is said to be missing in traditional public programs. According to this logic, private firms and NGOs help reduce government's monopoly power as provider, an important source of its inefficiency. The ensuing competition among potential providers yields results that are more responsive to consumer needs and preferences, and more tailored to local conditions.

The evidence from donor evaluations and other studies, including my own, does not support these assertions. First, it revealed that private providers can be as standardizing and insensitive to user needs or local conditions as considered typical of the public sector.[49] Second, NGOs were barely present on the scene, accounting for no more than 15 percent of expenditures by most Latin American SFs.[50] When they *were* involved, their projects were among the least sustainable,[51] and often suffered from incompetence and politicization.[52] This raises questions about leaning so heavily on NGOs for decentralization's benefits to materialize.

Another troubling assertion is that many SFs are demand-driven. The evidence suggests that many of these particular SFs can be more accurately described as *supply-*driven in that they substitute a new cast of "supply-driving" characters for the traditional bureaucrats of faraway agencies. These new characters include building contractors, equipment suppliers, and project design firms, together with the more familiar political personages (mayors, legislators, ward bosses) and government technical agents themselves—this time from the SF.[53] To the extent that these actors determine the choice of projects, rather than community members, it is not surprising that sustainability and ownership often fail to materialize. But continuing to describe these programs indiscriminately as reflecting community preferences makes it difficult to understand exactly what goes wrong—and, more importantly if things work well, what goes right. If there is a distinction to be made between SFs and other government programs, then, it may lie less in bringing beneficiary choice into the picture than in substituting another array of supply-driven forces. Supply-drivenness, however, is exactly the critique that is made of *traditional* government provision. This shifts the focus of attention from the matter of demand-driven vs. supply-driven, and the SF model vs. traditional government, to which kinds of supply-driven programs are better than others.

Information Asymmetries: The New Spoilers

Some of the afflictions of SFs and other programs serving poor and rural populations originate in "asymmetries" of information and power. These figure importantly in the recent literature of the new institutional economics. Information asymmetries can cause trouble in various kinds of contractual relationships—between buyers and sellers, service providers and users, and central governments and local governments. If one side knows much more than the other and keeps that information to itself, the underinformed and less powerful party to the transaction does not fare well. In fact, the new institutional economists have warned that when these kinds of asymmetries prevail, the usual bets on the gains to be made from decentralization and its associated measures are off. The economist Joseph Stiglitz played a seminal role in developing this literature of information asymmetries and transactions costs in the 1980s.[54] Later in the 1990s, when Stiglitz was Senior Vice President and Chief Economist for Development of the World Bank, he warned of the stranglehold that these asymmetries could exert on the benefits normally expected from decentralization, as well as from privatization.[55]

Those who worry about asymmetries of information and power typically assign to government the role of correcting or counterbalancing them—as regulator, mediator, and broker for the weaker party to the contract, and as provider of information. Indeed, this is exactly what SF units are meant to do. Social Fund project designs, or at least the evaluations of existing SF programs, typically call for strong public information campaigns about the new choices available to communities, and the procedures for taking advantage of them. But the evidence shows information and community choice to have been surprisingly low in many of the assisted communities, even in the Brazilian programs of my field research where project design included information campaigns and the donor paid serious monitoring attention to them. Combined with the typical political, bureaucratic, and market forces present in many SF environments, ironically, the model may actually reinforce the very asymmetry of information that it was meant to reduce.

The findings from my Brazil research projects shed light on this strange outcome. Three separate sets of actors turned out to have a distinct interest in *limiting* information rather than broadcasting it: contractors and project-design firms, elected leaders and other politicians, and SF management and staff.[56] It is important to note that their information-limiting behavior was not simply motivated by rent-seeking and other forms of mean-spiritedness. Just as often, these actors were doing what they thought was right—maximizing profits or efficiency, enacting a particular vision of the public good, insisting on standards representing the profession's consensus about best practice, or making the best of a work environment in which demand for projects exceeded supply. This means that even when actors thought they were serving the public good, or when firms were behaving at their best, the results were not that different from those said to be produced by rent-seeking behavior! This explanation for SF shortcomings is in some ways more troubling than that of rent-seeking and corruption: It

suggests that even when the decentralization dynamic of the SFs is working as it should, it cannot produce the desired results.

Unfortunately, SFs typically work in environments where asymmetries of information and power are particularly common—rural areas and poor communities. Population densities are lower, illiteracy is higher, and travel and other means of communication are more difficult. Government is less present, whether as provider or regulator, partly because this kind of presence is more difficult and costly under such conditions. For this and other reasons, then, the SF model might actually work *least* well in such environments, not better. An indicator of this problem can be found in the remedies suggested by the donors to fix SF shortcomings.

A representative sampling of such remedies includes: more monitoring and supervision, more transparent and objective selection criteria for projects, more training, more public information campaigns about project choices available to communities, more tolerance by project managers for "participation," more poor-targeted selection criteria, more "demand orientation" and community participation in helping communities to choose their projects, more attention to organizing users around operations and maintenance or to committing line agencies to that responsibility, and finally, more coordination with line agencies and their sectoral programs.[57] Many of these remedies would require a significant increase of SF agency presence in the countryside in terms of time, personnel, resources, and effort. This kind of change, moreover, would compromise one of the SFs' most acclaimed strengths—their "leanness" and low administrative costs. More constructively, if becoming more supply-driven is the solution rather than the problem, these conclusions suggest that donors might look with greater enthusiasm and diligence to reform prospects within existing public institutions.

Getting Out of the Fix

The difference between my judgments about SFs and those of the donors turns less on the empirical findings—given that much of the aforementioned case evidence comes from the donor evaluations themselves—than on our differing interpretations of the problems revealed by this evidence. To their credit, the donors take the flaws they report seriously. But they also assume that these flaws can be readily fixed without compromising the strengths of the model. I see these findings, in contrast, as meriting greater pause. If informed community choice, sustainability, and reduction of inequities of service provision are incompatible with the SFs' most marked achievements, then they are not much better in the long run than existing approaches to reforming traditional agencies, or in dealing with similar problems in the recent decentralization experience.

Finding incompatibility among basic goals or instruments within a particular program is not unusual. Scholars of the behavior of organizations have long shown how the goals of any particular organization often conflict, one with the other. Indeed, a mix of conflicting goals often serves various organizational purposes and constituencies well. Treatises on organizational leadership show how the best agency managers are those who manage these contradictions artfully, and in a way that presents a unified face to the outside world. It is not the incompatibilities themselves that are cause for concern, then, but the lack of recognition of them and, hence, their implications.

Trimming the perception of SFs down to size would make it possible to look at the SF experience and that of traditional government agencies with a more open and curious mind. At their best, for example, SFs may represent a "deconcentrated" version of supply-driven service—rather than demand-driven or decentralized service—that leads to the construction of small infrastructure projects more quickly and at lower cost. It must be kept in mind, however, that these programs seem to do no better than traditional agencies in generating maintenance and operational support. Social Funds may also show the way for traditional public agencies to simplify procurement regulations. At the same time, no such demonstration effect has yet been reported in SF evaluation studies.

The reported achievements of SFs in rapid disbursement rates and lower unit costs, in turn, may represent such significant progress in service delivery that the approach is well worth pursuing.[58] If these gains are so palpable, it is important to pay attention to how they can be applied to reducing costs and delays in existing agencies and programs. At the same time, however, this mode of operation can also jeopardize participation, locally tailored solutions, and sustainability. Similarly, SFs may work at their best only for certain kinds of communities—better off, better organized, or less remote. But what works best for the rest, who are less well off and so much the object of policy concern?

Finally, it should be noted that one of the best SFs is actually most *unlike* the average SF—the Chilean SF. In this case, the SF is not an autonomous unit and works instead through a line agency of the central government. (A study comparing the Chilean with the Venezuelan SF cited the unusual integration of the Chilean SF with the line ministries as an explanation for why it was more successful.)[59] It does not circumvent procurement and civil-service regulations. And it is financed mainly by the Chilean government, in comparison to the continuingly heavy donor funding of most other SFs.[60] These traits place the Chilean SF closer to existing government than the average. Outlier cases like this raise questions about what actually makes SFs work when they do. More importantly, these cases should be mined for an understanding of how to reduce some of the important limitations of SFs, while at the same time showing how the experience can be made more germane to reform efforts in the traditional public sector.

The findings reported here, in sum, raise important questions about SFs and other reforms, whether decentralizing, deconcentrating, or neither. If SFs and traditional public institutions all tend to be supply-driven, that is, then we should be asking which of these interventions leads to better results, in which particular circumstances and places, and for which particular tasks. Correspondingly, what are the circumstances under which private firms providing public goods and services are, à la Stiglitz, actually likely to be more responsive than public institutions to user needs? These questions will not yield answers that are necessarily pro-SF or anti-SF, or pro- or antitraditional government. Importantly, however, they do not start out by assuming that programs with demand-driven designs actually *are* demand-driven, or that private and decentralized provision always elicits more user choice and customer-tailored results. Turning the assumptions into questions instead could generate considerable empirical material of value about how communities decide, how markets work under outsourcing and partial privatization, and how politics influences outcomes—whether for the better or for the worse.

Gaining Favor

If SFs do not measure up to the broadly held understanding of how they work and what they accomplish, then why are they so popular? Why do the very documents relating the shortcomings previously cited conclude on such a positive note? If SFs are afflicted with some of the same grave problems that afflict existing government agencies, then why has this model elicited so much enthusiasm in comparison to efforts to reform traditional agencies working on similar problems? If many staff members of the donor agencies themselves share these skeptical views about SFs, then why has the more enthusiastic interpretation won out, and so strongly influenced policy?

In part, the popularity of SFs is itself supply-driven, but in this case the "supply-drivers" are donor agencies rather than traditional government agencies in borrower countries. The reason for SF popularity, that is, relates not only to the acclaimed features of the model, but also to the workings of the donors as large bureaucracies. As such, they are subject to the same dynamics that drive all large organizations, including their complex relationship with and sensitivity to their outside environments. For perfectly understandable reasons, many donor professionals find it more satisfying to work with SFs and on SF projects than with traditional agencies. The management and staff of SF agencies in borrower countries have far fewer bureaucratic masters to serve than ministries and other existing agencies, and are therefore more easily accessible to donor project officers and more able, if willing, to carry out their suggestions for improved service. All this provides a greater sense of control and accomplishment to donor project officers, making it easier to design such projects and monitor them, and to see things happen before one's eyes. To dedicated professionals working within the bureaucratic constraints of a large donor organization, this makes for satisfying work.

Adding to this liberating effect, the regulations of both the World Bank and the IDB endow SFs with something akin to fast-track status compared to other categories of projects. The World Bank suspends conditionality requirements on SF projects, which normally slow down and complicate the trajectory of project approval in the Bank. IDB rules require that funding for SFs and other projects falling in this more subsidized category must be approved before some other categories of projects offered on less subsidized terms can go forward. This requirement turns a more numerous and influential group of IDB professionals and directors into SF advocates—in itself contributing to faster project approvals. To the same end, the SF agency's association with an international donor is an important source of power and prestige in its own bureaucratic world. This helps counterbalance the jealousies and resistance of other bureaucratic actors on whom SF projects are dependent for maintenance and operation, and who resent the special status of SFs and their freedom from civil-service and procurement regulations.[61]

Borrower-government elected leaders also support SFs, though this is partly in reaction to donor suggestion. Because donors often suggest SFs as part of a larger lending package, borrower governments tend to favor their creation as a surefire way of obtaining donor financing. In addition, donors have invested considerable effort in creating and supporting a network of SF professionals from various countries, funding them to travel to international meetings where they share their experiences and learn about best practices in other SFs.[62] This

nurturing has led to the formation of an articulate and visible support group for SFs within and across borrower countries themselves, which must surely boost morale and enhance learning. Support for such sustained cross-country networking is usually not available to public servants trying to carry out reform within line agencies, although they face at least as daunting and isolating an environment as those working at SFs.

Social Funds are also popular because of their crucial role in helping donors sell austerity reforms to borrower countries. Because donors present SFs to governments as safety-net measures that help reduce poverty and unemployment (despite the evidence that SFs do not really fulfill these goals), they help counteract the widespread public criticism of these governments that austerity measures fall disproportionately on the poor. The belief that SFs will help ease the adoption of austerity packages, in turn, attracts support from macroeconomists in international financial institutions whose task is to convince countries to adopt the macroreform packages. This support represents an influential and powerful voice for SFs—the voice of professionals who would otherwise have no particular interest in such programmatic interventions.

Social Funds also draw powerful support because they help leaders out of the political dilemma created by such austerity programs and other unpopular reform measures. The political assist from SFs does not necessarily work directly through their actual impact on the poor, but through their use by elected leaders to selectively court groups of voters, whether among the poorest or not. In that the macroreform programs inevitably cause governments to lose votes from important constituencies, this leads to the aggressive courting by leaders of new constituents to make up for the losses, often through the dispensing of patronage. Social Funds, like all "distributive" programs that provide numerous individual grants for small projects that are spatially dispersed, are an excellent vehicle for such patronage—as demonstrated in richly chronicled accounts of SFs and electoral politics in Peru and Mexico.[63] That elected leaders can distribute these funds in a discretionary manner to some districts and not others, and that they are exempt from existing formulas for revenue-sharing with local governments, also contributes to their suitability for patronage purposes.

Social Funds' prized autonomy and freedom from bureaucratic encumbrances, in sum, also makes them vulnerable to political meddling. While donors are praising SF autonomy, presidents and other elected officials are viewing it as almost the opposite kind of blessing. To them, SFs offer *easier* access than regulation-bound ministries for meeting their electoral needs. This politics-as-usual side of SFs tends to be obscured by the accounts of SFs as a "modern" model of management, and by their inclusion in packages of "modernizing" reforms to be carried out by "serious" leaders.

The final reason for SF popularity among donors relates to their effectiveness as a powerful "development narrative," to use the words of Emery Roe and others. Roe writes that in environments with great ambiguity as to cause and effect, such narratives offer convincing and simple explanations for the causes of certain problems and provide appealingly straightforward blueprints for action (1991, 1999). Because of their power as narratives, he argues, these accounts are rather invulnerable to empirical evidence that challenges their accuracy—such as the evidence of SF shortcomings, and of insignificant impacts on poverty and unemployment.

Roe develops three examples from Africa of such development narratives and contrasts them with extensive empirical findings to the contrary.[64] In each of these cases, he shows how remarkably resistant these narratives have been to case evidence that contradicted them. He draws on his empirical material to make programmatic suggestions that differ from the "blueprint for action" attached to each of the three narratives. At the same time, however, he chides academics and consultants like himself for "naively" thinking that carefully gathered empirical evidence could have the same kind of power the narratives have in influencing the way institutions think about and act upon such problems. The talk about SFs would seem to meet Roe's qualifications of a successful development narrative, with a corresponding blueprint for action. This also helps explain why donors remain so enthusiastic about SFs, and so accepting of the causal assumptions underlying the model, despite the questionable evidence that they themselves have unearthed.

Bibliography

Abrúcio, Fernando Luiz. 1998. *Os barões da federação: Os governadores e a redemocratização brasileira.* Departamento de Ciência Política da USP [Universidade de São Paulo]. São Paulo: Editora Hucitec.

Ames, Barry. 1995. "Electoral Strategy under Open-List Proportional Representation." *American Journal of Political Science* 39(2, May): 406–33.

Ames, Barry. 2000. *Institutions and Politics in Brazil.* Ann Arbor, MI: University of Michigan Press. (Relevant material drawn from Part 1, Chapter 4 of "Institutions and Politics in Brazil," draft manuscript, 1996.)

Angell, Alan, and Carol Graham. 1995. "Can Social Sector Reform Make Adjustment Sustainable and Equitable? Lessons from Chile and Venezuela." *Journal of Latin American Studies* 27(1, February): 189–219.

Barnett, Richard A. 1994. "Publicity Strategy Evaluation, Northeast Rural Development Project." World Bank, Recife Office. August 11.

Bianchi, Tito. 1997. "Supply-led Technology Adoption in Maranhão, Brazil: A Case of Development Trade in the Small-scale Furniture Sector." MIT/State of Maranhão Project. Master's Thesis, Department of Urban Studies and Planning, Massachusetts Institute of Technology. May. Cambridge, Massachusetts.

Bianchi, Tito. 1998. "Built to Last: A Couple of Well-Known Secrets About Cooperatives and What Keeps Them Alive." Report to the MIT/BNB (Banco do Nordeste) Project. July 14. Cambridge, Massachusetts.

Bonfim, Washington L. de Souza. 1999. "Qual Mudança? Os Empresários e a Americanização do Ceará." Unpublished Ph.D Dissertation in Political Science, Instituto Universitário de Pesquisas do Rio de Janeiro (IUPERJ). Rio de Janeiro.

Boschi, Renato. 1998. "Democratic Governance and Participation: Tales of Two Cities." Universidade Federal de Minas Gerais/Instituto Universitário de Pesquisas do Rio de Janeiro.

Cornelius, Wayne A., Ann L. Craig, and Jonathan Fox. 1994. *Transforming State-Society Relations in Mexico: The National Solidarity Strategy.* San Diego: Center for U.S.–Mexican Studies, University of California.

Cornia, Andrea Giovanni. 1999. "Social Funds in Stabilization and Adjustment Programmes." United Nations University/World Institute for Development Economics Research, Helsinki. Forthcoming. In Andrea Giovanni Cornia, ed., *Inequality and Poverty Under the Washington Consensus.* New York: Oxford University Press.

Cornia, Andrea Giovanni, and Sanjay Reddy. 2000. "The Impact of Adjustment-related Social Funds on Distribution and Poverty." Manuscript.

Costa, E. 1978. "An Assessment of the Flows and Benefits Generated by Public Investment in the Employment Guarantee Scheme of Maharashtra." Working Paper No. 12. Geneva: International Labour Organisation/World Employment Programme.

Damiani, Octavio. 1996. "Report for the Government of Brazil—World Bank Commission: Rural Poverty." Cambridge, MA: Department of Urban Studies and Planning, Massachusetts Institute of Technology. February.

Deolalikar, Anil B., and Raghav Gaiha. 1996. "What Determines Female Participation in Rural Public Works? The Case of India's Employment Guarantee Scheme." University of Washington and the University of Delhi. April.

D'Silva, E. H. 1983. "Effectiveness of Rural Public Works in Labour-surplus Economies: Case of the Maharashtra Employment Guarantee Scheme." Ithaca, NY: Cornell International Agricultural Monograph No. 97, Cornell University.

Echeverri-Gent, John. 1988. "Guaranteed Employment in an Indian State: The Maharashtra Experience." *Asian Survey* 28(12, December): 1294–1310.

Echeverri-Gent, John. 1993. *The State and the Poor: Public Policy and Political Development in India and the United States.* Berkeley, CA: University of California Press.

Eicher, Carl K. 1999. "Institutions and the African Farmer." CIMMYT [International Maize and Wheat Improvement Center] Third Distinguished Economist Lecture. Mexico, DF: CIMMYT

Fox, Jonathan, and Josefina Aranda. 1996. *Decentralization and Rural Development in Mexico: Community Participation in Oaxaca's Municipal Funds Program.* Monograph Series, 42. San Diego, CA: Center for U.S.–Mexican Studies, University of California.

Gaiha, Raghav. 1998. "Do Anti-Poverty Programmes Reach the Rural Poor in India?" New Delhi: Faculty of Management Studies, University of Delhi. May.

Gay, Robert. 1990. "Popular Incorporation and Prospects for Democracy: Some Implications of the Brazilian Case." *Theory and Society* 19: 447–63.

Gay, Robert. Forthcoming. "The Broker and the Thief: A Parable (Reflections on Popular Politics in Brazil)." *Luso-Brazilian Review.*

Gay, Robert. Forthcoming. "Rethinking Clientelism: Demands, Discourses and Practices in Contemporary Brazil." *European Review of Latin American and Carribean Studies.*

Gershberg, Alec Ian. 1994. "Distributing Resources in the Education Sector: Solidarity's Escuela Digna Program." In Wayne A. Cornelius et al., eds., *Transforming State-Society Relations in Mexico: The National Solidarity Strategy.* San Diego, CA: Center for U.S.–Mexican Studies, University of California, pp. 233–54.

Gibson, Edward L. 1997. "The Populist Road to Market Reform: Policy and Electoral Coalitions in Mexico and Argentina." *World Politics* 49(April): 339–70.

Graham, Carol. 1994. "Mexico's Solidarity Program in Comparative Context: Demand-based Poverty Alleviation Programs in Latin America, Africa, and Eastern Europe." In Wayne A. Cornelius et al., eds., *Transforming State-Society Relations in Mexico: The National Solidarity Strategy.* San Diego, CA: Center for U.S.–Mexican Studies, University of California, pp. 309–28.

Graham, Carol. 1998. "The Capitalization and Popular Participation Programs in Bolivia." In Carol Graham, ed., *Private Markets for Public Goods: Raising the Stakes in Economic Reform.* Washington, D.C.: Brookings Institution Press, pp. 139–87.

Graham, Carol, and Cheikh Kane. 1998. "Opportunistic Government or Sustaining Reform? Electoral Trends and Public-Expenditure Patterns in Peru, 1990–1995." *Latin American Research Review* 33(1): 67–104.

Heller, Patrick. 1999. *The Labor of Development: Workers and the Transformation of Capitalism in Kerala, India.* Ithaca, NY: Cornell University Press.

Herring, Ronald J. 1983. *Land to the Tiller: The Political Economy of Agrarian Reform in South Asia.* New Haven, CT: Yale University Press.

Herring, Ronald J. 1998. "Agrarian Reform, Path Dependency and Persistent Poverty: Lessons from the United States and India." For the Conference "What Can be Done about Poverty?," Institute of Development Studies, University of Sussex, June 29–July 1, 1998.

Herring, Ronald J., and Rex M. Edwards. 1983. "Guaranteeing Employment to the Rural Poor: Social Functions and Class Interests in the Employment Guarantee Scheme in Western India." *World Development* 11(7): 575–92.

Hesse, Fernando J. 1996. Against All Odds: Successful Cases of Collective Use of Tractors in Rural Ceará, Brazil." MIT/State of Ceará Project II. Master's Thesis, Department of Urban Studies and Planning, Massachusetts Institute of Technology. June. Cambridge, Massachusetts.

Hutchful, Eboe. 1994. " 'Smoke and Mirrors': The World Bank's Social Dimensions of Adjustment (SDA) Programme." *Review of African Political Economy* 62: 569–84.

Inter-American Development Bank (IDB). 1997a. *Social Investment Funds in Latin America: Past Performance and Future Role.* By Margaret Goodman et al. Evaluation Office, Social Programs and Sustainable Development Department. March. Washington, D.C.

Inter-American Development Bank (IDB). 1997b. *Chile: Fondos de Solidaridad de Inversión Social (FOSIS).* Informe de la Consultora Srta. Dagmar Raczynski. Evaluation Office, EVO. June 1996. In *Social Investment Funds in Latin America: Past Performance and Future Role,* Chapter 2. A Joint Project Between the Evaluation Office and the Social Programs and Sustainable Development Department. June. Washington, D.C.

Inter-American Development Bank (IDB). 1998. "The Use of Social Investment Funds as an Instrument For Combating Poverty." A Bank Strategy Paper. July. Washington, D.C.

Joshi, Anu. 1999. "Mobilizing the Poor? Activism and the Employment Guarantee Scheme, Maharashtra." Draft. Institute of Development Studies, Sussex.

Lowi, Theodore J. 1964. "American Business, Public Policy, Case-Studies, and Political Theory." *World Politics* 14(July): 677–715.

Lustig, Nora, ed. 1995. "Coping with Austerity: Poverty and Inequality in Latin America." A study jointly sponsored by the Brookings Institute and the Inter-American Dialogue. Washington, D.C.: The Brookings Institution.

Lustig, Nora. 1997. "The Safety Nets which Are Not Safety Nets: Social Investment Funds in Latin America." Draft. October 31. Washington, D.C.

Molinar Horcasitas, Juan, and Jeffrey A. Weldon. 1994. "Electoral Determinants and Consequences of National Solidarity." In Wayne A. Cornelius et al., eds., *Transforming State–Society Relations in Mexico: The National Solidarity Strategy.* San Diego, CA: Center for U.S.–Mexican Studies, University of California, pp. 123–42.

Morrison, Judith A. 1997. "What Works in Rural Afro-Brazilian Communities of Maranhão? Impressions of Successful Agency Interventions." Master's Thesis, Department of Urban Studies and Planning, Massachusetts Institute of Technology. MIT/State of Maranhão Project. May 12. Cambridge, Massachusetts.

Natalacchio, Marcela. 1998. "Organization and Empowerment of Rural Women in the Babassu Areas of Maranhão, Brazil." MIT/State of Maranhão Project. Master's Thesis, Graduate School of Arts and Sciences, Boston University. Boston.

Nelson, Joan. 1997. "Reforming Social Sector Governance: A Political Perspective." Paper prepared for a conference on Governance, Poverty Eradication, and Social Policy, Harvard University, 12–14 November. November 7. Overseas Development Council, Washington D.C.

Nordhaus, William D. 1975. "The Political Business Cycle." *Review of Economic Studies* 42(2): 1969–90.

Pinhanez, Monica F. 1997. "Shattered Power, Reconstructed Coalitions: An Analysis of Rural Labor Unions in Maranhão, Brazil." MIT/State of Maranhão Project. Master's Thesis, Department of Urban Studies and Planning, Massachusetts Institute of Technology. May. Cambridge, Massachusetts.

Quirós, Rosa. 1996. "Rural Water Supplies that Work, Endure and Reach the Poor: Lessons from Ceará, Brazil." MIT/State of Ceará Project II. Master's Thesis, Department of Urban

Studies and Planning, Massachusetts Institute of Technology. May. Cambridge, Massachusetts.

Roberts, Kenneth M. 1996. "Neoliberalism and the Transformation of Populism in Latin America: The Peruvian Case." *World Politics* 48(1): 82–116.

Roberts, Kenneth M., and Moises Arce. 1998. "Neoliberalism and Lower-Class Voting Behavior in Peru." *Comparative Political Studies* 31(2): 393–407

Roe, Emery M. 1991. "Development Narratives, Or Making the Best of Blueprint Development." *World Development* 19(4): 287–300.

Roe, Emery M. 1999. *Except Africa: Remaking Development, Rethinking Power*. New Brunswick, NJ: Transaction Publishers.

Rogoff, Kenneth. 1990. "Equilibrium Political Budget Cycles." *The American Economic Review* 80(1, March): 21–36.

Rogoff, Kenneth. 1994. "Equilibrium Political Budget Cycles." In Torsten Persson and Guido Tabellini, eds., *Monetary and Fiscal Policy*, Vol. 2, pp. 47–70. Cambridge, MA: MIT Press.

Schady, Norbert R. 1999. "Seeking Votes: The Political Economy of Expenditures by the Peruvian Social Fund (FONCODES), 1991–1995." Policy Research Working Paper 2166. The World Bank. August. (Page references in the chapter are to a 1998 draft.)

Scott, James. 1998. *Seeing Like a State: How Certain Schemes to Improve the Human Condition Have Failed*. New Haven, CT: Yale University Press.

Seabright, Paul. 1997. "Is Co-operation Habit-Forming?" In Partha Dasgupta and Karl-Göran Mäler, eds., *The Environment and Emerging Development Issues*, Vol. 2, pp. 283–307. Oxford: Clarendon Press.

Serrano Berthet, Rodrigo. 1996. *Who Knows What's Best for the Poor: Demand-Driven Policies and Rural Poverty in Northeast Brazil*. MIT/State of Ceará Project II. Master's Thesis, Department of Urban Studies and Planning, Massachusetts Institute of Technology. May 22. Cambridge, Massachusetts.

Serrano Berthet, Rodrigo. 1997. "Fruitful Policies: The Adoption of Cash Crops by Subsistence Farmers in Maranhão, Brazil." First-year Doctoral Paper, Department of Urban Studies and Planning, Massachusetts Institute of Technology. MIT/State of Maranhão Project. May. Cambridge, Massachusetts.

Skocpol, Theda, and Kenneth Finegold. 1982. "State Capacity and Economic Intervention in the Early New Deal." *Political Science Quarterly* 97(2): 255–78.

Souza, Celina Maria de. 1997. *Constitutional Engineering in Brazil: The Politics of Federalism and Decentralization*. New York: St. Martin's Press.

Steffes, Ann. 1997. "An Organizational Analysis of Rural Drinking Water Provision in Ecuador and Maranhão, Brazil." Department of Urban Studies and Planning, Massachusetts Institute of Technology. MIT/State of Maranhão Project. February 10.

Stewart, Frances, and Willem van der Geest. 1995. "Adjustment and Social Funds: Political Panacea or Effective Poverty Reduction?" In Frances Stewart, ed., *Adjustment and Poverty*, pp. 108–37. London: Routledge.

Stiglitz, Joseph E. 1985. "Information and Economic Analysis: A Perspective." *Economic Journal* 95: 24–41, Supplement.

Stiglitz, Joseph E. 1998. "More Instruments and Broader Goals: Moving toward the Post-Washington Consensus." World Institute for Development Economics Research (WIDER). WIDER Annual Lectures 2. January.

Tagle, Laura. 1996. "Inadvertently Reaching the Poor: The Diffusion of Small Scale Irrigation in Northeast Brazil." MIT/State of Ceará Project II. Master's Thesis, Department of Urban Studies and Planning, Massachusetts Institute of Technology. June. Cambridge, Massachusetts.

Tendler, Judith. 1982. *Rural Projects Through Urban Eyes: An Interpretation of the World Bank's New-style Rural Development Projects*. Staff Working Paper No. 532. Washington, D.C.: World Bank.

Tendler, Judith. 1993a. *New Lessons from Old Projects: The Workings of Rural Development in Northeast Brazil*. A World Bank Operations Evaluation Study. Washington, D.C.: World Bank.

Tendler, Judith. 1993b. "Tales of Dissemination in Small-farm Agriculture: Lessons for Institution Builders." *World Development* 21(10, October): 1567–82.

Tendler, Judith. 1997. *Good Government in the Tropics*. Baltimore, MD: The Johns Hopkins University Press. [Paperback version, 1998; Portuguese version published by Editora Revan and ENAP (Escola Nacional de Administração Pública) (Rio de Janeiro) 1998.]

Tendler, Judith. 1999. *The Rise of Social Funds: What Are They a Model Of?* Monograph for the United Nations Development Program (UNDP). January.

Tendler, Judith, and Monica Amorim. 1994. "Small Firms and Their Helpers: Lessons on Demand." *World Development* 24(3, March): 407–26.

Tendler, Judith, and Sara Freedheim. 1996. "Trust in a Rent-seeking World: Health and Government Transformed in Northeast Brazil." *World Development* 22(12, December): 1771–91.

Thomas, John W. 1986. "Food for Work: An Analysis of Current Experience and Recommendations for Future Performance." Development Discussion Paper No. 213. Cambridge, MA: Harvard Institute for International Development, Harvard University.

United Nations Educational, Scientific, and Cultural Organization (UNICEF). 1998. *Social Funds in Developing Countries: Recent Experiences and Lessons*. By Sanjay Reddy. UNICEF Staff Working Papers. Evaluation, Policy and Planning Series Number EPP-EVL-98-002. June. New York.

Vieira da Cunha, Paulo, and Maria Valeria Junho Peña. 1997. *The Limits and Merits of Participation*. Policy Research Working Paper No. 1838. The World Bank, Office of the Senior Vice President and Chief Economist. October. Washington, D.C.

Vivian, Jessica. 1994. "NGOs and Sustainable Development in Zimbabwe: No Magic Bullets." *Development and Change* 25(1): 167–93.

Vivian, Jessica, and Gladys Maseko. 1994. "NGOs, Participation and Rural Development: Testing the Assumptions with Evidence from Zimbabwe." United Nations Research Institute for Development. Discussion Paper DP 49. United Nations Research Institute for Social Development. January.

von Braun, Joachim, Tesfaye Teken, and Patrick Webb. 1992. "Labor-Intensive Public Works for Food Security in Africa: Past Experience and Future Potential." *International Labour Review* 131(1): 19–34.

Webb, Kathryn Vandever, Kye Woo Lee, and Anna Maria Sant'Anna. 1995. *The Participation of Nongovernmental Organizations in Poverty Alleviation: A Case Study of the Honduras Social Investment Fund Project*. Discussion Paper No. 295. Washington, D.C.: World Bank. January.

Weyland, Kurt. 1998. "Swallowing the Bitter Pill: Sources of Popular Support for Neoliberal Reform in Latin America." *Comparative Political Studies* 31(5, October).

White, Robert, and Carl Eicher. 1999. "NGOs and African Farmers: A Skeptical Perspective." Staff Paper No. 99-01. Department of Agricultural Economics. East Lansing, MI: University of Michigan. January.

Woodall, Brian. 1996. *Japan Under Construction: Corruption, Politics, and Public Works.* Berkeley, CA: University of California Press.

World Bank (WB). 1995. *Decentralized Rural Development and Enhanced Community Participation: A Case Study from Northeast Brazil.* Policy Research Working Paper No. 1498. By Johan van Zyl et al. Agriculture and Natural Resources Department, Sector Policy and Water Resources Division. August. Washington, D.C.

World Bank (WB). 1997a. "Portfolio Improvement Program Review of the Social Funds Portfolio." The Working Group for the Social Funds Portfolio Review, headed by Ishrat Husain (PREM). Forthcoming as World Bank Technical Paper. May.

World Bank (WB). 1997b. "Innovations in the Delivery and Organization of Social Assistance and Poverty-Targeted Programs." In K. Subbarao et al., *Safety Net Programs and Poverty Reduction: Lessons from Cross-Country Experience.* Washington, D.C.: World Bank.

World Bank (WB). 1998a. *Designing Rules for Demand-Driven Rural Investment Funds: The Latin American Experience.* By Thomas Wiens and Maurizio Guadagni. World Bank Technical Paper No. 407. May. Washington, D.C.

World Bank (WB). 1998b. *Social Funds and Reaching the Poor: Experiences and Future Directions.* Anthony Bigio, ed., Washington, D.C.: World Bank.

World Bank (WB). 1998c. *Getting an Earful: A Review of Beneficiary Assessments of Social Funds.* Social Protection Discussion Paper No. 9816. By Daniel Owen and Julie Van Domelen.

Wright, Gavin A. 1974. "The Political Economy of New Deal Spending: An Econometric Analysis." *The Review of Economics and Statistics* 56(1): 30–38.

Notes

1. I am most grateful for comments on an earlier version of this chapter from Meenu Tewari, Rodrigo Serrano, Hubert Schmitz, Anna Maria Sant'Anna, Sanjay Reddy, Sonia Ospina, Joan Nelson, Anu Joshi, Maurizio Guadagni, Margaret Goodman, Raghav Gaiha, Osvaldo Feinstein, Octavio Damiani, and John Briscoe. For a very detailed reading of the chapter and extensive comments, I am indebted to Mounir Tabet, Mick Moore, Richard Locke, Robert Kaufman, Anu Joshi, Steen Lau Jorgensen, Carol Graham, Ruth Dixon, and Soniya Carvalho. I also benefited substantially from feedback received at seminars at the World Bank, the Inter-American Development Bank, the David Rockefeller Center for Latin American Studies at Harvard, the Institute for Development Studies at Sussex, and the School of International and Public Affairs at Columbia University. I thank Sandra Hackman for excellent editing.

Funding for the field research in Brazil was graciously provided by the state governments of Ceará and Maranhão, the Bank of the Northeast, and the World Bank. For financial support for writing the larger document from which this chapter was drawn, I thank the MIT/UNDP Decentralization Project and the Division of Management Governance and Development of the United Nations Development Program. For support for my research with students and for leave time, I thank Bish Sanyal, Chair of the Department of Urban Studies and Planning of the Massachusetts Institute of Technology. None of these persons or institutions is responsible for or necessarily agrees with my findings.

2. These numbers are approximate and a few years out of date because of the difficulty of finding consistently defined cross-donor data on SFs. In May 1997, the World Bank (WB) reported having committed US\$1.367 billion to SFs in 34 countries (WB 1997a: 5, and Attachment 1, end-fiscal year 1996); the Inter-American Development Bank (IDB) reported an additional US\$1.3 billion in 16 countries, 8 of which involved SFs to which the WB also contributed, making a net total of 41 countries for these two largest donors (IDB 1997a: 10, Table 2.1). The IDB reported an additional US\$558.2 million in its Latin American SFs as coming from "other donors"—mainly European donors, which does not include SFs funded outside Latin America by these other donors. For the latter reason, and because the numbers do not capture the past few years' SF commitments in Southeast Asia and Eastern Europe in particular, the totals in the text are an underestimate. Also, in several countries, the WB and IDB have more than one project, or have given second loans to existing SFs; in the 34 countries with WB-funded SFs, 60 projects have been funded—some representing follow-on loans and others the creation of a second SF in that country. For the 16 countries with IDB-funded SFs, this includes 18 projects.

3. This chapter is not meant to be a thorough review of the SF experience or of the arguments for and against them. For this, the reader can turn to several comprehensive donor-funded reviews of the evidence and other excellent studies of SFs by outside researchers, cited in the endnotes throughout or appearing in the Bibliography at the end of this chapter.

4. Nora Lustig (1997) contests this statement persuasively, which has been frequently repeated in donor documents. With respect to the Latin American SFs, at least, she shows that donor-funded SF projects were actually underway well before the structural adjustment programs began to show any hint of adverse effects on the poor.

5. For example, WB (1997b: 104) reports savings of 30–40 percent in school construction in Mexico's SF, PRONASOL; and savings of up to 35 percent in Mexico's Mendoza Provincial Program for Basic Social Infrastructure (MENPROSF). (PRONASOL is one of the SFs initiated without donor assistance—though it has subsequently received donor funding—and to which the Mexican government has committed more funds than all of the Latin American SFs combined.)

The WB itself also spends less on SFs for project preparation and supervision than on other projects run through existing ministries or agencies in education and health, economic infrastructure, and for targeted or participatory poverty projects. The cost of WB input into the SF projects varied from 39 to 85 percent of equivalent costs for comparator projects [WB (1997a: 42–43, including Table 6)]. These lower costs, however, are not necessarily related to the SF model in itself, but to the fact that the WB does not make disbursements on SF loans contingent on "policy conditionality," which can slow down disbursements on these other projects substantially [WB (1997a: 42, and note 55)].

6. IDB (1997a: 71), and WB (1997a: vi).

7. See, in particular: (1) *Portfolio Improvement Program Review of the Social Funds Portfolio* (WB 1997a); see also WB 1998a

(by Wiens and Guadagni); WB 1998b (edited by Bigio *et al.*); and WB 1998c (by Owen and Van Domelen); (2) *Social Investment Funds in Latin America: Past Performance and Future Role* (IDB 1997a, 1997b; see also IDB (1998); (3) a chapter on SFs in *Safety Net Programs and Poverty Reduction: Lessons from Cross-Country Experience* (WB 1997b); and (4) a review for UNICEF by Sanjay Reddy, *Social Funds in Developing Countries: Recent Experiences and Lessons* (UNICEF 1998). All these studies are thoughtful and candid attempts to review the SF experience. To the extent that half of the Latin American SFs are funded by both the WB and the IDB (9 out of 18), there is a significant overlap in the experience on which they both report. As of May 2000, the Operations Evaluation Department of the World Bank is initiating a comprehensive study of SFs; in addition, the WB has undertaken a set of six case studies of SFs to look into their relationship to local government.

For the interested reader, I have included in the Bibliography to this chapter additional relevant works that were cited only in its longer version (Tendler 1999).

8. See, in particular, Lustig (1995, 1997); Stewart and van der Geest (1995); Cornia (1999); Cornia and Reddy (2000); and Hutchful (1994).

9. I report on this research in a longer version of this chapter (Tendler 1999), where extensive evidence and citations for the claims made here can be found; see also Serrano (1996). The field research looked into the SFs of four states in Northeast Brazil—Ceará, Maranhão, Bahia, and Pernambuco.

10. Not all SFs are explicitly demand-driven. A recent WB review reported that between 10 and 40 percent of the SFs use demand-driven mechanisms (WB 1997a: 24). The narratives about SFs and their strengths nevertheless often describe them as "participatory," if not demand-driven.

11. The evidence on quick disbursement is actually somewhat mixed, as reported by the WB study of three social funds in Latin America (1998: xvii), Stewart and van der Geest (1995), and in the complaints of project agency managers about the way community decisionmaking "slows down" the rate of disbursement. The WB report attributes cases of slow disbursement to delays by the central government in providing counterpart funding to the projects. Stewart and van der Geest attribute the problem to the demand-driven structure itself, which results in a time-consuming process of community- and municipal-level organizing and decisionmaking. They also point to the concern of project agencies about "clientelism" and political meddling in such decentralized project selection and location, which causes agency managers to impose criteria and requirements that slow things down. Their concern about reducing delay is at odds with the WB study (1997a) that suggests that *more* time and attention be paid to imposing project criteria that assure better participation and inclusion of the poor.

12. Most importantly, the earlier funds were fashioned to be temporary and emergency interventions—usually bearing the name of *Social Emergency Funds* (SEFs). Subsequent SFs, or later phases of earlier ones, were viewed as more permanent—both in terms of their institutional design and the community projects themselves, and as reflected in the slight name change to Social *Investment* Funds (SIFs); the WB made an even later distinction, stressing those SFs with particularly explicit demand-driven features and designating them as *Demand-driven Rural Investment Funds* (DRIFs). I thank Maurizio Guadagni for pointing out this latter distinction to me in reacting to an earlier version of this chapter (see also his co-authored contribution, WB 1998a). The programs I researched in Brazil, funded by the WB, are now characterized in the WB SF lexicon as DRIFs.

13. This dynamic is chronicled for Peru's SF by Schady (1999), Roberts (1996), Roberts and Arce (1998), and Graham and Kane (1998); and for Mexico's SF, by Gibson (1997). See also endnote 63.

14. IDB (1997a: 71). Lustig reports that even the most well-known, older, and highly praised Latin American SF, the Bolivian Social Emergency Fund (starting in 1986), employed roughly only 6–8 percent of workers in the two lowest income deciles. The Honduran fund employed only 7 percent of the unemployed (1990–1995), the Peruvian fund, 2.7 percent (1991–1995), and the El Salvadoran fund, 2.5 percent (starting in 1990). (For the Guatemalan fund, no data on employment generation were even gathered.) Data are from Lustig (1997: 4–5), citing as sources the WB (1997a) for Bolivia; and IDB-funded studies of El Salvador, Guatemala, and Honduras.

15. IDB (1997a: 71). In a study of the employment-creating works programs in various developing countries funded out of U.S. agricultural surpluses (Food for Work), Thomas (1986: 26) reports an average 52 percent of total expenditures on labor, with a maximum of 77 percent; von Braun et al. (1992) stipulate at least 60 percent for labor expenditures as desirable for African programs. Studies of the Maharashtra Employment Guarantee Scheme in India (Costa 1978; D'Silva 1983) show how labor intensity varies with the kind of project—water projects using the largest percentage (80 percent) and road projects the lowest (55 percent). More recently, the Maharashtra Scheme has required that at least 60 percent of total costs be spent on unskilled labor (Deolalikar and Gaiha 1996).

16. IDB (1997a: 22, 71). The WB found similar results in Honduras (Webb et al. 1995). The evaluators also note that estimates of SF job creation are often overestimated because of the large amount of temporary employment that usually lasts only a few months (p. 22).

17. In reporting these findings, Stewart and van der Geest (1995) note that these unimpressive outcomes for benefits are partly a result of the fact that governments in SF countries committed more resources to these non-donor-funded programs than they did to the SFs. But even if SF countries had committed more resources, the authors claim that their calculations show that the SFs would still have reached only a smaller share of the unemployed in the lower deciles because of their greater difficulty in targeting (p. 126).

18. IDB (1997a: 22–23).

19. IDB (1997a: 23).

20. Peru is one of the exceptions, and perhaps for this reason one of the most studied cases with respect to this particular kind of outcome. Schady (1999), among others, show that the Peruvian SF succeeded in concentrating a large percentage of its expenditures in the poorest districts. (Because of difficulties of available data, as is typical, measures of the distribution of project benefits within districts could not be made).

Given the bad name that political meddling has in these types of programs—and the donor claim that SFs can operate autonomously—it is important to note that this success at targeting is directly attributed to President Fujimori's electoral strategy to court this most marginalized rural population in his second electoral bid (they had not voted for him in a previous referendum on allowing him a second term); more generally, he needed to find a new constituency to make up for voter disaffection in urban areas resulting from his macroreforms (Schady 1999; Roberts 1996; Roberts and Arce 1998).

Similarly, it is interesting that the Peruvian SF has also been characterized negatively for this political direction as one of the most "politicized" programs—where support for projects was centrally directed according to political criteria (Graham and Kane 1998; Schady 1999). It is ironic, in this case, that one of the SFs' most important objectives—reaching poor communities—was achieved through means that are considered antithetical to the program model: SFs are said to be better at service delivery, that is, partly because they are "autonomous" and "apolitical."

21. As reported by WB (1997a: 18, WB 1998a: xv), IDB (1997a), Lustig (1995, 1997), IDB (1997a), and Stewart and van der Geest (1995). For the 1990–92 period with respect to Mexico's PRONASOL, Cornelius et al. report that middle-income states received more funds per capita than poor states (as measured in terms of indices of poverty and underdevelopment) (1994: 22–3). Graham (1994) reports that, more generally, none of the poverty alleviation programs in Latin America, Africa, or Europe has been particularly successful in targeting the poorest members of the population. The IDB study points out that even after its own calculations, it is very difficult to determine targeting from the data, which does not distinguish between rich and poor within municipalities or higher-level administrative units from which the data are drawn.

22. WB (1997b), as cited in WB (1997a: 18).

23. Lustig (1997: 5), citing WB (1997b). More recent commentaries have suggested that in the Bolivian cases, the units of study are so large and diverse—whole departments—that intradepartmental comparisons would be more valid.

24. Some of the studies show that whereas the SFs did not reach the poorest communities, they often reached communities that were poor. The IDB study found that the poorest decile municipalities received less than the others, but that the nonpoorest poor received more than the best off. As noted earlier, a study of the Peruvian SF FONCODES (Schady 1999) found that poorer communities actually get more SF funding per capita.

25. Lustig (1995, 1997) for the comparator programs and SFs in Latin America, and Stewart and van der Geest (1995) for comparator programs in Latin America, Africa, and South Asia. In Lustig's review of the Latin American SFs (1995: 31), she noted that they "compare unfavorably" with such direct-transfer programs (she is considering only the direct-transfer aspects of SFs in the comparison). Lustig, a researcher at the Brookings Institution at the time of her study, drew on various SF evaluation studies by the donors.

26. Cornia (1999) and Cornia and Reddy (2000).

27. The IDB review of SFs found that, for all but one of the countries (Peru), it was not possible to determine the extent to which those employed by SFs were poor. [In Peru, an unrelated survey from the ongoing WB Living Standards Measurement Project had included a question about employment in the SF; 36 percent of the jobs went to the extremely poor, and 57 percent to the poor (IDB 1997a: 32).]

28. IDB (1997a: 15). The study notes that baseline data are not available for employment and income in the regions served by SFs, making the estimate of changes in poverty and income not possible. Data have been collected in several cases, however, on the employment and income generated by the projects themselves, their benefits, and surveys of project beneficiaries.

29. WB (1998a: xv–xvi, edited by Wiens and Guadagni). The WB text uses the acronym "DRIFs" rather than SFs; DRIFs are a subspecies of SFs called "Demand Driven Rural Investment Funds" that, according to this classification, support mainly productive infrastructure and natural resource management. The study reports on three DRIFs in Latin America—in Mexico, Colombia, and Brazil—the latter being the same program looked at in my Brazil research. (Actually, the Brazil SFs/DRIFs did not exactly fit this particular description.)

30. IDB (1997a: 71).

31. Lustig (1997: 2–4). Stewart and van der Geest (1995) arrive at similar conclusions in a study including African as well as Latin American countries.

32. IDB (1997a: 23).

33. IDB (1997a). The citation (p. 16) comes from a December 1996 version of this report, as cited in WB (1997a: 47, note 58).

34. The evaluators also pointed to the inability to truly compare the demand-driven SFs to other programs due to the lack or poor quality of the data, the classic apples-and-oranges problem of such a comparison, and the limitations of their data and methodology. The sample size was small (ranging from 8 to 69); they did not compare SFs to non–Bank-funded programs [as Stewart and van der Geest (1995) did]; and they were not able to separate out, on the SF side, the sectoral piece of the SF program that corresponded to the comparator project in a functional ministry—health, education, water, roads, and so on. (They also did not rank the kinds of impacts of unemployment and poverty reported above.) WB (1997a)

35. IDB (1997a: 68). The study notes that this is because of the reliance on *ex-post* beneficiary questionnaires for these evaluations, and the lack of *ex-ante* data. The report does mention, however, that the impact evaluations are a valuable source of information on whether projects are operating and whether selection and construction were satisfactory.

36. IDB (1997a: 6, 46, 73). The evaluators attributed this finding to the "inflexibility" of the donors, and their "rules and limitations," which inhibited the ability of local officials to experiment with innovative solutions. One interesting example of this donor "inflexibility" related to the use of private contractors for works projects. In trying to serve the poverty-reducing goals of the SFs, donors typically emphasized works projects that trained and employed local people. This stipulation faced the resistance or noncompliance of private contractors, who usually preferred bringing in their own workers from outside, particularly for skilled work, and complained that this would compromise their efficiency. In focus-group meetings convened by the IDB, interestingly, mayors and community representatives expressed more concern about project quality than local employment, and therefore preferred that contractors use their own skilled labor. With respect to "inflexibility," then, the IDB evaluators were making the same critique of the donors that the latter had been making of line ministries.

37. The WB review of African and Latin American projects reported concerns about sustainability, particularly with respect to the economic infrastructure and microfinance components of such projects, noting that such concerns had "been raised in other reviews as well" (WB 1997a: vii, 15–16, including footnote 9). Another WB study (1998a: xvii–xviii, 46) found that none of the three Latin American projects (DRIFs/Demand-Driven Rural Investment Funds) it reviewed "performed partic-

ularly well in achieving" sustainability, and that "information from local or partial surveys suggests that a high proportion of subprojects may not be sustainable." A WB appraisal report for a Senegal SF/AGETIP noted that the "sustainability of many AGETIP investments is uncertain," due to a lack of ownership and participation in the project identification and preparation phase and in the post-project operations and maintenance phase [WB Senegal PAR Public Works and Employment Project, 1996 draft, page 2 notes, as cited in WB (1997a: 15:note 9)].

The IDB came to similar conclusions (1997a: 35–41), and an earlier 1994 IDB study cautioned that "[s]ustainability remains a potentially serious problem . . ." [Glaessner, Lee, Sant'Anna, and de St. Antoine, "Poverty Alleviation and Social Investment Funds: The Latin American Experience," p. 22, as cited in WB (1997a: 15)].

38. WB (1997a: 31).

39. Eighty percent of the project descriptions did not mention sustainability, nor concern themselves with its three key components: (1) evidence of demand (range of options offered, information made available, evidence of commitment through contribution in cash or kind); (2) appropriateness of technical standards; and (3) soundness of arrangements for operations and maintenance (funding, and training) (WB 1997a: 30).

40. WB (1997a: 30–31).

41. WB (1997a: 15–16, and note 9). The WB evaluators reinforce their concerns about sustainability with citations from their sister SF financing institution, the IDB, and from other reviewers within the WB itself. They also question whether SF designers and managers even thought about project designs and technical standards that would be more likely to elicit user maintenance and financing for recurrent costs. They point out, it should be noted, that their findings relate more to "likely," as opposed to actual, sustainability, because only a limited number of the individual country evaluations it drew on involved SF projects with long-term objectives (p. 4).

42. WB (1997a).

43. The aforementioned study of SFs now being studied will hopefully yield more evaluation information on this issue. In addition, six country studies now being carried out by the WB by Andrew Parker (Africa) and Rodrigo Serrano (Latin America) to explore the impact of SFs on local governments may also provide illuminating findings on the issue.

44. IDB (1997a: 74). In Latin America, out of 16 countries and 17 SFs (Guatemala has two), Chile's FOSIS has the lowest level of external financing—11 percent. The next lowest are Guatemala's FONAPAZ (12 percent), and Colombia's RED SOLIDARIDAD (20 percent). (The IDB evaluators, as already noted, ranked these three as the most successful in terms of innovative practices.) For the rest, external financing ranges from 58 to 94 percent, with only three countries being lower than 80 percent (albeit higher than 60 percent)—Peru, Uruguay, and Venezuela (IDB 1997a: 10, T. 2.1). The Mexican SF, PRONASOL, is also one of the SFs most "owned" by its government: It was also initiated by the Mexican government without donor funding and is one of the largest in terms of absolute resources, share of the budget, and coverage (Cornelius *et al.* 1994: 14). It does not appear in this particular table of the IDB because it is currently not receiving donor funding, though it has in the past.

45. IDB (1997a: 64, 74).

46. WB (1997b); IDB (1997a: 15, 43). Based on studies of the Bolivian and Honduran SFs, Stewart and van der Geest

(1995: 128) reported that poorer communities present fewer proposals for funding than richer communities. Herring (1983) and Gaiha (1998) found the same kinds of results in similarly targeted and deconcentrated programs in India. A study of the education projects financed by the Mexican SF found that the program's requirement that a community have an effectively functioning Solidarity School Committee before seeking funding explained why fewer per capita funds went to poor indigenous communities as compared to others (Gershberg 1994: 249–51).

There may be an inherent tendency for exacerbation of this problem in that the better-off communities that are successful in getting one project will come back for subsequent ones, and prepare them better, while communities that are turned down or have a difficult time will become discouraged and desist, a point made by Schady (1999). I thank Mick Moore for pointing out the importance of looking at subsequent choices of projects because of the learning that results from "repeated games."

47. IDB (1997a: 15).

48. In another twist on the tradeoff theme, the Stewart and van der Geest (1995) comparator study of SFs with earlier supply-driven programs claims that SFs actually disburse less rapidly than the comparators, and pointed to the consultation process and the demand-driven design: if taken seriously and at its best, it resulted in a time-consuming process of organizing and decisionmaking by communities or municipal councils.

49. See Serrano (1996), and Tendler (1999, Sections III and IV).

50. IDB (1997a: 39). In many communities, the report said, NGOs are not that active. In addition, NGOs tended to specialize more in training and community development programs than in managing the construction projects that constitute an important activity of many SFs. In the SFs where NGOs played a greater role, then, it was because the program did not focus on building infrastructure (like Chile's FOSIS). Other exceptions were cases in which the government was "institutionally extremely weak" to the point that NGOs had more capacity to generate projects than government (Haiti) and, in general, because the SF was formally required to use them. The usual tension that exists between NGOs and government also seemed to get in the way. The NGOs disliked being the mere executors of a "paternalistic" government program and wanted to participate more in early phases of the project cycle. The SF managers and staff, presumably, were not anxious to do this.

51. The IDB review reported that the "recurrent-cost problem" was most acute in the case of NGOs (IDB 1997a: 41). A WB Project Completion Report [cited in WB (1997b: 107) and also in the previous IDB reference] noted a study of the Bolivian SF showing NGOs to be disproportionately represented among the projects that were *least* likely to be sustained. The projects were in health and education, and the study was conducted one to two years after completion. (Lower performers on the "sustainability" measure also included projects requested by regional government, as opposed to central-government, institutions.)

52. Reddy's review for UNICEF (1998: 58) noted that "[f]avouritism in the disbursal of contracts to NGOs" was a serious issue in various countries, as was the "proliferation of NGOs of dubious grassroots credentials" as a result of the new availability of SF funding.

53. Some SF managers expressed a certain distaste for, and therefore sometimes discouraged, genuine processes of community decisionmaking. These processes, they said, "slowed down"

the rates of disbursement so prized by these managers and their donors (WB 1997a; IDB 1997a). [Other managers, interestingly, actually liked the eligibility criteria which, even though slowing down disbursement, gave them some kind of protection against political interference (Stewart and van der Geest 1995)].

54. See, for example, Stiglitz (1985).

55. See, for example, his speech to the World Institute for Development Economics Research (WIDER) (1998).

56. Rodrigo Serrano (1996) reported this three-part set of actors in driving community decisions, which emerged from the larger Brazil research program; see also Tendler (1999), Sections III, IV, and V. The IDB evaluation also points to the importance of contractors in driving community decisions in many cases. The practice was apparently common enough that the IDB evaluators baptized it as "persuasion by contractor," and cautioned that "the real beneficiaries" in these cases might well be "the contractors" rather than the final users (IDB 1997a: 41, 43).

57. For example, WB (1997a: vii, ix, 15).

58. Some question the evidence on this claim on the grounds that systematic and comparable cost data are not available or not collected (sometimes even across different SF offices in the same country), and important costs—such as donor monitoring—are not included. Some SFs, for example, do not include their own overheads in reporting unit costs; for Peru, see Schady (1998: 5).

59. Angell and Graham (1995).

60. IDB (1997a: 34, and 1997b: 38–76, particularly pp. 46, 48, 73, 74). Also different, the Chilean government viewed FOSIS as a *permanent* program from the start (it was created during a time of high economic growth of 7 percent a year); this contrasts with the originally temporary status of the majority of Latin American SFs and the origins of most SFs in "temporary" periods of low growth, high unemployment, and structural-adjustment or other crises.

61. It should be noted that this recognition of the problems of special autonomous institutions is definitely not new, particularly the way such special status exacerbates the fabled lack of in-

teragency cooperation. This same problem plagued the earlier integrated urban and rural development projects, so much in vogue in the 1970s and 1980s, with their autonomous project units. The problems of this autonomy contributed to the keen distaste today among the donors for such integrated projects, and hence their rapid fall from grace in the late 1980s. An even earlier donor penchant for creating special autonomous state enterprises, in the 1950s and 1960s, also fell out of fashion, for partly similar reasons. If donors were slapping their own hands about the pitfalls of independent units created solely for their programs in the 1980s, what is different about SFs or the 1990s that would reverse this judgment?

62. One such recent meeting was held in Mexico in December of 1999, and another is planned for Washington, D.C. in June of 2000.

63. These arguments have been made at great length and with detailed case study evidence by Gibson (1997) for Argentina and Mexico, and, for Peru, by Schady (1999), Roberts (1996), and Roberts and Arce (1998). In developing the evidence from their cases, these authors specifically link the compensatory patronage-dispensing policy to the SFs in Mexico and Peru. I elaborate on this point and the evidence in Tendler (1999, Section VI).

64. The examples are (1) the tragedy of the commons, which predicts that collective-action attempts to prevent overuse of grazing lands and other common-property resources will always be doomed to failure because of the free-rider problem; (2) the belief that the lack of secure and privately held land titles holds back farmers from investing in increased productivity, which formed the basis for much policy advice and intervention directed to convert common holdings to individually held parcels; and (3) the concept that the integration of economic activities (such as livestock management in his study) into larger systems requires that programmatic interventions also be integrated by bringing together various agencies in one program and requiring them to coordinate—which led, in turn, to a generation of "integrated" rural and urban development programs.

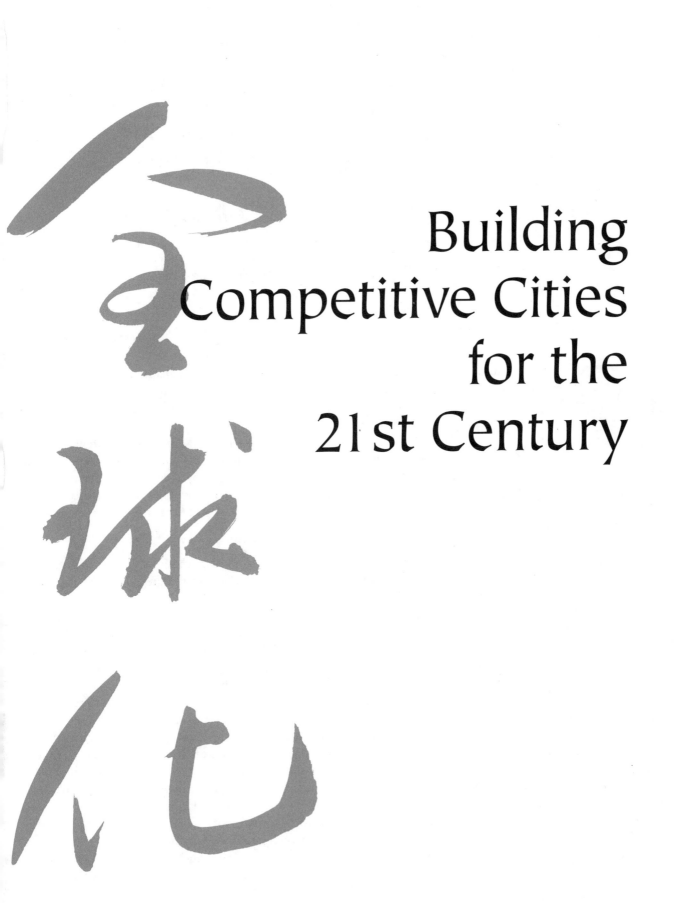

Building Competitive Cities for the 21st Century

chapter 15

What Distinguishes Success among Second-Tier Cities?

Ann Markusen

Urban and Regional Planning Program, Humphrey Institute
University of Minnesota
Council on Foreign Relations

In many countries "second-tier," or midsized, cities have been growing faster than first-tier cities over the past few decades. In Brazil, Japan, the Republic of Korea, and the United States, the employment growth rates of at least half a dozen medium-sized cities have exceeded those of the largest metropolitan areas in each country (see Table 15.1). Why have these second-tier cities grown so fast? What can be learned from their patterns of development and economic structure?

This chapter summarizes the results of five years of comparative research on the fastest-growing second-tier metropolitan areas in Brazil, Japan, the Republic of Korea, and the United States by a team of economists and geographers based in universities in each country (Markusen, DiGiovanna, and Lee 1999). Specifically, we research the structural and voluntaristic features of three to five of the fastest-growing second-tier metropolitan areas in each country. Our research uncovers several prominent contributors to the success of such cities:

- Specialization in innovative and/or income-elastic economic sectors
- Favorable national government policies (investment, infrastructure, and industrial and regional policies)
- Leadership in economic development by the local public or private sector
- Flexibility and openness to new and emerging industrial ensembles.

In the course of our study, we develop two new structural prototypes, contrasted to the Marshallian industrial district, depicting the dominant relationships among firms and other agents in urban economies. We conclude that national governments should continue to monitor and shape urban growth patterns, selectively intervening in dynamic patterns that are worsening inter- and intraregional disparities. We warn that wholesale devolution, when unmatched by adequate financial resources, training, or institution-building at the subnational level, may paradoxically set back economic development.

Three Urban Economic Prototypes

Since the early 1980s, economic geographers and regional economists have elaborated on Alfred Marshall's insights to focus on the industrial district as a core component of economic regions (Markusen 1996). Relying heavily on the experience of the "third Italy" and Silicon Valley in "flexible specialization," some analysts have claimed that these "new industrial districts" constitute a novel regional form that is growing disproportionately fast (Scott 1988). However, we found that the characteristics associated with such districts explain only a modest number of rapidly growing second-tier cities. Many more fully reflect two other new industrial models: the hub-and-spoke structure and the satellite platform.

In investigating these three prototypical structures, as well as the keys to success of second-tier cities, we identified metropolitan areas with growth rates significantly higher than the national average. We then chose a subset as case studies, including at least one in each of the four countries that conformed to the new industrial districts (NID) formula, and three to five others whose industrial structure and organization appeared to be different. Although we have not attempted to fit all fast-

Table 15.1

Second-Tier City Employment, Brazil, Japan, Republic of Korea, and the United States, Selected Years 1970–90

Brazil	Employment (thousands) 1970	1991	% Change 1970–91
Second Tier			
Manaus	10	57	477
Londrina/Maringa	13	46	246
Curitiba*	38	128	237
Joinville	22	73	234
Fortaleza*	25	80	223
Caxias do Sul	23	75	221
Belo Horizonte*	62	173	182
Franca	9	27	182
Campinas	71	193	172
Piracicaba	19	50	166
Salvador*	28	71	156
Blumenau	29	74	156
Sorocaba	35	88	151
Santos/Cubatao	35	88	151
Belem*	14	33	128
Americana	13	28	122
São Jose dos Campos	47	100	114
First Tier			
São Paulo*	907	1,410	55
Rio de Janeiro*	224	313	39

Republic of Korea	Employment (thousands) 1981	1991	% Change 1981–91
Second Tier			
Ansan	na	134	na
Changwan	44	141	220
Taejon	122	284	133
Kwangju	127	275	117
Kumi	52	110	112
Inchon	272	560	106
Pohang	55	107	95
Ulsan	111	207	86
Masan	86	136	58
First Tier			
Taegu	360	558	55
Seoul	2,372	3,629	53
Pusan	734	1,108	51
Korea	6,602	11,356	72

Japan	Employment (thousands) 1970	1990	% Change 1970–90
Second Tier			
Sayama	13	23	73
Anjyo	24	41	70
Hatano	12	21	69
Komaki	20	33	65
Kasugai	22	31	44
Oita	18	26	40
Kawagoe	22	30	35
Yao	35	47	33
Sagamihara	41	53	28
Atsugi	20	25	26
Hiroshima	56	69	23
Kohriyama	22	27	22
Suzuka	22	27	20
Kariya	40	47	18
Nagaoka	21	24	17
Ueda	18	21	14
First Tier			
Nagoya*	981	957	-2
Osaka*	1,126	863	-23
Tokyo*	1,394	785	-44
Japan	11,675	11,173	-4

United States	Employment (thousands) 1970	1990	% Change 1970–90
Second Tier			
Orlando, FL	164	569	246
Anaheim-Santa Ana, CA	532	1,552	192
Austin, TX	169	471	178
Reno, NV	57	145	155
San Jose, CA	445	1,015	128
Albuquerque, NM	136	305	125
Tucson, AZ	142	316	123
Raleigh-Durham, NC	230	513	123
San Diego, CA	635	1,397	120
Seattle, WA	626	1,339	114
Melbourne/ Titusville, FL	95	202	112
Colorado Springs, CO	112	228	104
Huntsville, AL	93	163	76
Madison, WI	151	262	73
Elkhart, IN	71	116	64
First Tier			
Los Angeles, CA	3,333	5,200	56
Boston, MA	1,286	1,672	30
Chicago, IL	2,986	3,673	23
New York, NY	4,671	4,765	2
United States	70,719	110,321	

Sources and notes: Data are compiled and explained in separate tables in Ann Markusen, "National Contexts and the Emergence of Second Tier Cities," in Ann Markusen, Yong-Sook Lee, and Sean DiGiovanna, eds., *Second-Tier Cities: Rapid Growth beyond the Metropolis, Minneapolis:* University of Minnesota Press, 1999.

* Brazil: connote metropolitan area data. Japan: Figures are for industrial employment only. Data for Tokyo, Nagoya, and Osaka are for the prefectures, not metropolitan areas.

growing cities into this typology, it is our working hypothesis that most such cities can be characterized as possessing one or an amalgam of these structures.

Building on enterprise studies and corporate interviews as methods for studying regions (Markusen 1994), we relied on interviews with business firms, trade associations, trade unions, and regional economy watchers to map the relationships among firms and other economic actors inside and outside the region. We specifically focused on features in the NID formula: firm size, upstream and downstream industrial links, vertical integration, networks among district firms, local governance, innovative capabilities, and the organization of production. We also scrutinized the role of large firms and that of the state at both the national and regional/local level, as rule maker, producer and consumer of goods and services, and underwriter of innovation. Finally, we investigated the longer-term dynamic of major industries to determine their resiliency.

The Flexibly Specialized Industrial District

The literature on new industrial districts focuses on regions where the business structure is composed of small, locally owned firms that make investment and production decisions locally (top of Figure 15.1). Scale economies are relatively modest, forestalling the rise of large firms. Buyers and sellers transact substantial trade within the district, often based on long-term contracts or commitments, and often for eventual export from the region. Such a district also encompasses a relatively specialized set of services tailored to its unique products and industries. They include local financial institutions offering "patient capital"—that is, they are willing to take longer-term risks because they have access to inside information and trust local entrepreneurs.

What makes this type of industrial district so vibrant and productive, in Marshall's account, is the nature and quality of the local labor market, which is highly flexible. Individuals move from firm to firm, committed to the district rather than to any one company. Labor outmigration is minimal, while in-migration occurs as growth permits. Owners and workers live in the same community, where all benefit from the fact that "the secrets of industry are in the air." This relatively stable community enables a local cultural identity and shared industrial expertise to evolve.

Scholars of new industrial districts hypothesize that robust growth rates are due, too, to cooperation among competitor firms to share risk, stabilize markets, and share innovation. Disproportionate shares of workers are engaged in design and innovative activities. Activist trade associations provide management, training, mar-

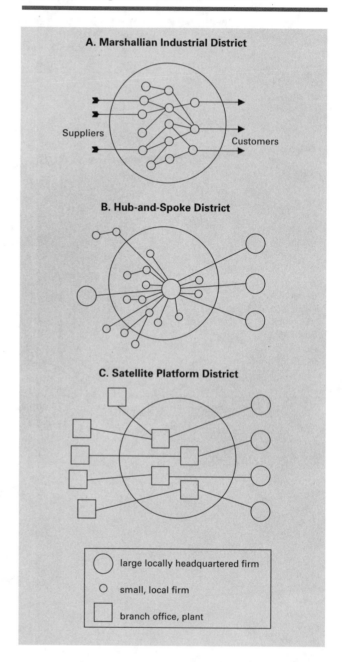

Figure 15.1
Alternative Regional Industrial Structures

A. Marshallian Industrial District

Suppliers

Customers

B. Hub-and-Spoke District

C. Satellite Platform District

○ large locally headquartered firm

∘ small, local firm

☐ branch office, plant

keting, technical, and financial help, as well as forums to hammer out collective strategy. Local and regional governments may be central in regulating and promoting core industries (Markusen 1996).

The Hub-and-Spoke Industrial District

In the hub-and-spoke region, a number of key firms or facilities act as hubs for the regional economy, with suppliers and related activities spread out around them like spokes of a wheel (B in Figure 15.1). The dynamism in hub-and-spoke economies is associated with the position of the large firms in their national and international markets. Key investment decisions are made locally but their consequences are spread globally. For example, a single large firm such as Boeing in Seattle or Toyota in Toyota City buys from local and external suppliers and sells chiefly to external customers, who may be large (as in the case of Boeing) or numerous (as in the case of Toyota). Other examples include central New Jersey in the United States, Ulsan and Pohang in South Korea, and San Jose dos Campos in Brazil.

Unrelated or loosely linked hubs may coexist in a region. The Seattle economy, for instance, encompasses paper manufacturer Weyerhauser as the dominant resource sector company, Boeing as the dominant industrial employer, Microsoft as the leading services firm, the Hutchinson Cancer Center as the progenitor of biotechnology firms, and the Port of Seattle as the transportation hub. Core firms or institutions are embedded nonlocally, with substantial links to suppliers, competitors, and customers outside the district. Internal scale and scope economies are relatively high, and turnover of firms and personnel relatively low.

Hub-and-spoke districts may exhibit intradistrict cooperation, but generally on the terms of the hub firm. Markedly lacking is cooperation among competitor firms to share risk, stabilize the market, and share innovation. Larger firms are more apt to forge strategic alliances with partners outside the region. Workers' loyalties are to core firms first, then to the district, and only after that to small firms. If jobs open up in hub firms, worker will often abandon smaller employers to get on the hub firms' payroll, but turnover of firms and personnel is relatively low.

In hub-and-spoke districts, the few trade associations are relatively weak, often because top hub managers absent themselves from their activities. Hub firms concern themselves with state and local governmental activities that impinge upon their land use, taxes, and regulations, and try to ensure that area politicians represent the interests of their firm and industry at the national and international levels. They may also be actively involved in issues that affect their workforce and ability to do business, especially in improving area educational institutions and infrastructure.

The Satellite Platform

A third distinctive industrial form is the satellite platform—a congregation of branch facilities of firms based elsewhere. National or provincial governments often assemble these platforms to stimulate economic development in outlying areas and lower the cost of business for firms bristling under high urban wages, rents, and taxation. Tenants of satellite platforms may perform functions ranging from routine assembly to relatively sophisticated research, but they must be spatially independent of upstream or downstream operations in the same firm, and of agglomerations of suppliers, customers, and competitors.

The most conspicuous feature of this model is the absence of any networks within the region and the predominance of links to the parent corporation and branch plants elsewhere (C in Figure 15.1). Large, externally situated firms make key investment decisions, and orders and commitments to local suppliers are noticeably absent. Since platforms generally host heterogeneous firms, they do not share risk, stabilize the market, or engage in innovative partnerships. The labor market is internal to the vertically integrated firm rather than to the district, producing high rates of migration at the managerial, professional, and technical levels.

Almost all countries have satellite platforms. An outstanding U.S. example is North Carolina's much-admired Research Triangle Park, a collection of unrelated research centers of major multinational corporations (Luger and Goldstein 1990). In South Korea, Kumi constitutes a low-end textile and electronics platform, while Ansan operates as an intentional ensemble of disparate industrial polluters (Park and Markusen 1994, 1999). Even Taeduck can be regarded as a satellite platform because R&D centers in the science park have few local links (Jeong and Park 1999). Some of the better-performing Japanese technopoli, such as Oita and Kumamoto, fall into this category (Markusen and Sasaki 1999). A remarkable Brazilian case is the state-sponsored expansion of Manaus as an import/export zone (Diniz and Borges Santos 1999).

Satellite platforms can and do evolve into rapidly growing second-tier cities, but they have little "patient capital" to draw on because outside corporate headquarters are the main sources of finance, technical expertise, and services. Satellite platforms also lack industry-specific trade associations that would provide shared infrastructure and assist with management, training, and marketing. Strong efforts by national or local governments and services from Chambers of Commerce and other associations of local fixed capital can compensate only partially for these drawbacks.

Industrial Specialization

One of our most interesting findings regarding second-tier cities, no matter what their economic prototype, is that they must specialize more than ever before, given rapidly integrating world trade and investment. Some continue to rely on hinterlands that specialize as agricultural processing centers or mining districts, but most have lost hinterland markets to competitors, as distance costs or hinterland competitiveness shrinks.

In general, the more successful cities—especially those we classify as Marshallian or hub-and-spoke—are built on one or more specializations that are well positioned in national and international trade because they are innovative or income-elastic, or simply because they exhibit comparative advantage (Howes and Markusen 1993). Autos, for instance, are an income-elastic sector because as people's income rises in host and neighboring nations, they spend a larger share of their earnings on cars. Port cities with containerization facilities and good rail and highway links to the interior are similarly favored by growth in the volume of trade (Noponen, Markusen, and Driessen 1997). Examples of successful specialization include autos and auto parts in the Republic of Korea's Ulsan and Changwon, electronics and telecommunications in Brazil's Campinas (Diniz and Razavi 1999), electronics in Japan's Oita and Kumamoto (Markusen and Sasaki 1999), and aircraft and software in Seattle (Gray, Golob, and Markusen 1996).

Of course, not all cities specialize, especially satellite platforms. But when they do, specializations tend to emerge on their own, as did pharmaceuticals and electronics in North Carolina's Research Triangle Park (Luger and Goldstein 1990). A number of government attempts to confine new industrial complexes to certain sectors have failed or required modification. For example, the Republic of Korea's Kumi, designed as an electronics export complex, ended up with a significant number of textile plants (Park and Markusen 1999).

Public-Sector Investment and Directives

Most of the cities we studied benefited extraordinarily well from public-sector investment, procurement, and/or regional programs, including national defense. United States examples include Silicon Valley, Seattle, and Colorado Springs (Gray, Golob, Park, and Markusen 1999; Gray, Golob, and Markusen 1996; Markusen and Gray 1999). Brazil's San Jose dos Campos, which hosts the nation's publicly owned defense-related aircraft sector (Diniz and Razavi 1999), and the Korean city of Changwon, built in the 1970s to serve as the nation's defense industrial complex (Markusen and Park 1993), are other examples.

Land-grant universities in the United States, funded first by the national government and later by state governments, have contributed to the decentralization of urban growth and the remarkable postwar success of several dozen cities. Similarly, investment by the state of Sao Paulo in its university in Campinas played a pivotal role in that city's growth (Diniz and Razavi 1999), while Korean investment in research institutes and the Korea Institute of Technology in Taeduk have spurred growth in their host cities (Jeong and Park 1999).

However, the presence of excellent research universities does not guarantee superior economic performance. Many of America's best research universities have had no appreciable impact on regional development, while cities like Colorado Springs have thrived without research universities. Still others, such as San Diego and Seattle, have used revenues to create such universities after the fact.

Explicit regional policy, often as a component of national industrial policy, has played a strong role in shaping the placement and growth of second-tier cities (Markusen 1995). Examples are Korea, where the central government built and still runs entire industrial complexes within which firms are directed to locate (Park and Markusen 1994), and Japan, where incentives for industrial location have long been used to stimulate regional growth, most recently via the technopolis program (Funaba, Sasaki, Lee, and Markusen 1999).

Public investments in infrastructure have also been significant in explaining the relative growth of cities within nations. The U.S. investment in railroads—and more recently the interstate highway system—made a major contribution to postwar population growth in second-tier cities (Isserman, Rephann, and Sorenson 1989). Brazilian infrastructure investments have done likewise, although since states have contributed much of the investment, decentralization has tended to occur mostly within richer regions such as São Paulo (Diniz 1994).

Of course, not all second-tier cities owe their success to high levels of public investment or activity. The Research Triangle area, while it did land a major federal facility early on, today attracts very low levels of defense or other procurement spending. The park owes its success to other features, particularly its pioneering activities as a satellite platform (Luger and Goldstein 1990). Nor do public-sector investments and directives inevitably turn out well. Despite heavily subsidizing Manaus as an export platform in the Amazon, and draconian attempts to suppress manufacture of consumer electronics elsewhere, the Brazilian government has created a deformed industrial district that is now largely an entrepot for electronics imports and a major drain on the national treasury (Diniz and Borges 1999).

Public and Private Leadership

Porter (1990), among others, has shown that state and local politicians, business leaders, and economic developers have often designed unique and effective strategies by playing to their regions' strengths. And indeed, subnational leadership helps explain the relative success of some cities in our study. A U.S. governor along with local developers played a key role in creating Research Triangle Park (Luger and Goldstein 1990). A Japanese governor in the prefecture of Kumamoto played a similar role (Markusen and Sasaki 1999). In Colorado Springs, a private economic development group composed mainly of local business interests ("fixed capital") recruited the Air Force Academy and the North American Space Command, and later electronics branch plants from Silicon Valley (Markusen, Hall, Campbell, and Deitrick 1991). In the case of these satellite platforms, leaders have focused on recruiting firms from outside the area. However, other localities cannot always emulate such strategies, as the number of beneficiaries depends upon the available private and public facilities.

Leaders in some cities have attempted to retain and strengthen existing, often mature firms and encouraged entrepreneurship and startups by existing residents, managers, and employees. In the northeastern United States, this form of development leadership has emerged as prospects for successfully competing with southern and overseas localities have declined.

To confound matters, we identified robust instances of metropolitan growth without much public- or private-sector leadership at all. Seattle has benefited from very little concerted economic development activity over the decades. And, with the possible exception of Boeing's attention to the region's elementary and secondary educational system, neither Boeing nor Microsoft has exerted much local leadership (Gray, Golob, and Markusen 1996).

Private-sector entrepreneurship—the incidence of startup firms—has proved important in some American cities, but the conditions that promote (or suppress) such entrepreneurship are not well understood (Gray, Golob, and Markusen 1996). Such entrepreneurship proved important in Seattle, for example, through the work of Bill Boeing and Bill Gates. However, in other U.S. cases—including Research Triangle and Colorado Springs—and most of the other countries we studied, private-sector entrepreneurship was not particularly important in explaining the growth of second-tier cities. The relative absence of small entrepreneurial firms in lead sectors in second-tier cities led us to speculate that startups are more likely to cluster in the largest metropolitan areas.

Openness to New and Emerging Industrial Ensembles

Second-tier cities that have done well, especially more mature ones facing declining sectors, do have business and public cultures that embrace new sectors. Although

we do not yet know much about this process, certain regions seem to possess an ability to learn and to shift gears to new types of activities when threatened with obsolescence or decline caused by trade or shifting national policy. Seattle had the good fortune that Boeing, despite its active suppression of local suppliers and spin offs from the parent company, was relatively indifferent, if not welcoming, to the rise of Microsoft and the region's new, small biotech industry (Gray, Golob, and Markusen 1996).

The most outstanding instance of a deliberately—even aggressively—flexible strategy is Colorado Springs. Having once hedged against its dependence on military installations by attracting electronics branch plants, it responded to the exit of a number of such plants by recruiting telemarketing firms, then sports organizations (including the U.S. Olympic Committee), and most recently Christian organizations such as Focus on the Family, with its publishing and TV empire. In this "recruit and parlay" activity, local business elites transformed fixed assets (physical structures, labor force, culture) accrued in one era into attractors for a next round of economic activity (Markusen and Gray 1999).

We found instances of this in other countries as well. In Changwon, the complex was able to parlay its machining expertise into attracting an auto parts sector (Markusen and Park 1993). In Campinas, a similarly open environment has encouraged diversification of sectors in that metropolitan area (Diniz and Razavi 1999). Masan, South Korea, originally designed for Japanese branch plants but subject to recent plant closings on a relatively large scale, has attracted smaller Korean firms in diverse sectors (Lee 1999).

The antithesis of this kind of culture is that of Detroit, where a dominant, often oligopolistic industry uses markets in land, labor, capital, and politics to suppress other sectors (Chinitz 1960; Checkland 1975; Markusen 1985).

Implications for Urban Policy in the Twenty-First Century

Several conclusions from our study are germane to the prospects for subnational economic development. First of all, while there are remarkably successful second-tier cities, many benefited from one-of-a-kind circumstances, making their success difficult for other regions to replicate. What's more, there are no magic bullets. Although some factors contributed to growth of multiple second-tier cities, no one factor was present in all cases.

However, investments by national governments in the form of infrastructure, facilities, procurement, and revenue sharing have clearly been important determinants of metropolitan growth. Action by urban and regional leaders has also been important, although of somewhat more limited effect. Overall, we found ample evidence that good regional policy still matters. Smart and informed choices by national and urban leaders regarding the number of urban centers to nurture, the optimal location of infrastructure and other public investments, and the deployment of development incentives can have a major impact on the distribution of economic activity as well as on national growth.

Successful U.S. second-tier cities like Seattle, Colorado Springs, Silicon Valley, and Research Triangle have served as objects of admiration and emulation for economic developers around the world. But admiration for the U.S. system must be coupled with a recognition that significant national public investments, accompanied by two centuries of practice in democratic local governance, are largely responsible for the sustained growth of multiple metropolitan areas.

Overall, our results cast doubt on the ability of decentralization and devolution to adequately spur urban development, balance regional growth rates, and ensure national economic efficiency in allocating resources. For example, both Korea and Japan have arguably used top-down means to disperse employment more successfully than the more federally structured Brazil. Devolution does not automatically foster balanced regional development. In Brazil, where federal and state governments have long shared responsibilities and taxing powers, development remains concentrated in a polygon around the São Paulo–Rio–Belo Horizonte axis (Diniz 1994). This has occurred mainly because the "haves," such as the state of São Paulo, are able to use state tax revenues to build infrastructure and educational institutions. Economic activity has decentralized from the city of São Paulo, but mainly to medium-sized cities within the state.

Our research documents the past success of and contemporary need for explicit regional policy at the national level. The recent trend toward devolution, accompanied by a retreat from regional policy, may result in wasteful allocations of resources, especially if dynamics are set in place that eschew some communities in favor of concentrated and high-income growth in others. For devolution to work, it must be complemented with shared revenues, training, and subnational institution-building. Expecting urban areas to be responsible for their own growth and livability is naïve now that—more than ever before—they are subject to the eclectic choices of outside producers, consumers, governments, and international institutions. Since urban economies must specialize to ensure growth, their leaders will require good economic data (on regional trade, industry, and oc-

cupations), guidance in economic development, and assistance in building their capacity to meet this challenge

Bibliography

Checkland, S. 1975. *The Upas Tree*. Glasgow: Glasgow University Press.

Chinitz, Benjamin. 1960. "Contrasts in Agglomeration: New York and Pittsburgh." *American Economic Association, Papers and Proceedings* 40: 279–89.

Diniz, Clelio Campolina. 1994. "Polygonized Development in Brazil: Neither Decentralization nor Continued Polarization." *International Journal of Urban and Regional Research* 18: 293–314.

Diniz, Clelio Campolina, and Fabiana Borges Santos. 1999. "Manaus: Vulnerability in a Satellite Platform." In Ann Markusen, Sean DiGiovanna, and Yong Sook Lee, eds., *Second Tier Cities: Rapid Growth Outside the Metropole in Brazil, Korea, Japan and the U.S.* Minneapolis: University of Minnesota Press: 125–46.

Diniz, Clelio Campolina, and Mohamad Razavi. 1999. "San Jose dos Campos and Campinas: State-Anchored Dynamos." In Ann Markusen, Sean DiGiovanna, and Yong Sook Lee, eds., *Second Tier Cities: Rapid Growth Outside the Metropole in Brazil, Korea, Japan and the U.S.* Minneapolis: University of Minnesota Press: 97–124.

Funaba, Masatomi, Masayuki Sasaki, Yong-Sook Lee, and Ann Markusen. 1999. "Japanese Technopolis Policy: A View from Four Cities." In Ann Markusen, Sean DiGiovanna, and Yong Sook Lee, eds., *Second Tier Cities: Rapid Growth Outside the Metropole in Brazil, Korea, Japan and the U.S.* Minneapolis: University of Minnesota Press: 239–66.

Gray, Mia, Elyse Golob, and Ann Markusen. 1996. "Big Firms, Long Arms, Wide Shoulders: The 'Hub-and-Spoke' Industrial District in the Seattle Region." *Regional Studies* 30 (7): 651–66.

Gray, Mia, Elyse Golob, Ann Markusen, and Sam Ock Park. 1999. "New Industrial Cities? The Four Faces of Silicon Valley." In Ann Markusen, Sean DiGiovanna, and Yong Sook Lee, eds., *Second Tier Cities: Rapid Growth Outside the Metropole in Brazil, Korea, Japan and the U.S.* Minneapolis: University of Minnesota Press: 267–90.

Howes, Candace, and Ann Markusen. 1993. "Trade, Industry and Economic Development." In Helzi Noponen, Julie Graham, and Ann Markusen, eds., *Trading Industries, Trading Regions*. New York: Guilford.

Isserman, Andrew, Terance Rephann, and David Sorenson. 1989. "Highways and Rural Economic Development: Results from Quasi-Experimental Approaches." Discussion Paper, University of West Virginia, Discussion Paper 8907.

Jeong, Jun Ho, and Sam Ock Park. 19993. "Taeduk Research Park: Formation of Spin-offs and Local Linkages." In Ann Markusen, Sean DiGiovanna, and Yong Sook Lee, eds., *Second Tier Cities: Rapid Growth Outside the Metropole in Brazil, Korea, Japan and the U.S.* Minneapolis: University of Minnesota Press: 199–222.

Lee, Yong-Sook. 1999. "The Masan Free Export Zone: Conflict and Attrition." In Ann Markusen, Sean DiGiovanna, and Yong Sook Lee, eds., *Second Tier Cities: Rapid Growth Outside the Metropole in Brazil, Korea, Japan and the U.S.* Minneapolis: University of Minnesota Press: 183–98.

Luger, Michael, and Harvey Goldstein. 1990. *Technology in the Garden.* Chapel Hill, NC: University of North Carolina Press.

Markusen, Ann. 1985. *Profit Cycles, Oligopoly and Regional Development.* Cambridge, MA: MIT Press.

Markusen, Ann. 1994. "Studying Regions by Studying Firms." *The Professional Geographer* 4(4): 477–90.

Markusen, Ann. 1995. "The Interaction of Regional and Industrial Policies: Evidence from Four Countries." *Proceedings, Annual World Bank Conference on Development Economics 1994*: 279–98.

Markusen, Ann. 1996. "Sticky Places in Slippery Space: A Typology of Industrial Districts." *Economic Geography* 27(3): 293–313.

Markusen, Ann. 1999. "Fuzzy Concepts, Scanty Evidence, Wimpy Policy: The Case for Rigor and Policy Relevance in Regional Studies." Paper presented at the American Association of Geographers. Boston. March.

Markusen, Ann, and Mia Gray. 1999. "Colorado Springs: A Military-anchored City in Transition." In Ann Markusen, Sean DiGiovanna, and Yong Sook Lee, eds., *Second Tier Cities: Rapid Growth Outside the Metropole in Brazil, Korea, Japan and the U.S.* Minneapolis: University of Minnesota Press: 311–32.

Markusen, Ann, and Sam Ock Park. 1993. "The State as Industrial Locator and District Builder: The Case of Changwon, South Korea." *Economic Geography* 69(2): 157–81.

Markusen, Ann, and Masayuki Sasaki. 1999. "Oita and Kumamoto: Technopolises without Brains." In Ann Markusen, Sean DiGiovanna, and Yong Sook Lee, eds., *Second Tier Cities: Rapid Growth Outside the Metropole in Brazil, Korea, Japan and the U.S.* Minneapolis: University of Minnesota Press: 223–38.

Markusen, Ann, Peter Hall, and Amy Glasmeier. 1986. *High Tech America: The What, How, Where and Why of the Sunrise Industries.* Boston: Allen and Unwin.

Markusen, Ann, Peter Hall, Scott Campbell, and Sabina Deitrick. 1991. *The Rise of the Gunbelt.* New York: Oxford University Press.

Markusen, Ann, Sean DiGiovanna, and Yong Sook Lee, eds. 1999. *Second Tier Cities: Rapid Growth Outside the Metropole in Brazil, Korea, Japan and the U.S.* Minneapolis: University of Minnesota Press.

Noponen, Helzi, Ann Markusen, and Karl Driessen. 1997. "Trade and American Cities: Who Has the Comparative Advantage?" *Economic Development Quarterly* 11(1): 12.

Park, Sam Ock, and Ann Markusen. 1994. "Generalizing New Industrial Districts: A Theoretical Agenda and an Application from a Non-Western Economy." *Environment and Planning, A*27: 81–104.

Park, Sam Ock, and Ann Markusen. 1999. "Kumi and Ansan: Dissimilar Korean Satellite Platforms." In Ann Markusen, Sean DiGiovanna, and Yong Sook Lee, eds., *Second Tier Cities: Rapid Growth Outside the Metropole in Brazil, Korea, Japan and the U.S.* Minneapolis: University of Minnesota Press: 147–62.

Porter, Michael. 1990. *The Competitive Advantage of Nations.* New York: Free Press.

Porter, Michael. 1996. "Competitive Advantage, Agglomeration Economies and Regional Policy: A Response to Ann Markusen," *International Regional Science Review* 19(1 & 2): 85–94.

Saxenian, Annalee. 1994. *Regional Advantage: Culture and Competition in Silicon Valley and Route 128.* Cambridge, MA: Harvard University Press.

Scott, Allen. 1988. "Flexible Production Systems and Regional Development: The Rise of New Industrial Space in North America and Western Europe." *International Journal of Urban and Regional Research* 12(2): 171–86.

chapter 16

Globalization and Urbanization: The Case of Thailand

Utis Kaothien

National Economic and Social Development Board
Royal Thai Government

Douglas Webster

National Economic and Social Development Board
Royal Thai Government and Asia Pacific Research Center, Stanford University

Thailand exemplifies a new form of urbanization that is occurring throughout East and Southeast Asia. Although Bangkok—with some 8 million people—still reigns as the primate city, most new urbanization is occurring in areas extending beyond traditional municipal boundaries. This periurbanization is driven by manufacturing, which is increasingly located in modern industrial estates, with residential development and commercial facilities such as megamalls following, often in a dependent and non-planned fashion.

This new form of urbanization differs from the edge cities found in western countries, particularly the United States, in that periurban areas generally have minimal business services and thus lack office (particularly regional headquarters) and research and development parks. Meanwhile, growth rates are slowing in core Bangkok, which is based on tertiary—or knowledge—activities. Much of the deconcentration is occurring within 200 kilometers of core Bangkok, driven by motorization and changes in communications and transportation infrastructure, production processes, housing preferences (people's desire for more space at an affordable price), and government location incentives (which are being withdrawn consistent with World Trade Organization regulations).

However, growth around the intermediate-sized cities of the Northeast—the poorest region of Thailand—now outpaces even that in the extended Bangkok region. This growth is fueled by rural–urban migration and the increasing integration of the southern portions of the northeast corridor into the core Eastern Seaboard Area

and the national economy (see Map 16.1). As a result of government policy, as well as cooperation between international lenders and multinationals investing in Thailand, the center of manufacturing has shifted to the three Eastern Seaboard provinces of Chonburi, Chachoengsao, and Rayong. In fact, this periurban area is emerging as the manufacturing center of Southeast Asia, not just Thailand. One can argue that the Eastern Seaboard, with 2.5 million people, is the second-largest city. As a result, Thailand's urban system is becoming less primate nationally.

Although periurbanization has been an important factor in gross domestic product (GDP) and employment growth and declining poverty levels, it has generated social costs in terms of low environmental quality and inadequate services.[1] For example, while the number of people living in slums in Bangkok fell during the 1990s, slums are proliferating throughout the industrial heartland to the north and east of core Bangkok, along roads, rivers, and around industrial estates.

Periurbanization also means that essentially rural-oriented, low-capacity governments are attempting to deal with the cutting edge of globalization, while more sophisticated local governments manage slower-growing core areas. Urgent measures must be taken to shape and better manage periurban development while Bangkok itself builds on its attempts to become a knowledge economy supporting a largely middle-class population. Thailand will especially need to ensure the competitiveness of its extended urban economy as lower-cost producers such as China and Indonesia emerge. Although the private sector will be the prime investor in restructuring the economy of the Bangkok region and boost-

Map 16.1 Dynamic Urban Regions: Thailand

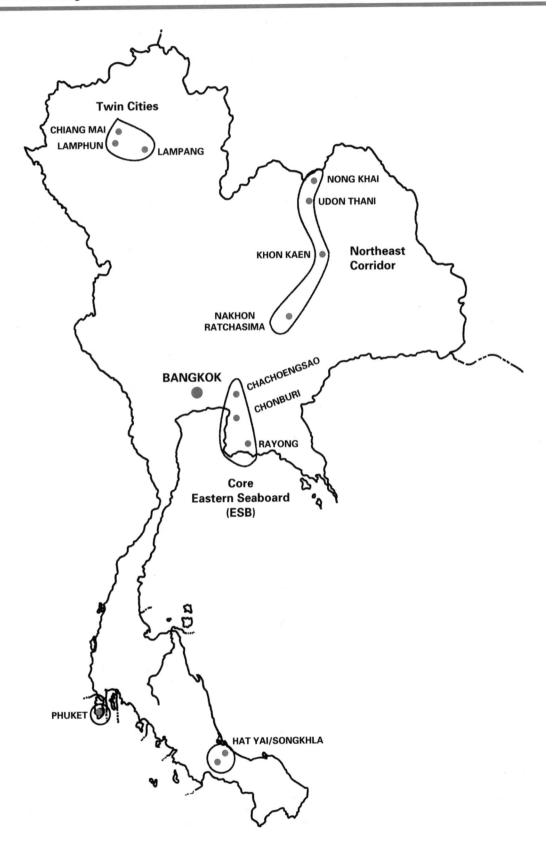

Source: Urban Development Co-ordination Division, National Economic and Social Development Board, 1998

ing its position among Southeast Asian cities, the role of the public sector in strategically shaping the extended urban region will continue to be essential.

Building Regional Coordination

To strengthen the ability of local governments to deliver infrastructure and services, the Thai government has made decentralization a priority. However, the problem in Thailand is a plethora of local governments. The extended Bangkok region contains close to 1,000 local governments, and even intermediate-sized urban regions have 10 or more. Thus, decentralization could enable local areas to tailor development strategies to global opportunities, or it could result in lost opportunities if extended urban regions lack the capacity and resources to support new economic activities.

What is needed are new forms of regional coordination, especially in larger extended urban regions such as the Eastern Seaboard. A variety of possibilities to address this challenge exist, from regional government to regional development corporations to voluntary associations of local governments. In the case of Thailand, pure regional government and regional development corporations are unlikely to be politically feasible or locally acceptable. However, in November 1999, the King signed the National Decentralization Committee law, which makes possible the creation of special local administration organizations (SLAOs) modeled on the Bangkok Metropolitan Administration (BMA). SLAOS would take responsibility for regional-scale governance, with local councils operating below the SLAO level to provide meaningful local participation, as is currently the case in the BMA. Thus, services that are best planned or delivered at a regional scale, such as treatment of wastewater and solid and toxic waste, transportation, and development, could be coordinated by one regional-scale government.

SLAOs would oversee urban regions that are economically and politically more developed, often where a special economic zone exercises considerable influence on developmental dynamics. SLAOs coterminous with an existing province would exercise approximately the same wide range of powers and have the same revenue-generating opportunities as the BMA will have under the new decentralization law. SLAOs smaller than a province would hold the powers of a senior municipality.

The first SLAO will probably be implemented in Phuket, and the second in the Nakhon Ratchasima (see Map 16.1), which contains Thailand's second-largest city (excluding the Eastern Seaboard), with approximately 1 million people in the extended urban region. If successful, the concept can be applied in areas experiencing strong development pressures such as the Eastern Seaboard, and in the Hat Yai extended urban region in the South (see Webster 1999). Although the new law does not provide for multiprovince SLAOs, it could be amended to create SLAOs covering dynamic multiprovince regions such as the Eastern Seaboard.

Addressing Quality of Life in Extended Urban Regions

Slum communities are only a rough surrogate for poverty in many emerging economies, as some households prefer to invest in small businesses and their children's education rather than higher-quality housing. In fact, in Bangkok, one-third of slum renters—usually considered the poorest residents—have household incomes higher than the mean (Pornchokchai 1992).

What's more, the percentage of people living in poverty, the number of people living in slums, and the number of slum communities in the BMA declined during the 1980s and 1990s (although the recession has reversed these gains somewhat).[2] These changes reflect reduced migration to the area as well as upward socioeconomic mobility supported by the buoyant economic conditions from 1984 to 1996.

Nevertheless, urban slum communities do reveal Thailand's failure to deliver acceptable living standards to substantial numbers of citizens—approximately 20 percent of the population of the extended Bangkok region. And slums are dispersing to suburban and exurban areas, a process that is not receiving enough attention. These slums are prevalent along expressways, rivers, roads, and near industrial estates. For example, in the Rayong urban area, as much as 50 percent of the population may be "unregistered"—mostly living in slums—creating significant demand for services while providing little local government revenue.[3] The proliferation of local governments has not helped the situation.[4]

Unfortunately, fewer state agencies, nongovernmental organizations (NGOs), and community-based groups are available to address this challenge in newly urbanizing areas. NGOs, government agencies, and international development agencies must recognize that the geography of poverty is shifting and change their priorities accordingly to help communities deal with this challenge. In particular, government grants based on registered rather than actual population hamper the ability of fast-growing communities to address the needs of the poor. Furthermore, the high capital costs for social services and infrastructure associated with fast-growing urban populations should be recognized in dynamic areas such as the Northeast Corridor and the Eastern Seaboard.

To address the problem of urban poverty, the National Economic and Social Development Board and the National Housing Authority established the Urban Community Development Office. This agency, which began operating in 1992 with startup capital of US$53 million, offers residents of poor urban areas microcredit for livelihood improvement—such as vocational or small business training, or loans to establish or upgrade a small business—and for housing and community improvement, including security of tenure. To be eligible, a low-income community must first establish a community savings group, which lends money to households or groups within the slum community. The agency focused its first activities in Klong Tooey, Bangkok's largest slum, adjacent to the port, but its activities are spreading throughout the extended Bangkok region and beyond to smaller cities, increasingly in the rapidly urbanizing but poor Northeast.

What is lacking in Thai urban areas are public–private partnerships that develop and operate large-scale projects for the public good (see Kaothien and Webster 1996). Hopefully, public-sector reform, such as legal change enabling private enterprises to hold more than 50 percent equity in public–private partnerships, and allowing public servants to openly negotiate with the private sector, will make such partnerships more attractive to the private sector. Even more importantly, governments need to establish a track record of delivering on plans and honoring commitments, thus making the private sector more willing to engage in joint ventures. For its part, the private sector will need to better recognize emerging opportunities and community needs and act prudently; its past performance in overbuilding property in inappropriate places indicates that it could benefit from paying closer attention to government development plans and socioeconomic data.

As the global economy demands new forms of urban infrastructure, such as convention districts with high-level amenities, public–private cooperation will become not an option but a necessity. Until recently, decision-makers in Thailand have consistently underestimated the role that such amenities play in attracting high-value activity to urban regions. Numerous surveys of Japanese, American, and European corporate leaders have shown the value they place on amenities in deciding where to locate production and knowledge-based activities (Webster 1992). Those that control capital are demanding even more amenities for high-level corporate, service, and production activities, and Thailand's urban citizenry is increasingly demanding that government confront traffic congestion and "brown issues"—wastewater treatment, garbage pickup, solid waste processing and disposal, and air pollution. Urban residents are also demanding more public space, particularly green, in the city, including access to the river.

The national government was relatively slow in identifying the key role that quality of the urban environment plays in attracting corporate headquarters, tourism, and producer services. However, high-profile reports such as the 1996 Urban Environment Strategy highlighted the importance of amenities such as public space and the need to address brown issues. Although considerable progress has been made, further alleviating traffic congestion—which accounts for a loss of at least 2.1 percent of gross regional product in the Bangkok area alone—is an obvious step. Although Bangkok still trails some competitor cities in environmental quality, public commitment to improving the urban environment—as well as developing human resources—is now evident. For example, in the most recent *Asia Week* poll of Asia's best cities, Bangkok climbed from a 26th-place ranking in 1998 to 13th in 1999 despite (or perhaps because of) economic constraints imposed by the economic recession.

Developing Human Resources in Extended Urban Regions

The Royal Thai Government has made considerable progress in improving enrollment rates at both primary and secondary school levels through stay-in-school programs that include student loans. (Many children from poor families do not attend or drop out of secondary school because of lost income, plus the costs of modest school fees, books, school clothes, and transportation.) The challenge is to develop post–secondary technical education that will dovetail with existing and future employment needs in Thailand's diverse urban regions. Because of a shortage of qualified instructors—over 30 percent of post–secondary faculty positions are vacant outside Bangkok—this will require more emphasis on cutting-edge telecommunications infrastructure to allow distance learning.

Distance learning can also help improve education in rural areas, indirectly benefiting urban regions through rural–urban linkages and migration. Today there are enormous differences in educational attainment between rural and urban areas: Some 33 percent of urban residents have attended secondary school, while only 11 percent in rural areas have done so; 27 percent of urban residents have some post–secondary education versus 6 percent in rural areas.

Considerable promise also lies in public–private partnerships that involve corporate leaders in operating state-of-the-art training facilities. General Motors and

Honda, as part of their decisions to locate or expand production for Southeast Asian markets in Thailand, are developing automotive technical colleges in the periurban area. Similarly, UNOCAL is operating a training facility in partnership with the Department of Mineral Resources in Songkhla. Governments must maintain regulatory control over such human development facilities, but they do represent an effective means for technology transfer, and almost invariably provide a springboard to good employment after graduation. An education system that produces entrepreneurs and managers as well as technical personnel will set the stage for more Thai ownership of firms in industries such as automobiles, petrochemicals, tourism, and agribusiness. A current weakness in Thailand's development is that small manufacturing enterprises are not developing rapidly enough to supply lead firms in periurban industrial clusters such as automobiles and electronics.

Harnessing Global Capital Flows

When Thailand suffered a severe recession in the early 1980s, the national government decided to implement an export-led development policy propelled by foreign direct investment (FDI). This policy was more successful than even its strongest supporters expected. Virtually all the resulting FDI flowed into Thai urban areas. Inadequate regulation of capital flows, particularly portfolio investment, clearly underlay the urban bubble that burst in 1997.

FDI was dominantly in manufacturing early on but it shifted toward real estate by the latter 1990s. The impacts of this shift—as well as a 19-fold increase in commercial lending from foreign banks between 1991 and 1997, resulting from introduction of the Bangkok International Banking Facility in 1991—on the property market of the extended Bangkok region were enormous. However, the high levels of investment did enhance Bangkok's role as a financial center and diversified its rapidly growing service economy. The result was a property bubble: Approximately 340,000 housing units remain vacant in the extended Bangkok region (see Figure 16.1). Although overbuilding can make middle-class housing and office and industrial space more affordable, it encourages urban sprawl, misallocates capital better used to fund employment-creating enterprises, and results in "ghost" buildings throughout the urban landscape.

A secondary but significant use of available financing was for purchase of consumer durable goods, mainly automobiles. Thus, the opening up of Thailand to capital flows and motorization were powerful forces in shaping Thailand's urban region, particularly the extended Bangkok region. Inexpensive loans for automo-

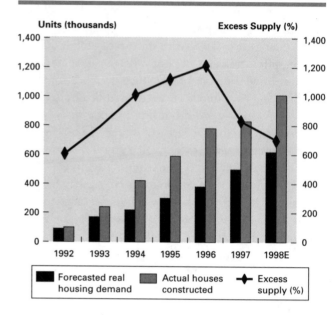

Figure 16.1
Oversupply to Remain for a Long Time

Note: Forecasted real housing demand contrasted to actual housing construction in the extended Bangkok region from 1992 to 1998. Excess supply peaked in 1996.
Source: Government Housing Bank, National Housing Authority, Real Estate Sub-committee.

biles made living or producing in more remote locations possible.

The Thai Government also recognized a decade ago that telecommunications would become vital in international competition, and partially deregulated and privatized the telecommunications industry. Private operators installed wideband fiber optics networks in many urban areas and in corridors connecting major urban areas, often using railway rights-of-way.[5] Ironically, middle-income developing countries such as Thailand, particularly their urban areas, often leapfrog technologically. In this case, backlogs in orders for fixed telephone lines have encouraged rapid acceptance of new technologies such as mobile phones. Today virtually all settled areas possess state-of-the-art wireless systems, often more advanced than those in Europe.[6]

Focusing on Software instead of Hardware

Recent Thai urban development has focused largely on "hardware"—or physical systems. In cases where full or nearly full cost recovery is possible, such as urban expressway projects serving core urban areas are operating effectively, but new expressways into lesser-developed areas are having difficulties achieving full cost recovery. However, in other cases, such as wastewater treatment and solid waste disposal, expensive facilities are not operating well because local operating funds or technical skills are not available, and because appropriate policy frameworks, including incentive structures, are not in place. For example, Bangkok's wastewater treatment system is operating at 20 percent of capacity because there is no regulation, or incentive, for households or firms to hook up (see Webster 2000). This problem is exacerbated by international companies that promote inappropriate technology such as costly solid waste incinerators, multilateral and bilateral development agencies that favor loans for such hardware, and central and local government politicians and bureaucrats who stand to gain through large-scale capital projects.

Managing demand in vehicle use and consumption of electricity and water must become a priority. Although demand management will obviously not negate the need for incremental infrastructure, it will dampen the need for costly new hardware. The fact is that the price of many conventional technologies, such as wastewater systems, which cost as much as US$1,000 per household, or urban incinerators, which usually cost at least US$50 million, are disproportionately high relative to incomes in Thai urban areas. Thus, capital costs alone make cost recovery difficult, and in times of economic recession subsidies are not available to keep these systems operating.

Decentralization should reduce this problem, as local authorities may be less likely to invest in facilities that they cannot maintain. Policymakers, politicians, and managers responsible for Thai urban regions must determine whether there are more cost-effective means of delivering urban infrastructure, such as through demand management, recycling, more informed choice of technology, market-based incentives, or user fees. Globalization forces will demand better urban management; given real resource constraints, this will force a move away from a simplistic focus on urban hardware to a more challenging focus on urban software.

Thailand's overall goal should be to aim for higher-value-added urban activities, employment based on skilled human resources, and amenities such as access to a full range of social and recreational services. All these activities need an urban framework: Comprehensive planning may be dead for good reason, but strategic planning/management and coordinated programming at local and regional levels are essential.

The reality is that today government has limited power to control capital flows; the notion that governments in guided capitalist systems in East and Southeast Asia can pick winners and allocate capital accordingly has largely been abandoned. The government's role will instead be to inform, advise, and regulate key users of capital—especially by producing and widely disseminating information on flows and uses of capital. For example, the government can educate the banking industry on the need to consider the region's supply and demand in making loans for urban development projects. Even at the microlevel of loan applications, future income flows based on business plans and market analysis should take precedence over collateral-based loans.

All these efforts could result in more effective use of capital in structuring and shaping urban systems. To a large extent, urban regions rather than nations will be competing. They cannot afford to grossly misallocate scarce capital in either the private or the public sector.

The Bangkok Plan

The case of the extended Bangkok region demonstrates how positive outcomes and additional challenges may arise from such policy approaches. In 1995 the Ministry of the Interior gave the Bangkok Metropolitan Administration permission to prepare its own urban plan. This was an important precedent in Thailand, as it allowed a local authority to establish priorities and a vision of the future. Until this point all urban plans in Thailand had been produced centrally.

The rapid development of the Bangkok financial sector reflected a wider trend toward a knowledge economy. The National Economic and Social Development Board and the Bangkok Metropolitan Administration therefore promoted Bangkok as a "knowledge city"—a characterization that increasingly came to reflect reality. Governor Krisda Arunvongse of the BMA commissioned the Massachusetts Institute of Technology, in conjunction with BMA's city planning department, to develop a physical plan based on a vision of Bangkok as a knowledge-based economy playing a key role in Southeast Asia—and even the world. The ensuing administration of Governor Bichit Rattakul augmented this plan with local district-level initiatives and strong measures to make the city more livable and green.

For example, hundreds of thousands of trees have recently been planted in the city and sidewalks have been upgraded with interlocking bricks. Measures are being taken to limit growth in flood-prone areas on the periphery of the city. In 1997 Bangkok initiated a citywide antilittering campaign based on extensive public awareness, including posters, street booths, and airport advertisements, as well as strict enforcement, with violations incurring 2,000-Baht fines. The program has been a success: Bangkok streets are litter free. Other efforts to make BMA more attractive to global knowledge industries include improved sidewalks, more landscaping, and new "pocket" parks. In fact, the Bangkok administration justifies the initiatives as both improving the quality of life for local residents and positioning Bangkok as a leading knowledge city.[7]

The Bangkok Transit System (BTS) is a direct response to the rapid growth of the knowledge economy, particularly the financial sector. Bangkok has no one distinct downtown but rather several key areas specializing in different kinds of business such as media, finance, fashion, tourism, international governance, and diplomacy. The 24-kilometer elevated BTS, which opened in December 1999, connects these areas, with the exception of the new Rama III business area. The system was driven and justified by the fact that office-based employment and tourism generated traffic beyond road capacity. To increase densities demanded by the need for face-to-face contact in these industries, the government was forced to build a mass-transit system linking the city's key nodes.

The BTS system, opened in November 1999, with a capacity of 700,000 riders per day, is attracting worldwide attention because it aims to recover its costs fully—a rarity in urban rail systems. This is considered possible because time-savings afforded by the system will be among the highest in the world. However, full cost recovery might not be feasible in the near-term because vehicle traffic is growing more slowly than before the recession, several new toll freeways have recently opened, and a portion of the loans is denominated in U.S. dollars, while revenue will be in Baht. Nevertheless, the project will undoubtedly be highly economical.

The missing link is commuter rail. As the urbanized area grows far faster than population, the failure to develop commuter-rail systems becomes more serious. Rail systems would economize on energy and human time and provide urban structure by stimulating higher densities around stations. The State Railway of Thailand is now taking action to revive a 60-kilometer elevated commuter rail project to serve the northern and eastern suburbs.

Overall, the Bangkok metropolitan area, like the national Thai government, is beginning to understand the importance of amenities in attracting and retaining high-value economic activity, but much remains to be done. In many cases, small amounts of money would make a significant difference. For example, several hundred kilometers of elevated expressways and rapid-transit systems crisscrossing the Bangkok area are greatly improving the quality of life. However, landscaping of the vast concrete structures has been very limited, and the chaos created underneath these behemoths, resulting from population relocation and construction, is not being adequately addressed despite the fact that doing so would represent only a trivial percentage of the cost of the projects. Local

residents would benefit from such quality-of-life initiatives as well as the resulting income, as employment and educational levels would rise along with the influx of high-value businesses.

Rama III, the new business district, is emerging to the east of the present Silom area, known as the Wall Street of Thailand. This new district is almost completely the product of corporate interests such as Esso Petroleum and local property developers, who responded to a new road into the area built by BMA. As more multinational and national corporations are attracted to the area, the BMA has belatedly tried to shape this new business district and improve access to it by proposing a light-rail connection.

However, the business community is wary of government planning and management of urban infrastructure—the chief complaint being that the government often does not deliver on its commitments, leaving private investments stranded. Private entities are also reluctant to become involved in municipal ventures they would not control, as regulations prohibit more than 49 percent private ownership. Nevertheless, business communities increasingly drive local priorities. For example, businesses are promoting high-quality industrial estates with cutting-edge infrastructure including social facilities and programs, as well as vocational training focusing on the region's comparative advantages.

Shaping the Future

As the dominant city-region in a country that is one of the most open in East Asia, Bangkok has seen its economy and society change rapidly over the past 15 years. The resulting demands, such as improved job opportunities for households, more amenities and higher environmental quality, regional-scale infrastructure delivery in periurban areas, and faster transportation in the core, have required numerous changes in governance, service delivery, and the mix of public-sector programming. The BMA, suburban and periurban governments, as well as the national government, have often been in a reactive position, running to catch up with these changes.

However, much progress has been made, reflected in the rapid climb of Bangkok in city-quality ratings in Asia. For example, the SLAO form of organization could improve governance considerably in periurban areas, a rapid transit system and several new toll expressways are now operating, the city's streets have been cleaned and trees planted, low-income households have access to microcredit to improve their income capacities, and technical education is being improved to better match the emerging knowledge-based economy in the Bangkok area. The challenge now facing those responsible for the

Bangkok region's future—and with decentralization and the growth of civil society, there are many stakeholders—is to move policy and programming to a more proactive stance. It is to be hoped that, within a decade, local governments in the extended Bangkok region will be shaping socioeconomic and physical development, not just responding to the strong and often beneficial but rapidly changing forces of globalization.

Bibliography

Bangkok Metropolitan Administration (BMA). Various years. *Statistical Profile of BMA.* Bangkok: BMA, Department of Policy and Planning, published annually.

Bank of Thailand. Various issues. *Monthly Bulletin.* Bangkok: Bank of Thailand, published monthly.

Dowall, David. 1992. "A Second Look at the Bangkok Land and Housing Market." *Urban Studies* 29(1): 25–38.

Garreau, Joel. 1988. *Edge City: Life on the New Frontier.* New York: Doubleday.

Graham, Stephen, and Simon Marvin. 1996. *Telecommunications and the City: Electronic Spaces, Urban Places.* London: Routledge.

Kaothien, Utis, and Douglas Webster. 1996. "Public–Private Cooperation in Urban Development." *Proceedings of the 10th AAPH Biennial Convention on the Impact of Globalization on Urban Development in the ASEAN Region.* Bangkok: National Housing Authority.

Kaothien, Utis, and Douglas Webster. 2000. "The Bangkok Region." In G. Hack and R. Simmonds, eds., *Global City Regions.* London: Routledge.

Kaothien, Utis, Douglas Webster, and John Lukens. 1997. "Infrastructure Investment in the Bangkok Region." In *Proceedings of Conference on The Infrastructure Instrument: How to Use It to Manage the Function and Form of Global City Regions.* Global City Regions Project, Madrid. Madrid: Universidad Complutense.

Kaothien, Utis, Douglas Webster, and Voravit Vorathanyakit. 1996. "Country Report of Thailand." In Royston Brockman and Allen Williams, eds., *Urban Infrastructure Finance.* Manila: Asian Development Bank.

National Economic and Social Development Board (NESDB)/ Leman Group. 1995. *Chao Phraya Multipolis Structure Plan (Metropolitan Region Structure Study).* Bangkok: NESDB.

National Economic and Social Development Board (NESDB)/ Danish Cooperation for Environment and Development. 1996. *Urban Environmental Management in Thailand: A Strategic Planning Process.* Bangkok: NESDB.

National Economic and Social Development Board (NESDB)/ Norconsult. 1997. *A Spatial Development Strategy for Thailand, Bangkok.* Bangkok: NESDB/Norconsult.

Pornchokchai, Sophon. 1992. *Bangkok Slums: Review and Recommendations.* Bangkok: Agency for Real Estate Affairs.

Rohlen, Thomas. 1995. *A Mediterranean Model for Asian Regionalism: Cosmopolitan Cities and Nation States in Asia.* Asia Pacific Research Center, Stanford: Stanford University, Monograph (The Urban Dynamics of East Asia Series).

United Nations Conference on Trade and Development (UNCTAD). 1996. *World Investment.* New York and Geneva: United Nations.

Webster, Douglas. 1992. "The Role of Amenity in Canadian Regional Development." *Plan Canada.* July.

Webster, Douglas. 1998. "Infrastructure Development Policies and Economic Development: A Perspective from Thailand." Paper presented to Workshop on ASEAN Infrastructure Planning and Management, Bangkok, September 30.

Webster, Douglas. 1999. "Strengthening of Area Based Development in Thailand." In *Proceedings of Policy Workshop on Area Development and Rural–Urban Transition,* Bangkok: National Economic and Social Development Board.

Webster, Douglas. 2000. *Financing City Building: The Bangkok Case.* Asia Pacific Research Center, Stanford: Stanford University, Monograph (The Urban Dynamics of East Asia Series).

World Bank. Various issues. *Thailand Economic Monitor.* Washington, D.C.: The World Bank, published quarterly from October 1998.

Notes

1. Numerous high-profile environmental problems have been documented in the Extended Bangkok Area. For example, a school in Map Ta Phut had to be moved because of severe air pollution from a nearby petrochemical complex.

2. Because BMA's population grew substantially during the 1980s and 1990s, the percentage of people living in poverty and slums declined much faster than the absolute numbers. See *Statistical Profile of BMA* (published annually).

3. Personal communication, mayor of Rayong, September 1998.

4. Introduction of SLAOs, discussed previously, would solve the government proliferation problem.

5. Because deregulation often resulted in regional monopolies, the price of international telecommunications has remained high relative to competitor cities such as Singapore, but the Baht devaluation has brought the cost of Thai-sourced international telecommunications close to international prices. For details, see Kaothien, Webster, and Lukens 1997, and Kaothien and Webster 2000.

6. For a description and analysis of the acceptance of new technologies in Thailand, see Kaothien and Webster 2000, and Kaothien, Webster, and Lukens 1997.

7. Personal communication, Deputy Governor Banasopit Mekvichai, November 20, 1998.

chapter 17

The Impact of Decentralization on Cities' Fiscal Health: Lessons from the United States

Andrew Reschovsky

Robert M. La Follette Institute of Public Affairs
Department of Agricultural and Applied Economics
University of Wisconsin-Madison

Throughout the world, in both developed and developing countries, responsibilities for the provision of public services are being shifted to subnational governments.[1] Examples of decentralization can be found in a number of developing countries, for example, in South Africa and Kenya in Africa, and in China and India in Asia. Even in the United States, which has long been highly decentralized, recently passed legislation has shifted primary responsibility for cash assistance for the poor (welfare) from the federal government to the states.

Decisions to decentralize are usually motivated by a desire to improve the effectiveness of governments at all levels. Transferring the responsibility for both the provision and financing of public services from central governments to subnational governments means that decisions about the mix and the level of service will more closely reflect the preferences and tastes of the residents of each local community. As local governments are presumably more in touch with the desires of their constituents, they should be in a better position than higher-level governments to develop innovative and cost-effective methods for providing public services.

The strength of a decentralized fiscal system must be tempered, however, by the realization that when urban areas are divided into a number of fiscally independent local governments, each local government has an incentive to exclude those individuals who require extra expenditures in excess of their marginal contributions to locally raised revenues. If, as in the United States, the poor tend to be concentrated in the central city and in a few older suburbs, there exists a strong incentive for the nonpoor to escape fiscal responsibilities for the poor by moving to suburban communities where the poor are often effectively excluded through the use of zoning ordinances and the existence of housing market discrimination. The fiscal health of central cities can then be further weakened because the out-migration from the city of both businesses and moderate- and high-income families creates *fiscal externalities* by further weakening the fiscal capacity of the central city and raising the average cost of providing public services.

The governance of most American metropolitan areas is highly fragmented. For example, the Chicago metropolitan area contains 262 separate general-purpose governments. When one counts all school districts and special districts, there are nearly 1,200 different governmental bodies within the metropolitan area. The existence of a large number of governments is not necessarily bad. A large choice among governments enhances consumer well-being by matching public good preferences and willingness to pay. Furthermore, competition among governments may force local governments to operate more efficiently.[2] Fiscal externalities, however, may lead to central city fiscal problems when local revenue sources provide a substantial portion of the financing of public services provided by local governments, and when local governments are ultimately responsible for providing services for large concentrations of the poor and otherwise needy.

In this chapter, I argue that many U.S. cities are in a structurally weak fiscal position, and their long-run fiscal health may be further weakened by the recent devolution of responsibilities for welfare to the states. The U.S. situation provides a cautionary tale for countries throughout the world that are in the process of decentralization. By understanding the structural fiscal problems faced by many central cities in the United States, it is hoped that other countries will be able to avoid some of the hardships and distortions that result from the fiscal system that has evolved within metropolitan areas in the United States.

Measuring the Fiscal Condition of Local Governments

In *State of the Cities in 1998*, the U.S. Department of Housing and Urban Development (1998) declared that "driven by a robust national economy, cities are fiscally and economically the strongest they've been in a decade." Yet despite this rosy assessment, many U.S. cities continue to struggle. Even though their residents face relatively heavy tax burdens, many provide inadequate levels of public services—police are not available, trash is collected infrequently, and students perform poorly.[3]

These problems stem largely from the fact that decentralization is burdening many cities with growing service responsibilities even as federal assistance is declining. While the tax base (or more broadly, the revenue-raising capacity) of most cities is growing, the rate of growth is generally less rapid than in surrounding communities with whom cities must compete for both residents and business.

It is helpful to summarize these developments by using a single measure to represent and compare the *structural* fiscal condition of local governments. Drawing on the work of Bradbury et al. (1984), and Ladd and Yinger (1991), a *need–capacity gap* can be calculated for each local government. It is defined as the gap between *expenditure need* and the *revenue-raising capacity* of each local government. Expenditure need indicates the minimum amount of money a government must spend per resident in order to provide a standard or average level of public services for which it is responsible. Revenue-raising capacity indicates the amount of revenue per resident a local government has available if its residents face a standard or average tax burden. Revenue-raising capacities can be enhanced by cities' receipt of grants from higher-level governments. It is important to emphasize that this measure of the fiscal condition of local government focuses on factors that are generally outside the control of local government officials. In this way, need–capacity gaps provide an objective measure of the structural fiscal problems faced by local governments.

Fiscal Disparities within Metropolitan Areas

Within metropolitan areas, differences in the fiscal conditions of local governments, whether measured by need–capacity gaps or by alternative measures, are gen-

erally referred to as *fiscal disparities*. The existence of fiscal disparities has both equity and efficiency implications. Fiscal disparities result in horizontal inequities among metropolitan area residents. These inequities occur when residents of two metropolitan area communities face identical tax rates but receive different levels of public services. Alternatively, inequities exist when residents of communities that provide similar levels of public services face different tax rates.

The claim is sometimes made that these inequities are short-run phenomena that will be ameliorated by market forces as individuals living in communities in weak fiscal condition are motivated to move to places in stronger fiscal health.[4] The existence of zoning and other land-use control mechanisms in the United States, however, places severe constraints on the residential mobility of low-income households and helps explain why metropolitan area fiscal disparities are not self-correcting. The use of zoning regulations allows suburban communities to effectively set a minimum price (and rent) for housing within their boundaries, thereby providing an effective way to exclude low-income households. There is also considerable evidence that racial discrimination in the housing and rental markets is widespread (Yinger 1997). These discriminatory practices make it more difficult for minority residents to move out of central cities in order to find housing in communities in better fiscal health than the central city.

To the extent that individuals and businesses make locational decisions within metropolitan areas based on fiscal considerations, a pattern of inefficient location decisions is likely to occur.[5] By encouraging suburbanization, fiscal considerations may result in a pattern of business and residential locations that increases metropolitan area congestion and environmental degradation. To the extent that high-income residents and businesses are most sensitive to fiscal conditions, their out-migration from central cities will have the effect of further exacerbating the fiscal health of the city. These fiscal externalities are likely to occur because private decisions to leave the city will not only reduce the revenue-raising capacity of the city, but by changing the mix of residents remaining in the city, may result in increases in the average per capita cost of providing public services. For example, because of "peer-group" effects in education, the departure of middle-class children from central city schools is likely to raise the costs of educating those children who remain (Henderson, Mieszkowski, and Sauvageau 1978).

Reasons for Weak Fiscal Health

In the following paragraphs I consider a number of reasons why many American central cities are in weak fiscal health relative to their suburbs. They can be grouped into the following areas: (1) relatively low revenue-raising capacities in many cities; (2) growing service responsibilities; (3) higher uncontrollable costs in cities relative to their suburbs; and (4) policies of higher-level governments.

Low Revenue-Raising Capacity

Urban economists have argued that rising incomes and declining transportation and communication costs induce both individuals and businesses to move away from the city center and toward outlying areas where land is generally less expensive. Of the 24 U.S. cities with populations over one-half million, 8 had smaller populations in 1994 than in 1980. The population of these 24 central cities grew an average of 6 percent during those years, while the population of their suburbs grew 25 percent annually—over four times faster.

Of the 10 most populous cities in the Northeast and Midwest, only one, Columbus, Ohio, experienced a population increase between 1970 and 1990. Population in the other 9 cities fell an average of 17 percent. The population loss was mostly caused by out-migration of high- and middle-income families and individuals; in all 9 cities the ratio of per capita income in the city to per capita income in the suburbs fell between 1960 and 1989.

The out-migration of middle-income city residents tends to reduce the capacity of the city government to raise revenue, especially when people with lower incomes replace departing residents, or no one replaces them at all. To compensate, the city must increase tax rates or reduce public spending—further convincing middle-class residents to leave.

Regardless of what taxes city governments use, concentrations of poor people reduce their capacity to raise funds. Yet reducing spending on direct services to the poor in response may prove self-defeating. For example, while eliminating youth recreation or summer job programs may save money in the short run, cities may have to spend more on public safety and gang control in the long run.

The traditional role of central cities as centers of employment is also diminishing. Brennan and Hill (1999) studied private-sector job growth in 92 large metropolitan areas between 1993 and 1996—a period of rapid economic growth in the United States. They found that 23 percent of the central cities in their sample lost employment during this period, while their suburbs gained employment. The number of jobs increased in 52 percent of the central cities, but at a slower rate than in their suburbs. The result of these patterns of job growth

is that the central cities' share of metropolitan-area employment fell in 82 percent of the metropolitan areas studied.

Not only the level, but the structure of employment in cities is changing. Cities are losing manufacturing jobs while gaining some white-collar employment in business services, finance, insurance, and real estate. The holders of high-paying city jobs in these sectors often prefer to live in the suburbs and commute to work. Cities' ability to capture a share of the higher wages paid by new high-productivity industries therefore depends on whether they can tax the income of nonresidents.

Yet doing so is difficult because city governments that want to levy an income or sales tax must seek authorization from state government. And suburban-dominated legislatures often refuse to allow cities to expand their tax base because such a move would mean higher taxes for suburban residents. Only 8 of the nation's 24 largest cities impose an income or wage tax, and those 8 cities tax income earned by nonresidents at a very low rate or not at all. Even if a city does succeed in taxing earnings, businesses may move to the suburbs to avoid paying a wage premium to attract workers. And if a city imposes a sales tax, the higher the tax the smaller the chance that suburban residents will choose to shop in the city.

While central cities may no longer dominate their regions' economy as they did in the past, they continue to serve as their regions' cultural and entertainment centers. Although, cities' museums, concert halls, and sports facilities continue to be popular with residents, suburbanites, and tourists, the fiscal benefit to cities of these facilities is often limited. To the extent that these facilities are owned by governments or nonprofit organizations, they are exempt from property taxation. As a result, cities that rely heavily on the property tax get limited fiscal benefit from their cultural, educational, and sports facilities. In general, tax-exempt property is concentrated in central cities. For example, in New York City nearly one-third of property value is exempt from taxation, while 13 percent of property value is exempt from taxation in suburban Nassau County and 22 percent in Westchester County.

Broad Service Responsibilities

In the United States, local governments are responsible for providing a wide array of public services. In fact, many of the core services most people associate with governments are provided, and in most cases financed, by local governments. Although the assignment of functions differs across states, local governments generally play the role of *service provider of last resort*, required by state governments or by the courts to provide shelter to the homeless and medical aid to the indigent. Policy changes at higher levels of government often end up having fiscal implications for local governments. In practice, expanded public service responsibilities often come in the form of mandates from both the federal government and state governments. For example, the widespread de-institutionalization of the mentally ill that has occurred over the past couple of decades in effect forced cities to deal with the mentally ill who ended up on the street, became public nuisances, committed crimes, or needed medical care.

Service responsibilities tend to be greater in central cities than in most suburban communities. As demonstrated by recent research by Anita Summers and her colleagues at the University of Pennsylvania, one reason why public expenditures tend to be high in central cities relative to their suburbs is that city governments finance a number of direct services to poor persons, especially in the areas of public welfare and public health.[6] In 1998, the average poverty rate in American central cities was 18.5 percent, a rate that is over twice as high as the average suburban poverty rate (U.S. Bureau of the Census 1999). Not only are the poor concentrated in central cities, but many of the nation's social problems, problems that hardly existed 20 years ago, such as crack cocaine, homelessness, and the AIDS epidemic, also tend to be spatially concentrated in central cities.

The fiscal consequence for central-city governments that must provide special services to citizens with various social and economic problems is that other city residents and businesses must either pay higher taxes or contend with lower levels of basic public services, such as public safety and sanitation. The fact that the concentration of the poor within central cities results in broader service responsibilities for central-city governments relative to their suburbs serves to weaken the relative fiscal condition of cities.

The High Cost of Providing Services

To the extent that fiscal considerations influence locational decisions, it is reasonable to imagine that both businesses and individuals compare the level and mix of public services the city provides and the taxes and fees they must pay to receive these services. Available evidence suggests that the relationship between benefits received and expenses incurred is generally less favorable in central cities than in their suburbs. This central-city fiscal disadvantage may occur either because city governments operate inefficiently compared to the average suburban governments or because factors beyond city control require that city governments spend more money than suburban governments in order to deliver the same

bundle of public services. Economists refer to the minimum amount of money that a government *must* spend in order to provide any given level of public services as the *costs* of public services.

Although it certainly is not difficult to find examples where city government spending is inflated due to ineffective management, inefficient and outdated union work rules, and wasteful administrative structures, there also exists strong evidence that central cities face above-average costs due to factors over which they have no control. On the basis of a number of econometric studies, it is possible to conclude that costs tend to be higher in central cities for the following reasons.[7] First, the costs of achieving any given level of public safety or of educating children to meet any given level of educational performance are generally higher in locations with concentrations of low-income households. Not only is the incidence of crime higher in poor neighborhoods, but community attributes associated with poverty, such as high density and poor housing conditions, increase the amount of resources required to provide public safety in these neighborhoods. Studies also suggest that smaller class sizes, specially trained teachers, and extra classes are necessary to compensate for the social and economic disadvantages faced by most children from poor families.[8]

Second, in many cases, cities have higher costs than their suburbs because their infrastructure is older, and consequently the costs of maintenance, and often of fire prevention, are higher.

Third, there is evidence that, at least for some public services such as education, costs in large central cities are above average because of diseconomies of scale attributed to their large size.

Finally, costs, measured on a per resident basis, tend to be higher in central cities relative to suburbs because cities must provide services for significant numbers of nonresidents, whether they be suburbanites commuting to central-city jobs or taking advantage of the city's cultural, entertainment, and commercial attractions. In particular, nonresidents contribute to the costs of public safety, sanitation, and cultural and recreation services provided by city governments.

To the extent that city governments need to spend more money than their suburban neighbors in order to provide services for the poor and for nonresidents, there are fewer resources available for improving public service delivery for businesses and for the middle class. City governments face the difficult task of having to either cut services or raise taxes, either of which may increase the chances of out-migration by these relatively mobile groups.

Policies of Higher-Level Governments

One policy response to the relatively low fiscal capacity, broad public service responsibilities, and high costs faced by central-city governments would be for the federal and state governments to provide cities with direct grants. In principle, city governments' relatively weak fiscal conditions could be improved by a lump-sum grant allocated in proportion to a city's fiscal condition, with local governments in weaker fiscal positions receiving larger per capita grants.

In contrast to many, if not most, other countries, the federal government in the United States provides its local governments with no general-purpose aid. Most federal funds that are allocated to local governments are in the form of categorical grants designated for specific purposes, such as mass transit, education for disabled children, and community development. Since the late 1970s, financial assistance from the federal government to city governments has declined sharply as a percentage of city government spending. The cuts in direct federal assistance have been particularly steep for the nation's 23 largest cities. The share of expenditures financed by the federal government in those cities fell from 14 percent in fiscal year 1977 to under 7 percent in fiscal 1996 (the latest year for which such data are available).

Grants-in-aid from state governments to their cities have in aggregate remained quite stable over time. In a few cases, state financial assistance to city governments has taken the form of direct state financing of services previously funded by city governments. This is the case in New York City, where the state assumed responsibility for most of the operating costs of higher education and the courts in response to the fiscal crisis of the mid-1970s. The role played by state financial assistance in city budgets varies considerably among the states, depending in part on the range of services provided by city governments.[9] With the exception of Boston, Detroit, and Milwaukee, however, state general-purpose aid to cities is quite limited, accounting for only 3.5 percent of city direct expenditures in the nation's 23 largest cities.[10]

Perhaps even more important for the long-run fiscal health of cities than direct federal aid are the unintended pro-suburban spatial biases in a number of federal policies. The most salient examples are found in transportation, housing, and tax policies used by the federal government. These policies tend to reinforce both the market incentives that cause middle- and upper-income residents to migrate to the suburbs and the growing concentration of the poor in the central cities (McGeary, 1990; Chernick and Reschovsky, 1997). For example, by building most large low-income public housing projects in central-city low-income neighborhoods, the fed-eral government has increased the concentration of the poor in urban neighborhoods and also fostered immobility among project residents. This occurs because project residents pay a rent that is restricted to 30 percent of their income, while many low-income urban residents not living in public housing projects must pay over half their monthly income as rent.[11]

A number of features of the federal tax code also may have an implicit pro-suburban bias. The most important of these are the tax treatment of owner-occupied housing. In the United States, homeowners are entitled to deduct the value of their mortgage interest and property tax payments from their incomes subject to taxation. Given the progressive structure of the U.S. income tax system, this feature of the tax code provides more generous subsidies to middle- and upper-income families than to those with modest incomes. Ongoing theoretical and empirical work by Joseph Gyourko and Todd Sinai suggests that deductibility is providing larger subsidies to suburban than to central-city residents and may be having the effect of encouraging suburban homeownership among middle-income households.[12]

Continued Decentralization in the United States

Although the United States is already one of the world's most decentralized countries, policy changes implemented in the past few years have resulted in further decentralization. In 1996, the Congress enacted the Personal Responsibility Act. This legislation, commonly referred to as "welfare reform," devolved responsibility for the major program providing cash assistance to low-income families from the federal government to the states. Prior to 1996, families that met income and other eligibility criteria were *entitled* to a monthly cash grant funded jointly by the federal and state governments, with the amount of the grant determined by the legislatures in each state. With the passage of the welfare reform legislation, this entitlement was eliminated, and states became responsible for determining the level and the scope of cash transfers. Prior to 1996, the financing of these transfers was in the form of a matching grant from the federal government to the states. The new legislation replaced the matching grant with a block grant to the states.

Due both to the current strength of the American economy and to stringent new eligibility requirements that limit the lifetime receipt of cash assistance to five years and require most welfare-eligible adults to seek work, the number of welfare cases has fallen dramatically.[13] At least in the short run, the decline in caseloads combined with the switch to a system of block grants fixed in nominal value has resulted in substantial fiscal windfalls in most states. The evidence suggests that at least in some states these excess funds have been used to finance general tax relief or to fund programs unrelated to the well-being of the poor.

The important question, however, is whether this decentralization of cash assistance for the poor to the states will in the long run have an adverse effect on the fiscal health of central cities. Although it is obviously too early to have a definitive answer to this question, on both empirical and theoretical grounds there are some indications that welfare reform will further weaken the fiscal condition of many central cities.

The Impact of Devolution on the Fiscal Health of Central Cities

Although welfare caseloads have been falling everywhere, recent data indicate that the rate of decline is more rapid in the suburban ring of metropolitan areas than in central cities. The consequence of this pattern is that the remaining caseloads are becoming more concentrated in central cities. Katz and Allen (1999) report that between 1994 and 1998 welfare caseloads in the counties containing the 30 largest American cities fell by 35 percent, while the caseload in the states that are home to these counties declined by 44 percent. In ongoing research Howard Chernick and I are finding evidence that when one divides urban counties into their central-city and suburban portions, caseloads are falling less rapidly in central cities. For example, in July 1995, the City of Milwaukee, with less than 12 percent of the state of Wisconsin's population, was home to 51.2 percent of the entire state's welfare caseload. By July 1998, Milwaukee housed 85.1 percent of Wisconsin's welfare population.[14]

Although city governments are not responsible for the direct payment of cash transfers to the poor, the growing concentration of families on welfare in central cities has several important fiscal implications. First, those individuals remaining on welfare are probably those with the severest problems—the least education, the highest probability of drug or alcohol dependency, and the greatest incidence of mental illness or retardation. It is precisely these people who are likely to place the greatest demands on city services. To the extent that they are becoming increasingly concentrated in central cities, the *relative* fiscal position of central cities within their metropolitan areas will diminish.

The central goal of welfare reform in the U.S. is to move people away from dependency on government cash assistance and into permanent jobs. The falling caseload indicates an initial success in moving a large number of poor individuals into the labor force. Whether welfare reform will also prove successful in reducing poverty is unclear, however. Several recent studies that have been monitoring the employment and earnings history of individuals who are leaving welfare have found that earnings, even for those with full-time jobs, are very modest (Meyer and Cancian 1998; Parrott 1999; Cancian et al. 1999). These findings suggest that even in those cities with large drops in caseloads, fiscal need may not drop proportionately to caseload declines.

In the long run, the greatest danger to central-cities' fiscal health may come from the conversion of federal aid for cash assistance to the poor from an open-ended matching grant to a block grant. Because of their relatively short work histories and limited skills, individuals who have recently left welfare will be most vulnerable to unemployment when the economy slips into recession. Under a system of matching grants, the amount of federal money states receive increases if an economic downturn increases the need for welfare. The conversion of matching aid to block grants implies that state governments must now bear the full fiscal burden of any increased spending on the poor.[15] An economic recession will put further strain on the fiscal health of states because state tax revenues generally decline during recessions.[16]

Even in the absence of a recession, economic theory suggests that the long-run state government response to a shift from matching grants to a block grant for welfare will be a reduction in state government spending on the poor. Under a matching grant, an extra dollar of welfare benefits paid to the poor will cost state taxpayers less than a dollar, while an extra dollar spent on most other state-provided public services will cost a full dollar. The shift to a block grant means that the tax price of welfare rises to a dollar and becomes identical to the tax price of spending on other state objectives.[17] Although economic theory indicates that this increase in tax price will lead to a reduction in spending on the poor, empirical estimates of the magnitude of the reduction vary widely.[18] Although a precise estimate of the long-run state government fiscal response to welfare reform is not possible, the weight of evidence supports the contention that state government spending on the poor will decline over time (Chernick and Reschovsky 1999).

There are likely to be both direct and indirect consequences for central-city fiscal health if state government support for the poor is reduced. First, as the poor are concentrated in central cities, any policies that reduce the level of economic resources flowing to the poor will negatively impact on the revenue-raising capacity of city governments. Furthermore, as local governments serve as public service providers of last resort, the reduction of federal and state programs to aid the poor will in effect shift the responsibility for the poor to municipal governments. Even if welfare reform results in a permanent reduction in the number of individuals dependent on government transfer payments for support, central cities will in all likelihood remain the place of residence of a disproportionate share of those most in need of government assistance. To the extent that central cities serve increasingly as the home of those most in need, the fiscal position of cities will worsen relative to that of their suburbs.

One possible response to devolution would be for state governments to provide additional fiscal assistance to central-city governments. As already indicated, relatively few states provide much general-purpose assistance to their local governments. Although there are no nationwide data available on recent trends in the spatial patterns of state assistance, an analysis of the evolution of state assistance in two states suggests that state financial support for suburban governments may be increasing at a faster rate than support for central cities. The first example comes from the State of Wisconsin, where between 1991 and 1997 per capita aid to Milwaukee, the state's largest city, increased by 64 percent, while per capita aid to Milwaukee's suburbs rose by 117 percent. This distribution of aid, highly favorable to the suburbs, occurred despite the fact that between 1990 and 1997, per capita property values grew over $2\frac{1}{2}$ times faster in Milwaukee's suburbs than in the central city. In New York State, two recent policy changes appear to weaken the fiscal position of New York City relative to its suburbs. First, a school property tax relief initiative is replacing a portion of local property taxes with increased state aid. The initiative has been structured so that the greatest relief goes to communities with the highest rates of homeownership, highest property tax rates, and highest housing values. Because New York City has a relatively low rate of homeownership and low property tax rates on owner-occupied housing, in part because of its heavy reliance on nonproperty taxes, relatively little of the new state aid will flow to New York City (City of New York, Independent Budget Office 1997). Second, the New York State Legislature has recently passed legislation that repeals a commuter tax New York City levied on suburban New York residents who worked in the City. This tax had, at least in part, reimbursed the City government for the costs of services it provided to suburban residents.

The recent experiences in Wisconsin and New York are not sufficient evidence to prove that state governments in the United States are systematically shifting state government assistance away from central cities. The fact, however, that around the country the population of many central cities is growing more slowly than the population of their states suggests that city governments may be losing power in state legislatures (Weir 1996). To the extent that most state legislators vote for changes in state and local grants only if the residents of the communities they represent gain, it is not surprising that recent changes in intergovernmental aid policies are not favorable to central cities. If current population trends continue, it is unlikely that state governments will play an important role in ameliorating the structural fiscal problems faced by many central-city governments.

Lessons from the U.S. Experience

I have argued in this chapter that the decentralization of expenditure responsibilities and taxing power to local governments within metropolitan areas in the United States often results in a situation where central cities are in weak fiscal health relative to their suburbs. Unless some remedial actions are taken, the structural fiscal problems of cities are likely to continue to worsen. The concentration of the poor in many central cities will only serve to heighten existing inequalities in the provision of basic public services.

It is very important, however, to emphasize that by highlighting problems with the American fiscal system, I am not suggesting that fiscal decentralization should be avoided. Quite the contrary, the decentralization of both revenue-raising authority and expenditure responsibilities has large potential benefits, especially in developing countries that have a history of highly centralized government. Many developing countries are characterized by great local and regional differences. A decentralized system of local government finance has the advantage that decisions concerning the provision of public services can better reflect local economic, social, cultural, and political conditions. Decentralization also has the potential benefit of increasing citizen participation in fiscal decisionmaking and in enhancing political stability in countries where there exist strong pressures to break up along ethnic or geographic lines (World Bank 1999).

The fiscal problems of central cities that I have highlighted here do not result from decentralization per se. They occur because of the way decentralization interacts with a set of political, economic, and institutional factors that characterize American metropolitan areas in the beginning of the twenty-first century. As an example, zoning ordinances frequently used by suburban local governments serve to concentrate the poor, and in particular, racial minorities, in central cities. And as we have seen, the concentration of the poor in central cities has important implications for the fiscal health of city governments.

The general lesson from the American experience is not that developing countries should not pursue decentralization, but rather that great care must be taken to design an intergovernmental fiscal system that avoids some of the pitfalls that characterize metropolitan-area public finance in the United States. Implementing change in a mature intergovernmental system, such as that in the United States, is extremely difficult. As most changes involve winners and losers, the potential losers will work very hard to impede any change. Developing countries often have the opportunity to design intergovernmental arrangements and grant systems where none existed before. This puts these countries in a unique position to be able to learn from the experiences of other countries with well-developed systems of intergovernmental finance and to act upon the lessons learned.

In the next few paragraphs, I suggest three specific lessons that can be drawn with from the American experience of financing central-city governments.

Responsibility for the Poor

One of the basic precepts of the theory of fiscal federalism is that within an economy, the central government should pursue any efforts to redistribute resources. The argument, first articulated by Musgrave (1959) and Oates (1972), is that all attempts by subnational governments to redistribute resources through spending programs or progressive taxation are doomed to fail because high-income individuals can leave for other jurisdictions which pursue fewer pro-poor policies. In the United States, spending on redistributive programs is found at all levels of government.[19] By shifting more responsibility for cash assistance for the poor to the states, the recently enacted welfare reform legislation has obviously moved in the opposite direction from the principles articulated by Musgrave and Oates.[20] One way to improve the fiscal health of central cities and to reduce the incentive for local governments to attempt to exclude individuals with low incomes, is for the central government to play a dominant role in financing redistributive programs. It should be emphasized that central government financing of poverty alleviation and other social programs does not imply that these programs should be administered by the central government. In most cases, program administration, especially when the delivery of social services is involved, is more efficiently done at either the local or regional level.

Targeted Equalization Aid

As long as there are differences in the fiscal conditions of local governments within a metropolitan area, both businesses and individuals have an incentive to relocate to a community in stronger fiscal health. If a local government's weak fiscal condition were caused by inefficient government actions, then such intrajurisdictional mobility would be efficiency enhancing. If, however, weak fiscal health is due to factors outside the control of local government officials, then this mobility can further weaken city fiscal health and augment metropolitan-area fiscal disparities. One policy response to this situation would be the establishment of a system of local government grants from a higher level of government, with the grants being targeted to governments in the weakest fiscal health.

In the United States, there are no general-purpose grants to local governments. While state government grants to local school districts are found in all states, only a handful of states distribute general-purpose aid to their local governments. Even when state aid does exist, the formulas used to distribute the aid usually account only for differences across communities in property values per capita and ignore differences in costs and service responsibilities.[21] A number of other countries, such as the United Kingdom, France, and Switzerland, distribute general-purpose grants to local governments. In France, the largest government grant to local governments, the Dotation Globale de Fonctionnement (DGF), is distributed using a formula that includes a measure of "needs" (Gilbert 1999a). In a study based on the calculation of Gini coefficients, Guengant (1996) has found that the DGF reduces disparities in the fiscal capacity of local governments in France by about 40 percent.[22]

Metropolitan Cooperation

To avoid some of the problems faced by U.S. cities and to ensure that city governments will be able to continue to provide adequate levels of essential public services to their citizens, countries must work hard to counter the fiscal externalities that arise when local governments within metropolitan areas compete for tax bases and when the provision of services to the poor and the needy becomes an important responsibility of local governments.

One important strategy is to take steps to enhance metropolitan cooperation. On one extreme would be the creation of metropolitan-area governments that would be given the responsibility for the provision of core local government services. This approach has been taken in South Africa, which has established metropolitan-area governments that are responsible for the local public good provision in the central city and the surrounding communities. These communities include both high-income (mainly white) suburbs and the former black townships. It is too early to know whether these new metropolitan governments will be able to reduce the great inequities in public-service delivery (and in capital infrastructure) that currently exist within metropolitan South Africa.

In most countries local governments in metropolitan areas are already well established. This will make it politically very difficult to establish metropolitan governments. Nevertheless, various forms of metropolitan-area cooperation are possible. On the one hand, these can involve metropolitan-wide provision of specific services. Ideal candidates for metropolitan provision are public services for which scale economies exist or public services that are characterized by metropolitan-wide externalities. On the other hand, cooperation can take the form of suburban government contributions to the financing of central-city public services, especially those that provide direct benefits to suburban residents or that respond to problems that are arguably metropolitan in scope, such as homelessness.

In the United States, with the exception of metropolitan governments in Indianapolis and Jacksonville, and a tax-base sharing scheme in the Minneapolis–St. Paul metropolitan area, there are very few examples of metropolitan-area governance. In a number of other countries, however, one finds examples of intergovernmental grant systems within metropolitan areas. In these systems of horizontal equalization, relatively rich communities or districts contribute funds that are distributed directly to poorer municipalities or districts within the same metropolitan area. This type of metropolitan-area sharing scheme can be found in Beijing, China and in some cantons in Switzerland.[23]

The lesson that can be drawn from the experience of the United States and from other countries is that metropolitan cooperation, especially cooperative arrangements that are beneficial to central cities, is unlikely to occur unless local governments are provided with specific incentives to cooperate. In recent years the French government has been trying to induce local governments to cede both service responsibilities and a portion of their tax base to new metropolitan or regional governmental bodies (Gilbert 1999b). As the incentive mechanism, the government provides an increase in grants to local governments that agree to cooperate (mutualisation volontaire). It appears that this incentive mechanism has been quite successful in encouraging metropolitan cooperation in France.

An alternative form of metropolitan cooperation that would benefit central cities would be the imposition by local governments of income or payroll taxes that are payable in the jurisdiction where income is earned. Such a tax levied by central-city governments would be opposed by individuals who work in the city but live in the suburbs. One way to overcome this opposition would be to grant suburban residents at least a partial income or property tax credit against the payment of the city income or payroll tax. The problem with implementing such a scheme is that it would be opposed by suburban governments that would, in effect, be transferring fiscal resources to the central city. One possible way to overcome this suburban opposition would be for the state or central government to provide incentives to suburban governments to accept this type of tax-sharing scheme. The incentives could take the form of direct grants to suburban governments or income tax credits to suburban residents (Chernick and Reschovsky 1997).

Conclusion

Compared to most countries in the world, the fiscal structure of the United States is highly decentralized. Local governments are responsible for providing a wide range of public services, including many services provided by higher-level governments in other countries. Although the property tax is the most important local source of revenue, local governments, especially central cities, also employ a wide range of other taxes and user fees. As is well known, fiscal decentralization is assumed to enhance economic efficiency and encourage political participation in government decisionmaking. I argue in this chapter that given the political and cultural institutions present in the United States, fiscal decentralization within American metropolitan areas has led to long-run fiscal problems for many central cities.

Central cities often bear the responsibility of providing public services for the metropolitan area's neediest people in an environment where both businesses and individuals can easily move to suburban communities that provide a more favorable fiscal climate. As a result, city residents often face a below-average level of public services, yet an above-average rate of local taxation. I have suggested that one likely impact of the recently enacted decentralization of responsibility for cash assistance to the needy will be further fiscal pressure on central-city governments.

The fiscal problems of American central cities are not an inevitable outcome of decentralization. Newly decentralizing countries and countries in the midst of reforming their fiscal arrangements can learn from the U.S. experience. Countries should assign responsibility for providing services for needy populations to the central government, implement a system of equalizing grants from higher-level governments that accounts both for the expenditure needs and revenue-raising capacity of local governments, and take appropriate steps to internalize fiscal and economic externalities within metropolitan areas. Such countries should then be able to exploit the considerable benefits of decentralization and enjoy fiscally strong central cities.

Bibliography

Bahl, Roy. 1999. *Fiscal Policy in China: Taxation and Intergovernmental Fiscal Relations.* South San Francisco: The 1990 Institute.

Bradbury, Katharine L., Helen F. Ladd, Mark Perrault, Andrew Reschovsky, and John Yinger. 1984. "State Aid to Offset Fiscal Disparities Across Communities." *National Tax Journal* 37(June): 151–70.

Brennan and Edward W. Hill. 1999. "Where Are the Jobs?: Cities, Suburbs, and the Competition for Employment." *Survey Series.* Center on Urban and Metropolitan Policy, The Brookings Institution, Washington, D.C.: November.

Cancian, Maria, Robert Haveman, Daniel R. Meyer, and Barbara Wolfe. 1999. "Before and After TANF: The Economic Well-Being of Women Leaving Welfare." *Institute for Research on Poverty Report*, University of Wisconsin–Madison, December 14.

Chernick, Howard. 1998. "Fiscal Effects of Block Grants for the Needy: An Interpretation of the Evidence." *International Tax and Public Finance* 5(May): 205–33.

Chernick, Howard, and Therese J. McGuire. 1999. "The State, Welfare Reform, and the Business Cycle." In Sheldon H. Danziger, ed., *Economic Conditions and Welfare Reform.* Kalamazoo, MI: W. E. Upjohn Institute for Employment Research, pp. 275–304.

Chernick, Howard, and Andrew Reschovsky. 1997. "Urban Fiscal Problems: Coordinating Actions Among Governments." In Burton Weisbrod and James Worthy, eds., *The Urban Crisis: Linking Research to Action.* Evanston, IL: Northwestern University Press.

Chernick, Howard, and Andrew Reschovsky. 1999. "State Fiscal Responses to Block Grants: Will the Social Safety Net Survive?" In Max Sawicky, ed., *The End of Welfare? Consequences of Federal Devolution for the Nation.* Armonk, NY: M.E. Sharpe, pp. 157–93.

City of New York, Independent Budget Office. 1997. "School Tax Relief and Education Aid Proposals: Impacts on New York City." IBO Fiscal Brief, New York: April.

Council of the Great City Schools. 1999. "Closing the Achievement Gaps in Urban Schools: A Survey of Academic Progress and Promising Practices in the Great City Schools." Preliminary Report, October [available at http://www.cgcs. org/ ACHGAP.pdf].

Duncombe, William, and John Yinger. 1997. "Why Is It So Hard to Help Central City Schools?" *Journal of Policy Analysis and Management* 16(1): 85–113.

Gilbert, Guy. 1999a. "Local Taxation and Intergovernmental Fiscal Relations in France." In Amedeo Fossati, Amedo Fossati, and Giorgio Panella, eds., *Fiscal Federalism in the European Union.* Routledge Studies in the European Economy, No. 9, London: Routledge.

Gilbert, Guy. 1999b. "Quelles réformes pour le Financement des Collectivités Locales?" *Cahiers Français* 298(octobre–décembre): 61–69.

Glaeser, Edward L. 1998. "Are Cities Dying?" *Journal of Economic Perspectives* 12(Spring): 139–60.

Green, Richard K., and Andrew Reschovsky. 1992. "Fiscal Assistance to Municipal Governments." In Donald A. Nichols, ed., *Dollars & Sense,* Volume III. Madison, WI: The Robert M. La Follette Institute of Public Affairs, University of Wisconsin.

Guengant, Alain. 1996. "Evaluation du Pouvoir Péréquateur de la Dotation Globale de Fonctionnement des Communes." In Guy Gilbert, ed., *La Péréquation Financière Entre les Collectivités Locales.* Paris: Presses Universitaire de France.

Gyourko, Joseph, and Richard Voith. 1997. "Does the U.S. Tax Treatment of Housing Promote Suburbanization and Central City Decline?" *Working Papers.* Economic Research Division, Federal Reserve Bank of Philadelphia, Philadelphia: September.

Henderson, Vernon, Peter Mieszkowski, and Yvon Sauvageau. 1978. "Peer Group Effects and Educational Production Functions." *Journal of Public Economics* 10(August): 97–106.

Jeanrenaud, Claude, and Andreas Spillmann. 1997. *La Péréquation Financière dans le Canton de Berne.* Stuttgart: Verlag Paul Haupt.

Katz, Bruce and Katherine Allen. 1999. "The State of Welfare Caseloads in America's Cities: 1999." *Survey Series.* Center on Urban and Metropolitan Policy, The Brookings Institution, Washington, D.C.: February.

Ladd, Helen F., and John Yinger. 1991. *America's Ailing Cities; Fiscal Health and the Design of Urban Policy.* Baltimore, MD: Johns Hopkins University Press.

Ladd, Helen F., Andrew Reschovsky, and John Yinger. 1992. "City Fiscal Condition and State Equalizing Aid: The Case of Minnesota." *Proceedings of the 84th Conference on Taxation of the National Tax Association, 1991.* Columbus, OH: National Tax Association.

McGeary, Michael. 1990. "Ghetto Poverty and Federal Policies and Programs." In Laurence Lynn, Jr. and Michael McGeary, eds., *Inner City Poverty in the United States.* Washington, D.C.: National Academy Press.

Meyer, Daniel R., and Maria Cancian. 1998. "Economic Well-Being of Women Following an Exit from AFDC." *Journal of Marriage and the Family* 60(2): 479–92.

Musgrave, Richard A. 1959. *The Theory of Public Finance.* New York: McGraw-Hill.

Oates, Wallace E. 1972. *Fiscal Federalism.* New York: Harcourt Brace Jovanovich.

Oates, Wallace E. 1999. "An Essay on Fiscal Federalism." *Journal of Economic Literature* 37(September): 1120–49.

Pack, Janet R. 1995. "Poverty and Urban Public Expenditures." Working paper no. 197, Wharton Real Estate Center, University of Pennsylvania, October.

Parrott, Sharon. 1998. *Welfare Recipients Who Find Work: What Do We Know About Their Employment and Earnings?* Washington, D.C.: Center on Budget and Policy Priorities, November 16.

Reschovsky, Andrew, and Jennifer Imazeki. 1998. "The Development of School Finance Formulas to Guarantee the Provision of Adequate Education to Low-Income Students." In *Developments in School Finance, 1997.* Washington, D.C.: National Center on Education Statistics, U.S. Department of Education, 1998: 121–48.

Summers, Anita A. and Lara Jakubowski. 1996. "The Fiscal Burden of Unreimbursed Poverty Expenditures in the City of Philadelphia: 1985–1995." Working paper no. 238, Wharton Real Estate Center, University of Pennsylvania, August.

U.S. Bureau of the Census. 1997. *Statistical Abstract of the United States 1997.* [available at http://www.census.gov/statab/www].

U.S. Bureau of the Census. 1999. *Poverty in the United States, 1998*, Current Population Reports, Series P60-207, Washington, D.C.: U.S. Government Printing Office.

U.S. Department of Health and Human Services, Administration for Children and Families. 1999. "Change in Welfare Caseloads Since Enactment of New Welfare Law." [available at http://www.acf.dhhs.gov/news/stats/aug-sept.htm], December.

U.S. Department of Housing and Urban Development. 1998. *State of the Cities in 1998*. Washington, D.C.: Office of Policy Development and Research.

Wasylenko, Michael. 1997. "Taxation and Economic Development: The State of the Economic Literature." *New England Economic Review* (March/April): 37–52.

Weir, Margaret. 1996. "Central Cities' Loss of Power in State Politics." *Cityscape: A Journal of Policy Development and Research* 2(May): 23–40.

World Bank. 1999. *World Development Report 1999/2000.* Washington, D.C.

Yinger, John. 1997. *Closed Doors, Opportunities Lost: The Continuing Costs of Housing Discrimination.* New York: Russell Sage.

Notes

1. For an excellent review and analysis of decentralization efforts around the world, see Chapter 5 of the World Bank's *World Development Report 1999/2000.*

2. See Oates (1999) for a good discussion of the conditions under which competition among local governments will be efficiency enhancing.

3. In a recent report, the Council of the Great City Schools (1999) reports on the low test score results achieved by many students in the public schools of the nation's largest cities.

4. Fiscal advantages and disadvantages are likely to be at least partially capitalized into housing prices. While this capitalization will reduce the cost of housing for individuals living in communities in weak fiscal condition, it does not eliminate intercommunity inequities in both access to public services and tax prices faced by residents.

5. There is a large empirical literature in both the United States and Europe addressing the role of fiscal factors in the intrametropolitan locational decisions of households and businesses. Although these studies present a wide range of findings, there appears to be broad support for the contention that fiscal factors play a significant role in locational decisions within metropolitan areas. For a good summary of the U.S. literature on the role of taxes in locational choices, see Wasylenko (1997).

6. After completing a detailed analysis of the budget of the City of Philadelphia, Summers and Jakubowski (1996) concluded that in 1995 the City devoted 7.6 percent of its own source revenues to direct poverty-related services. In another study, Pack (1995) reports that larger cities spent more money per capita on direct poverty functions than smaller cities.

7. Examples of these studies include Bradbury et al. (1984), Ladd and Yinger (1991), Ladd, Reschovsky, and Yinger (1991), and Green and Reschovsky (1992).

8. Two recent studies that estimated cost functions for public education and found a strong relationship between concentrated poverty and educational costs are Duncombe and Yinger (1997) and Reschovsky and Imazeki (1998).

9. City governments responsible for elementary and secondary education and for public health generally receive substantially more state financial assistance than city governments with narrower responsibilities.

10. Excluding Boston, Detroit, and Milwaukee, general-purpose state aid equaled only 2.5 percent of direct expenditures in the nation's largest cities. These calculations are based on data from the U.S. Census Bureau's *City Government Finances for 1993–94* (available at http://www.census.gov/govs/city/).

11. Although recent federal housing policy has emphasized housing subsidies that low-income households are able to use in city as well as suburban locations, existing evidence suggests that this policy has done little to stimulate mobility by low-income households to the suburbs.

12. For some early work on this subject, see Gyourko and Voith (1997).

13. Between August 1996 (the date of the signing of the welfare reform legislation) and June 1999, the number of welfare recipients in the United States has declined by 44 percent (U.S. Department of Health and Human Services 1999).

14. We have also found that the rate of decline in welfare caseloads between 1995 and 1998 was less in the eight largest central cities in California than in their respective suburbs.

15. The current welfare reform legislation does allow limited state borrowing (with interest) from a "rainy day" fund if a state's economy slips into recession.

16. See Chernick and McGuire (1999) for a discussion of the empirical issues involved in estimating the impact of a recession on state welfare spending in light of the shift to a block grant for welfare.

17. In fact, the story is more complex. Because increases in family income lead to reductions in the amount of Food Stamps to which a family is entitled, the tax price of a state increase in cash assistance is actually greater than one (Chernick 1998).

18. See Chernick (1998) for a comprehensive review of the econometric literature.

19. Edward Glaeser (1998) has suggested that cities' fiscal health is improving because they have learned the Musgrave and Oates lesson that attempts at redistribution are destined to fail. Glaeser ignores the fact that although some cities, such as New York, have reduced programs targeted to the poor, many cities have limited ability to do so because state governments or court rulings mandate city responsibility for the homeless, the mentally ill, and others in need of some type of public assistance.

20. In a recent article, Oates (1999) suggests that by shifting the responsibility for welfare to the states, the U.S. Congress may have wanted to adopt a system that would (in theory) encourage states to experiment with new ways to end dependency and alleviate poverty.

21. In a study of the distribution of state aid to local governments, Ladd, Reschovsky, and Yinger (1992) found that per capita aid was uncorrelated ($r = 0.10$) with an index of local government fiscal health that included measures of local government revenue-raising capacity, costs, and service responsibilities.

22. In ongoing research Gilbert and Guengant are evaluating the entire system of grants to local governments in France. They are attempting to assess the extent to which grants reduce inequalities in both the fiscal capacity and expenditure needs of local governments.

23. See Bahl (1999) for a description of the grant system used in Beijing metropolitan area and Jeanrenaud and Spillmann (1997) for a discussion of the system used in the Berne metropolitan area.

chapter 18

How Singapore Regulates Urban Transportation and Land Use

Sock-Yong Phang

School of Business
Singapore Management University

Singapore is a small island city-state with a population of 3.9 million and a land area of 648 square kilometers. Without any natural resource except its strategic location, the country is economically dependent on trade and capital flows. To attract mobile capital, the government has tried to ensure that immobile factors—including land use, housing, infrastructure, public services, and labor—complement growth. In particular, the city-state has pursued a highly regulated approach to urban transportation and land use—an approach that contrasts sharply with its willingness to embrace foreign direct investment.

These policies have yielded stunning success. The 1998 *World Development Report* ranks Singapore fourth worldwide in gross national product (GNP) per capita, after Switzerland, Japan, and Norway. Annual growth has averaged 7 percent per capita since the 1960s, and the government has posted a budget surplus since 1968. Income tax rates have declined steadily, corporate income taxes have dropped from 40 percent to 26 percent, and there is no payroll tax. Meanwhile, over 5,000 foreign companies have located in Singapore, and many have made it their regional operating and manufacturing base. These experiences reveal that, despite the city-state's somewhat unique size and sovereign status, the argument for extensive government control and planning remains persuasive in the area of urban development.[1]

Controlling Land Use

Nineteenth-century economist Henry George made a strong case for 100 percent taxation of rents from land, which he regarded as common property. George claimed that such taxation would abolish poverty and economic crises, as the latter, he said, resulted from speculation in land values. In its approach to urban transportation and land regulation, Singapore has embraced a large dose of George's prescription (Phang 1996). The state not only owns four-fifths of all land but also controls the rights to road use.

This approach began in 1965 when the country faced severe unemployment and an acute housing shortage after gaining independence from Malaysia and Britain. State ownership and control of land were considered essential to attracting industrial investments and building public housing on a large scale.

In 1966 the government enacted the Land Acquisition Act, which permitted the state and its agencies to acquire land for any public purpose. A 1973 amendment set payments independent of market conditions and the landowner's purchase price. In 1951, to better enforce government control over private land use and development, the British colonial government enacted the Planning Ordinance (now the Planning Act). The Planning Act then spawned a Master Plan, which designates the type and intensity of use for privately owned areas. Higher densities and zoning alterations incur a surcharge, and all developers must obtain written permission before subdividing their holdings or making any alterations. The government reviews the Master Plan every five years.

Public-sector projects were subject to the 1971 Concept Plan, a strategic blueprint for land use and urban transportation for the entire city-state. The revised Concept Plan, released in 1991, includes comprehensive urban-design guidelines for a projected population of 4 million people.

However, unlike in former socialist cities where government ownership of land and the absence of markets undercut efficiency, productivity, and environmental quality, Singapore actively relies on markets to promote efficient land use. First, the one-fifth of land and associated real estate that belong to the private sector provides valuable price information to urban planners. Second, as in Hong Kong where the state owns all the land, the Singapore government uses a competitive bidding process to allow private development of state land. The bidding process for a particular plot of state land is administered by either the Urban Redevelopment Authority or the Housing and Development Board as agent for the Land Office. The reserve price for each plot is determined by the chief valuer. The bidding process is usually a closed tender exercise for which detailed procedures for the agent and bidders have been laid down as financial regulations. The process is subjected to both internal and external inspection and audit to ensure competition and fairness. Invitations to tender or participate in open auctions (which are sometimes held instead) are given the widest possible circulation to attract the largest number of competitive tenders. Government-owned and government-linked companies also compete with each other and with privately owned companies to develop both private and public land. For example, the Jurong Town Corporation develops and manages 30 industrial estates, including high-tech and business parks.

The government announces the total supply of units that its land sales program is expected to generate one year ahead of time and conducts a midyear review before finalizing the program for the latter half of the year. Tender documents for government land sales typically specify use, plot ratio, building height and layout, parking, time frame for completion, and open spaces. Through this process government leases have allowed private development of offices, hotels, shopping centers, warehouses, recreational facilities, and residential projects. Such leases, which typically run for 99 years or less, direct development toward priorities such as the new downtown and the financial district, conservation and renewal of specific buildings and areas, and new housing (Urban Redevelopment Authority 1995), as do tax exemptions and deductions. Government receipts from such leases totaled S$11 billion in 1995–96—nearly half of the government's operating revenue of S$28 billion that year.

Financing Public-Built Housing and Home Ownership

Singapore's extensive public housing program provides living quarters for more than 80 percent of the population and ensures affordable housing prices and rents in a land-scarce city. Some 22 public housing estates and new towns are comprehensively planned, with the number of dwelling units in each ranging from 20,000 to 62,000. Yet more than 90 percent of households are homeowners: The state leases 90 percent of the housing it builds on a 99-year basis to eligible household owners.

The government offers price discounts on newly constructed public housing and grants to households that purchase housing on the resale market. Households, in turn, finance their purchases through a compulsory savings scheme known as the Central Provident Fund, which requires all employees and their employers to contribute 20 percent of monthly wages. (The employers' share recently dropped from 20 to 10 percent because of the 1997 recession.) People may withdraw these compulsory savings at age 55, use them to finance mortgage payments, education, and medical expenses, or invest them in approved financial assets.

Rules encourage submarkets in government land and property leases but discourage speculation. For example, there is an active resale market for government-leased flats—but only after owners occupy the units for a minimum period of time. In fact, the volume of transactions on the housing resale market exceeds the volume of new flats, and resale prices help the government set prices of new flats. (Similarly, a successful bidder for the development of a government site cannot resell to another single party before completing the project without permission from the government, but after completing it faces no restrictions on resale.)

The government uses zoning and careful screening of hazardous industries to control emissions and imposes buffer distances from housing according to industries' classification as light, general, special, and hazardous. Together these land-use and planning efforts have completely eliminated slums and squatter settlements, and the population enjoys universal access to clean water and sanitation.

Regulating Urban Transportation

Despite a gross domestic product (GDP) per capita of S$37,214 in 1999, only one Singaporean in ten owns a car. To allocate rights to car ownership, Singapore again combines market mechanisms with taxation and active restrictions designed to contain congestion. The rationale for such an approach is simple: Roads already constitute 12 percent of the island's area, about the same percentage as housing, so room for continued expansion is clearly limited. To the extent that road use rights represent access to a land-related resource, taxation of those rights is completely in line with Henry George's prescription.

A quota system restricts the number of motor vehicles: Before buying a vehicle, a prospective owner must obtain a certificate of entitlement through competitive bidding. This bidding set the price of a certificate for a medium-sized car at S$43,802 in January 2000. The owner must also pay an import tax of 41 percent, a registration fee of 140 percent, and annual road taxes that depend on the vehicle's engine capacity. As a result, a typical medium-sized car costs up to three times per capita GDP—in most high-income countries that ratio is less than one. For example, a new Toyota Corolla with an import value of S$18,000 cost approximately S$110,000 (or US$65,000).

The government also tackled road congestion directly—and early, in 1975—by instituting an "area licensing scheme" in which motorists entering heavily trafficked sectors had to purchase and display a coupon. Electronic road pricing (ERP) replaced this scheme in 1998. ERP charges vary by type of vehicle, time, and location, and involve a combination of radio frequency, optical detection, imaging, and smart card technologies. ERP relies on a pair of gantries: The first has antennas that check smart cards on approaching vehicles and debit the card. The second gantry pinpoints the location of the vehicle, identifies the vehicle type, and verifies that the correct deduction has been made. A controller links information from the antennas and detectors to check for possible violations (no smart card, insufficient balance on the card), and cameras transmit an image of the rear license plate to a central computer in the event of a violation.

The Land Transport Authority conducts quarterly reviews to adjust charges to yield targeted "optimal" speed ranges of 45 to 65 kilometers per hour for expressways and 20 to 30 kilometers per hour for arterial roads. Other charges for vehicles include parking fees and fuel taxes, which are high enough that the tank of any vehicle leaving the country must be three-quarters full. Total levies on motor vehicles generally accounted for nearly one-quarter of the government's operating revenue and nearly one-half of the government's operating expenditure in recent years.

Because of such policies, Singaporeans use public transport to make 5 million of 7 million trips daily—of which 3.1 million occur on buses, 0.9 million are on rapid transit, and 0.9 million are in taxis. The government completely funded the cost of the 83-kilometer rapid-transit system, and fares are low, ranging from 35 cents to $1.60 per trip, compared with the quality of service. An integrated ticketing system allows commuters to use a single stored-value card to travel on both buses and trains. Two major private companies enjoy a monopoly on bus routes while a government-owned company operates the rapid-transit system and a linked 8-kilometer light-rail system. The government has announced plans to allow the development of two major multimodal public transport operators. Because of this comprehensive approach to transport, levels of carbon monoxide, sulfur dioxide, nitrogen oxide, and lead in the air all fall within the guidelines of the U.S. Environmental Protection Agency.

Creating an Effective Public Sector

Singapore's ability to pursue such effective planning stems from a network of competent, noncorrupt institutions that together provide rich public-sector capacity. Public-sector entrepreneurs at numerous government-linked companies (such as the world-renowned national airline) also compete with private firms both domestically and internationally in activities as diverse as telecommunications, airlines, shipping, banking, shipyards, manufacturing, health care, and trading.[2] Government-linked companies are self-financing and most public-sector institutions have also been structured to be self-financing. Table 18.1 lists the key public-sector agencies involve in urban transport and land-use activities.

Why and how does the public sector in Singapore perform so well? The government has developed a rigorous recruitment system: It sponsors the nation's "best and brightest" to attend top universities in the United Kingdom and United States, who then return to become public officials. Senior civil servants earn perhaps the highest salaries among bureaucrats in the world, with their pay benchmarked against private-sector salaries.[3] This system helps the government minimize corruption and recruit and retain talent, including midcareer officials from the private sector.[4] And recruitment and promotion are based on merit rather than seniority, kinship, or ethnic ties. Supervisors assess employees' ultimate potential and promote high flyers quickly so they will reach the top ranks by age 45. Finally, extensive computerization enhances public employees' productivity.

The civil service has developed a culture where corruption is viewed as a "high risk, low reward" activity (Quah 1996, p. 76). The powers of the Corrupt Practices Investigation Bureau are defined under the Prevention of Corruption Act 1960. The Corruption (Confiscation of Benefits) Act of 1989 provides for the confiscation of benefits derived from corruption. Whether the Singapore style of public administration is transferable elsewhere is debatable because of the high economic and political costs involved (Quah 1996). Competitive public-sector pay and large-scale computerization are economically costly and may be politically costly as well. Introducing

Table 18.1

Public Sector Institutions and Agencies Involved in Urban Transportation and Land Use Activities

Institution/agency	Primary responsibilities

Ministry of Law:
  Land Office
  Registry of Land Titles and Deeds
  Survey Department
  Land Surveyors Board
  Land Systems Support Unit
  Appeals Board (Land Acquisition)
  Strata Titles Board
	Primary responsibilities
	• Oversees land use and registration
	• Acquires private land under the Land Acquisition Act
	• Manages and controls state land
	• Alienates state land to both the public and private sectors for development
	• Collects land revenue

Urban Redevelopment Authority: statutory board under Ministry of National Development	• Acts as the national land-use and conservation planning authority • Formulates long-range land-use Concept Plan and translates it into specific planning guidelines for local areas, which then form the Master Plan • Enforces planning regulations and determines and collects development charges • Acts as agent to the Land Office in "packaging" and selling state land to the private sector to facilitate focused development
Jurong Town Corporation: statutory board under Ministry of Trade and Industry	• Acts as main developer and owner of industrial land in Singapore • Manages 30 industrial and business parks
Housing and Development Board: statutory board under Ministry of National Development	• Develops comprehensive estates that house 86 percent of the population and include infrastructure facilities, commercial, industrial, recreational, and public premises • Provides subsidized mortgage loans that enable people to purchase its homeownership flats • Administers the allocation system for subsidized public housing • Administers resale transactions • Provides housing grants for resale units • Upgrades and redevelops older housing estates • Acts as an agent of the Land Office in the sale of state land for private residential development and land reclamation
Land Transport Authority: statutory board under Ministry of Communications and Information Technology	• Acts as agent of the government in administering, assessing, collecting, and enforcing motor vehicle taxes, fees, and charges • Plans, designs, constructs, manages, and maintains road and rail network, and coordinates land transport services
Public Transport Council: statutory board under Ministry of Communications and Information Technology	• Regulates entry and exit of bus service providers by issuing bus licenses • Approves increases in fares for public transport • Ensures that bus operators comply with PTC's service standards, which include route planning and design specifications, service efficiency, hours of operations, affordability, and service information

a meritocratic system and minimizing corruption also require the widespread support of the population.

Transferability of the Singapore Experience

Not every government may find it feasible to make housing and competitiveness in attracting foreign investment high priorities. Indeed, one could argue that the draconian land policies that help facilitate integrated planning in Singapore work because of its peculiar circumstances. For example, few large private landowners existed in the 1960s and 1970s, when separation from Malaysia and the withdrawal of British troops created a sense of urgency. However, numerous city governments in former socialist countries and in Asia are also major landowners, yet the absence of markets often makes these cities inefficient (Bertaud and Renaud 1995). Those cities can learn much from Singapore's planning process and its active role in creating markets.

Larger countries cannot raise taxes on vehicle ownership to Singaporean levels because doing so would impose a heavy penalty on intercity transport. However, the Singapore experience does show that larger cities can use road pricing to manage congestion and that revenues can cover and even exceed the cost of providing and maintaining roads.[5] Despite this experience, only a few other governments have implemented congestion pricing: Congestion pricing has been implemented on the intercity A-1 highway in France and on toll rings in the Norwegian cities of Bergen, Oslo, and Trondheim.

Winning political approval for congestion pricing is admittedly difficult: In Hong Kong, Stockholm, London, and the Randstad, intense controversy defeated or delayed congestion pricing proposals. Many motorists feel they stand to lose under such a policy, particularly if the government does not return the toll revenue to them in some form. According to Oldridge (1994), "No city anywhere in the world that is run on democratic principles will be politically able to accept congestion pricing unless it is gained through a slow evolutionary process."

Such political problems, though difficult, are not insoluble, particularly in developing countries where rates of car ownership are still relatively low. Those countries should note that Singapore introduced its area licensing scheme some 25 years ago. Growing cities would do well to begin to regulate and enforce road-use pricing now, as well as develop their ability to manage efficient mass transit.[6]

The tactics on which Singapore relies—state land ownership, regulatory takings, and compulsory savings, complemented by an extensive public sector—could easily have spawned widespread inefficiency and corruption, as they have in other countries. But voters have returned the People's Action Party to power continuously since independence because it is honest, efficient, and effective in delivering a high quality of life. This political stability contributes to the city's ability to attract foreign investment.

Intervention by cities whose government and leadership are weak and corrupt may carry a higher cost than inaction. However, many cities, regions, and countries would benefit by developing efficient and effective public-sector institutions and emulating the coincidence of interests between Singapore's government and its people.

Bibliography

Bertaud, A., and B. Renaud. 1995. *Cities Without Land Markets: Location and Land Use in the Socialist City.* World Bank Policy Research Working Paper 1477.

Cmd 13. 1994. *Competitive Salaries for Competent and Honest Government: Benchmarks for Ministers and Senior Public Officers.* White Paper, 21 October, Singapore.

George, H. 1879. *Progress and Poverty.* New York: Robert Schalkenbach Foundation, 1979 edition.

Hau, T. D. 1992. *Congestion Charging Mechanisms for Roads: An Evaluation of Current Practice.* WPS 1071. Washington, D.C.: The World Bank.

Heggie, I. G., and P. Vickers. 1998. *Commercial Management and Financing of Roads.* World Bank Technical Paper No. 409. Washington, D.C.: The World Bank.

Oldridge, B. 1994. "Congestion Metering in Cambridge City, United Kingdom." In Borje Johansson and Lars-Goran Mattson, eds., *Road Pricing: Theory, Empirical Assessment and Policy.* Boston: Kluwer Academic Publishers.

Phang, S. Y. 1996. "Economic Development and the Distribution of Land Rents in Singapore: A Georgist Implementation." *The American Journal of Economics and Sociology.* October: 489–501.

Quah, J. S. T. 1996. "Public Administration in Singapore: Managing Success in a Multi-Racial City-State." In A. S. Huque, J. T. M. Lam, and J. C. Y. Lee, eds., *Public Administration in the NICs: Challenges and Accomplishments.* Basingstake: Macmillan Press.

Toh, R., and S. Y. Phang. 1997. "Curbing Urban Traffic Congestion in Singapore: A Comprehensive Review." *Transportation Journal* 37(2): 24–33.

Urban Redevelopment Authority, Singapore. 1991. *Living the Next Lap: Towards a Tropical City of Excellence.*

Urban Redevelopment Authority, Singapore. 1995. *Changing the Face of Singapore through the URA Sale of Sites.*

World Bank. 1998. *World Development Report 1998.* Washington, D.C.

www.gov.sg for web sites of Singapore government ministries and statutory boards.

Yuen, B., ed. 1998. *Planning Singapore: From Plan to Implementation.* Singapore Institute of Planners, pp. 81–132.

Notes

1. Recent literature on various aspects of land use and urban transport regulations in Singapore includes a collection of papers edited by Yuen (1998), which details different dimensions of the planning process, including sustainable development, the Master Plan, renewal of public housing estates, urban transport planning, and urban conservation. Toh and Phang (1997) reviews the literature analyzing policies to curb traffic congestion in Singapore. Quah (1996) describes and analyzes the contribution of the public sector to the economic success of Singapore. The Web sites of various government ministries and public institutions (see Table 18.1), found at www.gov.sg, contain much detailed information on current policies, prices, and other indicators of market conditions.

2. A government-linked company is one in which the government has equity holdings and is formed under the Companies Act.

3. A new minister earns two-thirds of the average income of the top four individuals in six sectors: banking, accountancy, engineering, law, local manufacturing, and multinational corporations. Meanwhile a good administrative officer at age 32 earns the average income of the 15th person aged 32 in the same six sectors (Cmd. 13, 1994). Other salaries are extrapolated from these two points. In 1992 the private benchmark figure for a new minister was S$800,000 (US$500,000) and that of a 32-year-old public administrator $199,000 (US$120,000).

4. The ability to attract private sector expertise into the public sector has been particularly important for the judiciary and for central banking.

5. For more on various combinations for cost recovery, see Heggie and Vickers (1998).

6. See Hau (1992), pages 62–63, for guidelines on congestion charges appropriate for developing countries.

chapter 19

To Plan or Not to Plan: Southeast Asian Cities Tackle Transport, Communications, and Land Use

Peter J. Rimmer

Department of Human Geography, Research School of Pacific and Asian Studies
The Australian National University

Howard Dick

Department of Management
University of Melbourne

The megacities of Southeast Asia intrude into world consciousness at opposite extremes (Rimmer 1986; Dick and Rimmer 1998 1999, forthcoming). Singapore has earned a justifiable reputation as a model world city. Bangkok has become notorious as arguably the globe's most congested city. Meanwhile Jakarta and Manila resemble Bangkok rather than Singapore, while Hong Kong and Kuala Lumpur are closer to the Singapore model. What accounts for such a marked difference among these major cities?

This chapter will show how different cities utilize land use, transport, and communications—as well as planning underlying all three—to produce very different outcomes. We will also contrast the experiences of megacities with those of medium-sized and smaller cities. Although cities of varying sizes often need to focus on different priorities, all would gain from greater access to local revenue sources and more responsiveness to local constituencies.

Planned Cities: Singapore, Hong Kong, and Kuala Lumpur

In Singapore urban planning is a task of national government and is a national priority. The land constraint is so tight and reclamation so expensive that the cost of planning errors is high. Moreover, the city itself is Singapore's prime resource: To compete on the world stage it must coordinate port, airport, and telecommunications with industry, commerce, and housing.

Integrated transport and land-use planning began in Singapore in 1967 with the Urban Renewal and Devel-

opment Project (Crooks Michell Peacock Stewart 1971). The infant republic had just separated from the larger state of Malaysia—an event soon followed by the staged withdrawal of British forces. To avoid soaring unemployment and political tensions, the government sought to attract foreign investment, especially in labor-intensive manufacturing. One aspect of a reliable workforce was a transport system that could get people to work on time, especially from new high-rise public housing.

Singapore's transport policy focused on both medium- and long-term horizons while also benefiting from continuous learning. The first measures involved rationalization of the existing slow-speed bus transport system. During the 1970s the government merged four main bus companies into one public corporation, while bus routes integrated with housing estates and new towns and industrial estates to allow for affordable and reliable commuting.

Although the government invested substantial funds in new highway links, by the mid-1970s it recognized that accommodating rapid motorization would only lead to worsening congestion. The subsequent initiative for tackling downtown congestion restricted access to the central business district through the pioneering Area Licensing Scheme and raised license and parking charges until the cost of car ownership became probably the highest in the world. In 1998 electronic monitors began to record and charge vehicles entering the central business district—an innovation in which Singapore again leads the world.

The government also decided that the transport system's dependence on buses and private cars was no longer a viable long-term strategy. Construction of a mass rapid-transit system began in 1983 at a cost of US$2.3 billion, and the first trains ran in 1989 (Rimmer 1986; JUTS 1997). Ten years later this network has become the backbone of a well-articulated transport system. Planning has also ensured that most new housing and employment locates along the rapid-transit corridors, reducing demand for cross-city movement. Both the port and airport are situated within these axes. No other Southeast Asian city has achieved this level of sophistication.

Singapore has also led the way in telecommunications development, pushing beyond basic functions into data networks that facilitate global trade and finance. The government has recently eased its restrictive policy on Internet access and media censorship, reinforcing its commitment to promoting Singapore as a high-tech information processing and research center.

The case most comparable to Singapore is Hong Kong. Both function as transport hubs, international business centers, and tourist destinations. And both have experienced the switch from basic to high-value manufacturing, services, and logistics and the need to develop cross-border links as part of their larger regional roles. Like Singapore, Hong Kong planned infrastructure development along expressway and fixed-route public-transport corridors. High-capacity metro, rail, light-rail, and cross-harbor tunnel projects extend the reach of older bus, ferry, paratransit, and tram networks. The long-term aim is to reduce commuters' reliance on road-based transport by integrating employment centers with rail stations, adding pedestrian walkways to selected roads, and providing segregated overhead walkways.

Despite their similarities in linking transport and industrial development, Hong Kong and Singapore do show marked differences in long-term planning. There is more private ownership of land in Hong Kong. The latter also relies more heavily on private investment to fund infrastructure (such as in developing a container port). Hong Kong has preferred franchised private bus and ferry companies, accompanied by public regulation of any transport monopolies. And Hong Kong has made more use of paratransit, though its operation in the metropolitan area has been constrained to scheduled services on fixed routes at fixed fares. After some early experiments, Hong Kong has not applied stringent traffic restraints in downtown areas.

The only other capital city in Southeast Asia that has implemented long-term planning is Kuala Lumpur. Because land is cheap, transport development has until recently been almost entirely road-based and facilitated settlement at lower density than in any other Southeast Asian city. The city's freeway/tollway system has accompanied low-rise new towns, producing a sprawling low-density city-region with a high rate of vehicle ownership that resembles a small Los Angeles. Authorities are now trying to retrofit the 24-kilometer elevated light-rail system opened in 1996 to serve this less-than-ideal situation for public transport use. Authorities are also making another attempt to retrofit the recently electrified commuter railway into the Kelang Valley corridor, which combines infrastructure, manufacturing, and both middle-class and working-class housing, along with a seaport and domestic airport.

Like Singapore, the Malaysian government aims to develop a high-tech information corridor in the hinterland of Kuala Lumpur on the model of Silicon Valley (Malaysia 1996). Taking advantage of large tracts of land formerly used for plantations, the Multimedia Super Corridor (MSC) covers an area stretching 50 kilometers by 15 kilometers. The corridor encompasses the twin Petronas Towers of the Kuala Lumpur City Center, the new administrative capital of Putra Jaya, the new manufacturing center known as Cyber Jaya, and the relocated Kuala Lumpur International Airport (Sirat 1998). Almost 300 information technology companies—including 30 world-class enterprises—have been attracted by the liberal cyber laws and received MSC status. The degree to which these firms will attract the latest information technology and stimulate the Malaysian economy will depend on the recovery in foreign investment after the Asian crisis.

Unplanned Cities: Bangkok, Jakarta, and Manila

Bangkok, Jakarta, and Manila, in contrast, have applied modern transport technologies piecemeal—uncoordinated by any consistent long-term strategy. Policy has focused on accommodating rapid growth in private vehicle traffic. Jakarta has built the most integrated toll-road network, with port, airport, and radial expressways connecting via a central ring road. Manila has built an elevated ring road that connects with northern and southern toll roads. Bangkok has managed to build only a few sections of freeway network, which have, if anything, exacerbated inner-city congestion. These cities have also implemented one-way streets, truck bans in daylight hours, dedicated bus lanes, minimum car occupancy, odd and even access days, and freight distribution terminals, but have paid almost no attention to the needs of pedestrians and bicyclists. The urban poor have thus seen their access impeded and dangers from vehicle traffic worsen.

Public transport in these cities has until very recently relied on buses supplemented by paratransit such as minibuses and jeepneys. Ambitious plans to modernize bus fleets have invariably foundered on lack of sustained funding and bad management. Competition has produced some air-conditioned, limited-stop buses charging premium fares, but most passengers put up with crowded, poorly maintained, and heavily polluting vehicles.

Notwithstanding the lack of comfort, flat-rate fares of the bus systems do allow cheap urban commuting—albeit at slow speed. And though criticized as a cause of traffic congestion, minibuses (in Bangkok and Jakarta) and jeepneys (in Manila) carry a large number of passengers over short-to-medium distances with stops on demand and minimal waiting times. The perception that such vehicles obstruct private vehicles and cause congestion—though influential in the making of transport policy—ignores the fact that paratransit vehicles have much higher productivity per unit of road space and dollar of road investment. Their drawback is slowness over long distances.

Despite substantial investment in urban roads and expressways, speed per kilometer in these three cities has remained constant or, as in Bangkok, even fallen. Expressways typically feed into and out of bottlenecks, so travel time is unpredictable and consists largely of idling, which is costly and leads to scheduling problems, despite the widespread use of mobile phones. These and other Southeast Asian cities can further streamline traffic, but even costly expansion of expressway systems can only delay other solutions to the problem.

Telecommunications access is much better than transport: All three cities have installed widespread basic infrastructure. Satellites provide television and telephone access to virtually the entire urban population. The less well-off gain access to the network through public telephone booths—even using them to make international calls. (Because of the high number of overseas Filipino workers, the Philippines has one of the highest rates of incoming international calls in the world.)

Confronting High Costs

Because a fixed-route public-transport network is either nonexistent or rudimentary in Southeast Asian cities other than Singapore, the dilemma is the high initial cost of a public-transport network. Virtually all large European and Northeast Asian cities, in contrast, have subway networks, while medium-sized European and some Japanese cities maintain tramway systems and discourage vehicle access. These systems feed into commuter railways and link to rail terminals and often airports.

The high cost of investing in such systems stems not only from the need for new lines and stations but also from the high price of land in central cities. To minimize such costs, Manila and Bangkok have begun to invest in overhead rail lines along main thoroughfares. Manila's 14-kilometer light-rail line, opened in 1984–85, is only now

developing into a minimal network. In December 1999 the first 10 kilometers of the new elevated mass rapid-transit system opened along the ring road between Quezon City and Makati; the full loop line is scheduled to connect back into the original line in 2002. In Bangkok the 23-kilometer elevated Skytrain also commenced operation in December 1999, but connections to main traffic nodes await integration with two other projects deferred because of the Asian economic crisis. Jakarta has rehabilitated its electric railway system, including an urban loop line, as a potentially high-volume commuter network, but further investment will be needed to harvest significant passenger flows. Funding constraints, political squabbling, and outright corruption have further ensured that little has been built. The region's economic crisis will further defer completion indefinitely and tempt policymakers to restrict infrastructure spending to incremental development of expressways.

However, Manila, Bangkok, and Jakarta should seize the opportunity to formulate 20-year land-use plans. The clear lesson from Singapore and Hong Kong is that efforts to funnel new industry and housing along primary transport corridors optimize returns from long-term investments in rail infrastructure. Incremental road and expressway investment and the lack of a long-term transport plan, in contrast, allow private and often speculative land-use decisions to shape the urban structure. Transport planning becomes reactive and unstable as each new increment reinforces the existing pattern.

The underlying problem is that Southeast Asia has seen both industrialization and rapid urbanization over the past three decades. High rates of investment in and around main capital cities have attracted steady in-migration, producing spectacular growth in city size, whether measured by population, area, or regional domestic product (Ginsburg, Koppel, and McGee 1991). The urban economies of Bangkok and Jakarta are now larger than the economy of Singapore, and greater Kuala Lumpur and Manila are following close behind (Table 19.1).

Urban sprawl is exacerbated by governments' tendency to tackle the symptom rather than the cause. New expressways are invariably accompanied by new sites for industrial estates and new towns, and they allow executives and managers of large factories to live in exclusive residential areas such as Pondok Indah in Jakarta or Forbes Park in Manila. Time has run out for these cities to adopt a long-term transport plan.

How Cities of Different Size Can Tackle Transport and Land Use

Cities of different sizes often need to approach transport, land use, and communications differently. One option for large cities—a technique that Japan has used

Table 19.1
Urban Agglomerations by Gross Regional Domestic Product, 1995

	Current int'l GRP US$billion adjusted for Purchasing Power Parity (PPP)	National total (percent)
SINGAPORE	68.3	100.0
THAILAND	438.8	100.0
Bangkok metropolis	172.5	39.9
Bangkok and vicinity		
(5 provinces)	226.0	51.5
INDONESIA	734.5	100.0
Jakarta DKI	112.4	15.3
Jabotabek	148.0	20.0
PHILIPPINES	195.5	100.0
Manila national capital region	63.5	32.5
MALAYSIA	181.3	100.0
Kuala Lumpur (Wilayah)	23.5	13.0
Kuala Lumpur & Selangor	60.4	33.3
VIETNAM	17.6	100.0
Ho Chi Minh City	3.0	17.2

Source: *World Development Report 1997: The State in a Changing World.* World Bank, Oxford University Press 1997, and national statistical yearbooks.

with success—is to encourage private companies to finance infrastructure by relying on earnings from related development. For example, Japanese railroad companies build their own department stores, hotels, and leisure facilities at downtown terminals, and create new towns, housing, shopping, and parks or resorts at outlying destinations. In Bangkok, Jakarta, and Manila in the 1980s and 1990s, in contrast, governments financed expressway construction but developers reaped the gains (and losses) from induced investment in towns, malls, and leisure facilities.

In addressing their transport problems, large cities need to pay particular attention to the needs of the poor. Very often decisions designed to relieve vehicular bottlenecks have ignored the needs of slow-speed and pedestrian traffic. These decisions have forced nonmotorized rather than motorized traffic to make longer detours, notwithstanding the considerable human energy required to travel extra distances in a tropical climate. Poor siting of bus stops and rail stations and design of overhead pedestrian bridges impose considerable inconvenience and discomfort, and schoolchildren can no longer safely ride bicycles to school. To address these problems, international lending agencies should integrate major infrastructure projects with local needs and plans, especially in densely populated neighborhoods with low motor vehicle ownership.

Integrated planning for transportation and land use may be one way out of megacities' transportation crises. Urban corridors such as the Kelang Valley, which combine infrastructure, manufacturing, and both middle-class and worker housing, are likely to generate the greatest benefits, especially if seaport and airport are located along or adjacent to the corridor. The Malaysian government has explicitly pursued such rational decisionmaking in planning the new information corridor. In Thailand, by contrast, the siting of the airport (Don Muang) well north and the new deep-sea container port (Laem Chabang) well south of Bangkok has made it particularly difficult for companies to decide where to locate (Rimmer 1995). Resiting the international airport to a new location southeast of Bangkok will facilitate industrial concentration along the corridor from Bangkok down the Eastern Seaboard. Jakarta's airport and container port also sit on opposite sides of the city center, but in this case completion of ring-road connections moderates travel time and eliminates the substantial advantage of any one axis.

Cities of 1 million or less, in contrast, typically do not suffer any serious transport crisis. They are compact enough to be served by slow-speed road and ferry links without significant peak-hour congestion, even in downtown areas. Some have modest private bus networks, but paratransit can make journeys from the urban fringe to the central business district cheaply and in reasonable time. Motorcycles are more important than motor cars, while bicycles and pedestrian traffic often account for a substantial share of trips.

In these cities prestige rather than need often drives investment in large infrastructure projects such as traffic arteries and transport terminals. Overinvestment based on grants from central governments and multilateral loans is particularly noticeable in nearby airports, which are often poorly sited in terms of efficient access. As in larger cities, these major projects often disadvantage pedestrian and slow-moving traffic. Ambitious bureaucrats in medium-sized and smaller cities also often needlessly interfere with paratransit. Large projects to modernize transport systems generate both political kudos and slush funds for the officials in charge. They have little incentive to investigate low-cost investments in better and more direct walkways, all-weather footpaths, and dedicated bicycle lanes.

Governments of these cities need to focus more on specific projects rather than overall infrastructure. Central governments can help by monitoring local projects and holding officials accountable, and by earmarking grants or loans for construction of sewerage systems. A modern sewerage network is desirable on both public health and environmental grounds, and can be designed and constructed more cheaply when cities are still relatively small. And planners should note that the design of a sewerage system is as fundamental to long-term urban planning as transport networks.

Most urban governments, whether large or small, find themselves caught between rising public needs and aspirations and their limited powers: These governments do not administer functional urban areas, have little national political clout, and retain only limited access to their tax base. During the property boom of the 1980s and 1990s, for example, public revenue captured very little of the escalation of land prices, even where they stemmed from investments in public infrastructure. A good example was the huge increase in land values adjacent to Jakarta's urban ring roads built on what formerly was mainly *kampung* land.

Dealing with this situation will entail changes in public finance and the application of good government as much as transport engineering. First, urban governments, whether local or provincial, must oversee enough area to allow sound planning and political accountability. Second, to finance infrastructure programs, urban governments need much greater leverage over their tax base, especially growth in land values, and require substantial borrowing powers.

Finally, local governments that receive matching grants from the central government need to be accountable to that government, but their relationship to local citizens and interest groups is even more important. Cooperation with business makes decisionmaking more effective and promotes local investment and innovation, while a good relationship with citizens facilitates revenue raising and public initiatives. In Southeast Asia such ideas may still seem radical, but the Asian eco-

nomic crisis has highlighted the weakness of highly centralized decisionmaking and provoked domestic pressures for reform, especially in Indonesia. Local energies and initiatives are clearly one of Southeast Asia's great untapped resources.

Bibliography

Crooks Michell Peacock Stewart. 1971. *The Urban Renewal and Development Project, Singapore: For the United Nations Development Programme (Special Fund)*. Singapore, Crooks Michell Peacock Stewart Graphics and Printing Division (5 parts and summary volume).

Dick, H., and Rimmer, P. J. 1998. "Beyond the Third World City: The New Urban Geography of Southeast Asia." *Urban Studies* 35(12): 2303–21.

Dick, H., and Rimmer, P. J. 1999. "Privatising Climate: First World Cities in the Third World." In *East–West Perspectives on 21st Century Urban Development*. Aldershot, Ashgate/Vancouver: University of British Columbia: 305–24.

Dick, H., and Rimmer, P. J. Forthcoming. *Cities, Transport, and Communications: The Economic Integration of Southeast Asia since 1850*. London: Macmillan.

Ginsburg, N., Koppel, B., and McGee, T. G. (eds.). 1991. *The Extended Metropolis: Settlement Transition in Asia*. Honolulu: University of Hawaii Press: 3–25.

JUTS. 1997. *Janes Urban Transport Systems 1997–98*. Coulsdon, Janes Information Group.

Malaysia. 1996. *Seventh Malaysia Plan 1996–2000*. Kuala Lumpur: Economic Planning Unit.

Rimmer, P. J. 1986. *Rikisha to Rapid Transit: Urban Public Transport Systems and Policy in Southeast Asia*. Sydney: Pergamon Press.

Rimmer, P. J. 1995. "Urbanization Problems in Thailand's Rapidly Industrializing Economy." In Medhi Krongkaew, ed., *Thailand's Industrialization and Its Consequences*. London: Macmillan: 183–217.

Sirat, M. 1998. "Producer Services and Growth Management of a Metropolitan Region: The Case of Kuala Lumpur, Malaysia." *Asia Pacific Viewpoint* 39(2): 221–35.

World Bank. 1997. *World Development Report 1997: The State in a Changing World*. New York: Oxford University Press.

20

Public Participation in Urban Environmental Management in Japan

Ryo Fujikura

Faculty of Economics
Ritsumeikan University

In Japan, farmers and fishermen have traditionally managed natural resources, beginning with the cultivation of rice 2,000 to 3,000 years ago. Community rules strictly controlled the amount of water introduced into each field, and farmers managed surrounding forests and grasslands as common resources as well. Fishing cooperatives similarly determined when people could fish, by what method, and for which species.

As Japan modernized during the late 19th and early 20th centuries, farmers and fishermen protested economic losses from industrial pollution, but the Imperial government suppressed the movements. When Japan's economy rapidly developed anew during the 1960s, fishers and neighborhood associations again protested serious pollution, and victims of pollution-related diseases filed suit against industrial enterprises. These protests, as well as those of other local groups, raised public awareness of environmental issues throughout Japan and proved essential in turning local and central governments away from a sole focus on economic development at any cost. Public participation has since become the key not only to local urban planning and environmental management, but also to the country's approach to global environmental sustainability.

The Birth of Local Protest

The first industrial pollution in Japan stemmed from the Ashio copper mine and refinery in Tochigi Prefecture during the 1890s and the 1900s. To catch up to developed nations, the Imperial government had established the Rich and Strong Empire Policy, which en-

tailed heavy reliance on copper exports to obtain foreign currency. The country's large-scale copper refineries did nothing to abate pollution, and the results around the Ashio mine were typical: Sulfur dioxide emissions killed trees on surrounding mountains while sludge and effluent polluted rice fields downstream. Farmers protested, but the Imperial government transferred them to other areas (Ui 1985). Protests against air pollution from another copper refinery, which began operating in 1904 on Shikoku Island and damaged rice and wheat crops, ultimately yielded more results: The company moved to another island and finally solved its problems in 1939 after experimenting with several flue gas treatment technologies (Himi 1987).

In urban areas, such as Tokyo and Osaka, air pollution and noise from factories bothered citizens beginning in the prewar period, and their complaints prompted central and local governments to take some action. However, governments regarded the problems individually—the concept of environmental pollution did not exist—and citizens could not easily speak out against the Imperial government. With the onset of the Japan–China war in 1937, industrial production became a national priority, and the ability to tolerate pollution became a virtue. Industry did adopt antipollution measures during the war but only to increase productivity, avoid disaster, or enhance military strength (Institute for Pollution Control Studies 1970).

Citizens' Movements during the Postwar Period

The primary object of the Japanese government after World War II was reconstruction, and in 1960 the Cabinet instituted the Income Doubling Plan, which aimed to double per capita gross domestic product (GDP) in 10 years. As iron and steel production, the leading industry, quadrupled, rapid industrialization caused serious pollution in cities throughout Japan. But as ordinary citizens began to afford TV sets, refrigerators, and washing machines—previously symbols of rich families—most considered pollution an unavoidable side effect of their new prosperity.

Fishing communities again became the first obvious victims of this pollution, and when effluent from a paper factory killed a high percentage of fish at a fishery in Tokyo Bay in 1958, fishermen asked for compensation. When the company did not respond, angry fishers burst into the factory, prompting the government to pass two laws controlling water pollution in the same year—although those could not prevent pollution.[1] Fishing communities similarly protested water pollution from large petrochemical complexes in Yokkaichi City when the catch began to smell of industrial effluent and plummeted from 17,000 tons in 1956 to 4,000 tons in 1964. Fifteen fishing cooperatives requested compensation from industry and the Mie Prefecture government for falling prices in 1960, while neighborhood associations began to complain of noise, vibration, and offensive odors (International Center of Environmental Technology Transfer 1992).

Meanwhile, in the mid-1950s Minamata City saw evidence of a strange illness known as Minamata disease, whose cause was unknown—although fish caught in Minamata Bay were suspected. When they could not sell their fish and a research group of Kumamoto University concluded that organic mercury in fish was a possible cause for the disease, fishermen held demonstrations requesting compensation. Many members of fishing families suffered and died from the disease during the decade the government took to identify organic mercury in factory effluent as the culprit (Ui 1968; Social Scientific Study Group on Minamata Disease 1999).

The first successful citizens' movement that changed the government's plan probably occurred in Mishima and Numazu City, where the central government planned to establish a petrochemical complex in the 1960s. The governments of Shizuoka Prefecture and both cities at first welcomed the project, but local people feared that the complex would produce the kind of air pollution Yokkaichi City had experienced. The mayor of Mishima City convened a study group consisting of experts and high-school teachers whose report confirmed that the project would cause serious damage. Some 25,000 citizens—corresponding to one-third of the city's eligible voters—demonstrated against the plan. This show of force convinced the mayor and the municipal assembly to oppose the project, which was abandoned.

Central government officials had not expected that local protests would prompt the city to abandon the project. The government and big business worried that soon, if things went on this way, they would not be able to build factories anywhere (Broadbent 1998). Thus, the central government established the Basic Law for Pollution Control in 1967, but it stipulated that pollution control should be implemented "in harmony with sound economic development." This halfhearted law failed to assign responsibility for conserving the environment to any national agency. But when the central government hesitated to enforce substantive antipollution measures, some local governments, often headed by socialists or communists, known as "reformists," began to act.

As these reformists began to replace conservative governors and mayors throughout Japan, Prime Minister Sato, the head of a conservative party, convened the "Pollution Control Diet" session in 1970. This session passed 14 pollution-related bills, deleted the controversial requirement that pollution control essentially take a back seat to economic development, and established the Environment Agency. The central government had finally changed its attitude toward the environment. The movement also reversed the direction of the justice system, as courts uniformly reached verdicts in favor of victims of pollution-related illnesses such as Itai Itai disease, Yokkaichi asthma, and Minamata disease in the early 1970s. Faced with no other choice, Japanese companies began to invest intensively in pollution control during the mid-1970s, and environmental quality significantly improved.

Overall, local people had at first kept silent because they considered pollution unavoidable and also hesitated to speak out against the government and big business, much as they had before the war. However, once they recognized that they suffered from pollution, they started to protest and used new political institutions, such as local elections and courts, to push the government toward a pro-environment policy (Broadbent 1998).

The experience in Kitakyushu City reveals that women often played a key role in training the spotlight on the need to clean up severe industrial pollution. Women's associations have formed in Japan since the prewar period, and during the Japan–China War and World War II, the central government relied on Patriotic Women's Associations or Nation Defense Women's Associations to enforce wartime policy. The women supported injured soldiers and bereaved families, and facilitated food rationing and obligatory household savings. In order to help democratize Japan after the war, occupation forces educated leaders of women's associations, who studied the problems they faced and learned how to solve them. Because of women's efforts, the government of Kitakyushu succeeded in improving the environment during the 1970s in close cooperation with industry, and is now trying to transfer its experience and technology to developing nations.

Kitakyushu City: Women Take the Lead

Kitakyushu City became one of four major industrial cities during postwar reconstruction and development. Its economic development was based on the production of iron and steel, chemical products, and cement. Because of these industries Kitakyushu suffered the worst air quality in Japan. However, its citizens remained quiet even while those in other industrial cities such as Yokkaichi, Osaka, and Kawasaki sued the government and private enterprises. They regarded Kitakyushu not as a place to live but as a place to work: Factory workers returned to their rural hometowns when they retired, and hesitated to speak out against Nippon Steel and other large companies.

As more laborers began to raise their children in Kitakyushu and remain after retirement, pollution awareness grew. Women found that they had to wipe the interior of their houses daily because of smoke from the factories, and that wash hung out to dry turned gray from oily dust. Children drew black and gray pictures of their surroundings and asked mothers why suburban skies were blue; many became sick and were often absent from school.

Women of the Tobata District Association in Kitakyushu, in particular, discovered that laundry hung outside grew dirtier with proximity to a power plant using low-quality coal. Because many of their husbands worked at the plant, they pressured the mayor and the city assembly instead, and the plant installed a costly precipitator to clean its emissions at the mayor's request.

Another women's group, the Sanroku District Association, monitored smoke and offensive odors from a factory manufacturing carbon black[2] and coke, alerting the municipal government and the factory when they observed serious pollution and showing the mayor dirty wallpaper and floor cloth. When the situation did not improve after the mayor visited factory headquarters in Tokyo accompanied by local citizens in 1961, the association members turned to a professor of engineering for help. The group of 500 women then measured airborne pollution by leaving white cloth and paper boxes outside and photographing smoke-emitting facilities. In 1963 the local people and factory owners concluded an agreement—mediated by prefecture and city officials—

that defined remedial action. This agreement was one of the few concluded before companies throughout Japan accepted responsibility for controlling pollution a decade later (Kitakyushu City 1998).

Dust decreased in the late 1960s as the companies substituted liquid for solid fuel, but airborne concentration of sulfur dioxide grew. This time the Sanroku District Association focused on health effects and enlisted the help of a professor of medicine. The group found a relationship between air pollution and the number of absent pupils from 1961 to 1964, uncovered 562 asthma or bronchitis patients among 817 families, and found that many children suffered respiratory diseases when they moved from rural areas to Kitakyushu. In 1967 the association measured air pollution by exposing plates outside for one month, finding that the weight of iron plates increased significantly while that of tin and stainless steel plates dropped. The group presented their results to other citizens while showing an original 8 mm film. Widespread media reports of these activities helped raise concern about pollution in the city (Hayashi 1971).

Meanwhile, the women endured pressure from the enterprises that employed their husbands—the families lived in company dormitories, and janitors monitored their activities. The association's leader received threatening telephone calls. Guards did not allow anyone to photograph the factory, even from outside. But during the 1971 municipal election the conservative mayor, who had not professed interest in pollution previously, proposed a policy of pollution control. His rival, supported by the Communist Party, criticized the mayor's policy as favoring the enterprises and appealed for more stringent control. An intensive campaign by the business community reelected the incumbent mayor, but many people who were not supporters of the Communist Party voted for his rival. These results prompted Kitakyushu officials to reverse course in the 1970s, and enterprises had no alternative but to clean up their act. City officials and business leaders alike feared that a communist would become the next mayor and impose harsher regulation, as reformist mayors had done elsewhere.

Public Participation Today

Today, most participation in urban environmental management is based on action-oriented activities and education. In fiscal year 1998, for example, the Environment Agency of the Japanese Government supported about 4,000 eco-clubs—voluntary clubs consisting of some 70,000 elementary and junior high school pupils throughout Japan that pursue environmental education—mainly by providing information and organizing meetings (Environment Agency 1999). Municipalities rely heavily on citizens' groups to support recycling activities, as citizens become more aware of the country's solid waste problems. In Tokyo's Minato Ward, home to numerous businesses and foreign embassies, over 160 groups collected 2,500 tons of recyclable waste in 1995 (Minato Ward 1996).

On the other hand, media reports on endocrine disrupters also have prompted 221 local disputes regarding planned and existing waste-treatment facilities, as citizens demand more information disclosure and participation in decisionmaking on such facilities (Environment Agency 1998).

The 1992 Earth Summit prompted more opportunities for local involvement in environmental policymaking. Japan's Basic Environmental Law, enacted in November 1993, represented the first attempt by any industrial nations to codify the concept of sustainable development. The Basic Environmental Plan, passed a year later after public hearings throughout the country, specifies comprehensive environmental goals for the next 50 years and lays out the responsibilities of central and local governments, businesses, and citizens in fulfilling those goals. In particular, the plan identifies participation as one of its basic concepts, facilitating public participation in formulating policy of both the central and local governments.

In 1993, moreover, the Urban Planning Law was amended to allow municipal governments to establish master urban plans defining long-term development goals and specifying how they will reach them.[3] Since then, public participation has been regarded as an indispensable step in preparing not only master urban plans but other local plans: Mayors must organize committees that include local citizens to prepare the plans, and they must also hold public hearings. Such participation often remains nominal—but Kamakura City, 50 kilometers southwest of Tokyo, is an exception.[4]

Kamakura City: The Public Role in Environmental Decisionmaking

The Japanese capital during the 13th century, today Kamakura City is home to many industry executives and high-ranking government officials, and numerous heritage sites and marine sports attract over 15 million tourists annually. In the mid-1990s the municipal government adopted an innovative approach to public participation in decisionmaking.

The government relied on over 200 citizens participating in two symposia to devise the basic framework for its new master urban plan. The government then held 25 public hearings and over two dozen meetings with representatives of local communities, cooperatives,

and business associations, and collected opinions from more than 400 citizens to further develop the framework (Fujikura 1995). This process convinced the planning committee to choose "creation of the environmentally sound municipality" as their basic goal—in marked contrast to other municipalities, which usually focus on population, the economy, and land use.

Kamakura City also relied on an environmental committee to prepare its Basic Environmental Plan (BMP). In Japan, the members of such committees are usually selected by the government, which tends to exclude critics. Kamakura City advertised for committee members and selected 5 representatives of different age groups and neighborhoods from among 60 applicants. Businesses and citizen groups prepared materials for the committee—in contrast to other municipalities, where the government usually prepares such materials. The city held two workshops and one symposium, attended by several hundred citizens, to provide information on the committee's discussions and feed citizens' opinions back to the committee before it produced its final document. The city used the same approach to prepare its Traffic Plan and Women's Plan, which facilitates women's participation in society.

In 1998 Kamakura City established two centers to support the activities of local nonprofit organizations working on social welfare, environmental management, international cooperation, and urban development. These centers, which provide meeting rooms, copying and printing equipment, and information on the activities of other nonprofit organizations, are designed by local people, funded by the municipal government, and administered by volunteers. Support for such activities is rare in Japan, which tends to lack organized environmental groups and other nongovernmental organizations (NGOs).

Nongovernmental Organizations in Japan

Although neighborhood associations and cooperatives have been instrumental in changing Japanese attitudes toward pollution control, the role of NGOs has been limited (Japan Environment Association 1996). Although the activities of NGOs are growing, most work locally—the country has almost no nationally influential environmental organizations.

The Japanese system of lifelong, seniority-based employment is one factor hindering the emergence of nationwide NGOs. Although attitudes are changing, most university graduates, particularly men, seek jobs at large enterprises or government agencies that assure long-term employment. More women brave short-term contracts and work in foreign companies and international organizations, partly because they find it difficult to obtain jobs in large Japanese enterprises. Changing jobs in Japan remains difficult and is doubly so for a full-time NGO staff member: Unlike in the United States, governments do not recruit NGO staff as high-ranking officials. Full-time NGO staff are poorly paid and the jobs lack prestige.

According to a survey by the Environment Agency, 57 percent of NGOs lack full-time staff—most cannot afford them. Few foundations provide financial support to Japanese NGOs; most rely largely on membership fees for revenue. And more than half have fewer than 200 members; the Wild Bird Society, the largest NGO in Japan, has some 50,000 members (Japan Environment Association 1996). Because of these constraints, Japanese environmental NGOs have great difficulty becoming as influential as those in the United States.

On the other hand, volunteer activities are becoming more popular and important. Neighborhood associations have traditionally cleaned towns, assisted vulnerable and aged people, and reconstructed communities after disasters. Although many Japanese today do not have the time or inclination to join formal groups, a number of young volunteers helped victims of the 1995 earthquake disaster in Kobe City, and volunteers largely removed oil spilled by a Russian tanker in the Sea of Japan in 1997. According to a government survey, over half of Japanese are interested in volunteer activities (Saotome 1995). More Japanese will undoubtedly participate, but it is unclear whether influential NGOs will grow from these largely project-oriented activities.

Many Japanese fear that NGOs will become too political. Conversely, politicians often try to coopt environmental NGOs, pretending to pay attention to them. For their part, Japanese NGOs are not good at cooperating: Small differences often erode alliances. During the Kyoto Conference on Global Climate Change in December 1997, Japanese NGOs working on climate change did organize a nationwide network and appeal for support from the nation and the media, but such activities have been limited.

Challenges for Japan and Lessons from Its Experience

The Japanese government has lagged behind other developed nations and international organizations in transparency and accountability. However, the situation has improved remarkably over the past few years. In 1999, the Cabinet adopted a procedure on public comment. Since then, all central government agencies invite comments from the public and respond to them when they want to introduce, amend, or abandon regulations.

The Law Concerning Access to Information Held by Administrative Organs was also established in 1999 and will become effective within two years. The purpose of the law is to strive for greater disclosure of information from administrative organs. It also stipulates that local governments establish ordinances for the same purpose.

Almost all prefecture governments and many municipal governments have already established such ordinances, and most documents of prefecture governments are accessible. But citizens are demanding more information. For example, many citizens concerned about hazardous emissions from industrial waste treatment facilities have not been able to get hard data. Information regarding emission from private facilities is not subject to disclosure.

Japan's experience suggests that democracy is indispensable in pushing for such laws and other aspects of environmental protection; the Imperial government successfully quashed protests against pollution. International efforts to promote democratization thus are essential.

The Kitakyushu experience shows the importance of public awareness and environmental education in building support for environmental protection. Many developing countries attempting to promote environmental education lack trainers, teaching materials, and methods; international sharing of methods and materials would also support these efforts.

Japan's experience reveals the importance of local governments in controlling industrial pollution: Local leaders understand their communities better than the central government, and careful advice from local officials to individual polluters has solved many problems. Unlike the central government, local people elect local leaders directly, and they must therefore be sensitive to constituents' opinions. Local people can also more easily participate in decisionmaking on a local rather than a national issue.

However, in many developing countries local governments exert little control over environmental management, and their capacity is weak compared with that of the central government and industrial enterprises. What's more, the central government often appoints municipal leaders who do not understand the local situation. Their staffs have little prestige and low incomes, making it difficult to attract engineers and scientists knowledgeable about controlling pollution.

In countries that do not mandate local governments, international cooperation could help build the ability of the central government to make sound environmental decisions. Where independent local governments do exist, such aid could greatly enhance their ability to incorporate public participation into development decisions.

Bibliography

Broadbent, J. 1998. *Environmental Politics in Japan.* Cambridge: Cambridge University Press.

Environment Agency. 1998. *Heisei 9 Nendo Kankyo Hakusho* (*The Quality of the Environment in Japan, FY1997*). Tokyo: Okurasho Insatsukyoku.

Environment Agency. 1999. *Heisei 10 Nendo Kankyo Hakusho* (*The Quality of the Environment in Japan, FY1998*). Tokyo: Okurasho Insatsukyoku.

Fujikura, M. 1995. "Kankyo Kihon Keikaku Sakutei De Kuhusareta Atarashii Shiminsankaku No Katachi" (An Innovative Approach of Public Participation for Establishment of a Local Environmental Plan). *Global Net,* pp. 18–19. Tokyo: Global Environmental Forum.

Hayashi, E. 1971. *Yahata No Kogai* (*Pollution in Yahata*). Tokyo: Asahishimbun.

Himi, K. 1987. "Showa 30 Nenndai Kara 40 Nendai Ni Itaru Madeno Wagakuni Ni Okeru Taikiosen Taisakushi No Gaiyo" (An Outline of Air Pollution Control Measures Taken from the Mid-1950s until the Mid-1960s). *Kenko Eikyo Ni Tuiteno Kakono Taikiosen Deta No Seirini Kansuru Kenkyu* (*Study Report on Past Data Regarding Health Effects Caused by Air Pollution*), pp. 1–30. Tokyo: Taikiosen Kenkyu Kyokai.

International Center of Environmental Technology Transfer (ICETT). 1992. *Yokkaichishi Kogai Kankyokaizen Heno Atumi* (*History of Pollution and Environment Improvement in Yokkaichi*). Yokkaichi: ICETT.

Institute for Pollution Control Studies, Tokyo Metropolitan Government. 1970. *Kogai To Toukyoto* (*Pollution and Tokyo*). Tokyo Metropolitan Government.

Japan Environment Association. 1996. *Kannkyo NGO Soshiki Unei Jittai To Anketo Chosa Kekka* (*Study Report on the Status Quo of the Management of Environmental NGOs*). Tokyo: Japan Environment Association.

Kitakyushu City. 1998. *Kitakyushushu Kogai Taisakushi* (*History of Pollution Control in Kitakyushu*). Kitakyushu: Kitakyushu Municipal Government.

Minato Ward. 1996. *Minato Eco-Life Plan.* Tokyo: Minato Ward Government.

Oya, K. 1998. "Sinrin Rinya No Chiiki Shakai Kanri" (Forestry Management by Regional Societies). *Asia No Kannkyo Mondai* (*Environmental Problems in Asia*) pp. 265–78. Tokyo: Toyokeizai.

Saotome, M. 1995. *The Volunteer.* Tokyo: International Development Journal.

Shoji, H. 1975. *Nihon No Kogai* (*Pollution in Japan*). Tokyo: Iwanami Shoten.

Social Scientific Study Group on Minamata Disease. 1999. *Minamatabyo No Higeikiwo Kurikaesanai Tameni* (*Not to Repeat Tragedy of Minamata Disease*). Minamata: National Institute for Minamata Disease.

Ui, J. 1968. *Kogai No Seijigaku* (*Politics of Pollution*). Tokyo: Sanseido.

Ui, J. 1985. *Gijutsu To Sangyo Kogai* (*Technology and Industrial Pollution*). Tokyo: Tokyo Daigaku Shuppankai.

Yokohama City. 1999. Press release and interview with an officer of the municipal government of Yokohama City, July.

Notes

1. The two laws for water pollution control and the Soot and Smoke Control Law enacted in 1962 did not prevent pollution because the government had not changed its pro-industry policy, and the laws established effluent and emission standards only within "designated areas." Almost no regulation was enforced outside of the areas. The two laws and the Soot and Smoke Control Law were replaced by the Water Quality Conservation Law and the Air Pollution Control Law in 1970 and 1968, respectively.

2. Carbon black is manufactured by heat decomposition of oil and used as material for pigment, ink, and rubber products.

3. Before the amendment, only prefecture governments could prepare their master urban plans.

4. Yokohama City also took an innovative approach to public participation in planning a road project. After a questionnaire survey to 40,000 families regarding participation to decision-making, municipal government presented citizens with several alternatives early in the process—including the option of "no development"—and information on the advantages and the disadvantages of each plan. It organized a committee consisting of 2 local experts, 7 representatives of local communities, and 12 citizens selected from applicants in order to identify which alternative should be adopted. The committee made another questionnaire survey to 10,000 families regarding the alternatives. In 1999, it prepared a draft report on the best route. The municipal government will start to prepare its road plan based on the draft report in 2000. It took already seven years from the first survey, and will take another some years until the completion of the projects. However, this is a test case: the municipal government has not decided to use this approach for all development projects (Yokohama City 1999).

chapter 21

Coping with Municipal Solid Waste in Developing Countries

David N. Beede

U.S. Department of Commerce

David E. Bloom

School of Public Health
Harvard University

lthough recent environmental issues such as global warming and stratospheric ozone depletion garner the lion's share of public attention, municipal solid waste—more colloquially known as garbage—has been with us for centuries. The implications of such waste for the quality of life of people living in many developing countries are also more urgent.

Municipal solid waste typically encompasses all solid wastes except industrial, agricultural, and human wastes. Local definitions may or may not include material such as tires, construction debris, and sludge and ashes from waste treatment plants. Reliable data on the generation, recovery, and disposal of municipal solid waste are somewhat hard to come by, as most countries do not keep good records. And cross-country comparisons suffer from a lack of common definitions and techniques for estimating amounts. Most estimates are based on either a sampling technique or a materials-balance analysis. Sampling techniques involve measuring municipal solid waste generated by samples of households, and using those to estimate the generation rate for the entire population. Materials-balance analyses indirectly estimate municipal solid waste generation by estimating annual rates (by weight) of the consumption of nondurable goods and the disposal of durable goods. Neither technique is very precise.

Despite these challenges, we have estimated that the world generates some 1.5 billion metric tons of municipal solid waste annually, and that this amount is growing by a substantial 2.7 percent per year. We base this estimate on data from the World Resources Institute and our own correlations between municipal solid waste, population size, and income per capita. Our figures show that on average, each person generates two-thirds of 1 kilogram of municipal solid waste each day—a finding broadly consistent with estimates using other data and methods.

Whether 1.5 billion metric tons is a lot depends on one's perspective. That amount exceeds the annual global production of wheat and rice. Yet if the waste occupied a 100-meter-deep landfill with the same density as U.S. garbage, it would cover only 28 square kilometers. Filling an area the size of Rhode Island—the smallest U.S. state and only 0.002 percent of the world's land area—would take 100 years.

The Municipal Solid Waste Problem

Not surprisingly, the amount of municipal solid waste is very sensitive to population size, growing at a one-to-one relationship. Municipal solid waste also rises with per capita income, although less than proportionately. Thus developing countries account for a disproportionately high share of municipal solid waste relative to their income, while rich countries account for a disproportionately high share relative to their population.

The problem stems not so much from the amount of waste but from its spatial distribution and growth rate. Although nature has an inherent ability to assimilate waste—depending on temperature, precipitation, the physical characteristics of soil, the height of the water table, and the extent of forest cover—the amount of waste in urban areas exceeds nature's absorptive and recycling capacities. And since urban population is growing rapidly—far faster than world population—the concentration of waste creates enormous health and environmental problems. Poor public management and transportation infrastructure compound these problems.

Many cities in the developing world dump great quantities of waste haphazardly on land or in uncovered and unlined landfills atop porous soils. Inefficient collection techniques exacerbate this problem. For example, the practice in some cities of discarding food wastes in the streets, from which it is collected by hand each day, appears to be much less efficient than household disposal in tightly closed bins combined with collection two or three times a week. Using uncovered collection trucks leads to significant spillage back onto streets. Such activities make public cleaning of streets and open areas critically important. Given that the per ton cost of street cleaning in developing countries is estimated to be between two and three times that of curbside collection (Cointreau-Levine 1994), using more costly collection equipment that reduces spillage, such as covered trucks, would likely be more efficient.

Because developing countries rarely separate long-lived hazardous waste such as insecticides, solvents, batteries, used car oil, and medical waste from the municipal waste stream, these substances commonly leach into the water table. Disposing of hazardous waste according to the standards set by developed countries may seem to be beyond the financial capacity of governments or the private sector in developing countries. Suppose, however, that codumping of municipal solid waste and hazardous waste means that within 15 to 25 years commingled wastes must be handled at a facility that isolates or treats the waste more thoroughly, and at much greater cost than for municipal solid waste alone. Our calculations show that it would be highly cost-beneficial to segregate and treat or dispose of the hazardous waste at the more expensive facility from the start (Beede and Bloom 1995).

Many communities also burn much municipal waste, without emission controls, and make no attempt to capture the resulting energy. Other communities dispose of municipal waste in waterways used for drinking and cooking. The result is growing air and water pollution and breeding grounds for disease-carrying rodents and mosquitoes. Poorly managed municipal solid waste also generates offensive and sometimes overwhelming odors. Overall, free markets clearly do not work very well in promoting socially efficient controls on solid waste, as delays seem easier and less costly, and dumpers and burners do not usually have to pay a direct price for their actions. And children and future generations do not have a vote or a say in the marketplace, even though

today's management practices will affect their health and environmental quality.

From Concern to Action

People in developing countries are acutely aware of the municipal solid waste problem. In a 1992 Gallup survey conducted in 12 developing countries, including Russia, Hungary, and Poland, 45 percent of respondents (weighted by population) considered inadequate sanitation and garbage disposal a "very serious" problem. That was higher than the percentage of respondents who considered water, air, or soil problems, overcrowding, or too much noise "very serious." By contrast, only 16 percent of respondents in 12 industrial countries rated solid waste as a very serious problem.

However, translating concern into action in the face of enormous financial constraints is difficult. This is compounded by the fact that unlike, say, specific health problems, where new vaccines, diagnostic tools, or drug therapies can have powerful beneficial impacts, the municipal solid waste problem has no technical magic bullet. Moreover, judging which municipal solid waste management options are cost-beneficial is hampered by poor, incomplete, or inconsistent data (see, for example, Spencer 1994).

The valuation of some costs and benefits for managing municipal solid waste is relatively straightforward, including out-of-pocket collection and transport expenses and revenues from the sale of recyclable materials, compost, and energy. However, other costs and benefits are less obvious but may be key, such as the opportunity costs of land (for transfer stations, processing facilities, and landfills) and of household labor (especially if households are expected to sort their waste or transport it to a central collection point). Savings from avoided disposal costs when new technologies are implemented are also sometimes overlooked.

Other costs and benefits may be extremely difficult to value, such as changes in public health and in the aesthetic quality of air, water, and land. Furthermore, valuations of the costs and benefits of changing one aspect of municipal solid waste management must reflect any impacts on the costs and benefits of other aspects of managing municipal solid waste. For example, the cost of producing agricultural-quality compost may fall sharply if households separate their compostable and noncompostable wastes. Finally, cost and benefit valuations must account for the value of resources over time, requiring the choice of a discount rate, which is often less straightforward than would appear at first.

The fact that much economic activity in developing countries is effectively outside the realm of state control and tax authorities further complicates the ability of policymakers to make effective choices. In addition, municipal managers in developing countries often lack the information they need to make well-informed decisions.[1]

Overall, developing countries face challenges in addressing the four main components of the problem of managing municipal solid waste: collecting the waste; transporting the waste; processing the waste to make it more disposable, to reduce its health threat, and possibly even to draw value from it; and disposing of the residue. On the first two counts, many developing countries lack the transport infrastructure needed to collect and transport waste. Narrow and unpaved roads limit the use of large and heavily loaded trucks, thus undermining economies of scale.

Three main techniques are available to process and dispose of waste: landfills, incineration, and recycling and composting. Landfills are expensive to design and operate. In addition to liners and covers, they also require systems for collecting and managing leachate, removing hazardous waste, and flaring or capturing the methane that results from anaerobic decomposition.

Incineration is also very expensive. In many developing countries, the waste stream includes a high proportion of organic matter, such as food trimmings. The water content in such waste means that burning it properly requires adding fuel, raising the cost of processing the waste. Most developing countries cannot afford to purchase and operate the capital-intensive (in both human and physical terms) incinerators that industrial countries have devised to minimize the emissions from burning municipal solid waste. Recycling and composting may be better alternatives in most developing countries, as they also capitalize on the resource value of the waste.

Efforts to collect and process recyclable materials in industrial countries are considerably more capital-intensive than in most developing countries.[2] The most capital-intensive method is mixed collection in which municipal solid waste is collected and delivered to a facility for mechanical extraction of recyclable materials, with the remainder often used to make fuels for electricity-generating incinerators. A somewhat less capital-intensive system is the separate collection of old newspapers and commingled glass, metal, and plastic materials, plus other waste. Generally this method requires special trucks that have two compartments, one for newspapers and the other for other recyclable materials. Households and firms perform the initial separation of recyclable materials, and the process is refined at materials-recovery facilities of varying capital intensity. These can include highly automated systems that use magnets to extract ferrous metals, air classifiers (which use blowers to separate light materials, such as plastics, by weight), eddy-current separators to extract aluminum (magnets above a conveyor belt that induce an opposing magnetic field in aluminum below and push it off into a separate bin), and "low-tech" conveyor belts that transport recyclable materials past workers who sort them.

The least capital-intensive, and hence most labor-intensive, recycling systems in industrial countries require that households sort and separate each type of recyclable material (paper, aluminum, steel cans, different types of plastic, and glass by color). Workers may also sort commingled recyclable materials as they collect them, placing each type in its own compartment in the truck. Households may also transport separated recyclable materials to containers scattered throughout a community or to staffed drop-off centers. Households may also take beverage containers to buy-back centers, in the case of deposit systems for bottles. Finally, even the least capital-intensive recycling systems in the industrial countries use mechanical shredders, balers, and pulverizers to make materials denser, thereby reducing transport costs—and rendering these systems relatively capital-intensive compared with systems in developing countries.

More labor-intensive collection and processing of recyclable materials are found throughout the developing world. These efforts can entail households bringing their recyclables to redemption centers, and small-scale entrepreneurs going door-to-door to purchase recyclables. Labor-intensive recycling can also involve municipal workers and informal sector scavengers rummaging through household wastes put out for collection, or scavengers sifting through municipal solid waste at transfer stations and final dumpsites. Often the privately run businesses that purchase, clean, sort, and sell recyclables in bulk to other middlemen or directly to factories are also highly labor-intensive.[3]

Composting will not fulfill its promise in developing countries until both quality control and demand improve significantly, since farmers, landscapers, and other potential users of compost typically insist on a product that is free from bits of glass, plastics, metals, and toxic materials. Eliminating subsidies for chemical fertilizers—common throughout the developing world—would help make compost more competitive and thus raise demand.

Paying for Proper Waste Management

Many economic schemes can help municipal officials pay for proper management of solid waste and cut the amount illicitly dumped into waterways and onto roadsides and open fields. However, these schemes often involve tradeoffs.[4]

For example, governments can provide municipal solid waste collection, transport, processing, and disposal services, charging either a flat fee per household or a fee per unit volume of waste collected. Besides financing such services, a fee per unit volume creates incentives for households to reduce their waste by encouraging recycling and altering consumption. Setting a per-unit fee equal to the net marginal social cost of managing municipal solid waste may lead to a more efficient outcome than charging a flat fee that effectively sets the marginal cost to households for managing municipal solid waste at zero.

However, per-unit fees may also encourage households to deal with their municipal solid wastes by dumping or burning them illegally, or by placing them into the dumpsters of other households and businesses. Because of such undesirable results, efficiency may be higher if per-unit fees are set lower than the marginal social cost of managing municipal solid wastes—as low as zero, as in the flat-fee option, particularly if a per-unit fee program costs more to administer than a flat-fee program.

For items such as batteries, paints, and motor oil whose burning or dumping are especially damaging to the environment and whose codisposal with nonhazardous municipal solid waste would drive up the cost of managing the entire solid waste stream, a deposit–refund mechanism may be more efficient than per-unit fees. Under a deposit–refund mechanism, households and firms pay a fee when they buy certain goods, which is refunded when they dispose of or recycle the associated waste acceptably. The advantage of deposit–refund mechanisms is that they provide households and firms with an incentive not to illegally dump or burn certain parts of the municipal solid waste stream, and they may be cheaper to manage than monitoring the behavior of many small–scale illegal dumpers.

Some governments use competitive bidding to contract out waste management and then monitor the quality of service, penalizing or canceling the contract of any trash hauler or processor that does not perform to standard. Profit-seeking firms generally have both greater flexibility and incentives than government bureaucracies to redeploy workers and physical capital quickly in response to changing circumstances, and to design and implement cost-cutting innovations. The better able the government is to specify the tasks it seeks to accomplish, including setting standards for environmentally sound practices, the more easily it can evaluate contractor performance. The more effective the government is at implementing a mechanism for penalizing poor performance and monopolistic behavior, the greater the likelihood that private municipal solid waste management will be more efficient than public management.

Competition under the vigilant eyes of government regulators and private citizens can also achieve appropriate economies of scale in solid waste management. In particular, governments can achieve operational efficiency by allowing free entry into and exit from relatively labor-intensive activities (such as curbside collection of solid waste), and by holding open competitions for the exclusive rights to operate large-scale, capital-intensive activities (such as landfill and incineration facilities).

Conclusion

There are no sure-fire solutions to the municipal solid waste problems of developing countries. Nevertheless, municipal solid waste is more a quality-of-life problem than a major impediment to economic growth,[5] and the one-two-three punch of economic growth, poverty reduction, and good governance will naturally enhance countries' capacity to address it. Income growth can help because garbage grows less than proportionately with income, and countries with rising per capita incomes can afford, and will typically desire, to spend more to address waste. The ratio of services to goods also tends to rise with income, and services tend not to be very waste-intensive. Finally, good governance is important because waste management is generally provided and financed publicly, or at least publicly regulated.

Bibliography

Beede, David N., and David E. Bloom. 1995. "The Economics of Municipal Solid Waste." *The World Bank Research Observer* August: 113–50.

Bloom, David E. 1995. "International Public Opinion on the Environment." *Science* 269: 354–58.

Bennett, Christopher P. A., David E. Bloom, Lakshmi Reddy Bloom, Marguerite S. Robinson, and Michael H. Simpson. 1993. *Enterprises for the Recycling and Composting of Municipal Solid Waste.* Jakarta, Indonesia: Center for Policy and Implementation Studies.

Cointreau-Levine, Sandra J. 1994. *Private Sector Participation in Municipal Solid Waste Services in Developing Countries*, vol. 1, *The Formal Sector.* Washington, D.C.: World Bank.

Kinnaman, Thomas C., and Don Fullerton. 1999. "The Economics of Residential Solid Waste Management." National Bureau of Economic Research Working Paper 7326 (August).

Kreith, Frank, ed. 1994. *Handbook of Solid Waste Management.* New York: McGraw-Hill.

Rosenberg, Larry, ed. 1996. *International Source Book on Environmentally Sound Technologies for Municipal Solid Waste Management.* Osaka: United Nations Environment Programme International Environmental Technology Centre.

Spencer, David B. 1994. "Recycling, Part E." In Frank Kreith, ed., *Handbook of Solid Waste Management.* New York: McGraw-Hill.

World Bank. 1997. "Turkey–Antalya Solid Waste Management." World Bank Project Information Document for Project Number TR-PA-40865 (March).

World Bank. 1999a. "Dominican Republic—Solid Waste Management in Tourism Centers." World Bank Project Information Document for Project Number DOPE59511 (January 6).

World Bank. 1999b. "West Bank and Gaza—Solid Waste and Environmental Management Project." World Bank Project Information Document for Project XOPE54051 (July 26).

Notes

Larry Rosenberg provided helpful comments on an earlier draft of this chapter. The views expressed in this article do not necessarily reflect the views of the U.S. Department of Commerce or the United States Government.

1. The U.N. Environment Programme's recent source book provides a good summary of current practices in both industrial and developing countries, along with recommendations. See Rosenberg 1996.

2. See Spencer 1994 for a description of recycling systems in industrial countries, and Kreith 1994 for an excellent reference on the technology and economics of capital-intensive recycling systems.

3. For example, see Bennett and others, 1992, for descriptions of the recycling industry in Jakarta.

4. Kinnaman and Fullerton 1999 review economic models and empirical evidence on the effectiveness of a wide range of incentive schemes for optimal municipal solid waster management.

5. Poor management of municipal solid waster management projects in the Dominican Republic, Turkey, and the West Bank and Gaza (see World Bank 1997, 1999a, and 1999b).

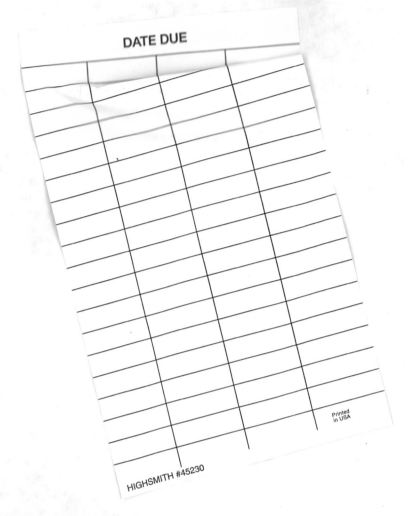

DATE DUE

HIGHSMITH #45230

Printed in USA

ven as globalization annihilates distance and brings countries closer together, pressure for local autonomy and a shift toward urbanization are diffusing economic and political power within countries. These changes are transforming the role of governments and enlarging the involvement of private and nongovernmental participants. The number of critical decisionmakers will multiply, calling for reform and the creation of new modes of governance, including institutions to harness efforts aimed at raising welfare.

One possible outcome of this dynamic is a shift away from a central state–led view of development toward a more complex, and potentially untidy, coalition of actors who will typically not confine themselves to operating in a single arena. A second implication is that the combination of local dynamics and global forces will catalyze the development of regions and cities. To the extent that such development does or does not occur, it may well widen the gap between the richer and poorer regions of the world.

An outgrowth of the *World Development Report 1999/2000, Local Dynamics in an Era of Globalization* is a collection of papers by leading authorities discussing some of the major aspects of decentralization and urban change in the context of globalization. These scholars have drawn upon the experiences of developing and industrial countries from every continent.

An essential reference for all those interested in one of the most important issues of the new millennium, this volume will be of special interest to governments, nongovernmental organizations, the private sector, economists, and those in the international development community.

The World Bank
1818 H Street N.W.
Washington, D.C. 20433 USA
Telephone: (202) 477-1234
Facsimile: (202) 477-6391
Telex: MCI 64145 WORLDBANK
MCI 248423 WORLDBANK
Internet: www.worldbank.org
E-mail: books@worldbank.org

Oxford University Press

ISBN 0-19-521597-4